Mastering

English Literature

readi

Books M
Family h
Faxing G

Pleas
date
card

You

- P

-

Palgrave Master Series

Accounting
Accounting Skills
Advanced English Language
Advanced English Literature
Advanced Pure Mathematics
Arabic
Basic Management
Biology
British Politics
Business Communication
Business Environment
C Programming
C++ Programming
Chemistry
COBOL Programming
Communication
Computing
Counselling Skills
Counselling Theory
Customer Relations
Database Design
Delphi Programming
Desktop Publishing
Economic and Social History
Economics
Electrical Engineering
Electronics
Employee Development
English Grammar
English Language
English Literature
Fashion Buying and Merchandising
   Management
Fashion Styling
French
Geography
German

Global Information Systems
Human Resource Management
Information Technology
International Trade
Internet
Italian
Java
Management Skills
Marketing Management
Mathematics
Microsoft Office
Microsoft Windows, Novell
   NetWare and UNIX
Modern British History
Modern European History
Modern United States History
Modern World History
Networks
Novels of Jane Austen
Organisational Behaviour
Pascal and Delphi Programming
Philosophy
Physics
Practical Criticism
Psychology
Shakespeare
Social Welfare
Sociology
Spanish
Statistics
Strategic Management
Systems Analysis and Design
Team Leadership
Theology
Twentieth Century Russian History
Visual Basic
World Religions

www.palgravemasterseries.com

Palgrave Master Series
Series Standing Order ISBN 0–333–69343–4
(outside North America only)

You can receive future titles in this series as they are published by placing a standing order. Please contact your bookseller or, in case of difficulty, write to us at the address below with your name and address, the title of the series and the ISBN quoted above.

Customer Services Department, Macmillan Distribution Ltd
Houndmills, Basingstoke, Hampshire RG21 6XS, England

Mastering

 English Literature

Second edition

Richard Gill

palgrave

First edition 1985
Reprinted 6 times
Second edition 1995

Published by
PALGRAVE
Houndmills, Basingstoke, Hampshire RG21 6XS and
175 Fifth Avenue, New York, N.Y. 10010
Companies and representatives throughout the world

PALGRAVE is the new global academic imprint of
St. Martin's Press LLC Scholarly and Reference Division and
Palgrave Publishers Ltd (formerly Macmillan Press Ltd).

ISBN 0–333–62529–3

This book is printed on paper suitable for recycling and
made from fully managed and sustained forest sources.

A catalogue record for this book is available
from the British Library.

14   13   12   11
07   06   05   04   03

Printed in China

Contents

PART III STUDYING DRAMA

Preface

I hope that this book will help you to enjoy English literature and be successful in public exams. I don't think those aims are incompatible; I've always found that the more I think about a book, the more I see in it and the more I enjoy and value it. I hope that this will also be your experience.

This isn't a course-book. The books studied at GCSE, A-level and at university differ according to syllabus and institution, so I can't rely on a common list of books that everyone will be studying. Moreover, each book is different from every other, and therefore it needs to be thought about in its own way. One of the themes of this book is that there is not a set of ready-made formulae which can be 'applied' to every work. As Kent says to Oswald in *King Lear*, 'I'll teach you differences'. That is what we have to learn; each book is different and must therefore be thought about in a way distinctive to itself.

In the light of the above, you might want to ask: 'How can a book help?' My answer is: 'In three ways'.

First, it can give you some questions to ask. Often when we are studying, we need help with our thinking. It is very difficult studying anything unless you have some idea of what you are 'looking for'. Questions can help you in this. They can open up areas of a book and they might alert us to some important features. Of course, there is no guarantee that they will. One of the things we learn about study is what approaches are or are not helpful. In fact, even when an approach proves to be unhelpful, it might tell us something. Sometimes, we see an important feature of a text when we realise that it doesn't work in a particular way. For instance, many novels work by showing us how the central character changes, but in *Huckleberry Finn* Mark Twain has produced a central character who is effective precisely because he does not.

Secondly, a book can provide you with examples. What I've tried to do is refer to many of the books that frequently appear on syllabuses. Altogether, there are references to over a hundred authors. You are unlikely to know all of them, but I think that many of the examples are intelligible, even if you are unfamiliar with the book. For readers who are looking for ideas about their set works, I suggest a glance at the index. I hope that what I say about individual works will be helpful; I have been partly guided by the kind of things examiners ask students to write about.

Thirdly, a book can give you help on how to write about literature. For a lot of the time, writing about books requires what we might call a general vocabulary; you might need to write about feelings of love or hope or discuss how a character is fired by revenge. Such topics don't require you to use a specialist language. But there are aspects of literature that do need to be talked about in a special way; for instance, how a poem is formed or the way a story is told. What I hope to do is to introduce you to some useful terms. I also hope I won't bring

Every effort has been made to trace all the copyright holders but if any have been inadvertently overlooked the publishers will be pleased to make the necessary arrangement at the first opportunity.

The following friends have helped me through discussion and advice: Jane Clarkson, John Florance, Pat Phillipps, Neil Roberts, John Spanos, Michael Sweeney, Eric Swift, Jan Todd and Joan Ward. This book has no formal dedication, but they and my many pupils over the years are the ones who have most helped me as a teacher, so it is to them that I offer my grateful thanks.

RICHARD GILL

Part I
Studying Poetry

Reading, thinking and writing

1.1 The poem on the page

When you open a book of poetry, it may strike you that poems are unusual things. For instance, look at this poem by A. E. Housman:

> This time of year a twelvemonth past,
> When Fred and I would meet,
> We needs must jangle, till at last
> We fought and I was beat.
>
> So then the summer fields about,
> Till rainy days began,
> Rose Harland on her Sundays out
> Walked with the better man.
>
> The better man she walks with still,
> Though now 'tis not with Fred:
> A lad that lives and has his will
> Is worth a dozen dead.
>
> Fred keeps the house all kinds of weather,
> And clay's the house he keeps;
> When Rose and I walk out together
> Stock-still lies Fred and sleeps.

What makes this and other poems 'unusual' is the way it uses words. Words are not usually used in the following ways:

- organised into fixed lines
- lines organised into verses
- lines that are rhythmical
- words that rhyme
- words arranged in non-standard order
- words used with special meanings ('clay' means the grave).

We don't usually speak or write in this way. This brings us to an important point:

Poems are not like ordinary speech or writing; they are specially made objects in words.

It is useful to remember that the word 'poetry' comes from a Greek word, which 'to make'.

1.2   A poem is made of words

We should investigate a little further what it means to say that a poem is a specially made object in words. In one sense, anything that we say, from talk about buying potatoes to saying 'I love you', is 'made'. Words, sentences, speeches and so on are not 'natural' things; we have to learn to speak, and whenever anything is said or written, the words are chosen and arranged by the speaker or writer.

The point about poetry (and other forms of literature) is that the choice of words and their arrangement is made so as to draw the listener's or reader's attention to those features of language which in everyday speech are usually ignored – rhythms, rhymes, non-standard word orders and so on. Poetry does this in order to stimulate a pleasure in these features and to enlarge or augment the meaning and impact of the poem.

Two points about poetry and all literature emerge in what has just been said:

(1)   poetry is specially made
(2)   poetry says something.

Poetry is specially made

We have already talked about this, but one more thing needs to be said about it:

To say that poetry is specially made is to say that it is art.

No matter how interested we might become in what a poem is saying, we must never forget that what it says is the result of the way it has been written. For instance, the meaning, and therefore the impact, of the Housman poem printed above depends in part upon the repetition of the phrase 'the better man'. We ask who is and what it means to be 'the better man' because the phrase is repeated, and that is a matter of art, of how the words are arranged. (You will see that in talking about the art of the poem, we have also spoken of what it says. We can't separate the one from the other.)

Poetry says something

Poetry is about ideas, about feelings, about places, about people and about events. It can argue, explore feelings, create pictures (either detailed or impressionistic ones) and, in the case of the Housman poem, tell stories. It is a fact of history that people have set down their most precious thoughts and feelings in poems – for instance, in 1992 Thom Gunn published a book of poems called *The Man with Night Sweats* about his friends who had died of AIDS. It's also true that readers have been able to appreciate and value experiences more fully because they have encountered them in the form of poems. When people have been particularly happy or particularly sad they have read or, in some cases, written poetry.

Poetry and female identity

At the moment there is a strong movement that uses verse to think about female identity. In bookshops and on syllabuses for public examinations you will find poems by women which explore the nature of female experience. For instance, Maya Angelou and Grace Nichols write about being black and female, while U. A. Fanthorpe implicitly and wryly presents a different view of human life from that which is often found in poetry written by men. Her 'Not My Best Side', a comical but not unkind subversion of a famous painting by Uccello of St. George and the Dragon, playfully presents the maiden whom St. George is rescuing as being more interested in the dragon – 'Well, you could see all his equipment/At a glance' – than she is in the conventionally heroic man:

> I didn't much fancy him. I mean,
> What was he like underneath the hardware?
> He might have acne, blackheads or even
> Bad breath for all I could tell

Fanthorpe is a very careful artist. The tone of the girl is cleverly captured in her choice of words; think, for instance, of how belittling of male pride in machinery (in this case St George's armour) is the workaday word 'hardware'. Through her artistry her interests are divertingly expressed – a woman might not value a man in the way in which he wants her to. Poetry that adopts a feminine perspective may be a relatively new thing, but what it's doing is not; poets have always explored what matters to them. Poetry says things that matter to people.

1.3   Two ways of talking about poetry

Most people who read this book will do so because they have to sit an examination in English Literature. That means they will have to think about what literature says and how it says it. To think about literature requires two kinds of language:

(1)   a specialised language that enables us to be clear about the art of literature
(2)   a more general language about the subject matter of literature.

For instance, one of the features of the Housman poem is the stanza (the verse form). It's written in what is sometimes called *common metre* (the same metre that the familiar Christmas hymn 'While shepherds watched their flocks by night' is written in), a form frequently used in ballads. This gives to the poem a traditional and even timeless quality; we feel that the violent rivalries of love are constantly recurring features of human life. Perhaps for this reason we, as readers, are distant and detached as we listen to what is a familiar story; we might say: 'Yes, this is what has always happened', and we might add, 'It'll go on happening.'

In what I have written above there are both kinds of language; 'stanza' and 'common metre' are specialised, while 'violent rivalries' is from that more general language we need when writing about the subject matter of poems. In what follows I hope to give advice about the specialised and the general languages. But before we move on, there are three points that need to be made, the first of which is a reply to a frequently made objection.

(1) Is a specialised language necessary?

Some people say that it's not necessary to have a specialised language. The reason they give for this is that readers should just rely on what they feel. There is some sense in this. Quite often we are attracted to a poem because of the feelings it rouses in us, and those feelings are a good place to start our thinking. All this is true. But if you only rely on your feelings you end up writing about them and not the poem itself. This applies to the more general as well as the specialised language. The words 'violent rivalries' refer to the subject matter of the poem and not the feelings of the reader.

This is not to say that when writing about poetry there is no place for the first person; you can say, for instance, 'I feel the poet is both happy and sad . . .' but you will also find that you need to write a good deal in the third person as well. It's useful to bear in mind two different complaints that examiners often make: they say that students often ignore the language of the poem and they also complain that they don't talk about the impact the poetry has on them.

(2) The two languages are inseparable

The specialised and general ways of talking can never be separated. The one requires the other, so in writing about literature the specialised language blends into the more general one. This, of course, is a repetition of what we have already said: poetry is both specially made and an important way of saying something. Hence the two different ways of talking about it are inseparable. For example, in Wordsworth's sonnet 'Upon Westminster Bridge Sept. 3 1820' there are these lines:

> This city now doth, like a garment, wear
> The beauty of the morning . . .

You might say of this that the simile 'like a garment. . .' (see pp. 25–6) expresses the glad surprise that at this particular moment ('now') the city is clothed in 'the beauty of the morning'. In that sentence 'simile' is specialised and 'glad surprise' general; both are needed to do justice to the words of the poem.

(3) There are no formulae

Since all poems (and all works of literature) are different from each other, there can be no single way of writing about them. Each work should be written about in its own particular way. The most therefore that a book like this can give is guidelines to help you come to see how each work might be thought and written about. There are no formulae, only approaches.

1.4   Reading poetry

One of the problems of thinking about poetry is that we find it difficult to recognise what is before us. To many of us, particularly when we are starting to study, the poems before us seem to be vague and blurred. It is as if we can't get them into focus. The first thing to remember is that this isn't unusual; most of us feel like this. Even after many years of reading, there are some poems which at first seem to me to be in a kind of mist.

One thing we can all do to cope with this is to read them carefully. The voice is as much the medium of a poem as the page on which it's written, so it's a good idea to read it aloud. This can be done in a number of ways.

- You can read the poem aloud to yourself when you are alone and undisturbed by noise. (Warning: you can't read poetry if music is playing!)
- When you read to yourself you should vary the speed from a deliberate one in which each word is pondered to one which is quicker and so keeps the shape of the whole poem in mind.
- You can read the poems you are studying into a cassette recorder, so you will be able to replay them again and again.
- In some cases you will be able to buy tapes and discs of the poems, sometimes these are read by the poets themselves.
- You can ask a friend to read the poems to you.

As you read you should try to do the following things:

- concentrate on each word as you hear it
- keep in mind how the poem is developing
- listen to what the poem sounds like (it might be gentle, angry, thoughtful, sad . . .)
- be aware of how you are reacting to what you are hearing
- notice any words that have a particularly strong impact on you.

It will be obvious from that rather demanding list that one reading will not be enough. When you are studying poems for the first time or revising them, it's a good idea to adopt the rule that several readings are better than one. The only other thing that needs to be said is that if a poem has a very powerful impact upon first reading, you should try to remember what you experienced, because it's likely that something very important about the poem was present in that experience.

1.5   Thinking about words

But what is it that you are reading? The simple but important answer is – words. Poems are made of words, and whatever is said in them is said in words, which are arranged in fixed lines. Any poem can be said to be: these particular words arranged in these particular lines. As you read, you should try to attend to the following points:

- how the words combine to create meanings
- how they create pictures in your mind
- how they work upon your feelings
- how they are organised to give the poem a shape.

Another way of putting this is: notice what you notice. That is to say, be aware of those features of the poem that advertise themselves to you in your reading.

Example

Let us look at Tennyson's 'The Eagle'.

> He clasps the crag with crooked hands;
> Close to the sun in lonely lands,
> Ringed with the azure world, he stands.
>
> The wrinkled sea beneath him crawls;
> He watches from his mountain walls,
> And like a thunderbolt he falls.

You may notice the slightly unusual combination of 'crooked hands' (a combination made more prominent because of its place at the end of the line). Neither words seem immediately appropriate; an eagle has claws not hands, and if they were crooked he would not be able to clasp the crag.

What then are the words pointing to? It may be that the fifth line is a clue. Perhaps the poem is also about a king or ruler looking down from his castle walls and dealing out punishment with the suddenness and power of 'a thunderbolt'. Hands would then be appropriate, and 'crooked' could suggest either that they are gnarled with age or that the man is crooked in the sense of unjust or dishonest. Even if this idea is merely, so to speak, a shadow cast by the image of the dominant eagle, it would still help the reader to recognise the presence of power and potential terror.

That discussion started when we looked at how the words combined to create meanings. In thinking about this we also looked at the picture that was created – the eagle on the crag and, possibly, the king on his castle walls. If we entertain the idea that we should think of a ruler as well as the eagle, our feelings have been aroused; the arbitrary authority of the absolute ruler (and an eagle might be thought to be ruler of the skies) is felt in the drama of the final line about the thunderbolt.

The fact that that is the final line shows us how the organisation of the poem matters. For instance, the fact that 'falls' is the closing word is important; we don't know what the eagle is falling on, so at the end of the poem its terror and mystery is preserved.

What that brief discussion of 'The Eagle' has shown is that points about words go hand-in-hand with points about how we read and respond. When we notice what we notice we become aware of how we are reacting to the poem. There are a number of questions you can ask about your reactions:

- How exactly am I reacting?
- Can I identify the thoughts and feelings these words arouse in me?
- Is this poem asking me to think about things in new and different ways?
- What kind of pleasure is this poem giving me?

In one sense you can't get round your reactions; they are the only way you have of finding your way into a poem. Yet you must remember that when writing about poetry, it is the words and not your feelings that matter. The questions above are only going to be helpful if they enable you to think about the words of the poem.

1.6 What the poem is about

To think about the words of a poem is to think about its meaning. That's an obvious statement, but saying it is useful because it addresses an anxiety some readers have about poems: do I understand what this poem is about?

- **The first thing you can do is be realistic.**

Some poems are so rich in their meanings that a lifetime is needed to appreciate them. If that is so, you can't expect to get very far with them on first acquaintance. If you can't expect that, it's not something you should worry about. Given that, it's wise to start with a modest aim.

- **Before you begin to think about a poem in detail, it's a good idea to have a general idea as to what it's about.**

For instance, if it's a narrative poem like the Housman quoted above, you need to be sure that you can follow the main events of the story. If, on the other hand, the poem presents an argument, you will have to make sure you can follow it at least in outline. You shouldn't be worried if there are some words, phrases or even whole sentences you don't understand. If you have an outline to work on, that's good enough for a start. In some cases you can probably guess what a word means. For instance, the word 'jangle' in the third line of the Housman means to talk in a noisy and discordant manner. You may be unaware of this, yet it doesn't matter; as long as you can see that the poem is about a dispute between two men over a woman you've got the gist of its opening.

1.7   Getting it clear

Some advice can be given about what you can do to get an outline of the poem's meaning. It's been said above that you should read a poem several times. You may find that as you do so the shape of the meaning becomes clearer. Also, as in the case of 'jangle', you can look up words in a dictionary if your ignorance of their meanings gets in the way of your achieving an overall understanding. As you try to come to terms with a poem's meaning, you may become aware of some features of poetic language that are not common in ordinary speech or writing. There are five which students often find difficult.

(1)   *Line and stanza endings are not always coterminous with units of meaning.*

That's to say, a phrase or sentence can run over from one line or one stanza to another. What you must do to avoid confusion is always follow the sense of phrases and sentences, and this means observing how the punctuation works. In other words, read on until you come to the comma, semi-colon, colon or full-stop. In the third line of the Housman, you have to read on beyond the line ending (this is called a run-on line) in order to make sense of 'till at last/We fought and I was beat.'

(2)   *Poems often shorten phrases, so a few words stand for what in speech would be conveyed by several more.*

This is sometimes called *compression*. Often we have to spell out the meaning by thinking of the words that might have been included. There are some puzzling lines in Hardy's 'Neutral Tones':

> And some words played between us to and fro
> On which lost the more by our love.

It's not immediately evident what the second line means. If, however, we realise that the words are compressed, we might read it as meaning: On the subject of which of the two of us lost the more by our love.

(3) *Poets have a habit of contracting words.*

Of course, we do this a great deal of the time, particularly in speech; for instance, 'don't' is a contraction of do not. In the Housman poem there is ''tis' in the tenth line. It sounds rather old-fashioned (and perhaps for that reason poetic), but in fact it simply is a contraction of 'it is'.

(4) *Poets use inversion – the changing or reversing of the normal order of words.*

The Housman poem ends: 'Stock-still lies Fred and sleeps.' In most conversation and writing we would probably have put it: Fred lies stock-still and sleeps. Inversion is not something we should ignore when we have worked out the meaning; it can subtly direct us to very precise and delicate effects. We see that, by placing it first, the poet shows that as far as the speaker is concerned, the most important thing about Fred is that he is 'Stock-still'; that is, dead.

The last feature is slightly different from the others.

(5) *Over the years poets have developed special meanings for words.*

In order to understand what they are saying, we have to be able to recognise exactly how the words are being used. Of course, it isn't only literature that does this; everyone uses language in special ways. Sometimes, these special uses are likened to codes, and recognising what is being said is referred to as reading the code or even decoding. We've already pointed to one of these in the Housman poem: 'clay' refers to the grave. In fact, there is a highly developed code for death in poetry; for instance, 'to sleep' can mean to die and 'bed' can mean the grave. Death is not the only subject for which there is a code; most subjects have created their own special vocabulary. There's no short cut to learning these. The best advice that can be given is: read a lot and you'll begin to see how they work.

1.8 Puzzlement, interest and pleasure

The best thinking about poetry gets under way when we ask questions. If, when you are reading a poem, something attracts your attention, you should try to frame it in the form of a question. This isn't always easy. Nevertheless, in most cases there are two general questions that can usually be asked.

- What do I feel about this poem?
- What is it about this poem that makes me feel this?

Both these questions are about the words of the poem. Whatever you feel, you feel because something about the words has prompted you, so whatever answer you come up with in relation to the second question, it will refer to the words the poet has used.

When you try to frame questions about the effect of the poem, you may find that they deal with three things:

(1)   puzzlement
(2)   interest
(3)   pleasure

Puzzlement

Puzzlement arises when you say: 'how strange' or 'that's odd'. You can frame these reactions as questions:

- Why does the poet say that?
- Why is this particular word used?
- Why does the poet move from that subject to this?

Example

Look at these lines from Wordsworth's 'Resolution and Independence' (sometimes known as 'The Leech-gatherer'); he is writing about the lives of poets:

> By our own spirits are we deified:
> We Poets in our youth begin in gladness;
> But thereof come in the end despondency and madness.

At least two words here might puzzle you. Why does Wordsworth use such an elevated word as 'deified'? (It means made god-like.) It takes a very high view of the poet. But then the poem goes in a very different direction. We move from 'gladness' through 'despondency' to the disturbing rhyme of 'madness'. This is certainly puzzling; Wordsworth introduces us to an emotional world of a vast and frightening range.

Interest

Interest arises when we say things such as 'that's intriguing' or 'how fascinating'. Such feelings can be framed as questions:

- Am I interested because it reflects the way I feel?
- Am I interested because I've felt a bit like that but could never quite find the words?
- Am I interested because the poet thinks in an unusual way?
- Am I interested because the poem entices me to further thought?

Example

Consider the example of Tennyson's 'Ulysses'. The speaker (sometimes called the *protagonist*) is the aged Greek hero Ulysses, who, perhaps surprisingly, is not content with ruling his island but yearns for the kind of adventures he had when younger. What is interesting is that his son, Telemachus, is content to stay on the island and carry out the duties of a ruler. He is 'centred in the sphere/Of common duties' whereas the older Ulysses wants

> To sail beyond the sunset, and the baths
> Of all the western stars, until I die.

It is the contrast to and the departure from what we might expect that arouses interest; the young man is 'centred', whilst the older wants to go 'beyond'. And the words 'common duties' are usually associated with the routine life of older people, not the exploits of the adventurous young. Such interest points to the difference (a crucial one in the poem) between the heroic attitude to life, represented by Ulysses, and one that settles for convention and routine.

Pleasure

Pleasure is present when we say: 'How beautiful' or 'How wonderful for someone to say that'. For many people this is their way into poetry; a line, a verse, even a single word might suddenly astonish them so that they find themselves going back to the poem again and again. Sometimes, like a tune, the words sing in your head for days. My own enthusiasm for poetry started when I heard with astonished pleasure a record of T. S. Eliot reading his 'The Love-Song of J. Alfred Prufrock'. I had never heard anything like it before, and I've read Eliot ever since. Whenever you find pleasure in poetry you can ask:

- What is it about these words that I find pleasurable?

___ **Example** _____

A poem that has given pleasure to many readers is Edward Thomas's
'Adlestrop'. Its ending is particularly haunting:

> And for that minute a blackbird sang
> Close by, and round him, mistier,
> Farther and farther, all the birds
> Of Oxfordshire and Gloucestershire.

Isn't our enjoyment of these lines something to do with the way the very
precise phrase 'And for that minute' captures the intensity and stillness of a
special moment? It is 'that moment' and not any other that the poet wishes
to remember and celebrate. Or could it be the contrast between the single
blackbird 'close by' and, in the misty distance, 'all the birds/Of
Oxfordshire and Gloucestershire', which, so to speak, opens up the landscape as it moves beyond Adlestrop to the remote regions of the two coun-
ties? You then might want to ask why such a movement is pleasurable. In
many areas of literary thinking, one question leads to another.

_____

1.9   Tone

One of the things that readers often find puzzling, interesting or pleasurable
about poems is their tone. Tone is a term that is both specialised and general.
What creates tone is the way the words work, and that is a matter which, in
some measure, can be described in a specialised language; but it is also part of
that more general vocabulary about thoughts and feelings because it refers to the
emotional colouring of language. It can therefore be spoken of as what emerges
from the poise, mood, voice, manner, attitude and outlook of a poet. In order to
describe what does emerge you need to master a vocabulary about a very broad
range of human responses. You may also need to blend the words you use; a
poem may not be simply sad – it may be regretfully sad or wistfully sad or
nostalgically sad, and so on.
    The best piece of advice that can be given about tone is:

- **Try to imagine the poet speaking and hear in the words his or her attitude to what is being said.**

This act of imagination is not always easy, so, as with all difficult procedures,
practice is essential. Since virtually every poem can be regarded as a communication of one person to others, every poem can be imagined as the spoken utter-
ance of the poet. The reader, therefore, can always ask:

- Can I hear the poet's voice in this poem?

Examples

Example 1

Milton opens his sonnet 'On the late Massacre in Piedmont' with these words:

> Avenge, O Lord, thy slaughtered saints, whose bones
> Lie scattered on the Alpine mountains cold

What kind of voice do we hear in these words? How do we imagine the poet speaking? The tone is certainly fierce and revengeful, but you might also say that because the poet is so certain that those who have been killed are 'saints', it is also assured in its demand that God should exact vengeance.

Example 2

We surely have to imagine a different voice in Christina Rossetti's poem, 'A Birthday', which opens:

> My heart is like a singing bird
>   Whose nest is in a watered shoot;
> My heart is like an apple-tree
>   Whose boughs are bent with thickset fruit

The voice that I imagine is one that is joyful, but is it possible to imagine what kind of joy? Given the images of 'a singing bird' and 'an apple-tree', we might say that it is a fresh, natural and spontaneous joy that flourishes with the ease of bird-song and the certain growth of fruit. It might also be helpful to say that the joy is securely possessed by the poet because it has the quality of safe isolation (the 'watered shoot') and is as closely related to her as are the apples on an apple-tree.

Example 3

To my ear at least the tone of Auden's 'Musée des Beaux Arts' is quite different. I may be right in discerning a secure self-possession in Christina Rossetti, but the stance of the poet here is very much cooler. The subject is the treatment of suffering by the famous painters of the past:

> They never forgot
> That even the dreadful martyrdom must run its course
> Anyhow in a corner, some untidy spot
> Where the dogs go on with their doggy life and the torturer's horse
> Scratches its innocent behind on a tree.

The voice sounds quiet, detached, even off-hand; the poet surveys the work of painters in a leisurely, nonchalant way. He is fascinated but hardly engaged emotionally. Note how easily he uses a word such as 'even' (it's like a nod of the head in acknowledgement of a recognised feature), and the sombre phrase 'dreadful martyrdom' is followed up with the casual throw-away 'must run its course /Anyhow', an idea that is casually qualified by the imprecision of 'some untidy spot'.

As with most issues in the understanding of poetry, reading and re-reading is necessary. Tone is often difficult, and it's not uncommon to find readers disagreeing about it. The important thing to remember is that because tone is a poem's emotional colouring, it can be heard in a number of ways:

- in the pace of a poem
- in the weight of its stresses
- in the length of its vowels
- in its juxtaposition of words
- in its choice of images.

Since many of these are intimately related to the voice, it is wise, once you have an idea of what the tone is, to practise reading the poem aloud to yourself or to another. When you do this, you will find that recognition of tone goes hand-in-hand with the question of how to describe it.

1.10   Enactment

There is one other aspect of poetry that, like tone, applies to every poem: *enactment*. When in the next three chapters a number of technical terms are introduced, you can think about them all in terms of how they enact the meaning of the poem.

Enactment depends upon an idea that is central to the study of literature. People often talk about

- what a book says – its subject-matter, meaning, or content; and
- the way it is written – its form, shape or structure.

Sometimes the distinction is useful when you wish to isolate a particular aspect of a literary work.

Yet it can be misleading. A poem is not made of two things – form and content, subject and structure, meaning and shape – it is made of words, and words are indivisible. You can't take from a word the aspects that create form, shape or structure – its sound, the rhythms it can help to establish, the rhymes it can effect, and the stanza shapes it can be used for – and leave the content. If you did remove those things, you would be left not with the content of the word but with nothing at all.

So every aspect of a word contributes to the word's meaning. In everyday language we are not usually aware of this, but in poetry we are. Poetry uses every aspect, or resource, of language to enact meaning. The word 'enactment' is useful because it suggests that all the aspects of words, so to speak, join together and act out their meaning.

Example

Arnold's 'Dover Beach' is about the thoughts and feelings the poet has when he hears the waves breaking on the shore. At one point he writes about the sounds and rhythms they make:

> Listen! you hear the grating roar
> Of pebbles which the waves draw back, and fling,
> At their return, up the high strand,
> Begin, and cease, and then again begin,
> With tremulous cadence slow, and bring
> The eternal note of sadness in.

The sounds and rhythms of those words enact two things – the ebbing and flowing of the tide, which begins, and ceases, and then again begins , and the overwhelming sadness those sounds stir in the poet. We can hear the tide lapping up the shore and then relapsing before its inevitable return, and then the poetry becomes more still as we listen to the delicacy of the 'tremulous cadence slow'. This stillness ceases as the tide brings in 'The eternal note of sadness'. The word, 'eternal' is long, yearning and weighty; and it enacts the immensity of the poet's sadness. The point about these words is that they are not just decorating the idea of tides and sadness, but words which actually enact the movements of the tide and the poet's feelings.

Enactment is the harnessing of the physical or material aspects of verse – the length of lines, the sounds of words, the rhythms of words, the presence or absence of rhyme – so poets who are aware of formal matters (matters to do with how a poem is made) will be likely to produce verse in which enactment is clearly evident. This inevitably means that in many modern poets, particularly those who don't write in regular lines or stanzas (sometimes called 'free verse'), we don't find it obvious that the material aspects of the verse are being used to enforce and augment the meaning in the way in which they are in, say, Tennyson or Arnold. Yet there are twentieth-century poets whose language, sometimes quite brilliantly, enacts what they are saying. This is one of the pleasures of reading Yeats. T. S. Eliot is another; he is adept at creating rhythms, and, in particular, cadences, that – to use a musical metaphor – orchestrate his thoughts and feelings. The lost, perplexed, anguished and yearning Prufrock is heard in the trailing lines and somehow unsatisfying rhymes of the opening of his poem:

> Let us go then, you and I,
> When the evening is spread out against the sky
> Like a patient etherised upon a table

Rhymes usually resolve matters; the chiming of words in rhyme gives them a harmony which, so to speak, securely places and orders them. Here, however, the rhymes don't sort out anything. There's something so aching and empty about 'I/sky' that what we are aware of is the unappeased longing of Prufrock. And then glum collapse; the flatness – inertness – of the third line enacts the hopelessness from which he wants to escape.

More recently, Sylvia Plath has written verse in which the physical properties of the language eerily enact the meanings. Listen to the opening of 'Mushrooms':

> Overnight, very
> Whitely, discreetly,
> Very quietly
>
> Our toes, our noses
> Take hold on the loam,
> Acquire the air.

The poem gives the reader a new perspective on this common vegetable. No longer do we see mushrooms as soft, bland and even characterless; they are furtive, sinister, determined and perhaps even irresistible. We feel this because that is what the verse enacts; the subdued, soft consonants, the stealthy tread of the adverbs and the unsettling recurrence of whispering sounds all make us see and hear mushrooms as disturbing and threatening.

Exercises

1.1 Read through the poems you are studying a number of times, trying to detect their tone. When you think you have grasped the tone, try to characterise what it is in writing.

1.2 Read the following poem by Hardy and answer the questions below. Hardy is writing about a folk tradition that on Christmas Eve all the animals kneel in honour of the birth of Christ.

The Oxen

Christmas Eve, and twelve of the clock.
'Now they are all on their knees,'

> An elder said as we sat in a flock
> > By the embers in hearthside ease.
>
> We pictured the meek mild creatures where
> > They dwelt in their strawy pen,
> Nor did it occur to one of us there
> > To doubt they were kneeling then.
>
> So fair fancy few would weave
> > In these years! Yet, I feel,
> If someone said on Christmas Eve,
> > 'Come; see the oxen kneel
>
> 'In the lonely barton by yonder coomb
> > Our childhood used to know,'
> I should go with him in the gloom,
> > Hoping it might be so.

(a)   It looks as if the elder believes the tradition. In what tone do you think the second line of the poem should be read?

(b)   When Hardy says:

> Nor did it occur to one of us there
> > To doubt they were kneeling then.

he is looking back upon the beliefs of his childhood from a position of doubt. What tone do these lines have?

(c)   Try to characterise the tone of:

> So fair a fancy few would weave
> > In these years!

You might think about why he calls the idea a 'fair fancy'.

(d)   What is the tone of the last two lines of the poem? What words can you find to characterise the mood of a man who would willingly return to the beliefs of his childhood, although he knows they were only a 'fancy'?

② Words and meaning

2.1 Looking at words

When you ask what puzzles you, interests you or gives you pleasure in a poem, you will find that the answer is something to do with the way that the *words work*. The particular function of words that will be dealt with in this section is the way they establish meaning.

You could write about every word in a poem, but if you did, your writing would be mechanical and you would probably lose sight of the poem as a whole. It is much better to read through the poem a number of times, looking out for the *striking* word. You should read a poem with this question in mind:

● Are there words here that are particularly puzzling, interesting or pleasurable?

Here are some lines of poetry. Read them through with that question in mind and see if any of the words strike you:

(1)   And stare into the tangled fire garden
                                    (R. S. Thomas, 'On the Farm')

(2)   And a tense, musty, unignorable silence
                                    (Philip Larkin, 'Church Going')

(3)   Now as I was young and easy under the apple boughs
                                    (Dylan Thomas, 'Fern Hill')

(4)   The blue jay scuffling in the bushes follows
                                    (Thom Gunn, 'On the Move')

(5)   Till with a sudden sharp hot stink of fox
                                    (Ted Hughes, 'The Thought-Fox')

In the first line the words 'tangled' and 'garden' might have struck you. 'Tangled' points to an interesting complication, and 'garden' is a surprise, coming as it does after 'fire'.

In the second line, a number of words might have struck you, though perhaps the most interesting is 'unignorable'. The word itself is that!

In the Dylan Thomas line, it is surely the word 'easy' which attracts attention. It is both unusual and comes with a delightful lilt after 'young'.

'Scuffling' in the fourth line attracts attention, largely because it is the word dealing with sound among others concerned with sight.

In the last line, you might be struck by one or all of the four 'sudden sharp hot stink'; they are emphatic and deliberate.

In all the above examples, words are used in a rich and intriguing way. You are being invited to think about them, and as you do, you see more and more in them. This is what poetry does with words – enriches and deepens their meanings.

Sometimes as you are reading, a word or group of words may strike you, but you don't know how to start thinking about them. Here are three questions you might ask:

● Why was this word rather than a similar one used?
● What meanings does this word have in everyday speech that might be exploited here?
● How does the context enrich the meaning of the word?

Have another look at our five examples. In the first line 'stare' is more power-ful than, for instance, 'look'; it's more intense and purposeful. In the third line 'easy' is effective because it picks up everyday connotations of pleasure, effort-less activity and lack of anxiety. In the fifth line the proximity of 'fox' to 'sudden sharp hot stink' enriches the meanings of all the words. The fox is imbued with intense drama – its appearance is 'sudden' and its smell pungent; and a word such as 'hot' is given an animal vitality – the heat of the chase, of mating, of fighting – by its proximity to 'fox'.

Two points need to be stressed.

● **It is useful to look at the connotations of a word**.

Connotations are the associations of meaning a word has acquired because of its various uses. When you encounter a striking word, you can look at how in the context, a number of connotations are brought into play. One of the reasons that poetry is valued is because its words exploit a wide range of associations.

● **You should not ignore 'little' words** – such as 'the', 'a', 'too', 'yet', 'in', 'and'. Sometimes, a poet can enrich even the simplest and humblest of words. In MacNiece's 'Prayer before Birth', each irregular stanza begins: 'I am not yet born.' That simple word 'yet' is very poignant as it shows the unborn child poised on the edge of life, innocent of any corruption but aware of the dangers of what is ahead. In Stevie Smith's 'Not Waving but Drowning', there is the line

Oh, no, no, no, it was too cold always

which is a plaintive line of someone who is beyond hope, and its plaintiveness is enacted in its simple words. The, 'it' – such an insignificant word, normally – refers to the seas and to life itself. The contract between the insignificant word and the large things 'it' stands for is quite moving. Likewise, the 'too' is simple and deep. The 'always' confirms that life was at every moment much too much for him. The art of Stevie Smith lies in her ability to convey so much sadness in so few, seemingly ordinary words.

2.2   How poets use words

You may feel that the advice to look for the striking word is too general. If so, what other more specific advice can be given?

Look for a change in tone

Sometimes this can indicate that a word is worth thinking about. In Blake's 'The Poison Tree', the tone is that of someone who obsessively nurses his anger, until in the words of the poem, 'it bore an apple bright', which tempts his hated enemy to theft:

> And into my garden stole
> When the night had veiled the pole;
> In the morning glad I see
> My foe outstretched beneath the tree.

When the enemy is dead, the tone changes from being dark and furtive to one of relief, and even rejoicing. This change is focused in the word 'glad'. If you had to write about that poem, you would have to discuss the shock that comes when a word as blithe and innocent as 'glad' is used in relation to death.

Look out for repeated words

When a poet uses a word more than once it is often because it is vital in the building up of the poem's meaning. Here is another example from Blake – the opening of 'London':

> I wander through each chartered street,
> Near where the chartered Thames does flow,
> And mark in every face I meet
> Marks of weakness, marks of woe.

Why does Blake repeat 'chartered' and 'mark'? It looks as if he is angry at the way in which everywhere in London – even the river! – is given over to trade (a charter being a licence to sell). This, he feels, has marked the people, and also marked him, for although he uses the word as a verb when he speaks of himself, it sounds harsh, as if he, too, is aware of 'marks of woe' in him.

Look for contrast

This is another guide to important words. Yeats's poem 'The Circus Animals' Desertion' ends with a striking contrast between two ideas. He writes of:

> ... the foul rag-and-bone shop of the heart.

The power of these words comes from the contrast between the filth associated with a 'rag-and-bone shop' and the word 'heart' with its associations of high and noble feelings. Such a striking contrast invites you to write about how the words work.

No word is more poetic than another word

When you are asking questions about words, you must not imagine that some words are more worthy of study just because they sound more 'poetic'. This is particularly important in modern poems where quite ordinary words are used. Eliot uses 'cheap hotels', 'window-panes', 'coffee spoons', 'shirt-sleeves' and 'white flannel trousers' in 'The Love-Song of J. Alfred Prufrock'; and in his poem, 'Lake District', Betjeman (a master of the ordinary word) uses 'cruet', 'non-alcoholic wine', 'the H.P. sauce' and 'Heinz's ketchup'. No word is more poetic than another word. What matters is *how the poet uses them.*

Figures of speech

When you write about words that puzzle, interest or give you pleasure, you will need to master some technical terms. The ones the examiners will expect you to know are:

- simile
- metaphor
- conceit
- personification
- symbol
- image
- paradox
- ambiguity.

These are called *figures of speech.* You must show tact in using these terms. It is never sufficient merely to identify and label. No examiner will reward you for pointing out that a word is a metaphor. Your aim should always be to show *how* a figure of speech contributes to the poem. In order to show that, you will need to master both the technical terms and the broader vocabulary concerned with thought and feeling. Of course, one way of showing how a figure of speech contributes to the poem is by writing about how it enacts its meaning.

2.3   Metaphor and simile

Metaphors and similes are features of everyday speech. We talk, for instance, about 'a blanket of fog' or about the fog coming down 'like a blanket'. In both cases we are talking about two things at the same time; in the first case, the metaphor, we are saying that the fog is a blanket, and in the second case, the simile, we are comparing fog to a blanket. It has been said that in metaphors and similes we get two things for the price of one. In everyday speech we don't always take much notice of what we are doing when we talk this way, but in poetry these figures of speech are important. By carefully choosing their words, poets are effectively inviting us to look afresh at what they are talking about and to consider how they are saying it. How they are saying it is part of the meaning.

This puts a special responsibility on the reader. Rather than glancing over metaphors and similes as we do in ordinary speech we should linger over them and think about the way they link the two things, and the imaginative process we have to go through in order to see the linkage.

Metaphor

Let us first look at a metaphor in the way we have just discussed.

Example ————————————————————————

In R. S. Thomas's 'On the Farm' the poet writes:

> Her pale face was the lantern
> By which they read in life's dark book

'Lantern' and 'life's dark book' work metaphorically. In the case of the first metaphor, we see together her face and a lantern. We might imagine the one, as it were, superimposed on the other. Because we see the two together, the meanings and associations of the one become fused with the other. Normally 'pale face' might suggest weakness or sickness, but when we see it in the light (another metaphor) of 'lantern' we are enabled to see her face as radiant.

We should also see the force of the verb 'was'. There is always an implied 'is' or 'was' in a metaphor. The poet is not just comparing one thing with another; within the poem one thing is said to be the other. The imaginative process of the metaphor asks us to respond not just to the suggestion that they are similar but to the concrete actuality of 'face' and 'lantern'.

This is why metaphors are often valued for their power; they make us see things with the punch of actual sight. Sometimes the tough statement 'this is that' is used to define the imaginative force of metaphors. Think, for instance, about how the words 'dark book' make 'life' vividly sombre. Rather than saying that life is a serious matter, we are made to feel its darkness and the grim fixed quality of it being set down in writing. Poets and other writers are, like philosophers, thinkers, but their thinking is often done through figures of speech such as metaphors, in which thought comes alive when two things are brought together.

From the above discussion we might conclude two things about metaphors:

(1) they are economical
(2) they are immediate.

The fusion of two things takes place in a few words. Sometimes, it occurs in one. In Wordsworth's 'Ode on the Intimations of Immortality from Recollections of Early Childhood' there is a line about the earth seeming to be 'Apparelled in celestial light'. The metaphor exists in 'apparelled'; that single word economically presents a picture of the earth gloriously clothed in resplendent light.

The immediacy of metaphors is a function of their economy and their implicit assertion of an identity. Because they rest upon the assertion that 'this is that', they come across to the reader with the force of actuality. In Tennyson's 'Mariana' he writes of 'When thickest dark did trance the sky'. In a single word – 'trance' – he gives us an immediate picture of the darkness hypnotising the sky.

Simile

In metaphor two things are brought together and asserted to be one (remember 'this is that'); in simile there are also two things brought together, but the connection is made clear to the reader by the use of the words 'like' or 'as'. This means there is not the intriguing element of identity (no implied 'is'), and nor is there usually the immediacy of the metaphor. This had led some people to regard similes as of less worth than metaphors. This is a mistake. Although similar, they work in distinctive ways and should therefore be valued for what they individually do.

Similes can sound natural, and readers can enjoy moving from one thing to the other. Similes are often successful when they have the ease of ordinary speech which makes you say: 'Yes, I would make that comparison if I were in that situation.'

For example, Sassoon's 'Everyone Sang' moves effortlessly from singing to a simile that freshly, yet naturally, expresses a sense of release:

> Everyone suddenly burst out singing;
> And I was filled with such delight
> As prisoned birds must find in freedom ...

Sassoon trusts that the reader will know what a sudden outburst of joy feels like and will therefore understand the quite standard comparison with free birds.

But similes can also be unusual, and when they are they offer, so to speak, an invitation to the reader to travel in imagination from one thing to another. In 'The Rime of the Ancient Mariner', Coleridge says this of a becalmed ship:

> Day after day, day after day,
> We stuck, nor breath, nor motion;
> As idle as a painted ship
> Upon a painted ocean.

The simile invites the reader to journey from a real ship to one that is only 'painted'. Notice how the repetition of 'painted' makes the picture seem more unreal and thus very distant from the actual ship. The unusual attraction of the simile lies in the distance the mind of the reader has to travel between two objects that are felt to be very different.

If you are studying Milton, you will encounter a special kind of simile: the *epic* or *extended* simile. This is a simile which is worked out in detail, so there are either several points of comparison or a detailed picture of the thing to which the subject is being compared. They usually add to the range of the poem by giving the impression (necessary in epics) of the poet dealing with many branches of knowledge and human endeavour.

Tenor and vehicle

Whether you are writing about metaphors or similes, there is a useful distinction that can help you to explain how they work.

- The subject of the simile or metaphor – the thing the poet compares to something else – it is called the 'tenor.'
- The thing to which the subject is compared is called the 'vehicle'.

The distinction is useful, particularly when writing about complex lines.

—— **Example** ——————————————————————————————————

In his Sonnet 73 Shakespeare writes of growing old in terms of the metaphor of Autumn, but then a transformation takes place in the metaphor itself. This is how the poem opens:

> That time of year thou mayest in me behold
> When yellow leaves, or none, or few, do hang
> Upon those boughs that shake against the cold,
> Bare ruined choirs, where late the sweet birds sang.

How can we describe what happens in those lines? If we use the distinction between tenor and vehicle we can get somewhere.

The poet compares himself to Autumn, which he represents with a vivid picture of a tree almost completely bare of leaves. The ageing poet is the tenor, and the autumnal tree is the vehicle. But then the vehicle of the tree becomes the tenor of the next metaphor, when it's compared to the ruined choirs of deserted abbey churches. It's actually more complex than that, because there is a further metaphor of the singing birds and the choirs or choristers of the abbey. Which is tenor and which vehicle? That's not an easy question; the only advantage in using these terms is that, as in the case of the other metaphors, the words 'tenor' and 'vehicle' help to frame the question.

2.4 Conceit

When a simile or metaphor is elaborate or far-fetched, and strikes you at first as being inappropriate and even outrageous, it is called a conceit. Conceits were very popular in seventeenth-century poetry, so if you are studying, say, the poems of Donne, Herbert, Marvell or Crashaw you are likely to find yourself in the position of having to say something about them. Faced with this problem, there are two things that you might try to do.

The strangeness of the comparison

A good conceit has the impact of something odd or unexpected. The initial reaction of a reader is usually that he or she is more aware of the differences than the similarities. Examiners often complain that students fail to bring over just how exciting (and even heady) reading conceits can be. It has to be said that this feeling often remains even when we know the poem well. This is why some readers find them to be 'flashy' rather than helpful in revealing the truth about a person, emotion or idea. Some see them as odd rather than true.

The need for persistence

The second thing that demands attention is the way we have to read them at length and in detail, pondering each development at it unfolds. (In this respect they are similar to epic similes.) Sometimes a conceit of Donne stretches over several lines. (See the entry under 'conceit' in the Glossary.) Reading a conceit is like going on a strange journey of exploration. At the end of the journey, we may imagine that the poet hopes the reader will see the point of the comparison; it may have seemed wilfully strange but it is, nevertheless, intriguingly right. That is the way the accusation of oddity can be met; if the reader persists, illumination will come.

Example

Look at this example from Crashaw; it is a short poem about the crucifixion, built around an astonishing conceit:

> They have left thee naked, Lord. O that they had;
> This garment too, I would they had denied.
> Thee with thyself they have too richly clad,
> Opening the purple wardrobe of thy side:
> O never could there be garment too good
> For thee to wear, but this of thine own blood.

It is strange (and perhaps shocking) to see Christ's naked, blood-stained body as an open wardrobe of purple clothes, and yet the horror of the conceit – its outlandish inappropriateness – drives home the point that no clothes but Christ's own blood were too good for him to wear. Both elements of the conceit are present: the weirdness of 'purple wardrobe' and the journey to an intelligible conclusion.

The conceit is not just a thing of the past. In the late 1970s and early 1980s a number of poets wrote in a deliberately playful manner. They would select a subject, sometimes from everyday life, and look at it from unusual angles. The result was that they turned to the conceit, because it allowed them to present what is familiar as if it were unfamiliar – what was common was made to look strange. For instance, in Christopher Reid's 'Arcadia', a poem about a picture of an ideal world, traffic is said to lurch down the road 'on its long sum of naughts'. Like all conceits the image of naughts is an initially puzzling one, but then with thought the reader sees that what is being talked about are the wheels of the vehicles, which, when viewed in a line, resemble a question in arithmetic made up entirely of naughts. The process the mind is invited to go through is the same as when reading Donne or Crashaw.

2.5 Personification, pathetic fallacy and mental landscape

Personification

Personification occurs when language gives human qualities to non-human things. Tennyson's metaphor 'When thickest dark did trance the sky' personifies the 'dark' by giving it the power to hypnotise. Personification can also work on an abstract noun, as in this line from Gray's 'Elegy':

> Can Honour's voice provoke the silent dust?

Here 'Honour', which to us is normally just an idea, becomes a person able to speak; and moreover, a person of grand and elevated character, whom we might picture clothed ceremonially and speaking eloquently. Perhaps that tells us something about honour – it requires us to be attentive and reverential. Honour's voice is something we should listen to; it may even be able to address the dead – 'the silent dust'.

There are two important effects that are very close to personification – pathetic fallacy and mental landscape. You are likely to come across both of these in nineteenth-century and twentieth-century verse.

Pathetic fallacy

Pathetic fallacy occurs when human feelings are given to objects which cannot by their very nature have them. In 'The Lotos Eaters' Tennyson writes:

> All round the coast the languid air did swoon,
> Breathing like one that hath a weary dream.

'Air' can't have feelings, but 'languid', 'swoon' and 'breathing' bestow them. As with personification there is the pleasing experience of seeing a figure – a weary, sleepy one – through whom we can appreciate the mood of the scene.

Mental landscape

In a mental landscape the feelings of a person find expression in his or her surroundings; the landscape (or townscape) expresses or reflects what that individual is feeling. It should be added that this is usually something that the poet makes evident to the reader and is not necessarily the conscious projecting of the protagonist's feelings on to the landscape. It should also be added that this is something that occurs in novels as well as in poetry. Mental landscape, when successful, unites a poem by making many of its elements work in the same way.

┌─ **Example** ───┐

In Tennyson's 'Maud' there is a bitter, resentful man on the edge of a
mental collapse, who speaks, as in these opening lines of the poem, with a
barely controlled violence:

> I hate the dreadful hollow behind the little wood,
> Its lips in the field above are dabbled with blood-red heath,
> The red-ribbed ledges drip with a silent horror of blood,
> And Echo there, whatever is asked her, answers 'Death'.

This grotesque and nightmarish picture of a heath is as much an image of
the speaker's mind as it is of an 'external' landscape. Its dreadfulness is his
dread, and 'Echo' reverberates his preoccupation with 'Death'. He doesn't
say: 'I see the connection between this place and my state of mind'; it is the
reader who makes the connection and sees that the landscape is a landscape
of the mind.

└───┘

Many poets employ mental landscapes to present the plight of the characters
who move through them. In Crabbe's 'Peter Grimes' the solitary landscape of
the Suffolk coast mirrors Peter's outcast state, and in Coleridge's 'The Rime
of the Ancient Mariner' the seascapes are an apt reflection of the mariner's
spiritual state. Many of Wordsworth's landscapes can be read as scenic
representations of the solitary and troubled characters that he so frequently
writes about.

There is one quality that personification, pathetic fallacy and mental landscape
have in common, and that is a feeling (or intuition?) in the poet's mind that the
world itself is not a dead thing but is itself alive. Perhaps we read the connections between feelings and landscape as bringing home to us the living nature of
the natural world.

2.6   Symbol

A symbol can be defined in the following way:

A symbol is a word that stands for, or points to, a reality beyond itself.

Sunrise, for instance, is often used for a symbol of a new beginning. That
example helps you to see something else about symbols:

Symbols often share in the reality for which they stand.

A sunrise not only stands for a new beginning; it is the new beginning of a day. Because it is actually a new beginning, it can stand for many other new beginnings. This is true of symbols that are not in words: a handshake is not just a symbolic way of welcoming someone; it is itself an act of welcoming. Thus in poetry we can say that Blake's 'The Tyger' is a symbol of terrifying, creative energy, and in itself a terrifying, energetic creature.

When you are reading poetry, you may be troubled by this question:

- How do I know whether a word is or is not being used as a symbol?

Unlike similes, there aren't linguistic features to look out for; symbols don't use words such as 'like' and 'as'. This is a real issue and it bothers many students. Often students are taught that poetry works by symbols and they respond by wrenching the most inappropriate meanings out of a poem. I have seen answers about Roy Campbell's poem 'Horses on the Camargue' (a poem about horses!), which have said it's about nuclear war! Many poems are about what they appear to be about; for instance, whatever subjects are touched on in Wordsworth's 'Daffodils' (and they include the place of memory and the flux of our emotional life) the daffodils in it are still daffodils.

How then can we tell whether something is a symbol? There is, of course, no foolproof 'method', but there are certain things we can attend to when thinking about this issue.

Traditional symbols

Most symbols are traditional; the more you read (and talk to readers of poetry) the more you will become acquainted with how words function symbolically. For instance:

- there are many symbols for death – sleep, sunset, night, the reaper – and many associated with what lies beyond death, such as a river reaching the sea or making a journey from which there is no return.
- Other frequently-used symbols are: flowers for the shortness of life, birds for the soul, a garden for perfect order, the sky for heaven and a tree for the whole created order of nature.
- Seasons are frequently symbolic – spring for new life and energy; summer for the joy and carefreeness of living; autumn for maturity and fulfilment; and winter for old age, decline and death.

Those are just a few. As you read and discuss literature you will become aware of how authors give a symbolic life to many of their words.

New symbols

In some cases, a poet makes new symbols. For Yeats the ancient city of Byzantium was a symbol of the perfect blending of the arts of living and the visual arts (or what is sometimes called art and nature). In our own day another Irish poet, Seamus Heaney, has found in the mummified remains of ancient people discovered in bogs a symbol of the tribal passions that are still present in Ireland. How, you may ask, can a reader hope to recognise these as symbols? The best you can do is ask three questions.

- Is there a word that has a prominent place in the poem?
- Is the word used in an elevated way?
- Does the word transform other elements in the poem?

Example

Consider the opening of Edwin Muir's 'The Horses':

> Barely a twelvemonth after
> The seven days war that put the world to sleep,
> Late in the evening the strange horses came.

The word 'horses' is prominent; it comes at the climax of the sentence and just before its main verb. And the horses are not any old nags; they are 'strange horses'. Although we don't know exactly what 'strange' means here, we can see that this word marks them out as different. Therefore they are 'elevated'; that is, raised above the level of the ordinary. You might also notice that they are elevated in another way – they appear amid the traditional symbols of creation and death ('seven days' is the biblical time for creation and 'put to sleep' is a traditional symbol of death). If you think about the order – creation, death, the coming of the horses – you can see that the horses have a transforming effect. They are a new beginning after a world-shattering catastrophe. Significantly, the poem ends with these words:

> Our life is changed; their coming our beginning.

Muir's horses are clearly symbolic, yet it is not easy to say *exactly* what they symbolise. This is often the case with symbols (particularly newly created ones), and you should try to capture this in your writing.

Final points

Symbols are often rich and complex, so you should be careful to suggest this when you discuss their function. We have used 'stands for' and 'points to'; you could also use:

- 'represents'
- 'suggests'
- 'evokes'
- 'expresses'

Your aim should always be to capture the way in which, so to speak, a symbol glows or echoes with meaning.

2.7   Images and imagery

GCSE, A-level and university questions often invite candidates to discuss the *imagery* of a poem. Because the term covers simile, metaphor, conceit, personification and symbol, what was said about those terms may apply to the more general word imagery. What, however, you must avoid is mere labelling; you must always try to write about its place in the poem. But what is that place? Whenever you are invited to write about imagery, there are three questions that you might ask.

- Does it help to create the atmosphere of the poem?
- Does it establish a pattern in the poem?
- Does it help to focus the meaning of the poem?

_____ **Example** _____

Look at this poem from Tennyson's *In Memoriam*, a sequence of poems on the death of his friend Arthur Hallam:

> Dark house, by which once more I stand
>   Here in the long unlovely street,
>   Doors, where my heart was used to beat
> So quickly, waiting for a hand.
>
> A hand that can be clasped no more —
>   Behold me, for I cannot sleep,
>   And like a guilty thing I creep
> At earliest morning to the door.
>
> He is not here; but far away
>   The noise of life begins again,
>   And ghastly through the drizzling rain
> On the bald street breaks the blank day.

> The atmosphere of a dreary morning in an anonymous and (we sense) unfeeling city is created through the imagery. The 'house' is 'dark', the 'street' 'long' and 'unlovely', and the morning (not here a symbol of new beginnings) breaks 'ghastly through the drizzling rain'.
>
> The recurrence of these images establishes a pattern; the poem starts with the 'dark house' and 'the long unlovely street', moves away to talk of the dead friend but then grimly returns with 'bald street'. It's as if the poet can't escape either from his feelings of grief or the ugly city.
>
> In doing this, the imagery focuses the theme of the poem. The house is dark, and so is the 'house' the friend has gone to – the house of death; the street is 'bald', the morning 'blank' as also, we infer, is the mind of the bereaved poet.

Tennyson's poem works by choosing one idea – a bleak morning in the city – and, by extending it, making it central to the whole poem. He is not alone in doing this. Quite often poets make all the images of a poem grow, as it were, from a single root. To take a modern example: in 'The Thought-Fox' Ted Hughes establishes the parallel between writing a poem and sighting a fox through images that all stem from writing – the blank page, the moving hand and the printed words.

The examples from Tennyson and Hughes can be used to make another point about how imagery focuses the themes of a poem – its concrete quality. Because images always appeal to the senses, they can be vivid and immediate. In an image the reader sees or hears something; it is not merely a matter of being informed, the thing is present, and it has an impact on us.

Example

> Yeats's 'The Second Coming' is about the break-up of order, an idea that is made forcefully present through the image of the falcon and the falconer ('gyre' means a spiralling movement):
>
> > Turning and turning in the widening gyre
> > The falcon cannot hear the falconer ...
>
> We are not just told that relationships are breaking up or that communication is becoming difficult; in the concrete image we see the bird spiralling out of reach, out of control and beyond hearing. In the smooth yet relentless movement, we see the frightening collapse of order as things move away from their controlling centre. There are ideas in images; but they are ideas that we see at work.

- **When writing about imagery, you should remember that, as in the Tennyson poem, one function does not exclude another.** As in all matters of understanding literature, you should look carefully at the poem to see exactly how it works. You can't expect every poem to work in the same way.

2.8   Paradox and ambiguity

Paradox and ambiguity are sometimes called figures of speech and sometimes simply regarded as ways in which language functions. Either way, you should learn to master the terms.

Paradox

A paradox is an apparent contradiction which says something strange yet true. For instance, in Keats's 'Ode on a Grecian Urn' there are these paradoxical lines on music:

> Heard melodies are sweet, but those unheard
> Are sweeter ...

That is contradictory; a melody you can't hear can never be sweeter than one you can. Nevertheless, the lines point to the strange truth that that which we imagine is often more beautiful than that which actually exists. When you write about paradoxes, you should bring out the element of surprise. What starts off as an apparent contradiction often yields truths that are more interesting than everyday ones.

Ambiguity

'Ambiguity' is a very useful term to master, when you want to write about the richness of meaning in poetry. Unlike its use in ordinary speech, it does not mean a confusing mistake but is used to indicate the many nuances of meaning that can be found in poetic language. Because language is ambiguous, a poem can do justice at the same time to quite different ideas. In Book I of *Paradise Lost* Milton writes of Satan's pride in seeing his host of fallen angels assembling before him:

> And now his heart
> Distends with pride, and hardening in his strength
> Glories ...

The word 'pride' is ambiguous because it has two meanings: a praiseworthy delight in one's own achievements, and the sin of placing oneself before others and God. Satan is rightly proud to see before him all the angels who remain his faithful followers, but this pride is also a sin in that Satan is setting himself up in opposition to God.

Ambiguity can also be created by the *syntax* of a poem: that is, by the order of words in a sentence. Consider these lines from the opening poem of Blake's *Songs of Innocence*:

> And I made a rural pen,
> And I stained the water clear.

What do these lines mean? They are about making ink to use in his pen, but do they mean that the pen stained the clear water, or is the meaning that the water was stained in order to make it clear? The syntax makes *both* meanings possible.

- You may find that the longer you think about poems, the more ambiguous they become. If this is the case, you should not try to simplify them. The best thing you can do when writing about them is to make clear that poems might mean a number of things. Indeed, the meaning of poems may be all the possible meanings that arise through the ambiguities.

2.9   Advice about technical terms

- As with all technical terms, you will learn to master them by usage.
- Whenever you take notes or write an essay, you should try to use the appropriate technical terms.
- When you first begin to use them, it is a good idea, particularly in the case of imagery, to think them through in detail. You can do this by picturing the effects created by similes and metaphors and listing all the shades of meaning that emerge in symbols. Although this is somewhat artificial, it will help you to see just how rich are the meanings that words convey.

There is, however, one warning to give. Sometimes it is not possible to identify a word as particular figure of speech. For instance, in Blake's 'The Sick Rose' it is not clear whether the rose is a real, a symbolic or a metaphoric one. There is, of course, no virtue simply in labelling, so when you cannot use an appropriate technical term, you should just concentrate on writing about the richness of the language.

_____ **Exercises** _____

2.1   Read through all the poems you have to study to see if there are any
      words that particularly strike you. If there are, try to write about them,
      bringing out why you feel them to be effective.

2.2   Read through all the poems you have to study for any of the figures of
      speech explained in this section. If you find some, try writing about
      how they help to establish the meaning of the poem.

2.3   Read 'To Autumn' by Keats a number of times, and then attempt to
      answer the questions below.

> Season of mists and mellow fruitfulness!
> Close bosom-friend of the maturing sun;
> Conspiring with him how to load and bless
> With fruit the vines that round the thatch-eaves run;
> To bend with apples the mossed cottage trees,   5
> And fill all fruit with ripeness to the core;
> To swell the gourd, and plump the hazel shells
> With a sweet kernel; to set budding more,
> And still more, later flowers for the bees,
> Until they think warm days will never cease,   10
> For Summer has o'er brimmed their clammy cells.
>
> Who hath not seen thee oft amid thy store?
> Sometimes whoever seeks abroad may find
> Thee sitting careless on a granary floor,
> Thy hair soft-lifted by the winnowing wind,   15
> Or on a half-reaped furrow sound asleep,
> Drowsed with the fume of poppies, while thy hook
> Spares the next swath and all its twined flowers;
> And sometimes like a gleaner thou dost keep
> Steady thy laden head across a brook;   20
> Or by a cider-press, with patient look,
> Thou watchest the last oozings hours by hours.
>
> Where are the songs of Spring? Ay, where are they?
> Think not of them, thou hast thy music too, —
> While barred clouds bloom the soft-dying day,   25
> And touch the stubble plains with rosy hue;
> Then in a wailful choir the small gnats mourn
> Among the river sallows, borne aloft
> Or sinking as the light wind lives or dies;
> And full-grown lambs loud bleat from hilly bourn;

Hedge crickets sing; and now with treble soft
The redbreast whistles from a garden-croft;
And gathering swallows twitter in the skies.

(a) Think about the ambiguous character of: 'Conspiring with him how to
     load and bless' (line 3), 'To bend with apples' (line 5). What view of
     Autumn emerges from these ambiguities?
(b) In the second stanza Keats speaks directly to a personified figure of
     Autumn. How does Keats build up this figure, and what is its effect in
     the poem?
(c) Compare the lush imagery of the first stanza with the more restrained
     imagery of the third one.
(d) What distinctive atmosphere is created by the following images: 'the
     soft-dying day' (line 25), 'in a wailful choir the small gnats mourn'
     (line 27), 'borne aloft / Or sinking' (lines 28–9) and 'gathering
     swallows' (line 33)?

2.4 Read 'Lights Out' by Edward Thomas a number of times and then
     answer the questions below.

I have come to the borders of sleep,
The unfathomable deep
Forest where all must lose
Their way, however straight,
Or winding, soon or late;
They cannot choose.   5

Many a road and track
That, since the dawn's first crack,
Up to the forest brink,
Deceived the travellers,   10
Suddenly now blurs,
And in they sink.

Here love ends,
Despair, ambition ends;
All pleasure and all trouble,   15
Although most sweet or bitter,
Here ends in sleep that is sweeter
Than tasks most noble.

There is not any book
Or face of dearest look   20
That I would not turn from now
To go into the unknown

I must enter, and leave, alone
I know not how,

The tall forest towers;   25
Its cloudy foliage lowers
Ahead, shelf above shelf;
Its silence I hear and obey
That I may lose my way
And myself.   30

(a) Think about how the word 'sleep' is used in the first line.
(b) Would it be helpful to describe the forest as a symbol; if so, of what is it symbolic?
(c) Throughout the poem there are images of travelling. Think about what they mean in the poem, and consider whether the image is a traditional or new one.
(d) Do all the images stem from one basic idea, and if so what is that idea?

③ Line and rhythm

One of the things I have noticed about thoughtless students is that when they are quoting poetry, they write it out as if it were prose; in other words, they ignore the fact that in all poetry the line is fixed. When Christina Rossetti wrote 'A Birthday' she made the first line end with 'bird' and the next line begin with 'whose':

> My heart is like a singing bird
> Whose nest is in a watered shoot

And that is fixed; whenever her poem is printed, it must be printed in that way.

There are three features of lines that are likely to come to your notice when you read and study poetry:

- the way lines end
- the breaks or pauses within lines
- the rhythms of lines.

3.1 Lines: end-stopped and run-on

A line can end in two ways:

(1) end-stopped; or
(2) run-on.

In an end-stopped line the meaning is complete by the close, so it finishes with a punctuation mark; in run-on lines the meaning is left unfinished, so there is no punctuation at the end.

The first lines of Yeats's 'Byzantium' are end-stopped:

> The unpurged images of day recede;
> The Emperor's drunken soldiery are abed;

whereas his 'Leda and the Swan' begins with two run-on lines:

> A sudden blow: the great wings beating still
> Above the staggering girl, her thighs caressed
> By the dark webs ...

40

There is, of course, no point in just identifying one line as end-stopped and another as run-on. You should only use these terms if you can go on to show that they contribute to the impact of the poem. The question, then, that should be asked is:

● What effects are created by end-stopped and run-on lines?

End-stopped lines

End-stopped lines usually sound firm and finished, because meanings are completed within them. Consider the first verse of Gray's 'Elegy':

> The curfew tolls the knell of parting day,
> The lowing herd wind slowly o'er the lea,
> The ploughman homeward plods his weary way,
> And leaves the world to darkness and to me.

In those lines there is the satisfaction of finding the lines completing their meanings as the subjects of those lines complete their tasks. The curfew bell rings to tell us that day is over, and as soon as we have learned that the line itself is over; likewise, the herd wind over the lea as the line that tells us that winds to a close. The termination of the end-stopped lines beautifully enacts the completion of the four things with which the first stanza deals.

Run-on lines

By contrast, run-on lines create feelings of expectation. At the close of a line the meaning is not yet complete, so you might ask:

● What is going to happen next?
● What is the full meaning going to be?
● Where is the thought of the poem going?

Hopkins's 'God's Grandeur', which is about the presence of the glory of God in the world, starts with two firm end-stopped lines, and then offers the reader an enticing run-on:

> The world is charged with the grandeur of God.
> It will flame out, like shining from shook foil;
> It gathers to a greatness, like the ooze of oil
> Crushed.

Because the line ends half way through a simile, a great deal of expectation is aroused. The expectation is dramatically gratified by the word, 'Crushed' –

easily the strongest word Hopkins has yet used in the poem. As a result of the expectation being suddenly fulfilled, the run-on line is far more emphatic than the two end-stopped ones.

Effects of combining end-stopped and run-on lines

Sometimes very telling effects are created by combining the two sorts of lines. Hopkins offered two end-stopped lines before moving to a run-on, but in Wordsworth's 'The Solitary Reaper' there are six restrained, end-stopped ones before the line runs on:

> Behold her, single in the field,
> Yon solitary Highland lass!
> Reaping and singing by herself;
> Stop here or gently pass!
> Alone she cuts and binds the grain,
> And sings a melancholy strain;
> O listen! for the vale profound
> Is overflowing with the sound.

As Wordsworth becomes ever more deeply enthralled by the girl's singing, the emotional pressure, so to speak, builds up. In the sentence that begins 'Alone she cuts' it is very strong, and after the powerful outburst to the reader 'O listen!', the line, like the song itself, overflows. Needless to say, it is also Wordsworth's emotions that have overflowed. The change, therefore, from end-stopped to run-on lines can be effective because it marks a change in the emotions of the poet.

End-stopped and run-on lines occur because two kinds of formal arrangements meet – poetry written in lines of a specific length and the structure of individual sentences. One way of defining an end-stopped line is to say that it is co-terminous (having the same ending) with a grammatical unit. A line is run-on because it is not co-terminous. One of the pleasures of reading poetry is enjoying the way the poet observes both the disciplines of verse and of grammar.

Example _____

Elizabeth Jennings' poem 'Afternoon in Florence' is a quiet, thoughtful poem which moves in a leisurely yet exploratory manner. The subject introduced in the first verse is an elusive one – the relationship between experience and time – but she doesn't abandon the discipline of either line length or rhyme. What she does is allow her verse to follow the drift of her thought, so the lines are all run-on until the final line, which, because the thought is complete, is end-stopped:

> This afternoon disturbs within the mind
> No other afternoon, is out of time
> Yet lies within a definite sun to end
> In night that is in time. Yet hold it here
> Our eyes, our mind, to make the city clear.
>
> Perhaps it feels as if the poet is holding the city clearly before her eyes and in her mind because of the discipline of the verse and the way the rhyme word 'clear' end-stops the line.

3.2   Caesura

A break within a line is called a *caesura*. It can only be located by attending to the pauses you are obliged to make when *reading* the line, though sometimes it occurs at a punctuation mark. If you wish to indicate the presence of a caesura, the customary sign is ‖. Caesuras are worth noting because they can have marked effects upon a poem. You should look out for three effects:

- the way they shape the emotional life of a poem
- the humour they can help to create
- the way they can dramatise a poem's close.

Shaping emotion

To say that caesuras shape the emotional life of a poem is to say that breaks in a line of verse help to create distinctive tones. Consider the three following lines:

(1)   Sweet day,‖ so cool, ‖ so calm, ‖ so bright!
                                        (George Herbert, 'Virtue')

(2)   All's over then: ‖ does truth sound bitter?
                                        (Robert Browning, 'The Lost Mistress')

(3)   I sit in the top of the tree, ‖ my eyes closed.
                                        (Ted Hughes, 'Hawk Roosting')

- The tone of Herbert's line is that of a quiet, loving appreciation of the day's qualities. Speaking to the day, the caesuras mark the pauses in his thought. It is as if he stops to think before he speaks, so the caesuras enact the very process of deep thought and careful speech.
- The line from Browning forms part of a question which is asked in a resigned tone. The caesura is a heavy one (emphatic and long) which comes

after the very final sounding 'then'. The sense of finality and the break create the tone of resigned acceptance.

- The tone of the Hughes line is firm and determined. The hawk coldly lists its position in the tree and the fact that its eyes are closed. The caesura marks the determined way in which the bird notes those things.

Changing emotional

Caesuras also mark a *change* in the emotions of a poem. If you attend closely to a poem's mood you may enjoy the pleasure of recognising and following changes in feeling.

Example

Some very moving examples of caesuras marking changes of emotion occur in 'Thyrsis', the poem in which Arnold mourns the death of his friend by thinking about how the landscape around Oxford, where they used to walk together, seems utterly changed. At one point he appeals to the hills to recognise him. Note how the caesuras mark the emotional pulse of his appeal:

> See, ‖ 'tis no foot of unfamiliar men
> To-night from Oxford ‖ up your pathway strays!
> Here came I often, ‖ often, ‖ in old days—
> Thyrsis and I; ‖ we still had Thyrsis then.

The first caesura marks his attempt to reassure the hills as to who he is; the second is light and indicates that his mind is travelling over the past pleasures he and Thyrsis shared as they strayed up the pathways. In the third line he hesitates regretfully over the word 'often', remembering, no doubt, that these walks were so much a part of his life 'in old days'.

The greatest change in emotion comes in the last line, where a heavy caesura marks the deep change from the companionship of the past to the desolation of the present; a desolation made all the more poignant by the knowledge, enacted in the finality of 'then', that the pleasures of companionship are over.

Creating humour

The humour made possible by a caesura also marks a change in mood. Consider these lines from Pope's *The Rape of the Lock*:

> Meanwhile, ‖ declining from the noon of day
> The sun obliquely ‖ shoots his burning ray;
> The hungry judges ‖ soon the sentence sign
> And wretches hang ‖ that jurymen may dine …

The caesuras here are all light; indeed in the second and third line they are hardly noticeable. The one in the fourth line is also light, but Pope cleverly uses it to mark the division between the wretches who are sped to the gallows and jurymen who retire to enjoy their dinner. The humour of the line is increased when we see so light a caesura marking a gross miscarriage of justice that leads to a grotesque contrast in fates – the rope for some, and, let us imagine, roast beef for the others!

Dramatising the close

At the end of a poem a caesura can dramatise the meaning. The pause before the final word or words allows the reader time to recognise what has happened in the poem before it is completed. The end, therefore, when it does come, is felt to be even more final.

Example

Consider Larkin's short yet very moving poem, 'Home':

> Home is so sad. It stays as it was left,
> Shaped to the comfort of the last to go
> As if to win them back. Instead, bereft
> Of anyone to please, it withers so,
> Having no heart to put aside the theft
>
> And turn again to what it started as,
> A joyous shot at how things ought to be,
> Long fallen wide. You can see how it was:
> Look at the pictures and the cutlery.
> The music in the piano stool. That vase.

The pathos of the poem lies in the way that objects are made to stand for ordinary but deeply felt hopes and longings. When these hopes and longings have come to nothing, the objects still remain expressive of them at the same time as recording their failure. The heavy caesura in the last line allows the reader to see all that. We are told to look at the pictures, the cutlery and the music in the piano stool. The pause allows us to see just how sadly expressive these objects are before the final words – 'That vase' – confirms the poignancy of items that remain when the hopes that put them there have come to nothing.

3.3   Movement

Because it takes time to read anything, all literature is, in one way or another, concerned with movement. The experience of reading is one of moving from one word, from one sentence to another. Therefore it's appropriate in all sorts of literature to use the term 'movement' to describe what's happening.

When people talk about movement in verse, they might be commenting on a number of things. For instance, they might mean the movement of the argument; the way, for instance, in Donne's 'The Sun Rising' the poet thinks through why he and his beloved are special. That movement is, of course, also a movement of feeling. The arguments issue from the poet with an interesting blend of intellectual and physical passion.

For our present purposes movement means the physical aspect of reading through a poem, and therefore it covers how all the material aspects of language – their sounds, pitch, pace and patterning – combine together to create a recognisable sequence. Some of those aspects are going to be treated in Chapter 4. At the moment we shall concern ourselves with what has just been called patterning – the way in which the words of a poem create rhythmical shapes.

3.4   Listening to rhythms

When thinking about the rhythms of poetry it's best to be honest, so I will start with a confession. It took me quite a time to 'hear' some rhythms. I don't mean the very obvious rhythms of nursery rhymes or the equally unavoidable galloping rhythms of a poem such as Browning's 'How they brought the Good News from Ghent to Aix' but the quieter, more subtle and certainly less insistent patternings of, say, Wordsworth or Hardy. I can recall reading about the rhythms of verse and prose and feeling very stupid because I was deaf to them.

I suspect a lot of people are like that. When it comes to rhythm we have to learn, and as with all learning , some of us are better at it than others. I've noticed over the years that musicians, perhaps not surprisingly, are better at hearing rhythm than most other students, but I suspect that even for musicians there is still the need to listen and learn. What then can be done? Here are a few suggestions:

- listen to poetry being read aloud
- read poetry aloud yourself
- read poetry that has a very clear rhythmical quality
- talk to people about how they hear rhythms.

Of these I've always found the last one very valuable. I recall one of my A-level teachers pointing out how tough and muscular were the rhythms of Dryden, and later at university a lecturer remarked on the rhythmical strength and power of the Scottish medieval poet, William Dunbar. Help didn't only come from teachers; a friend once enthused about the closing of Auden's 'In Memory of Sigmund Freud', commenting on its elevated yet lamenting quality:

> sad is Eros, builder of cities,
> and weeping anarchic Aphrodite.

The rhythm is measured, and the beats are carefully placed so that they single out the important words; for instance, a beat falls on 'sad' in the first line but not on 'and' in the second, so the first syllable of 'weeping' (a far more important word) is stressed.

In case you'd like some practice, here are some lines of poetry. Don't worry about what to say about the rhythms (that will be covered in a later section); just see if you can hear and enjoy them.

Examples

Example 1

This is the opening verse of Ben Jonson's 'Hymn to Diana':

> Queen and huntress, chaste and fair,
>   Now the sun is laid to sleep,
> Seated in thy silver chair,
>   State in wonted manner keep:
> Hesperus entreats thy light,
> Goddess excellently bright.

Did you enjoy the way the rhythm singled out 'excellently'?

Example 2

Andrew Marvell's 'Bermudas' opens like this:

> Where the remote Bermudas ride
> In th' ocean's bosom unespied,
> From a small boat, that rowed along,
> The listening winds received this song.

Those lines sound very smooth, yet the beats are not as regularly distributed as you would think.

Example 3

If you want a real helter-skelter of constantly changing rhythms, listen to the opening of Hopkins's sonnet 'The Windhover'. Don't worry about what it means; just enjoy the ride!

> I caught this morning morning's minion, king-
>   dom of daylight's dauphin, dapple-dawn-drawn Falcon, in his riding
>   Of the rolling level underneath him steady air …
>
> If you can't hear the rhythms there, keep reading and listening.

3.5   Why rhythms matter

Thinking about rhythm should start and finish with this simple point.

Rhythms matter because they contribute to the impact of the poem.

Poetry uses all the resources of language, and one of those resources is that the movement of words can form recognisable patterns. Having said that, there are two problems:

(1)   Is rhythm merely subjective?
(2)   Can any general statements be made about the function of rhythms?

Is rhythm merely subjective?

To say that hearing rhythms is subjective is to say that we imagine there's a rhythm when there isn't one. Of course there's an unavoidable element of subjectivity in hearing rhythms; for instance, two people may differ on where they think a beat falls and on how heavy that beat is. But this is different from saying there's no rhythm at all. There is a difference between, say:

> On either side the river lie
> Long fields of barley and of rye
> > (Tennyson: 'The Lady of Shalott')

and

> There are long fields of barley and rye
> On either side of the river

This difference is a difference in rhythm.

Can we generalise about the function of rhythms?

This second question is far more of a problem. The rhythm of one line is going to differ from another because of a number of factors: the length of the line, the subject matter, the word order, the sounds of individual words, the number of syllables in the words and so on. This is going to make generalisations difficult. Nevertheless, if we accept that generalisations in the study of English are only rough guides, we can say that readers over the centuries have valued certain things about rhythms.

(i)   Rhythm draws attention to individual words and so makes us think more about them.

For instance, in John Clare's haunting 'I am' the irregular rhythm picks out the word 'what' for a heavy stress:

> I am: yet what I am none cares or knows

'What' might be thought of as an insignificant word, but in this poem it's crucial; the poet is asking the big question: what is he?

(ii)   Rhythm can lend a significance and an urgency to what is being said.

The very fact that the words come to us in a pattern advertises their importance, so what is said feels as if it is more important. Listen, for instance, to this mysterious poem by Wordsworth. The pressure of the poet's thoughts and feelings are surely expressed with a compelling power in and through the poem's insistent rhythms:

> A slumber did my spirit seal;
>   I had no human fears:
> She seemed a thing that could not feel
>   The touch of earthly years.
>
> No motion has she now, no force;
>   She neither hears nor sees;
> Rolled round in earth's diurnal course,
>   With rocks, and stones, and trees.

(iii)   Rhythm can convey to the reader far more fully than mere statement what it feels like to have a particular feeling.

Hardy wrote a number of haunting poems about the death of his wife. They convey what it feels like to have lost someone in a way that 'I miss my wife' can't. The emotional weight of loss can be felt in the rhythms of 'The Voice':

> Woman much missed, how you call to me, call to me,
> Saying that now you are not as you were
> When you had changed from the one who was all to me,
> But as at first, when our day was fair.

In the repetition of the plaintive 'call', the emphatic stresses on 'woman' and 'missed' and the way the thought climaxes on 'not' in the second line, we can hear and feel the ache and the longing of bereavement.

The fourth point about rhythm is a variation of the third:

(iv)   When all the material aspects of verse work together – rhythm, sound, pitch and the form of the verse – the language can acquire an impressive finality.

We feel that the idea is really present, and that it has a convincing authority. Listen to the opening of Donne's 'The Undertaking':

> I have done one braver thing
> Than all the Worthies did,
> And yet a braver thence doth spring,
> Which is, to keep that hid.

Here the incisive thought is augmented by the punchy rhythms, and we might feel that the poet is entitled to boast because the physical properties of the verse reinforce what he's saying.

3.6   Beats

A lot has been said about rhythm without talking about what it is. I think this is the right approach. In public examinations you might be asked to write about its effects, but it's very unlikely that you'll be required to offer a detailed description of what constitutes rhythm. The only reason for offering an account is that it might help you talk about it. What follows here, then, is a simple guide to what makes rhythm.

What matters in English is the *beat*. Some syllables are emphasised more strongly than others, and if there is something approaching a pattern of these, then there is rhythm. It's traditional to mark a beat or stress like this: ´. When a word or syllable is not emphasised, it is marked like this: .

In a lot of English verse there are either four or five beats in a line.

What makes rhythm is a certain regularity of beats. This arouses expectation in the reader, who enjoys hearing what is expected. One of the pleasures of reading verse is that of hearing a line unfold smoothly. When an expected beat falls, the reader is satisfied. The pleasure here is a physical one, and it can be enjoyed even if the reader can't say exactly how the rhythm contributes to the meaning of the verse. We might say that the pleasure is like that in music; we tap our feet as the rhythm falls in the expected place.

All that was said above about why rhythm matters could be repeated here. The expected beat

- singles out words
- lends importance to what is being said
- acts out the feelings of the poem
- gives what is said a finality.

Those are the effects of a pattern of beats.

3.7 Variation

Rhythms that slavishly follow a single pattern soon tire readers, so variety is almost always welcome. But variation is only effective if it's expressive of the thought and feeling of the poem.

Variation is usually of two kinds:

- a change in the expected pattern; or
- stresses that are of different weights.

Example

Consider the opening of this poem by Wyatt:

> They flee from me, that sometime did me seek
> With naked foot, stalking in my chamber.

The first line is almost regular; there is a beat on every second syllable. The only doubt is whether only the first or both syllables of 'sometime' should be stressed. (Try reading it both ways.) In the second line the variation is more prominent. Is the first or both syllables of the crucial word 'naked' to be stressed? However you resolve that, it's clear that a beat falls on 'foot'. It's also clear that the next word (a crucial one because it continues the metaphor of hunting) requires a stress on the first syllable. Moreover, isn't 'stalking' given a heavier beat than any word in the first line? This heavy stress draws attention to the blend of the predatory and the timid; the creatures are out hunting and yet they tread with caution. The result is that the smooth rhythm gives way to a sequence of strong beats. This means that we notice those words and perhaps feel the excitement of the poet's recollection of secret, amorous encounters.

3.8   Metres

Metres have traditionally been classified. Whether or not it's useful to know the names they've been given is debatable, but occasionally questions are asked about them, so, just in case, here they are.

The foot

The idea that has traditionally controlled thinking about metre is that of the *foot*. This is the basic unit that, when repeated, creates a rhythm. Feet usually consist of two or three syllables. The most important thing about a foot is whether or not it starts with a beat.

- A two-syllable foot that starts with a beat is called a *trochee* (´ ˇ), and the rhythm so created is said to be *trochaic*.

- A three-syllable foot starting with a beat is a *dactyl* (´ ˇ ˇ), and its rhythms are *dactylic*.

- Feet that don't start with a beat are called *iambs* (ˇ ´) in the case of two-syllable feet and *anapaests* (ˇ ˇ ´) in the case of three-syllable feet. The rhythms so created are called *iambic* and *anapaestic*.

Trochaic metres

Trochaic metres, because they start with a stress, can sound assertive. Look at the opening of Blake's 'The Tyger':

> Týgĕr! Týgĕr! búrnĭng bríght
> Ín the fóreŝts óf thĕ níght ...

The 'Tyger' bursts upon the reader in assertive trochees. Not all trochaic metres will be as powerful as that, but it is a good idea to see if you can find this rhythm hammering out the meaning of the lines.

Lambic metres

By contrast, iambic metres, can be thoughtful and recollective since they move from the uncertainty of an unstressed syllable to the certainty of a stressed one. Wordsworth's 'Tintern Abbey', a thoughtful poem about recollected experiences, is written in gentle and not always regular iambic pentameters. In this passage he writes about how his mind works:

> Wĭth mány récŏgnítiŏñs dím ăñd faínt,
> Ăñd sómewhăt óf ă sád pĕrpléxĭty,
> Thĕ píctŭre of thĕ mínd rĕvivés ăgaíñ ...

The iambic rhythm of the last line beautifully enacts the revival of which it speaks; the stresses on 'Thĕ píctŭre', 'mínd', 'rĕvíves', and 'agaín' create the increasing certainty that comes with the mind's revival. This is particularly so in the di-syllabic 'rĕvíves' and 'agaín', where the poetry observes the natural iambic rhythms of speech, so that within one word there is movement from unstress to stress, from uncertainty to certainty.

Dactylic metres

Dactylic metres tend to be sad. The two unstressed syllables which follow the stress create a feeling of decline, of a falling away from certainty. It is not surprising, therefore, that a poem of regret – Browning's 'The Lost Leader' – should be written in sad, heavy dactyls:

> Wé that hăd lovéd hĭm sŏ, fóllowĕd hĭm, hónourĕd hĭm,
> Lívéd iň hĭs míld aňd mágnifĭčeňt eýe . . .

The sad regret of 'loved hĭm šo' is created by the two unstressed syllables that follow 'loved'. It is as if we hear the sighs of the protagonist as hope fades away. The dactyl, in other words, enacts the way love for the lost leader dies.

Anapaestic metres

Anapaestic metres, by contrast, build up emotional tension by hurrying the reader through unstressed syllables to the stressed one. A famous example is Byron's 'The Destruction of Sennacherib':

> Thĕ Ăssýriăn camĕ dówn liǩe thĕ wólf ŏn thĕ fóld,
> Aňd hĭs cóhŏrts wĕre gléamiňg iň púrplĕ aňd góld.

The unstressed syllables create an anticipatory tension, which is released in powerful monosyllables – 'dówn', 'wólf', and 'fóld'.

● **There are also names for the number of feet in a line.**

A one-foot line is called a monometer, two a dimeter, three a trimeter, four a tetrameter, five a pentameter, six a hexameter, seven a heptameter and eight an octameter.

3.9   Writing about rhythm

There are two reasons why you should master ways of writing about rhythm that are additional to the technical terms outlined above.

- Examiners won't reward you just for putting a label on a metre.
- Rhythm, because it affects the impact a poem has, should be spoken about in ways appropriate to that.

Examples

Example 1

Consider these lines from Blake's 'Spring':

> Sound the Flute!
> Now it's mute.
> Birds delight
> Day and Night . . .

The metre is trochaic, but what else can be said about it? The rhythm can be said to be light and carefree. If you want to say further what 'light' means, you might say that the rhythm is deft and tripping.

Example 2

A very different effect is present in the first two lines of Herbert's 'Affliction':

> Lord, how I am all ague, when I seek
> What I have treasured in my memory!

The opening is basically iambic, but its effectiveness depends upon the jerky and uncertain quality of the rhythm. The first line is about disease (that is what 'ague' means), and you can feel the discomfort in the stumbling rhythm. The second line, by contrast, is much more smooth and flowing.

Example 3

Our third example can be found in Shakespeare's Sonnet 12:

> When I do count the clock that tells the time,
> And see the brave day sunk in hideous night . . .

The metre is a regular iambic one, but it is still necessary to describe its effect. Would it be right to say the regular, insistent rhythm makes the poem grave, serious and slow? The rhythm is that of somebody deliberately counting time and being fully aware that it is ebbing inevitably away.

Example 4

A contrasting example can be found in Donne's 'The Canonization':

> For God's sake hold your tongue, and let me love,
> Or chide my palsy, or my gout . . .

The metre here is appropriately irregular. The poet is angrily turning upon the person who is interrupting him and gesturing him away defiantly.

Words to describe rhythm

- As you will see, some of the words used to characterise rhythm are concerned with *feeling*. Rhythms were said to be 'carefree', 'uncertain', 'grave' and 'serious'. If you can characterise the emotional impact of rhythm, you should, of course, do so.
- You may also have noticed that some of the words used to describe rhythm were drawn from the vocabulary of *physical movement*. The rhythms were said to be 'light', 'tripping', 'deft', 'jerky', 'stumbling' and 'slow'. When you consider how to describe the impact of rhythm, it is a good idea to draw on such words. Rhythm could be:

  — awkward
  — ponderous
  — heavy
  — swaying
  — rolling.

- Very close to physical movement is *physical gesture*. It is sometimes appropriate to use words dealing with gestures to describe the effect of rhythm. In the above examples, the Donne passage was described as a defiant gesture. Some lines of poetry, or even whole poems, might be described as:

  — expansive
  — dramatic
  — inviting
  — tense.

- Because rhythm is an element in music, it is often useful to turn to the *language of music* when you are looking for words to characterise rhythms. In the above examples a line was described as 'smooth' and 'flowing' – words often used to describe the effect of a piece of music. Other words that might be used are those associated with tempo, such as:

  — lively
  — quick
  — brisk;

and ones associated with the movement and volume of sound, such as:

— crescendo.
— diminuendo.

3.10   Cadence

A very useful word that has been borrowed from music to talk about the rhythmical aspects of literature is *cadence*. As the reader comes to the end of a line, a clause, a verse or a sentence, the voice goes up, goes down or remains steady. This movement is known as cadence. Sometimes another musical term *modulation* is used to talk about the change in the voice, and the levels of sound are sometimes spoken of in a further musical term – *pitch*.

Cadences often establish the emotional character of a line. A rising cadence is often expressive of hope, whilst a falling one can sound regretful. Listen, for instance, to these lines from the song in Shakespeare's *Cymbeline*:

> Golden girls and lads all must,
> As chimney-sweepers, come to dust.

The thought that even 'golden girls and lads' must come, in the end, to nothing but 'dust' is enacted in a falling cadence of wistful resignation.

At the close of the first stanza of Donne's 'The Anniversary' the poet makes a large claim for the strength of their love:

> Only our love hath no decay;
> This, no tomorrow hath, nor yesterday,
> Running it never runs from us away,
> But truly keeps his first, last, everlasting day.

Although the rhymes – 'decay'/'yesterday'/'away'/'day' – might lend themselves to a falling cadence, the poet rises to the climax with a triumphant assertion on 'everlasting' that concludes the line with a confident and elevated cadence.

Exercises

3.1   Read through the poems you are studying and consider the effects of end-stopped and run-on lines. You should also consider the impact of caesuras.

3.2   Read through the poems you are studying and consider the rhythm of the poetry. You should also consider any variations and try to write about how central rhythms are to the poems.

3.3 Read Sonnet 97 by Shakespeare a number of times, and when you feel you know it, answer the questions below.

> How like a winter hath my absence been
> From thee, the pleasure of the fleeting year!
> What freezings have I felt, what dark days seen!
> What old December's bareness everywhere!
> And yet this time removed was summer's time,
> The teeming autumn big with rich increase,
> Bearing the wanton burden of the prime,
> Like widowed wombs after their lord's decease:
> Yet this abundant issue seemed to me
> But hope of orphans and unfathered fruit
> For summer and its pleasures wait on thee,
> And, thou away, the very birds are mute.
> Or, if they sing, 'tis with so dull a cheer,
> That leaves look pale, dreading the winter's near.

(a) What is the emotional effect of the first line being run-on, and how is this increased by the heavy caesura after 'thee'? Think, too, about the effect of run-on and end-stopped lines in the sonnet.

(b) Think about the rhythms of the third line. What is effective about 'dark days seen'?

(c) What word is heavily stressed in the fourth line, and what effect does this have on the meaning and emotional quality of the poem?

(d) How would you characterise the effect of the cadence at the close of line 12? What is its emotional quality?

3.4 Read Hardy's 'At Castle Boterel' a number of times, and when you feel you understand it, answer the questions below.

> As I drive to the junction of lane and highway,
> And the drizzle bedrenches the wagonette,
> I look behind at the fading byway,
> And see on its shape, now glistening wet,
>   Distinctly yet
>
> Myself and a girlish form benighted
> In dry March weather. We climb the road
> Beside a chaise. We had just alighted
> To ease the sturdy pony's load
>   When he sighed and slowed.
>
> What we did as we climbed, and what we talked of
> Matters not much, nor to what it led, —
> Something that life will not be baulked of

Without rude reason till hope is dead,
And feeling fled.

It filled but a minute. But was there ever
A time of such quality, since or before,
In that hill's story? To one mind never,
Though it has been climbed, foot-swift, foot-sore,
By thousands more.

Primaeval rocks form the road's steep border,
And much they have faced there, first and last,
Of the transitory in earth's long order;
But what they record in colour and cast
Is — that we two passed.

And to me, though Time's unflinching rigour,
In mindless rote, has ruled from sight
The substance now, one phantom figure
Remains on the slope, as when that night
Saw us alight.

I look and see it there, shrinking, shrinking,
I look back at it amid the rain
For the very last time; for my sand is sinking
And I shall traverse old love's domain
Never again.

(a)   Think about how the basic rhythm is varied throughout the poem
      and consider the emotional effect of this.
(b)   Which words are heavily stressed in the third verse, and what
      contribution do they make to the meaning of the poem?
(c)   Think about the movement of the words in the fifth verse. You
      might like to think about the place of 'first and last', 'transitory',
      'long', and the effect of the run-on line.
(d)   Try to describe the emotional effects of the end-stopped lines,
      the run-on lines, the heavily stressed words and the closing
      cadence of the final verse.

4 Sound, rhyme and form

4.1 Listening to sounds

Every word that is spoken has a sound as well as a meaning. In everyday speech people do not usually call attention to the sounds that words make, but in poetry – a special way of using words – sounds are sometimes made to play a part in the meaning and impact of the poem.

As in the case of rhythm, you may find that when you first read poetry you are deaf to sounds. If so, don't worry; this is what a lot of people find when they start to read. Teachers tell them to listen, but they can't hear anything distinctive going on. As with many things in learning, you have to practise. It's a good idea to read a lot of poetry with the expressed intention of listening for the sounds. When you read or listen to any poem, try bearing this question in mind:

- What effects are being produced by the sounds of the words?

Listen, for instance, to these lines:

Thou mastering me
God! giver of breath and bread;
World's strand, sway of the sea;
Lord of living and dead ...
(G. M. Hopkins, 'The Wreck of the Deutschland')

Somewhere afield here something lies
In Earth's oblivious eyeless trust ...
(Thomas Hardy, 'Shelley's Skylark')

Beautiful lofty things: O'Leary's noble head ...
(W. B. Yeats, 'Beautiful lofty things')

It seemed that out of battle I escaped
Down some profound dull tunnel, long since scooped
Through granites which titanic wars had groined.
(Wilfred Owen, 'Strange Meeting')

Underwater eyes, an eel's
Oil of water body, neither fish nor beast is the otter ...
(Ted Hughes, 'An Otter')

- The passage from Hopkins sounds majestic and powerful; in the sounds of the words you can hear the authority of God. Listen, for instance, to the authority God has over the sea in the sounds of 'sway of the sea'.
- The sound of the Hardy is more difficult to describe. Could it be said that the passage is soft and lyrical, suggesting a safe keeping in the oblivious earth?
- The sound of the passage from Yeats is also lyrical. It is also elevated without being grand or oppressive.
- The Owen passage, by contrast, is grave and sonorous. In the very sounds of the words you can hear the descent into the earth and feel something of the power that opened up a way into the earth's core.
- The Hughes passage is agile and fluid; in the sounds of the words you can hear the lithe twisting of the otter, particularly in 'an eel's/'Oil of water body'.

You will have noticed that it was not possible to write about the effects of the sounds without also commenting on the meanings of the words. This is as it should be:

- **When writing about the sounds of words you must not separate them from their meanings.**

The reason for this is that every word is both a sound and a meaning; you can't have the one without the other. Used sensitively, sounds can enact meanings; that is to say, we can hear the meaning in the sounds. As Pope said in 'An Essay on Criticism':

> 'Tis not enough no harshness gives offence,
> The sound must seem an echo to the sense.

Writing about sounds is sometimes made easier by using some of the technical terms. The most popular ones are:

- alliteration
- consonance
- assonance
- onomatopoeia

4.2   Alliteration

Alliteration is the repetition of a consonantal sound. For instance, the 'w', 'l' and 'sh' sounds are alliterated in this line from Hopkins's 'Spring':

> When weeds, in wheels, shoot long and lovely and 'lush',

and in this line from Dylan Thomas's 'Over Sir John's Hill' the 's' is repeated:

> Stare for the sake of the souls of the slain birds sailing.

Many students find it quite easy to recognise alliteration, but are less sure about how to describe its effects. You can look out for two things:

(1) the way it helps to create tones
(2) its regularity or irregularity.

Alliteration often helps to create a poem's distinctive tone. Of any alliteration you can ask:

● Does the alliteration help to create the tone of the poem?

Listen, for instance, to the vigorous opening of Shelley's 'Ode to the West Wind':

> O Wild West Wind, thou breath of Autumn's being

The alliterated words powerfully enact the awe the poet feels in the presence of such a mighty force. You can hear that awe in the expansive sounds of 'Wild West Wind' and feel the power of the wind in 'breath' and the cleverly delayed echo of the 'b' sound in 'being'.

When alliteration strikes you as being interesting, it is worth asking:

● Are the alliterated sounds regularly or irregularly spaced?

When they are regular, they can sound very emphatic. Consider the last line of the 'dark house' poem from *In Memoriam*:

> On the bald street breaks the blank day.

The feeling of a lonely poet oppressed by the return of morning is enacted in the regularly spaced words beginning with 'b'; they hammer home his desolation. The irregularity of Hughes's 'Pike' is also impressive:

> Pike, three inches long, perfect
> Pike in all parts ...

The 'p' sound stands out, but because it does so irregularly it sounds more threatening. It is not relentless like the alliterated 'b's of Tennyson but sharp, quick and disturbing.

4.3 Consonance

You will not use the term 'consonance' very much. It describes the effect of *like* consonant but *unlike* vowel sounds, as in 'heat' and 'hate'. When you do come across consonance, it is worth while asking whether there is a relation in meaning between the words. If so, you can write about the pleasure of finding a closeness of meaning in the similarity of sounds. For instance, in Marlowe's 'The Passionate Shepherd to his Love', there is a clear relation between 'live' and 'love':

> Come live with me and be my love ...

To 'live' with someone is to share their life, and that sharing is close to what we mean by 'love'. The consonance gives the satisfaction of ear and mind working together.

4.4   Assonance

Assonance is the repetition of a vowel sound. The points that were made about alliteration often apply to it, though you will have to become used to assonance working on a smaller scale. Nevertheless, it can be effective. Consider the following two examples:

(1)   Prayer, the Church's banquet, Angels' age ...
                                                (George Herbert, 'Prayer')

(2)   Such weight and thick pink bulk
                 Set in death seemed not just dead.
                                                (Ted Hughes, 'View of a Pig')

- The 'a's in 'Angels' age' sound elevated and spiritual, and the line consequently sounds as if it is lifted to a higher plane.
- The 'i's in the 'thick pink' and 'in' sound blunt and insistent. In the assonance, you can hear the poet pointing to these features.

In both cases, however, the assonance is on a small scale.

4.5   Onomatopoeia

'Onomatopoeia' is the name given to the effect of sounds of words imitating, or miming, the sounds of the object. For instance, 'buzz' is the name for the sound a bee makes, and the sound of the word itself imitates that sound. Poets often write in such a way that the sounds of the words they use remind you of the sounds made by the objects about which they are writing. Listen to the way in which Owen uses his words to imitate the harsh, mechanical sounds of guns and rifles:

> Only the monstrous anger of the guns.
> Only the stuttering rifles' rapid rattle
> Can patter out their hasty orisons
>   ('Anthem for Doomed Youth')

'Monstrous anger' mimes the explosive power of big guns, and 'stuttering rifles' rapid rattle is close to the repetitive sound of infrantrymen's quick firing.

There is no point in writing about onomatopoeia unless you can show that it is effective. A good question to ask is:

• Does the onomatopoeia help to establish the atmosphere of the poem?

If the answer is 'yes' then you can write about its effectiveness. Consider the close of Tennyson's 'Morte D'Arthur':

> Long stood Sir Bedivere
> Revolving many memories, till the hull
> Looked one black dot against the verge of dawn
> And on the mere the wailing died away.

'Wailing' is an onomatopoeic word which in combination with 'away' creates a falling cadence which is expressive of the isolation and silence of the mere. It helps to establish the atmosphere of a solitary figure left on the edge of a vast lake.

4.6 Texture

A useful word, though not a technical term, is 'texture'. You can use it when you wish to talk about the physical impact of the words in a poem. The texture of a poem is the sum of all its material aspects – its lines, caesuras, rhythms and sounds. When you want to write about what all those various things add up to – the feel they have when they all work together – then it's the most obvious word to use.

--- **Example** --

Listen to (or feel) the texture of these lines from Browning's mysterious poem, 'Childe Roland to the Dark Tower Came':

> If there pushed any ragged thistle-stalk
> Above its mates, the head was chopped; the bents
> Were jealous else. What made those holes and rents
> In the dock's harsh swarth leaves, bruised as to baulk
> All hope of greenness?

The texture here is dense; there's a feeling that a lot of words (perhaps too many) have been packed into the line. The lines might also be said to be rough and even abrasive; we might use one of the words themselves and call it harsh.

> The texture is clearly the product of the sounds – 'bruised as to baulk' –
> and the caesuras (look at the second line) but as in many cases when the
> texture of lines is worth commenting on, the grammar plays a part. Note,
> for instance, the forceful verbs – 'pushed', 'chopped' – and the way many
> of the nouns are qualified by vivid adjectives – 'ragged', 'harsh swarth'.

One of the features of English is that it lends itself to so many different
textures. Within the same opening section of his lyrical poem 'Briggflatts', Basil
Bunting can write lines that are smooth:

> Brag, sweet tenor bull,
> descant on Rawthey's madrigal,
> each pebble its part
> for the fells' late spring

and as rough, scratchy and gritty as:

> harness mutter to shaft,
> felloe to axle squeak,
> rut thud the rim,
> crushed grit.

A poet who has very distinctive textures is Tony Harrison. He is now being set
for public exams, so you might face the enjoyable challenge of writing about his
rough textured and vigorous verse. Listen, for instance, to the rumbustious
opening of 'The Heart of Darkness' with its thickly textured and slightly comic
awkwardness:

> Disjointed like a baobab,
> gigantic first, then noonday blob,
> my shadow staggers, lurches, reels,
> elasticated at my heels,

As with rhythm and sound it's not always necessary to comment on the texture
of a poet's verse. There are, however, poets that almost demand some
comment. Bunting and Harrison are certainly two twentieth-century poets who
call for recognition in this respect, and in the nineteenth century there is
Hopkins.

4.7   Writing about sounds

In writing about the four technical terms alliteration, consonance, assonance and
onomatopoeia, it has not been possible to exclude other ways of characterising

sound in poetry. Let us now concentrate on a wider vocabulary that will help you to write about the effects of sound.

● You could turn to the words we use to describe how people speak. The sounds of words in a poem might be characterised according to *manner of speech*. Here are some possible words:

— gently
— whisperingly
— stridently
— mellifluously
— forthrightly
— smoothly
— incisively
— piercingly
— flatly

As you will see, most of these words are closely connected with tone.

● There are also words that describe *the nature of sounds*. 'Echo' and 'pitch' are useful, as are 'resonant' and 'sonorous'. Other words are:

— deep
— harsh
— grating
— light
— shrill

How might some of these words be used? Here are some examples.

Examples

Example 1

Listen to these lines from Tennyson's 'The Lotos Eaters':

> The lotos blooms below the barren peak:
> The lotos blows by every winding creek:
> All day the wind breathes low with mellower tone:
> Through every hollow cave and alley lone
> Round and round the spicy downs the yellow lotos-dust is blown.

How can the effect of the alliteration, assonance and onomatopoeia be described? Could it be said that because of the sounds of the words the lines sound gentle, mellifluous and smooth?

Example 2

Dryden's verse sounds very different. How can these lines from *Absalom and Achitophel* be characterised?

> Of these the false Achitophel was the first,
> A name to all succeeding ages curst:
> For close designs and crooked counsels fit,
> Sagacious, bold and turbulent of wit,
> Restless, unfixed in principles and place,
> In power unpleased, impatient of disgrace ...

The alliteration of the 'f' sound is forthright, and that on the 'c' incisive and even piercing in its forcefulness. Likewise, the 'p' sounds could be described as forthright.

Example 3

The sound of Milton's verse is very impressive. Listen to this passage from Book II of *Paradise Lost*, in which Satan, having left Hell, launches on his journey to Paradise:

> At last his sail-broad vans
> He spreads for flight, and in the surging smoke
> Uplifted spurns the ground, thence many a league
> As in a cloudy chair ascending rides
> Audacious, but that seat soon failing, meets
> A vast vacuity: all unawares
> Fluttering his penons vain plumb down he drops
> Ten thousand fathoms deep, and to this hour
> Down had been falling, had not by ill chance
> The strong rebuff of some tumultuous cloud
> Instinct with fire and nitre hurried him
> As many miles aloft ...

In the very sound of the words you can hear that Milton regards Satan as small and insignificant in the vastness of the universe. The words associated with his flight are light and mellifluous – 'flight', 'uplifted' and 'failing', but when he falls into the 'vast vacuity', the words that alliterate with these – 'fluttering' and 'falling' – stand in marked contrast to the deeply sonorous ones which enact his descent – 'plumb', 'down', 'drops', 'fathom' and 'deep'. The contrast between light and sonorous words enacts the slightness of Satan when compared to the fathomless tracts of space.

4.8   The effects of rhyme

The most common sound in poetry is that of rhyme. Most people's idea of poetry is of rhyming lines, and sometimes they are puzzled when they read poetry that doesn't rhyme. Their reaction is understandable. It is only in poetry that rhyme becomes an important feature. In everyday speech, for instance, it is treated as an embarrassment.

Whilst nearly everybody can recognise rhyme, few people can talk about its *effectiveness*. It is clearly not good enough to point out that lines rhyme. To help you think about it, five points will be made in guidance:

(1)   the technical terms
(2)   the harmony rhyme creates
(3)   its role in giving emphasis to the words of a poem
(4)   its ability to focus the meaning of a poem
(5)   its capacity to produce comic effects.

The technical terms

There are two technical terms associated with rhyme:

- masculine – which occurs when words are monosyllabic
- feminine – which occurs when words are polysyllabic.

'Bold' and 'old' are masculine, and 'leaving' and 'weaving' feminine. You will also notice that in the case of 'leaving' and 'weaving' the first syllable is stressed, whilst the second is not. This is called a feminine ending. The terms are of little use, as most rhyme in English is masculine.

Nevertheless, it is worth noting that masculine rhyme often sounds settled and determined, whereas feminine rhyme is fluid and musical.

___ **Examples** _____

Example 1

In Blake's 'Infant Sorrow' from *The Songs of Experience* the masculine rhymes create a hard and fixed effect:

> My mother groaned! my father wept.
> Into the dangerous world I leapt:
> Helpless, naked, piping loud:
> Like a fiend hid in a cloud.

The arrival of the child has a dramatic effect; the settled, determined rhymes give the impression that he is tough.

Example 2

By contrast with the first example, listen to the effect of these lines from Betjeman's 'Indoor Games near Newbury':

> Rich the makes of motor chirring,
> Past the pine-plantation purring
>   Come up, Hupmobile, Delage!
> Short the way your chauffeurs travel,
> Crunching over private gravel
>   Each from out his warm garage.

The feminine rhymes help to enact the sense of speed. Each flows musically after the other to create a feeling of quick yet smooth movement.

Creating harmony

When we hear one word rhyme with another, we usually experience pleasure in finding harmony between the two. Harmony creates a feeling of completeness, the sense that something has been resolved or finished. This is particularly true when we expect a rhyme; our ears wait for the rhyming word, and when it comes, we enjoy feeling that something – a meaning, a line, a stanza – has been completed.

___ **Examples** _____

Example 1

Listen to the neat first stanza of T. S. Eliot's 'Burbank with a Baedeker: Bleistein with a cigar':

> Burbank crossed a little bridge
> Descending at a small hotel;
> Princess Volupine arrived,
> They were together, and he fell.

That stanza is a little story in itself: Burbank, who is associated with small hotels, meets the exotic Princess Volupine and falls for her. The rhymes 'hotel' and 'fell' enact the sense of finality: Burbank, we feel, has fallen hopelessly in love, and nothing can be done about it. The rhyme, to put it simply, says: 'that's it'.

Example 2

Whereas Eliot's rhymes give a sense of completeness, in Stevie Smith's strangely moving little poem 'I remember', the rhymes, at the end, create a touching feeling of harmony:

> It was my bridal night I remember,
> An old man of seventy-three
> I lay with my young bride in my arms,
> A girl with t.b.
> It was wartime, and overhead
> The Germans were making a particularly heavy raid on Hampstead.
> What rendered the confusion worse, perversely
> Our bombers had chosen that moment to set out for Germany.
> Harry, do they ever collide?
> I do not think it has ever happened,
> Oh my bride, my bride.

The poem is full of interesting effects created by rhymes (look, for instance, at the deliberately clumsy yet amusing rhyme of 'overhead' and 'Hampstead'), but at the end the swell of emotion in the last line ('Oh') is completed by the rhyming word 'bride'. That creates harmony: in all the confusion, two people, one old and one young, can share in love.

Emphasising important words

When two words rhyme, you notice them. Poets can exploit this by using rhyme to emphasise important words. There are two particular ways in which this can be done:

- the frequent use of rhyme
- internal rhyme

Examples

Example 1 – frequent use of rhyme

In Betjeman's delightful 'Pot Pourri from a Surrey Garden', three lines of the last six-lined stanza rhyme. The poet is anticipating his marriage to Pam:

> Over the redolent pinewoods, in at the bathroom casement,
> One fine Saturday, Windlesham bells shall call:
> Up the Butterfield aisle rich with Gothic enlacement,
> Licensed now for embracement,
> Pam and I, as the organ
> Thunders over you all.

Rhyme brings together 'casement', 'enlacement' and 'embracement'. As well as admiring these polished, feminine rhymes, you might note that these prominent words are important to the poem's meaning. The 'casement' is open to admit the sounds that dominate the last stanza; 'enlacement' is a clever way of describing architectural detailing and it also suggests the loving ties that are made in marriage, an idea also present in 'embracement'.

Example 2 – internal rhyme

Internal rhyme, which occurs when a word within a line rhymes with the one at the end, surprises the reader, who is compelled to listen to what the words say. It also tends to quicken the pace of a line. In the last stanza of 'The Garden of Love', Blake sees with increasing horror how black gowned priests energetically destroy his beloved garden:

> And I saw it was filled with graves,
> And tombstones where flowers should be,
> And priests in black gowns were walking their rounds
> And binding with briars my joys and desires.

Internal rhyme emphasises that 'briars' are binding 'desires' and increases the pace of the line so that the dark, purposeful priests seem unstoppable. By emphasising, 'briars' and 'desires', internal rhyme enacts the conflict in the poem: the priests want to discipline and inflict pain upon someone who wants to express his feelings.

Focusing the meaning

Rhyme's ability to focus the meaning of a poem is an extension of the way it emphasises certain words. In the Blake poem in Example 2 above (p. 70) the theme is the conflict between 'briars' and 'desires'. Poets use rhyme to focus the reader's attention upon words that are central to the poem's meaning.

Example

There is a chilling moment in Chaucer's *The Pardoner's Tale* when this happens. Three reckless young men are in a town one morning:

> These riotoures three, of which I telle,
> Long erst er prime rang of any belle,
> Were set hem in a taverne for to drinke;
> And as they sat, they herde a belle clinke
> Biforn a cors, was carried to his grave.

It is a grim picture: early in the morning the wild young men are drinking but as they do so they hear the sound of a bell rung as a body is taken for burial. The central conflict of the poem between worldly, self-seeking pleasure and the inescapable presence of death is focused in the rhyme 'drinke' and 'clinke'. Their first pleasure in the morning is 'drinke', but this is interrupted by the sinister 'clinke' of a bell; not one for the first service of the day, but the one that precedes a body to burial. (Note how the run-on line dramatically leads to the grim word 'cors' – corpse).

When they learn the body is that of a friend of theirs, they rush out to find Death, a search which is successful in a grotesquely unexpected way, for they all die.

Of course, it will not be evident that 'drinke' and 'clinke' are the central words of the poem until you have finished it. Therefore, you will need to know a poem well before you will be able to see that rhymes focus words that are central to the meaning.

Producing comic effects

Rhyme can be comic, particularly when it comes in short lines. Belloc is a master of the short line; in 'Lord Lucky' he tells of how a Mr Meyer accidentally kills a lord while out shooting:

> As he was scrambling through a brake
> Discharged his weapon by mistake
> And plugged about an ounce of lead
> Piff-bang into his grace's head—
> Who naturally fell down dead.

The humour comes from the way the deft rhymes make a ghastly accident sound very clean and neat. The harmony of rhyme lends an inappropriate, and hence funny, smoothness to an unhappy event. Indeed, the sharp contrast between events that are ghastly or absurd and the neat harmony of rhyme may be the reason why comic poetry usually requires rhyme in order to be funny.

4.9   Half-rhyme

There is one poetic feature that is related to rhyme but which, strictly speaking, is not rhyme at all. This is *half-rhyme*, or *para-rhyme*. It is not rhyme because words either do or do not rhyme; nevertheless, it depends upon rhyme for its effectiveness, because the ear wants the full harmony of rhyme but instead experiences discord.

--- **Example** ---

Owen uses the incompleteness of half-rhyme to enact the destruction of order and harmony that occurs in war. In the first stanza of 'Insensibility' he writes of those who have become insensible to the horrors surrounding them:

> Happy are men who yet before they are killed
> Can let their veins run cold.
> Whom no compassion fleers
> Or makes their feet
> Sore on the alleys cobbled with their brothers.
> The front line withers,
> But they are troops who fade, not flowers,
> For poet's tearful fooling:
> Men, gaps for filling:
> Losses, who might have fought
> Longer; but no one bothers.

The half-rhymes 'killed' / 'cold', 'fleers' / 'flowers', 'feet' / 'fought', 'brothers' / 'bothers' and 'fooling' / 'filling' enact the disharmony of war by hinting at a rhyme which we do not get. There is discord in ideas as well as sound: 'brothers' are those for whom we should be concerned (that is what 'brother' means), but in war 'no one bothers' about them.

- **Remember**: When you write about half-rhyme, you should look for discord in meaning and sound.

4.10   Rhymes and rhyme schemes

Rhymes usually occur in three forms:

(1)   discrete units – couplets (or triolets)
(2)   interlaced
(3)   enclosed

Discrete units – couplets

When a poet writes in couplets (or very occasionally triplets), the rhyme sections form distinct units.

___ **Example** _____

Here is the closing passage from Pope's *The Dunciad*, a poem which ridicules dullness:

> Lo! thy dread Empire, Chaos, is restored;
> Light dies before thy uncreating word:
> Thy hand, Great Anarch, lets the curtain fall;
> And Universal Darkness buries All.

In those two couplets, the rhymes and the thought (the two are inseparable) work discretely; that is, they form isolated units that make sense on their own. Pope sees the triumph of dullness as a reversal of God's creation of the world, so when the empire of Chaos is restored (a word charged with irony), the word destroys rather than creates light. In the second couplet the hand is not the creative hand of God but one which brings down the final curtain in universal darkness. The rhyming words enact the theme: in this 'fall' / 'all' is buried.

- **Remember**: Couplets work like individual building blocks; their rhyming units are discrete – separate, distinct, detached.

Interlaced rhymes

The more usual pattern of rhyming is when the rhymes are interlaced. Our example is Yeats's 'No Second Troy', a poem about the devastating effect a woman of great beauty has upon the poet.

Example

> Why should I blame her that she filled my days
> With misery, or that she would of late
> Have taught to ignorant men most violent ways,
> Or hurled the little streets upon the great,
> Had they but courage equal to desire?
> What could have made her peaceful with a mind
> That nobleness made simple as a fire,
> With beauty like a tightened bow, a kind
> That is not natural in an age like this,
> Being high and solitary and most stern?
> Why, what could she have done, being what she is?
> Was there another Troy for her to burn?

The poem is built upon a number of rhetorical questions (questions that are asked for the effect of asking them rather than in expectation of an answer), and the urgency of these is expressed in the way the rhymes interlace – 'days' / 'ways' being woven into 'late' / 'great' and so on. The interlacing of the rhymes enacts the pressure of the poet's feelings.

That is not the only effect of interlacing rhyme; it can, for instance, show thought steadily growing or a mind in search of the satisfactory expression of an idea. Sometimes interlacing rhyme concludes in a couplet, so there is the pleasing effect of having arrived at a satisfying formulation.

Enclosed rhymes

The third way in which rhyme works is by enclosure. Our example of enclosed rhyme comes from the opening of Browning's, 'Meeting at Night'.

—— **Example** ——————————————————————————

The gray sea and the long black land;
and the yellow half-moon large and low;
And the startled little waves that leap
In fiery ringlets from their sleep,
As I gain the cove with pushing prow,
And quench its speed i' the slushy sand.

The stanza is built on three enclosing rhymes, so that the last line rhymes with the first, the second with the fifth, and at the heart is the couplet 'leap' / 'sleep'. It is a mysterious, stealthy and erotic poem about a secret journey at night, so the enclosing rhymes enact mystery by sealing it off, so to speak, from prying eyes. The poet speaks to us, but the rhymes suggest he wants to hide his journey from others.

————————————————————————————————————

- **Writing about rhyme schemes**   Should you ever want to write about the way in which a poem rhymes, there is an easy way of doing this. The first end-word is called A and any words that rhyme with it are also designated as such; the second end word is called B and so on. Thus the rhyme scheme of the Yeats poem is ABABCDCEDFEF and the Browning is ABCCBA. Of course, there's no point in just saying that; you have to go on to talk about how such a scheme helps to enact the meaning of the poem.

4.11   Stanza forms

The rhyming couplet

The simplest form of stanza is the rhyming couplet. Sometimes a couplet is the only structural unit in a poem, and sometimes it is part of a larger rhyme scheme. A very common couplet is rhymed iambic pentameters; these are called *heroic couplets*. The special effect this form creates is of self-affirmation; what is said in the first line is developed in the second, and then completed by the rhyme to make a strong, self-contained statement. In other words, the couplet is self-affirming because the second line and the rhyme develop and complete what the first line began.

Because the experience of reading couplets is of moving from one statement to another, it is a form that is particularly suited to argument. Let's look at an example of this.

Example

Dryden translated the Roman poet, Lucretius, who wrote about death. Here are two couplets:

> From sense of grief and pain we shall be free,
> We shall not feel, because we shall not be.
> Though earth in seas, and seas in Heaven were lost,
> We should not move, we only should be tossed.

You can see how appropriate the couplet is for argument by looking at the first one. The bold, monosyllabic words of the first line assert strongly that in death we shall be free from pain, while in the second a general statement – 'We shall not feel' – is followed by the reason, which, in rhyming, completes both argument and the couplet.

- This self-affirming quality of the couplet is often used by poets to conclude poems. By placing a couplet at the end, a firmness and strength is added to the whole poem.

Three-line stanzas

Stanzas of three lines are rare in English, though occasionally a *tercet*-three rhymed lines – is introduced to give variety or emphasis in a poem of couplets. Two three-lined stanzas which you might come across are *terza rima* and the *villanelle*. They are challenging forms, and, perhaps for that reason, rarely adopted.

The quatrain

The most common stanza is the quatrain. This four-line stanza is used in ballads and lyrical verse. It can be structured in a number of ways:

- ABCB
- ABBA
- ABAB
- AABB
- ABCA

There are also non-rhyming quatrains.

Quatrains can be neat and economical; there is pleasure in finding an argument or story, or a stage in either, neatly framed in four lines and held harmoniously together by rhyme.

Example

Consider the opening of Herrick's 'To the Virgins, to make much of Time':

> Gather ye rose-buds while ye may,
>   Old Time is still a flying:
> And this same flower that smiles today
>   Tomorrow will be dying.

The order of the argument is neat, and it is pleasing to find its four stages given a line each. Pleasing, too, is the contrast between the masculine rhymes which deal with what might be done and the flowing feminine rhymes that express the quick passing of time. Like all successful quatrains, this one creates the feeling that it needs just four lines to say all that needs to be said.

Other stanza forms

There are stanza forms of five, six, seven, eight and nine lines in length.

- Stanzas of seven lines that rhyme ABABBCC are called *rime royal*; they were used by Chaucer in some of his long, narrative poems.
- Eight-line stanzas that rhyme ABABABCC are examples of *octava rima*.
- Spenser used a nine-line stanza for his long poem *The Faerie Queene*; it rhymes ABABBCBCC.

Stanzas can be longer, but that is unusual.

4.12 Sonnets

A sonnet is a fourteen-line poem. It is usually formed in one of the two ways:

(1) an eight-line section (*octave*) followed by a six-line one (*sestet*) – this is called a *Petrarchan* sonnet; or
(2) three quatrains and a concluding couplet – this is called a *Shakespearian* sonnet.

It is important to understand that the way a poet structures a sonnet, or for that matter any verse form, shapes what the sonnet says.

The Petrarchan sonnet

In the Petrarchan sonnet the two-fold structure of octave and sestet makes possible an argument in two stages; in the first half the poet can explore a situation or an idea and then in the second come to a conclusion. If you look at sonnets written in the Petrarchan form you will often find the sestet beginning with words such as 'and', 'if, 'thus', 'so', 'but', 'for', and 'then'.

___

Example

___

In Sidney's sonnet, 'Loving in truth, and fain in verse my love to show', the persona is that of a poet who longs to find the right words to express the anguish of his love:

> Loving in truth, and fain in verse my love to show,
> That she, dear she, might take some pleasure of my pain,
> Pleasure might cause her read, reading might make her know,
> Knowledge might pity win, and pity grace obtain,
> I sought fit words to paint the blackest face of woe;
> Studying inventions fine, her wits to entertain,
> Oft turning others' leaves to see if thence would flow
> Some fresh and fruitful showers upon my sun-burned brain.
> But words came halting forth, wanting invention's stay;
> Invention, nature's child, fled step-dame Study's blows,
> And others' feet still seemed but strangers in my way.
> Thus, great with child to speak, and helpless in my throes,
> Biting my truant pen, beating myself for spite,
> Fool, said my muse to me, look in thy heart and write.

Sidney structures the poem in an octave, rhyming ABABABAB, and a sestet, rhyming CDCDEE. This division shapes the experience the poem deals with. In the octave he yearns and desires (you can feel the yearning in 'That she, dear she') to write in such a way that his beloved will realise his pain. To that end he studies and reads ('others' leaves' means pages of their books) in the hope of relief and inspiration. The sestet, however, begins on a note of disappointment:

> But words came halting forth, wanting invention's stay ...

Yet the 'But' does not mark the mood of the entire sestet; the poet, in an agony, which through a striking metaphor he compares to childbirth, gains inspiration (that is what 'muse' means here) to write, not from other poets' ideas but from his own feelings:

> Fool, said my muse to me, look in thy heart and write.

The sestet thus expresses both the disappointment of failure and the triumph of inspiration, and in so doing brings the sonnet to a satisfying close.

The Shakespearian sonnet

It is obvious that the Shakespearian, or English, sonnet, structured as it is in three quatrains and a couplet, will present a different set of opportunities to the poet. It is a more flexible form. The poet can develop an argument in two or three stages and then conclude it with a couplet, or produce one idea and two variations upon it before moving to the conclusion.

Another option is that of using the entire twelve lines to build up a picture, recount an experience, or develop a single argument, and then using the couplet to affirm, deny or modify what has been said.

You will see from this that the Shakespearian sonnet lays more importance on the concluding couplet. This, in itself, is a challenge, particularly when the couplet has to deny or overturn what the first twelve lines have been saying.

Example

Some of these points can be seen in Shakespeare's 'Sonnet 130'. It is a deliberately amusing poem which mocks the conventional language adopted by many poets when they imagine that their beloveds are more beautiful than they really are. Against the conventional ideal – sparkling eyes, red lips, white skin, golden hair and so on – we are offered a 'mistress' who has none of these qualities:

> My mistress' eyes are nothing like the sun;
> Coral is far more red than her lips' red;
> If snow be white, why then her breasts are dun;
> If hairs be wires, black wires grow on her head.
> I have seen roses damasked, red and white,
> But no such roses see I in her cheeks,
> And in some perfumes is there more delight
> Than in the breath that from my mistress reeks.
> I love to hear her speak, yet well I know
> That music hath a far more pleasing sound.
> I grant I never saw a goddess go;
> My mistress when she walks treads on the ground.
> And yet, by heaven, I think my love as rare
> As any she belied with false compare.

The three quatrains, rhyming ABABCDCDEFEF, do not develop an argument or produce variations on a basic idea; rather, Shakespeare builds up a picture (by no means a conventionally flattering one) of his mistress by comparing her features with those ideals honoured by other poets. By the end of the quatrains our picture of the mistress is fuller and more vivid, but it would be wrong to say that it has developed through a number of clearly defined stages.

The couplet is problematic. The persona tries to do two things: insist that his mistress is wonderful to him, and make clear that what other poets write is 'false compare', that is untrue. The latter works better than the former. By the end of the quatrains, it is, clear that the poet's mistress is a real woman; after all, don't most girls walk on the ground! But does the couplet sufficiently overturn the impression that his mistress is horrible: dull eyes, indifferent lips, wild hair, pale cheeks and, worst of all, breath that 'reeks'? (Are there stronger words concerned with smell than 'reeks'?)

Shakespeare tries to overcome this problem by saying 'And yet', following this with a colloquial phrase, the rhythm of which is very close to ordinary speech – 'by heaven' – and closing the line with the simple praise of one of his favourite words – 'rare'. But is it enough? If you feel it is not, then the reason for this is that Shakespeare, in structuring the sonnet this way, has given himself too much to do in the concluding couplet. The success of the poem, then, is related to the way it is constructed.

- The Petrarchan and the Shakespearian sonnets offer different opportunities to the poet, but they do have this in common. They allow a poet to handle difficult and varied ideas in a concentrated way. That is why readers value sonnets for their economy and complexity.

4.13   Why stanza forms matter

The question that should govern all your thinking about stanza forms is:

- How does the form of the poem shape the meaning?

Unless you can show that the form the poet has chosen is appropriate to the meaning and mood of the poem, it is pointless identifying and classifying stanzas.

___ **Example** ___

Let's look at the stanza Tennyson adopted for *In Memoriam*. Here is a quatrain in which he is writing about his puzzlement in the face of the cruelty of nature and his doubts about the presence of God:

> I stretch lame hands of faith, and grope,
> And gather dust and chaff, and call
> To what I feel is Lord of all,
> And faintly trust the larger hope.

The rhyme scheme is ABBA, a couplet enclosed by another couplet. This is appropriate in a poem which is inward-looking; the stanza contains Tennyson's thoughts in the way in which those very thoughts are contained within his mind. But the enclosing rhyme also creates another effect. Because the enclosing rhyme (the A rhyme) is separated by the couplet it seems, by contrast, less strong. In the above example 'all' directly answers 'call', but 'hope' is distant from 'grope', thus ending the stanza on an unresolved note of hesitancy and doubt. This is, of course, deeply appropriate to a poem that deals with doubts and uncertainties.

Exercises

4.1 Read the poems you are studying, paying particular attention to how the poets use sound. Write about how the sounds contribute to the meaning of the poems.

4.2 Read the poems you are studying, paying particular attention to the effects of rhymes and the appropriateness of stanza forms. Write about any rhymes you think are particularly successful, and about how the form of a stanza is appropriate to the meaning of a poem.

4.3 This is the first verse of the 'Song of the Lotos Eaters' by Tennyson. Read it through a number of times and answer the set questions below.

> There is sweet music here that softer falls
> Than petals from blown roses on the grass,
> Or night-dews on still waters between walls
> Of shadowy granite, in a gleaming pass;
> Music that gentlier on the spirit lies,
> Than tired eyelids upon tired eyes;
> Music that brings sweet sleep down from the blissful skies.
> Here are cool mosses deep,
> And through the moss the ivies creep,
> And in the stream the long-leaved flowers weep,
> And from the craggy ledge the poppy hangs in sleep.

(a) What is the effect of the rhyme scheme upon the mood of the poem?

(b) Tennyson has clearly made use of alliteration. What are the different patterns of alliteration, and what is their effect?

(c) What is the effect of the assonance in the poem?

(d) Would you describe the sound effects as onomatopoeic? If so, what is the effect created?

4.4   This is one verse from Shelley's 'Adonais', a poem written about the death of Keats. Read it a number of times and answer the questions below.

> Peace, peace! he is not dead, he doth not sleep —
> He hath awakened from the dream of life —
> 'Tis we, who lost in stormy visions, keep
> With phantoms an unprofitable strife,
> And in mad trance, strike with our spirit's knife
> Invulnerable nothings — We decay
> Like corpses in a charnel; fear and grief
> Convulse us and consume us day by day,
> And cold hopes swarm like worms within our living clay.

(a)   Describe the rhyme scheme and suggest what contribution it makes to the meaning of the poem.

(b)   What is the effect of rhyming 'life' with 'strife' and 'knife'? Do these words focus the meaning of the verse?

(c)   Think about the change in the sounds from the opening two lines to 'And in mad trance, strike with our spirit's knife'.

(d)   Are there any cases of alliteration in the verse, and do they contribute anything to the impact of what is being said?

⬡5 The poem as a whole

5.1 A poem is not lots of bits

Let's summarise what we have said on thinking about poetry.

- Each poem should be read several times (preferably aloud).

- Make sure you have a general idea as to what the poem is about.

- Start your thinking with what in the words of the poem puzzles, interests or . gives you pleasure.

- Always try to locate whatever you think or feel about the poem in its words.

- Think about the number of different ways in which the words create meanings (this will probably involve you in a consideration of figures of speech).

- Think about the particular arrangement of the lines.

- Think about what is contributed by the rhythms of the language.

- Think about the contribution of sounds, rhymes and stanza forms.

- Think about how all the above mentioned elements enact the poem's meaning and impact.

But you must not stop there. A poem is not just lots of bits. All the words of a poem add up to something – the poem as a whole. When, therefore, you study a poem, you should always do so with this aim:

- to write about the poem as a whole.

There are two ways in which you can prepare to do this.

(1) Think about what kind of a poem it is.
(2) Think about the ways in which poets design their poems.

In what follows, we shall look at different kinds of poems and then we shall follow that with ways in which poems are designed or constructed. The section will close with some thoughts on practical criticism and the challenge of writing about a poet's work as a whole.

5.2   Poems that tell stories

Many poems tell stories. The early border ballads such as 'Sir Patrick Spens' or 'Lord Randal' relate dramatic (and sometimes violent) tales against the background of a harsh natural (as well as social) world. In our own day, many of Tony Harrison's poems are narrative in content. In most cases there's no point in retelling the events of the story – your teachers or examiners can do that for themselves. It is, however, a good idea to ask yourself this question:

● Why does one event follow another?

If you can answer that question, you may begin to understand how the poem is designed. An example will help.

__ **Example** _____

Betjeman's 'A Subaltern's Love-song' tells a story. The created voice, or persona, is a breathless and ardent young man who, from the very start, is wildly in love with 'Miss Joan Hunter-Dunn'.

The first three stanzas are concerned with the tennis match, in which she beats him. In the fourth stanza we should picture them walking around her father's spacious garden, and in the fifth and the sixth they prepare for the Golf Club dance. In stanzas seven and eight they drive through the Surrey countryside, which is atmospherically full of the sounds and smells of high summer.

The order of events has led us to expect a scene at the dance, but here Betjeman springs his surprise – the last three stanzas record that the couple spent the whole evening ('until twenty to one') in the car park, with the result that the young man can proudly say 'And now I'm engaged to Miss Joan Hunter-Dunn'. The story thus depends upon a surprise.

Looked upon as a whole, you can also see that the story has a delightful shape. Its design is a happy reversal. At the beginning of the poem the young man is beaten by the lovely Joan – 'love–thirty, love–forty, oh! weakness of joy' – and at the end there is another love game which, you may gather from his pleasure, he thinks he has won.

It is worthwhile thinking about the three ways in which, in 'A Subaltern's Love-song', Betjeman engages the reader's interest in the story. He leads you to expect something, he surprises you, and he produces a reversal. These three elements

- expectation
- surprise
- reversal

are common to many poems that relate stories.

Look at how Keats arouses expectation at the beginning of 'La Belle Dame sans Merci':

> O what can ail thee, knight-at-arms,
> Alone and palely loitering?
> The sedge has withered from the lake,
> And no birds sing.

The poem starts with a question: what is the knight doing in this bleak and eerily silent place? Something is wrong, and the possibility that the scene might be a mental landscape reflecting his inner desolation raises the expectation that the knight has a strange story to tell. The rest of the poem fulfils that expectation.

Sometimes, particularly in ballads, the fulfilment of what we expect has a grim power. The ballad 'Sir Patrick Spens' is given shape by the expectation of disaster. Sir Patrick knows that the sea journey he has to undertake is dangerous, and when he and the whole ship's crew drown, there is a sombre feeling of fulfilment.

Likewise, in the dialogue poem 'Lord Randal' we know that he is very ill and probably dying, and we wait in expectation for him to realise that he has been poisoned by the one he thought was his true love. In both poems expectation helps us to see the design as a whole.

Surprise accompanies the reversal of expectation. Take, for instance, Scott's 'Proud Maisie'. The opening is fresh and beautiful:

> Proud Maisie is in the wood
> Walking so early;
> Sweet robin sits on the bush
> Singing so rarely.

The words suggest the coming of new life; Maisie is 'walking so early' in the woods, and the robin sings 'so rarely' – both symbols of new beginnings. Yet an uneasy tension creeps in when Maisie questions the robin; his answer is surprising:

> 'When six braw gentlemen
> Kirkward shall carry ye' …

The rest of the poem spells out this unnerving reply: what lies in wait for Maisie is death.

Most of the poems you are likely to study in public examinations are short, but there are occasions when examining boards set long poems. It's likely that these long poems will be narrative. Some ballads are lengthy, and one poem, deliberately written in the manner of an old ballad – 'The Rime of the Ancient Mariner' – has over 140 stanzas. Long poems (like long novels) can be intimidating. What are we to make of them?

If the poems tell a story, the best thing to do is to start with the events and think about how they link up with each other. (It might be helpful to look at Chapter 9 to see how authors create plots). If you keep clearly in your mind an outline of the events, you may be in a position to see what it is in the story that matters.

You can also hold on to images. Sometimes what is important in a narrative poem emerges, as it does in other kinds of poems, through strategically placed images. By using the word 'strategically' we are drawing attention to an important aspect of narrative poems – the place in the poem that something is mentioned.

Example

We can see both these points in Christina Rossetti's 'Goblin Market'. This is a magical poem about two sisters, who are tempted to eat goblin fruit. Early on in the poem the two girls are established as being different from each other; when faced with the temptation to eat, Lizzie is hesitant and Laura inclined to taste. Clearly, the two girls are going to act differently. And they do: Lizzie resists the offer of goblin food, but Laura eats. We know that this can be fatal, because we hear of another girl who ate and died. Then in the middle of the poem, after Laura has eaten but before the terrible effects start, there is an image of the girls asleep in each other's arms:

> Golden head by golden head,
> Like two pigeons in one nest
> Folded in each other's wings,
> They lay down in their curtained bed

The love and loyalty that is suggested by that image is very important in the plot. Because Lizzie loves Laura, she bravely attempts to rescue her. The image indicates the nature of the relationship between the girls, and it is because of that relationship that Laura acts. 'Goblin Market' is a teasing and elusive poem. It's not one that can be neatly interpreted. What, however, we can be sure about is the centrality of the love between these two very different girls. That is something we can identify by attending to the events and images of the poem.

5.3   Poems based on arguments

In poems that present an argument, you should try to attend to the structure of what is being said. If you can see the stages through which the argument passes, you will be aware of the design of the poem as a whole.

Stage 1

It's a good idea to make clear to yourself how the poem starts. Here are some questions you might ask:

- Does it start with a widely-held idea?

- Does it start with a question, a problem or a challenge to our thinking?

- Is there a situation out of which the poem arises?

Stage 2

Once the poem gets going, it's important to ask about its direction and the stages through which it passes. These questions might be appropriate.

- Why does the argument move from that stage to this?
- Are there directions the poem might have taken but didn't?
- Can we see the outcome of the argument, or is the poet keeping us in suspense?

Stage 3

The end or close of a poem is always important. We are taught to read books in such a way that the end is always a special and sometimes a memorable feature. You may find it helpful to ask some of these questions about endings.

- Is the end logical?
- Has the argument achieved what it set out to do?
- Am I convinced by this argument?
- Was I expecting this end at the opening of the poem?

___ **Example** _____

Marvell's 'To his Coy Mistress' is a poem with a distinctive design. It is an invitation to a lady to enjoy the pleasures of love while there is still time. The theme is popular in poetry (Herrick's 'To the Virgins, to make much of Time' is another example), but Marvell makes it distinctive by his almost philosophical approach. The poem opens in this way:

> Had we but world enough and time,
> This coyness, lady, were no crime …

That is the first stage in the argument; the poet starts with the condition that if they had a great deal of time, it would not be wrong for the lady to be coy, that is, reluctant to love. Marvell then launches into a delightful fantasy of what he would do if he had that much time, but the tone changes for the second stage. It begins:

> But at my back I always hear
> Time's winged chariot hurrying near …

His point is a simple one – time is short. He presses this point home by inviting her to think about the certainty of death. The argument of the poem has been: if we had much time, I would spend it courting you, and it would not be wrong for you to refuse me, but the fact is that we haven't. This leads to the third and final part of the argument:

> Now, therefore, while the youthful hue
> Sits on thy skin like morning dew …

The conclusion is logical: since we have only a little time, we had better love *now*.

  The structure of the poem is the structure of the argument. It arises out of a situation in which a man would love, and a woman would not. It moves from an impossible condition to a present reality, and then, in the eyes of the poet at least, to a logical conclusion. If you can grasp the order of the argument, you can understand the poem as a whole.

_____

5.4   Poems based on observations

In poems that develop from an observation you can see the poet at work. The poet is struck by something seen or heard, which starts a train of thought about its meaning or significance. In order, then, to see the poem as a whole, you have to follow those thoughts and reflections. One of the interesting features of this kind of poetry is the way the poet moves from observation to thought.

___ **Example** _____

Philip Larkin's 'Church Going' is a reflection upon the fact that the poet
stops and looks at churches. The first two stanzas recall familiar features –
the way the heavy door closes, the flowers, the organ, the unique silence of
the place and the lectern with its great Bible open. As he leaves, he says
that the place 'was not worth stopping for'. And then the questioning
begins:

> Yet stop I did: in fact I often do,
> And always end much at a loss like this,
> Wondering what to look for; wondering, too,
> When churches fall completely out of use
> What we shall turn them into …

The transition from detailed observation to thought comes with those questions. It is the last one that he concentrates on: will we keep cathedrals as
tourist attractions, or will we treat churches as places of magic? He then
asks who will be the last person to visit the church 'for what it was'. Will
he be a historian, someone who loves antiquity, a Christmas church-goer or
someone like the poet? That leads to the poem's conclusion. It is an answer
to the question of why he stopped:

> A serious house on serious earth it is,

and since it is a place where people can be serious about their lives, he concludes that someone will always be 'gravitating' towards 'this ground'
because he has discovered 'A hunger in himself to be more serious'.

5.5   Poems based on changes in emotion

Poems that trace the growth and development of an emotion are sometimes
similar to those based on argument and observation. Indeed, there are likely to
be changes in the emotional life of a poem that spells out an argument or follows
through the implications of an observation. For instance, the Marvell poem we
looked at on p.88 starts in a tone of cheerful playfulness, becomes broodingly
serious and closes on a note of urgent passion.

● When changes in a poet's feelings are the central feature of the poem, you
  will need to be alert to how the emotional life of the poem fluctuates.

This can be compared to following the contours of a landscape; you need to
notice the gentle rises, the sudden falls, the dips and the long declines. Particular
importance is sometimes given to the close: the poem might end because the

poet has found the words to express what he or she is feeling or because the act of expression has brought relief.

Example

Our example is a poem often studied at GCSE and A-level: Owen's 'Anthem for Doomed Youth'. It starts on a note of outrage:

> What passing bells for these who die as cattle?
> Only the monstrous anger of the guns.
> Only the stuttering rifles' rapid rattle
> Can patter out their hasty orisons.

Amid the mechanical noises of war, the poet angrily demands to know how the deaths of the soldiers are marked. It is not clear whether or not he wants bells tolled, because in the next line he calls the customary rituals of death 'mockeries':

> No mockeries for them from prayers or bells...

But it does not matter whether the poet is against funeral rituals or not, because the poetry should be read not as an argument but as a powerful discharge of emotion, as powerful, in fact, as the terrible guns. Yet that tone is not maintained. The second part (the sestet of the sonnet) begins more quietly:

> What candles may be held to speed them all?

and from then on the feelings of outrage give way to a sad contemplation of the very genuine ways in which the soldiers' deaths will be marked: tears in the eyes, the pale faces of grieving girls, the tender thoughts of the mind and, quietest of all, the image of a slowly darkening English evening, which is compared to the drawing of a blind:

> And each slow dusk a drawing-down of blinds.

The feeling at the end of the poem is of emotion that has been expressed, leaving a calm, resigned acceptance. If you are to understand this poem as a whole, you must trace the emotions as they move from outrage to sad acceptance.

5.6   Poems as games

Occasionally a poem is designed as a kind of game between poet and reader. Often the poet leads the reader to think the poem is going in a particular direction and then springs a surprise.

___ **Example** _____

A delightful example of this is Donne's 'Woman's Constancy'. The poet begins by mocking a woman for her unfaithfulness:

> Now thou hast lov'd me one whole day,
> Tomorrow when thou leav'st, what wilt thou say?

The tone is one of bitter amusement: she has loved 'one whole day' (so long!) and naturally will desert him tomorrow. Donne, again mockingly, furnishes reasons why she might go: she said she would, they are now different people from the ones who swore faithfulness, anyone may change a vow made in love, and so on. It appears that he is angry, and the reader may well pity his distress, until, that is, the poem ends:

> Vain lunatic, against these 'scapes I could
> Dispute and conquer, if I would,
> Which I abstain to do,
> For by tomorrow, I may think so too.

The reader, and the woman, have been caught out. The surprise of the ending reveals that the poem is not a bitter reaction to rejection but a cunning game he has been playing with an unsuspecting woman *and reader*. It looks as if the woman, after all, was the faithful one, and it was he who wanted to leave.

_____

5.7 Persona

Persona is not an easy idea to understand, so you should remember two things about it.

(1) The persona does not have to be the poet.
(2) Poets are free to adopt a number of different personas.

It is a mistake to assume that the 'I' that gives a poem its unity is the 'I' of the poet who wrote it; the voice inside the poem does not have to be the voice of the person whose name appears as the author. Just as in a novel there can be a narrator who is a character (for instance, Jane in *Jane Eyre*), so in a poem the 'I' can be a fictional presence created by the words the poet is using. In Browning's dramatic monologues the personas range from a perky and somewhat irreverent painter, 'Fra Lippo Lippi', to a disturbingly cool man who strangles his beloved with her own long (and beautiful) hair, 'Porphyria's Lover'. You can't identify either of them with Browning!

What, however, you might want to do is ask two closely related questions.

- Why has the poet created this particular persona?

- What opportunities does this persona offer to the poet?

Browning clearly enjoys (relishes even) minds that hover on the brink of horrors and atrocities and he also revels in the opportunity of presenting his personas living in exotic and tumultuous scenes and times.

In our own day, Craig Raine's 'A Martian sends a post-card home' gives the poet a chance to enjoy the perspective of an unengaged yet keenly observant alien, who sees our ordinary life in very different terms from ours. In 'Lady Lazarus', Sylvia Plath creates a persona with a strange, almost gleeful preoccupation with suicide. In studying her work, it's useful to ask why such a figure held such evident fascination for her.

In his dramatic monologues Browning creates lots of quite distinctive personas, each with his or her own characteristic voice. There are, of course, no limits to the number of personas a poet can create. This means that even when they are apparently similar, we should be wary of identifying them. In the early poetry of T. S. Eliot there are two poems in which a young man speaks, but in spite of their similarities – both are self-conscious, introspective and uncertain – they are different. The persona in 'The Love-Song of J. Alfred Prufrock' is a timid man who yet has wildly romantic fantasies, whereas the one in 'Portrait of a Lady' is rather bored, trivial and definitely embarrassed by the gushing older lady who befriends him.

5.8   The repetition of words

When a poet uses a word more than once, you should concentrate on it because it could reveal something of importance about the poem as a whole. It was said above that Blake's repetition of 'mark' in 'London' was important. It shows that life in London marks people like a disease; and that is what the poem is about – the outer and inner corruption that London generates in people.

Example

Read R. S. Thomas's 'Evans':

> Evans? Yes, many a time
> I came down his bare flight
> Of stairs into the gaunt kitchen
> With its wood fire, where crickets sang
> Accompaniment to the black kettle's
> Whine and so into the cold
> Dark to smother in the thick tide
> Of night that drifted about the walls
> Of his stark farm on the hill ridge.

> It was not the dark filling my eyes
> And mouth appalled me, not even the drip
> Of rain like blood from the one tree
> Weather-tortured. It was the dark
> Silting the veins of that sick man
> I left stranded upon the vast
> And lonely shore of his bleak bed.

You will notice that the word 'dark' occurs three times: the poet goes into 'the cold/Dark', the 'dark' that is 'filling' his eyes and mouth does not appal him, but 'the dark/Silting the veins of that sick man' does. 'Dark' is central to the atmosphere of the poem; together with words such as 'bare', 'gaunt', 'stark' and 'bleak', it creates the feeling of life reduced to a minimum, shorn of luxuries and pleasures.

Yet the word does more. If you follow the way the word's meaning is enriched, you will see it is central to the poem's meaning. 'Dark' at first is nothing more than the night. The next time it is used it is associated with the poet's feeling of being appalled, and its last use suggests it is something that has physically invaded Evans and left him lonely and stranded, beyond help. 'Dark' then, expresses Evans's condition: he is lost, isolated, and in the shadows of human life.

5.9   The use of contrast

When a poet employs contrasting words, the meaning of the whole poem emerges in and through the tensions created by the contrasts.

___ **Example** ___

Look at Owen's 'Futility', a poem about a dead soldier:

> Move him into the sun —
> Gently its touch awoke him once,
> At home, whispering of fields unsown.
> Always it woke him, even in France,
> Until this morning and this snow.
> If anything might rouse him now
> The kind old sun will know.
>
> Think how it wakes the seeds, —
> Woke, once, the clays of a cold star.
> Are limbs, so dear-achieved, are sides,

> Full-nerved – still warm – too hard to stir?
> Was it for this the clay grew tall?
> — O what made fatuous sunbeams toil
> To break earth's sleep at all?

The poem is built on a set of contrasts, one of which is between the sun and earth: the poet says 'Move him into the sun', and then speaks of the whispering fields and the snow. In the second stanza the sun 'wakes the seeds' and once woke the earth itself; but when it's evident that it can't wake the limbs of the dead man, the poem scornfully asks why it began the whole process of life at all. At this point the contrast between sun and earth links up with that between life and death – the sun can bring life to 'the clays of a cold star' but the 'limbs' and 'sides' remain dead. You may also find contrasts between warmth and cold and sleeping and waking. All these contrasts give the poem its shape and meaning.

5.10   Beginnings and ends

Owen's poem 'Futility', which we looked at in section 5.9, begins and ends with the sun warming the earth, but the poet's attitude changes from welcome to hostility. A change in attitude is one way of establishing the importance of the beginning and end of a work. There are others.

- The end can return the reader to the beginning and invite a comparison between the two states.
- The end can reveal what the poet has thought about the experience or event that has prompted the poem.
- The end can surprise the reader by revealing something previously concealed.
- The end can satisfy and please the reader by arriving at the point the reader was led to expect.

It is usually worth commenting on the end of a poem. Unlike the everyday experiences of our lives, poems (and other sorts of literature) have clear openings and closes. It is these which help to give works their formal shapes.

Example

Read Hardy's 'A Church Romance':

> She turned in the high pew, until her sight
> Swept the west gallery, and caught its row
> Of Music-men with viol, book, and bow
> Against the sinking sad tower-window light.
>
> She turned again; and in her pride's despite

One strenuous viol's inspirer seemed to throw
A message from his string to her below,
Which said: 'I claim thee as my own forthright!'

Thus their hearts' bond began, in due time signed.
And long years thence, when Age had scared Romance,
At some old attitude of his or glance
That gallery-scene would break upon her mind,
With him as minstrel, ardent, young, and trim,
Bowing 'New Sabbath' or 'Mount Ephraim'.

The delightful thing about this poem is the way it moves in a circle, a circle which gives the poem its shape and meaning, for Hardy, here as elsewhere, is concerned with the presence in our lives of past events. In the past the young girl's eyes swept the west gallery, where she saw the young man strenuously playing, and now, in the present, a glance of his can, in spite of age scaring romance, awaken that long-gone moment. It is worth asking what kind of an ending this is and how the poet has achieved it.

There is one other point that it's worth making about endings, and that is

● Endings are memorable.

Are Keat's lines about truth and beauty being all we need to know on earth ('Ode on a Grecian Urn') famous just for themselves, or is their force also derived from their place at the close of the poem?

Endings can also be memorable even when they are not obviously in keeping with the rest of the poem. Many readers of Arnold's 'Sohrab and Rustum' forget the events of the poem but recall with pleasure the haunting and unexpected end in which the river Oxus winds its way to the Aral Sea. The ending is oblique to the poem, but it impresses partly because it comes where it does.

5.11   Central images

The point about a poem being based upon a central, organising image has already been made. All that must be added is that you should be prepared to find the central image unusual.

Example

Hughes's short poem 'Snowdrop' is strangely impressive because its imagery is unexpected:

> Now is the globe shrunk tight
> Round the mouse's dulled wintering heart.
> Weasel and crow, as if moulded in brass,
> Move through an outer darkness
> Not in their right minds,
> With the other deaths. She, too, pursues her ends,
> Brutal as the stars of this month,
> Her pale head heavy as metal.

Hughes is writing about the flower that most people regard as both dainty and beautiful, but, as with many subjects, Hughes transforms the snowdrop into something hard, heavy and impressive. He does this by employing imagery associated with metal. The weasel and crow could be 'moulded in brass' an image that prepares us for the 'brutal' snowdrop with 'Her pale head heavy as metal'. The image transforms the everyday idea of a snowdrop and in doing so is central to the poem as a whole.

5.12   Practical criticism

In GCSE, A-level and university examinations you may well be asked to write about an unseen poem. This exercise goes by a number of names – *critical appreciation* and *analysis* being two – but the traditional title is *practical criticism*. There are no hard and fast rules or fixed procedures for tackling these questions. Most of what has been said in the previous chapters is relevant to the task. All that it's necessary to add is some advice.

- It's a good idea to read the poem several times in order to have a general idea as to what it's about.
- In your writing you should try to deal with all of the poem.
- You should try to write about the poem in as much detail as you can.
- Whenever you make a point you think is important you must support it by showing how the language of the poem bears out what you have said.
- You should remember that in many poems the meanings are not deliberately obscure – poems often mean what they appear to mean.
- It's a good idea to base your answer on the sequence of the poem, going through it section by section.
- When writing about the design of a poem, it's a good idea to draw together in one paragraph relevant features from all parts of the poem.
- Whenever you identify any technical features, always discuss their contribution to the meaning and impact of the poem.
- Don't be afraid of writing about your interest and pleasure, though be careful not to make your piece of work a list of your feelings.
- Don't be afraid of giving two different views about an issue; examiners like to see students teasing out difficult matters.

5.13   The whole work of a poet

At GCSE, A and university level you may well be asked to write about the work of a poet as a whole. Poets such a Donne, Milton, Pope, Wordsworth, Keats, Tennyson, Browning, Hardy, Hopkins, Yeats and Eliot are frequently set not in terms of individual poems in an anthology but as a single collection, featuring some of their best known works. What you are asked to do is understand this work not just as isolated poems but as a whole body of work.

Some students find this difficult. It's always difficult trying to see any work as a whole; the individual features can loom so large that the total picture is obscured. In the case of poetry, the lack of a connecting narrative, such as is present in novels and plays, makes an overall view difficult. The best that can be offered by way of advice is to think about certain rather general areas and see if they help you to gain a useful overview of the poetry. We shall briefly look at some of these and then see them at work in the case of one poet.

- Think about the kind of poems the poet writes. Consider not just the types (odes, sonnets, and so on) but the aim: is the poet arguing, narrating, reflecting…?
- Think about the subject matter. You might ask what the poet is interested in, whether certain situations frequently occur in the poetry and whether the range of interests is broad or narrow.
- Consider whether there is often a pattern in the poems. Does, for instance, the poet have certain habits of mind that make the verse move in particular directions?
- You might look at the presence of the poet or persona in the poems. Are there similarities both in the positions and attitudes of the voices?
- Are there discernible patterns in the poet's choice of imagery?
- Does the poet use particular kinds of words?
- You might look at the way in which the poet designs the poems. This will involve you in a consideration of stanza forms, rhymes, rhythms and even the way the sentences are constructed.
- Is there throughout the poetry a prevailing tone? This question brings you back to the earlier ones, because issues of tone are inseparable from the subject matter of the poetry.

That list is only a guide. In order to appreciate exactly what a body of poetry is like, you will need to think very precisely about how the poet's language works. Nor should the list be taken as indicating the order in which you must think about a poet's work. Nevertheless, it might form a useful starting point, so we'll see how the list works out in the case of a single poet – *Philip Larkin*.

Case study

- What kind of poems does Larkin write?

Larkin is a lyric poet. Some of his poems are like songs ('Love Songs in Age') and others are regular enough in their forms to be called lyrical ('At Grass'). What, however, is more important than the lyricism is the reflective attitude of the poet in the poem. Many poems open by describing, often in clear and refreshing detail, an event or experience and then go on to weigh the meaning and significance of what has been discovered in the experience. 'Church Going', for instance, is not just about the many things in a church – the roof, the font, the lectern, the hymn-books and so on – it's also about our sense of sacred places, and how they answer to something deeply within us.

- Think about the subject matter

Larkin's subject matter is largely drawn from the world around him; he is the poet of post-war England – a land of increasing prosperity, of subtle social change and the hopes and aspirations that prosperity and change bring in their wake. In one sense he's writing England, giving us back in the sharply focused images of his poetry the land which is both familiar and unfamiliar to us. Hence, there are poems about the central experiences of our lives. The obvious case is 'The Whitsun Weddings' – a poem about marriage and the way with a marriage the world is made (and seen) anew.

There are also poems about changes in our religious traditions ('Church Going'), our sense of the past ('Arundel Tomb'), holidays ('To the Sea'), hospitals ('The Building'), journeys ('The Whitsun Weddings' and 'Here'), sport ('At Grass'), the towns and cities in which we live and how we live ('The Importance of Elsewhere' and 'Here') and the kind of lives people live in those cities ('Toads', 'Toads Revisited', 'Afternoons' and 'Mr. Bleaney').

What Larkin finds in all experiences is the traditional stuff of poetry; in the ordinary and sometimes frankly drab lives of post-war England he rediscovers the themes of time, mortality, hope, expectation, disappointment, belonging and love. In one sense he is narrow; in another he attempts to do many of the things that poetry has always done.

- Is there a pattern in the poems?

When Larkin writes about how these aspects of life have a meaning for him (and by implication the reader), the poems tend to follow a common pattern. They start with what can be observed. Larkin is adept at capturing the exact feel of a place, person or event; he selects with a discerning eye those details that make something what it is. This part of a Larkin poem is usually clear, memorable but, emotionally speaking, low-key.

What then happens is that the poem builds up to a big climax in which the poet's thoughts emerge in striking images. In 'The Whitsun Weddings', for instance, the poem starts with the railway carriage and then moves on through sharply pictured images of the landscape and the commotion caused by the weddings. With the writing about the weddings, the poem becomes more emotionally involved, and this is a prelude to the big ending when the rhythms of the train and the picture of London like a rich wheatfield combine to create the experience of the sexual and procreative joy of a consummated marriage.

It must be said that this pattern is evident in the longer, serious poems; in some of the shorter ones the poems end on a low key, with a sort of casual shrug that seems to say with wry amusement: 'That's life'.

- Look at the presence of poet or persona

The issue of the presence of the poet in the poem is an interesting one in Larkin. As with many poets (and not just ones such as Browning who deliberately adopt different identities), it's not possible to see all of the poems as being the expressions of a single voice. But there are two voices that frequently occur; and often in the same poem.

One is an 'ordinary bloke' – the man who stands in the church and doesn't know what to look at and who talks about the cross and candlesticks on the altar as 'some brass and stuff'.

The other is the self-conscious poet who, in the closing stanzas of the same poem, delicately frames his thought about human identity and our hopes of fulfilment in an image which suggests that in church what we are and what we hope for are so clothed that we think they are our destinies.

In both cases, however, the poet is a detached figure who is an observer rather than a participant (there are many poems in which the poet looks on the world through a window). It's also true that the voice of the poet is very strong; whether it's the 'ordinary bloke' or the sensitive poet, the reader is very much aware of the presence of the poet in the poem.

- Is there a pattern in the choice of imagery?

It's already been said that the pattern of some of Larkin's poems is a gradual build-up to a big finish in which an image is a prominent feature. That point leads on to another: Larkin is a vivid poet but he is not a poet who crowds his poems with figures of speech. They are used sparingly, and possibly because of that they have impact when they do occur. Of the traditional figures of speech, he often opts for the simile. This sometimes gives the poetry a tentative and exploratory feel (as if he's saying: 'it might be thought of in this way') which is expressive of the distanced and even uncertain stance of the persona.

If imagery is taken in the wider sense of any language that makes an imaginative appeal to the senses, then Larkin can be said to deploy it abundantly. Many of his nouns are carefully qualified by discriminatingly chosen adjectives; sometimes he uses as many as three to define the exact nature of an experience or place. Many of his images appeal to the eye (though the ear is not neglected), and he delights in conveying the experience of looking at objects that are misty or unclear (one of his favourite words is 'blurred').

- Does the poet use particular kinds of words?

Larkin is often praised for the clarity of his poetic language (another name for this is *diction*). It's already been said that he carefully defines the things in his poems by a sensitive use of adjectives. He also uses a standard grammar (he doesn't write poetry as if it were music as does, say, Dylan Thomas). A feature of his language is his liking for the negative prefix; that is to say, he defines something negatively by adding the appropriate prefix (an addition to the beginning of a word which changes its meaning).

For instance, in 'At Grass', Larkin wants to suggest that the meadows in which the retired racehorses graze are comfortable and friendly. He creates this effect by calling them 'unmolesting'. When we come across a word such as this we have to stop and ponder how the language is working. It may be that this lingering (even if it's only momentary) is one of the ways in which the impression of Larkin as a discriminating observer and scrupulous craftsman is created.

● Look at the way the poet designs the poems

Larkin's craftsmanship is evident in the way in which he shapes his poems. Most of them (particularly the ambitious ones) have a regular stanza form and, again, most of them rhyme. But Larkin is not keen to draw attention to the form of his poems, so he has many run-on lines, allows sentences to run across stanzas and often uses near-rhymes. The result then is of a form that has been achieved naturally and, at its best, without strain.

● Is there a prevailing tone?

Students writing about Larkin very quickly judge his prevailing tone to be gloomy. This is understandable. One of his most frequent themes is failure (see the short 'As Bad as a Mile'), and, as a result, one of the common patterns in his poems is a contrast between what people hoped for and what they've ended up with. There aren't many people in Larkin poems, but those that do appear, such as Mr. Bleaney, are sad failures, whose meagre circumstances are an indication of what little they've achieved. And, of course, death is a frequent topic.

But this isn't all. A number of the poems are funny, and in the serious ones the attitude is often tough and honest rather than just defeatist. Above all, students should remember the big celebratory poem 'The Whitsun Weddings' in which the poet, in spite of his rather slighting remarks about fashion, feels the goodness of life that the newly married couples are experiencing.

Exercises

5.1   Read through the poems you have to study, trying to identify what kind of poems they are. See how this helps you to write about the meaning of the poem as a whole.

5.2   Read through the poems you have to study to see if they are formed upon recurring words, contrasts, a relation between their beginnings

and ends, or their imagery. Write about how these features help you
see each poem as a whole.

5.3   Read Wordworth's 'She dwelt among the untrodden ways' a number
of times and then answer the questions below.

> She dwelt among the untrodden ways
>   Beside the springs of Dove,
> A maid whom there were none to praise
>   And very few to love:
>
> A violet by a mossy stone
>   Half hidden from the eye!
> Fair as a star, when only one
>   Is shining in the sky.
>
> She lived unknown, and few could know
>   When Lucy ceased to be;
> But she is in her grave, and oh,
>   The difference to me!

(a)   How does each verse further the progress of the poem?
(b)   What is the effect of the contrasts between the 'none' and 'very
      few' in the first verse, and the 'few' and 'me' in the third?
(c)   Try to describe the importance of the imagery of the poem.
(d)   What do you think of the end of the poem? Is there anything in
      the poem that has prepared you for it, or does it come as a
      surprise?

5.4   Read Yeats's 'An Irish Airman foresees his Death' a number of
times, and then answer the questions below.

> I know that I shall meet my fate
> Somewhere among the clouds above;
> Those that I fight I do not hate,
> Those that I guard I do not love;
> My country is Kiltarten Cross,
> My countrymen Kiltarten's poor,
> No likely end could bring them loss
> Or leave them happier than before.
> Nor law, nor duty bade me fight,
> Nor public men, nor cheering crowds,
> A lonely impulse of delight
> Drove to this tumult in the clouds;
> I balanced all, brought all to mind,

> The years to come seemed waste of breath,
> A waste of breath the years behind
> In balance with this life, this death.

   (a)   The word 'balance' occurs a number of times in the poem. What is its significance, and what does it contribute to the whole meaning?

   (b)   What is the effect of the contrasts in the poem?

   (c)   Does the mood of the poem change at any point? If so, what is the contribution of these changes to the poem as a whole?

   (d)   The poem is about coming to a decision: trace the various stages of this decision by examining the changes in mood and argument.

5.5   If you are studying the works of a single poet, look through the poems in terms of the points made in 5.13. Try compiling notes about the features you've identified.

Part II
Studying Novels

⬡6 Authors

6.1 Novels are specially made worlds in words

One of the problems a lot of people have in trying to understand literature is that when we watch the television we are faced with art that looks as if it's a clear window on the world. To put that point another way: we are presented with art that looks like an unmediated slice of life. What we get, we are led to think, is life as it really is.

But no art is like this. No matter what it is – television and film as well as opera and ballet – art is something that has been specially made. Even art that tries to imitate as closely as possible some of the everyday features of life (soap operas, for instance) are works that have been designed, selected, edited, trimmed and packaged. All art is made.

This is why when people talk about novels, they say things such as: 'Have you read Jane Austen?' or 'You should read Alice Walker'. Novels – like poems, plays, pots, pans and pieces of music – have been specially crafted and constructed. Any novel, therefore, can be described as a world specially made in words by an author. Any novel exists in the way it does because an author has chosen to put it together in that particular way.

The traditional way of making this point is to say that novels are fiction; in other words, they've been made up. This is not in itself a difficult point to understand, yet it's surprising how many students write about novels as if the events are real and the characters the sort of people you might meet at the bus-stop. If you try to reflect on how you regard characters in a novel, you might find that there's a shadow of this idea present in your thinking. If there is, you should remind yourself that, for example, the only Jane Eyre there is is the one we meet in the pages of Charlotte Brontë's novel, and that if that book tells you she's short, dark and plain, you can't say: 'No, she's tall, beautiful and has long, fair hair.'

All this has a bearing on how you should write about novels. Instead of treating, say Jane Eyre, as if she were the girl next door, you need to bring out two things.

(1) Jane Eyre is a character created by Charlotte Brontë.
(2) We know Jane only by reading the novel.

It's not much help saying: 'Jane Eyre is badly treated when she is a child at Gateshead'. It's far better to say something like this: 'Charlotte Brontë ensures that the reader has sympathy for Jane by presenting her life at Gateshead as

105

hard'. In that last sentence, justice is done to the created status of Jane and the engagement of the reader – the two things that make a novel what it is. In fact, in any consideration of novels, three elements are present:

- the events of the book
- the author who made the book
- the reader who is responding.

Another way of making this point is to say that in the events of the book, the reader meets the author. Of course, of these two, it's the author that's the most important. The author controls what a character is like; the reader should try to respond to that character in a way that is true to what the author has done. Whenever, therefore, we look at a novel we should consider what the novelist is doing in his or her book.

6.2   How authors arrange events

A question you can ask of any novel is:

- With what purpose does a novelist arrange the events of a novel?

A number of answers can be given to that question. Among these are:

- to create excitement and suspense
- to produce mystery
- to show something important about the way people live their lives
- to arouse expectation.

That list could continue, but already one thing has emerged: what all those points have in common is the relationship between the reader and what the novelist has written. Therefore, a simple answer can be given to the question:

> *The author arranges events in order to control what the reader thinks and feels.*

What the reader thinks and feels will depend upon how the author allows him or her to see what is going on. You can, therefore, talk about the author controlling the reader's viewpoint or point of view. This is an important idea: because a novel is a specially written work, it always tries to encourage readers to look at things from a particular point of view. It may not succeed (have you ever read a novel in which you feel you are supposed to like a particular character but find that you don't?), but always the pressure of the writing is asking or inviting you to look at things in a particular way. This looking is always a matter of what is going on – the events, the characters and so on – and the angles from which they are seen. And, of course, we can't separate the one from the other – how it's looked at shapes what is seen.

Whenever you read a novel, you can always ask yourself this question:

- How is the author inviting me to view the events?

Example

In Charlotte Brontë's *Jane Eyre*, Jane, while at Lowood school, where life is hard, discipline strict and the buildings cold and damp, is befriended by a sickly girl called Helen Burns. When Helen is dying (a fact of which Jane is not completely aware) she creeps into Helen's bed. The passage ends in this way:

> She kissed me, and I her, and we both soon slumbered. When I awoke it was day: an unusual movement roused me; I looked up; I was in some-body's arms; the nurse held me; she was carrying me through the passage back to the dormitory. I was not reprimanded for leaving my bed; people had something else to think about; no explanation was afforded then to my many questions; but a day or two afterwards I learned that Miss Temple, on returning to her own room at dawn, had found me laid in a little crib; my face against Helen Burn's shoulder, my arms around her neck. I was asleep, and Helen was – dead.

- **How does the author invite us to view these events?**

The story is told from Jane's point of view, but after they have kissed and fallen asleep, there follows a set of disconnected statements: Jane awakes, there is movement, she looks, she is carried and so on. We are then told that she is not reprimanded, but we don't know whether Jane is referring to the time she is being carried or to a later time when explanations are given her. When explanations are given, we know they come from Miss Temple (the Headmistress) but we don't know whether they come directly or are relayed by someone else. It's only then that the truth becomes clear – Jane and we learn that she was asleep and that Helen was dead.

- **What is the effect of this and how is it achieved?**

The effect is such that we experience the commotion and the confusion of the event before we learn the truth. We are thus close to Jane because we can see and hear only what she does. As a result we have some feeling of what it's like being a child in an institution; neither Jane's nor our questions are answered, so the rush of events is a puzzle to both of us.

This is achieved by Jane reporting what she experienced and what others have told her. Jane tells the story, but we must imagine others, including

Miss Temple, also telling her what has taken place. One of the ways in which this is achieved is by witholding certain things. For instance, Jane is looking back on her life and therefore she knows what has happened, but in the passage she doesn't bring that knowledge into play at all. Also, as pointed out above, the fact that we don't know the exact circumstances in which Jane is told lends an air of mystery to the passage and makes us aware of Jane's minor position in the school.

Narration

The name usually given to the business of how authors relate events to readers is *narration*. Narration is a matter both of viewpoint and of attitude. In what follows we shall think about the number of different ways in which stories are narrated and how an attitude to the events and characters is present in the very manner in which the novel is narrated.

One of the basic features of narration is grammatical. A verb (a word that indicates an action or state of being) comes in three forms, known as the first, second or third person. Here is the singular form of the verb to write:

First person: I write
Second person: you write
Third person: he, she, it, one writes

A story can only be sustained in the first and third of these. (The only narrative I've ever seen in the second person was a sword and sorcery game book, which went something like this: 'You are Gondor the Mighty and you have to find a magic ring hidden in the deep forest of Glugg...'.) Narratives, therefore, are either first or third person. Both of these offer different opportunities to the author. What are they?

6.3   Narration: first person

When a novel is told in the first person (*Jane Eyre* is an example), it is as if the novelist (and the reader) is the 'I' of the book. Indeed, some novelists build on this by inviting the reader to imagine the 'I' of the book seated at a table with pen in hand. Others address the reader directly: 'Reader, I married him' (*Jane Eyre*).

In fact, there the first-person narrator is a specially-created persona. (Some people speak of him or her as a *construct*.) There is therefore always a potential distance between the narrating voice and the actual novelist. Sometimes this distance is so narrow that it can be ignored; in other cases we entirely misunderstand the novel if we overlook it. Of first-person narrators, you can always ask:

● How close are the author and reader to the narrator?

Let's look at some examples.

Examples

Example 1

The *strategy* (a useful way of talking about the means a writer employs) of *Jane Eyre* is to make the reader side with Jane from the very start; we see that Jane has been excluded from the family circle and is then disturbed by her awful cousin, John, when she's quietly reading in the window seat. That engages our sympathy. If we are at all in doubt as to how close Charlotte Brontë is to Jane and, consequently, how we should feel, the subsequent events make it clear to us: Jane is locked in the Red Room and even pushed back in by her cruel aunt when her distressed cries bring people to the door. In that moment, we are recruited to Jane's cause, so that we rejoice at her successes and deeply sympathise with her in her sufferings. Not only are we close to Jane, but we know that Charlotte Brontë is as well. She is directing us through the narration to approve of what her heroine does.

Example 2

A very different case is Mark Twain's *Huckleberry Finn*. In this first-person narrative we like Huck, but we are directed by the author to judge things differently from him. There is, therefore, an important distance between author and narrator. This becomes clear in the moral crisis of the book – the moment when Huck lies in order to save his friend Jim, a negro slave who is on the run. Huck has been born into a slave-owning society and he never questions that it's right for people to own slaves. As a result of this he feels that helping Jim to escape by lying is wrong.

> . . . I got aboard the raft, feeling bad and low;
> because I knowed very well I had done wrong. . .

But Twain doesn't want us to comply with this judgement. He invites us to see that what Huck is doing is right, even though his conscience tells him it's wrong. The passage works by Twain and the reader realising the distance (we might call it a moral distance) between ourselves and the narrator.

● **In first-person narrations you can always ask:**

What attitude does the novelist take towards the narrator?

The point is that there are any number of attitudes that an author (and there-fore a reader) can take. What you must never do is to decide beforehand what the attitude is going to be. You can't even be sure that the attitude is going to be consistent throughout the book.

Some other aspects of first-person narration

There are other aspects of first-person narration that are important in shaping our responses as readers. (We have already pointed to the first.)

- **We feel very close to the narrator.**

This is because we have access to the narrator's mind and feelings. We see and to a great extent share what Jane Eyre feels. Empathy – putting oneself in someone else's place – is something we are enabled to experience in first-person narration. All the questions that Jane has about Mr Rochester are our questions as well; we put ourselves in her place. First-person narrations allow the author to explore what it feels like to be frightened, guilty, apprehensive, grateful or whatever. It also allows the author to explore extreme states such as mental instability and night-mare. Charlotte Brontë herself does this in her very interesting novel *Villette*.

- **In many cases, all that we know is what the narrator knows.**

Reading first-person narrations is quite close to the way we know things in our own lives. We often know what other people think, but we don't know this in the same way in which we know what we ourselves think. We, like Jane, might guess what Mr Rochester thinks of her, but we don't know this in the same way in which we know what she thinks of him. But, as in the case of Huckleberry Finn, we don't always see exactly what Jane does. Sometimes the reader sees more. At the end of one chapter when we know that Jane loves him but can't be sure what he feels, there is this passage. Mr Rochester is speaking:

'Goodnight, my — ' He stopped, bit his lip, and abruptly left me.

It's surely evident to the reader that Mr Rochester is going to say: 'My dear' or 'My darling', and it's also pretty clear that he has to prevent himself from saying so. But it's not evident to Jane. She makes no comment at all.

- **Seeing into the heart and mind of the narrator allows the author to explore mental change and growth.**

When we follow a character through his or her life we can see how they adjust to experience. Jane Eyre is not always the passionate and wilful girl of her youth; she becomes disciplined and self-controlled as an adult.

A very interesting case of a character maturing is Pip in Dickens's *Great Expectations*. The novel is about what makes a true gentleman. Pip believes that wealth, London society, education and refined manners can make him one. But they don't. Pip has to grow up so that he can see through his snobbery and recognise his pretensions to gentility as false. Real maturity of vision comes when he sees that the true gentleman is kind, loving, generous and faithful Joe.

But not all narrators change; Huck never does. Even when he looks back on his life, there's no difference between the judgements he passes on himself now as opposed to when the events took place.

- **It's sometimes said that we know a first-person narrator better than any other character.**

This is often the case, but it's not always true. There are some characters presented through third-person narration whom we know through and through. This is particularly true of the novels of George Eliot and Henry James. And we can feel very close to characters so presented.

- **We can know the world from a viewpoint other than our own.**

It may be that this is one of the attractions of first-person narration. To follow Jane's or Pip's or Huck's narrative is to see the world from someone else's perspective. This may even spill over into our lives; through reading we might begin to understand how the world looks from someone else's point of view.

6.4 Narration: third person

Third-person narrations are more common than narratives in the first-person. Some narrators call attention to themselves as the narrators. George Eliot's novel *The Mill on the Floss* opens with the narrator looking at the mill. In fact, it looks as if the novel is going to be a first-person narrative, but after the opening passage it switches to a third-person mode. (A *mode* is a way of doing something.)

Some novels have narrators who are invisible; these have been compared to God: present everywhere but visible nowhere. It is always worth asking:

- How evident is the third-person narrator?

Let's look at some contrasting examples.

___ **Examples** ___

Example 1

Henry James begins *What Maisie Knew* in this way:

> The litigation had seemed interminable and had in fact been complicated; but by the decision on the appeal the judgement of the divorce-court was confirmed as to the assignment of the child.

The narrator as narrator is invisible; the litigation (legal proceedings) might have seemed 'interminable', but that is surely the experience of the characters, not that of the narrator.

Example 2

Compare, however, how Jane Austen starts the last chapter of *Mansfield Park*:

> Let other pens dwell on guilt and misery. I quit such odious subjects as soon as I can, impatient to restore every body, not greatly in fault themselves, to tolerable comfort, and to have done with all the rest.

The narrator is very evident, and we know what she's like – morally assured, understanding of some failures yet capable of dismissing those who have brought 'guilt and misery' upon themselves.

The intrusive narrator

Sometimes a narrator can be intrusive. This is not necessarily a criticism. It is merely a way of pointing out that they enter their narratives, usually to tell the readers what they think. George Eliot does this a lot in *The Mill on the Floss*. Some readers find this awkward; either they don't like what the narrator is saying or they prefer narrations to be uninterrupted.

In the first case, this is one of the challenges of literature. Authors often write because they want to present life in a particular light. George Eliot certainly does. She must hope we'll agree, but we may assume she's aware that we might not. Yet disagreement might not be negative or dismissive; it might show we are taking seriously what she is saying.

In the second case, it may be a mistake to expect an author to be consistent. For instance, one of the pleasures of reading Thomas Hardy is to see him switch narrative modes; sometimes he's the philosopher reflecting (often sadly) on the events of life, while at other times he's a natural historian writing about the changes of the season or an antiquary telling us what old Wessex was like or the keen observer of human feelings as they are seen in the faces of characters. Why should a narrator always do the same thing?

Degrees of knowledge

One of the opportunities third-person narration offers a novelist is degrees of knowledge. You can always ask:

- What does the narrator choose to know about the minds of his or her characters?

This is a very different situation from that of the first-person narrator. With first-person narration, it is only the narrator's mind that can be directly known; in third-person narration the novelist has a choice.

Some novelists don't choose to know very much. Hardy, for instance, often writes as if the narrator knows no more than an observer or a passer-by would (In fact, he often brings in travellers who look at a character and then pass on.)

Example

Think about this passage from *The Mayor of Casterbridge*, in which Michael Henchard enters a church:

> The hay-trusser deposited his basket by the font, went up the nave till he reached the altar rails, and opening the gate entered the sacrarium, where he seemed to feel a sense of the strangeness for a moment.

Everything we know about the character is conveyed through externals. The narrator chooses to know only what any other observer would see; there is no specially privileged insight into the mind of the character. Even the passage about feeling is from the point of view of an observer: '. . . he seemed to feel. . .'. This gives Hardy's novels their special character; we often view characters and events as if we were a bystander. This gives his writing if not an intimacy, at least a feeling that it's all happening before our eyes.

Sometimes a narrator chooses to have access to the mind of a single character. This is a way of combining the privilege of first-person narration with the scope that is characteristic of third-person writing. In William Golding's *The Spire*, the narrative is in the third person, but we are made intimately aware of what Jocelin, the central character, is thinking and feeling. This makes our feelings about him difficult to assess; because we are close to him there is sympathy, yet we can also see that he smug and presumptuous. Judgement is difficult because the narrative pulls us both ways.

When novelists choose to know everything about all the characters, they are called *omniscient*. George Eliot is a famous example. We come away from one of her novels with the feeling that we know the characters intimately, because Eliot writes about the thoughts, feelings and reactions of each in great detail in the hope that we will understand them.

Example

In *The Mill on the Floss* Eliot presents the brother and sister, Tom and Maggie Tulliver, eating jam puffs. It is an ordinary incident, but Eliot intimately explores their feelings. Tom has given Maggie the best piece, and she has gently protested that she doesn't want it:

> Maggie,thinking it was no use to contend further, began, too, and ate up her half puff with considerable relish as well as rapidity. But Tom had finished first and had to look on while Maggie ate her last morsel or two, feeling in himself a capacity for more. Maggie didn't know Tom was looking at her; she was see-sawing on the elder bough, lost to almost everything but a vague sense of jam and idleness.
>
> 'Oh, you greedy thing!' said Tom when she had swallowed the last morsel. He was conscious of having acted very fairly and thought she ought to have considered this and made up to him for it.

We can see into *both* of their minds. We know that Tom would like some more food – 'feeling in himself a capacity for more' – but we also know that Maggie is unaware of this. Hence, when Tom feels angry, we understand why. Yet we also know why Maggie might be surprised by this reaction. By showing us what is going on in both their minds, Eliot enables us to understand both their points of view.

6.5   Multiple narration

In some novels there are multiple narrators. For instance, in Emily Brontë's *Wuthering Heights* the whole of the book is narrated by Lockwood, a visitor who knows very little about the customs of the wild part of England in which the novel is set. He is the *primary* narrator. However, for much of the time the *secondary* narrator, Nelly, relates the incidents. She has known most of the main characters from their childhood, so is able to give Lockwood a broad view of events. But because she was not present when some of the incidents took place, she has to depend upon *tertiary* narrators – Cathy, Heathcliff and Isabella among others. Some are very minor figures – servants in the house – yet they all contribute something.

It's important to ask what are the effects of this. One effect is that we see the world of Wuthering Heights as a community. The characters in it owe their identity in part to the fact that other characters know who they are and what has happened to them. This is an important antidote to the view that *Wuthering Heights* is a book of rampant individualism.

Relativity of viewpoint

The other point about multiple narration in *Wuthering Heights* is that it opens up an issue that is often present in books that employ this narrative mode. This issue is that of the relativity of viewpoint. Because characters are different and because they see different parts of the story, the issue is raised as to how trustworthy are the various narrations. We may decide (I think we probably have to) that what they tell us is trustworthy, but many of the narrators also give us their views. It's much more difficult to know what to make of these.   Should we, for instance, take the protestations of Cathy and Heathcliff as the truth or should we rely more on the solid and sensible Nelly when we come to judge what has gone on? The point is that because the narration is multiple there is no way of coming to a final decision. What we have are different perspectives.

This problem is an even more difficult one in the case of Mary Shelley's *Frankenstein*. What she presents us with are a set of *enclosing* narratives. First there is a framing narrative from Robert Walton, an Arctic explorer who meets Victor Frankenstein. Frankenstein then tells his tale, and his narrative includes the account given by the monster of his own life. Frankenstein hates the monster he has made, but, nevertheless, he passes on the narrative, at times a very moving one, of the outcast creature to whom he has thoughtlessly given life. The novel closes with a return to Walton's framing narrative.

The narratives compete for our sympathy: do we side with Victor as the tragic scientist who has lost everything in his quest for the unknown or do we feel for the monster, who has turned to murder because of the misery of his life? The point is that the narrative gives us this problem; it doesn't sort it out for us. What we think can only be a matter of interpretation and judgement, never of unassailable knowledge.

What happens in *Frankenstein* is a pointer to how problems of perspective emerge in multiple narration: the more distinctive the characters are, the more likelihood there is that different attitudes and judgements will be present in the narrations. Increasing psychological complexity leads to the multiplication of viewpoints. Frankenstein and the monster are very different, so their views and judgements are sharply divergent.

But as with most literary strategies, this is not a matter of rules. There are multiple narratives that don't raise the issues of relativity. Take, for instance, Wilkie Collins's brilliantly ingenious narrative in *The Woman in White*. Here there are several narrators – three of the central characters and lots of minor ones – yet never once does Collins exploit the potential divergences of judgement. We trust everything that everybody says, and when a character offers a personal view, we always know that that is exactly what it is. And this happens in a book that has very distinctive characters.

Who narrates?

The Woman in White raises an issue that is always of some interest in multiple narration, and that is who does and who does not narrate. Because the novel depends upon discovering certain explosive secrets, some characters are never given the opportunity of narrating. If they were to speak, what they are trying to keep hidden would be bound to emerge. Also, not giving the narration to certain characters can help to place them. Neither Anne – the woman in white – nor Laura – the object of the hero's love – is allowed to narrate. The fact that they are both silent in this way allows the reader to see them as interesting doubles – both are deprived of their identity, both are treated badly by the same man and both are rescued, or at least aided, by another. The fact that they are both seen through others' narrations and yet don't speak directly to the reader drives us to see them together and to ask what it is they have in common. But I shall say no more, in case it spoils what is a dazzling example of the art of multiple narration!

6.6   Issues in narration

Because narration is the basis of novels (and other forms of literary art) it's not surprising that there are many aspects to it. This section deals with some of them. We shall start with issues that are related to what has already been said about the art of narrative.

Retrospection

Most first-person narrations are presented as a looking back upon what has happened. This is usually called *retrospective* narration. Even the diary sections in Collins's *The Woman in White* have a retrospective element, in that although we must imagine the diary to be written up at the end of each day and the writer to be unaware of the long-term consequences of characters' actions, it is retrospective to the extent of looking back on the day's events. Nelly Dean's narrative in *Wuthering Heights* is clearly retrospective, as also is Pip's in *Great Expectations*.

What retrospective narration allows a novelist to do is exploit the distance between the event narrated and the act of narration. Because the narrator looks back, there is a distance in time between the 'then' of the event and the 'now' of the narration. This allows narrators to think about the significance of the past that is being recalled. It also allows readers to think about the differences between the two times. Thus in *Great Expectations*, Pip recognises how his snobbery was the product of his false sense of values. In *Huckleberry Finn* there is no such judgement possible, because there is no narrative distance; Huck hasn't changed, so the Huck recalling and the Huck recalled are the same.

Sometimes, a retrospective narration is problematic. There are moments when *Jane Eyre* works retrospectively, but other moments when it doesn't. For instance, Jane never discloses until the final chapter that she is narrating the novel not as Jane Eyre but as Jane Rochester.

Knowledge

What a consideration of retrospective narration shows is that narrative deals with knowledge.

- **Knowledge in first-person narration**

In one sense this issue is simple: we know what the narrator thinks but, like the narrator, do not have the same assurance about other characters. If, however, something important hangs on what another character (a character to whom we do not have privileged access) is up to, then the issue of knowledge becomes crucial. In *Great Expectations* Pip is given a considerable fortune (his 'expectations'), but neither he nor the reader knows why he has been given it.

- **Knowledge in third-person narratives**

The problems here are different. The responsibility usually rests upon the reader to remember who knows what. In much literature knowledge is power, so *disparities* (a useful word when talking about different levels of knowledge among characters) in knowledge are the condition of very important effects.

___ **Example** _____

In *The Mill on the Floss* the central character, Maggie, is at one point staying with her cousin Lucy. Lucy is being courted (if rather languidly) by a wealthy young man called Stephen. When Maggie and Stephen first meet, there is awkwardness, but it is only the reader who knows that this arises from an interest – an immediate and compelling one – that they take in each other. Lucy thinks the awkwardness is hostility and is sad that her beloved and her cousin seem hostile. When, however, they later adjust to the shock of meeting, Lucy is comforted. While Stephen is talking about books, we are told what Lucy is thinking:

> but she, sweet child, was only rejoicing that Stephen was proving to Maggie how clever he was and that they would certainly be good friends after all.

What Lucy doesn't know, but the reader does, is that Stephen is becoming deeply fascinated by Maggie, so Lucy's judgement that they – Maggie and Stephen – will be good friends is on the way to being fulfilled in ways that will hurt her.

_____

In matters such as this it is a good idea to remind yourself what, as a reader, you know and what the other characters know. In doing this you will become aware of those disparities which form the basis of many of the important effects in a novel. As a guide, you can ask the following questions:

- What do I know?
- What do the characters know?
- What are the effects of these differences in knowledge?

Reliability

The most difficult area of knowledge is when there is a narrator whom the reader cannot wholly trust. Such a narrator (usually a first-person one) is called *unreliable*. Reliability is always a matter of degrees; if a reader did not believe anything that he or she was being told, the novel would not at any point make sense. What is more usual is a narrator who is so involved in the events of the novel that the reader wonders whether at some points the narrator's judgement has been affected and that, consequently, things are not quite as they are presented.

Examples

Example 1

A narrator who is on the brink of being unreliable is Nick Carraway in Scott Fitzgerald's *The Great Gatsby*.

Fitzgerald presents Nick with great care, so that the reader, for most of the time, finds him trustworthy. For instance, he's a stranger in New York who has grave reservations about the way of life he finds there. Also, he has a sense of humour, is aware of his own faults and, what is very important for the novel, he is troubled by a lot of what he sees in the central figure – Jay Gatsby.

But there are moments when we wonder whether Nick, in spite of himself, has been so attracted by the glamour of Gatsby, that what is presented is a Gatsby of Nick's own creation. He admits that when he first met him, there was nothing remarkable to see in the man, but at other points (near the beginning in fact) he talks of him in very elevated terms:

> there was something gorgeous about him, some heightened sensitivity to the promises of life . . .

Both at the beginning of the novel and at the end the reader may feel that such language is excessive. If the reader does feel that, then there is a dilemma: how much can we believe of what Nick says? Above all, how sure are his judgements? Countering these thoughts, however, is Nick's Mid-West commonsense. As I said above, Nick is on the brink of being unreliable, but there is enough for the reader to trust to make it an issue that the reader can think through without getting lost in a mass of uncertainties.

Example 2

Ford Madox Ford's novel *The Good Soldier* is now famous for the unreliability of its narrator. Here is a narrator who is not in the best position to tell the story. He is an American writing about the English gentry and, perhaps more important, a quiet, passionless man relating a story of passion. He calls what he has to say a sad story, but a reader having got to the end might feel that that is a serious understatement. Sometimes he says things which the reader later finds out to be untrue. He is frequently reminding the reader that he doesn't know the answer to the many questions and puzzles that face him, and this even extends to his very telling of the story: 'I don't know how it is best to put this thing down. . .' is how he begins one of his early chapters.

The effect of all this is that the reader is given more work to do. Should we trust this man who is involved and yet, in emotional terms, so detached? We know whom he feels sorry for, but should we? Do we want to endorse the judgements he has made? These are the kinds of questions the reader is left with; a firm answer is not to be had from the narrator. This is one of those books in which the reader is left to think things over for him or herself.

Perspective

Issues of retrospection, knowledge and reliability all turn on *perspective*. This is a word that comes from painting. It means what something looks like from a particular point of view. It's not difficult to see how this can apply to literature; all first-person narratives are from the perspective of the narrator. When it comes to third-person narrations, the issue is usually the perspective adopted by the narrator. There are two closely related questions that you can ask.

- From what perspective are the events viewed?

- What thinking about the events is implied in the chosen perspective?

Let's see how these questions work out in the case of Hardy's *Tess of the D'Urbervilles*.

The first thing that needs to be said is that the narrative distance shifts. The narrator (*Tess* is one of those novels in which it's difficult not to think of the narrator as Hardy) is sometimes very close – physically close – to the events and sometimes things are viewed from great distances. For instance, when, in the early morning, Angel Clare returns from visiting his parents, he finds Tess already up. The perspective of the writing comes from Angel's (and also the reader's) close proximity to Tess.

Example

> her eyes soon lifted, and his plumbed the deepness of the ever-varying
> pupils, with their radiating fibrils...
>
> The narrator is so close, he might be gazing down a microscope, a sugges-
> tion given some support by the almost scientific use of 'fibrils'. This close-
> ness is more than physical; Angel is emotionally close to Tess, but so also
> are the narrator and the reader. One of the effects of reading Tess is finding
> her precious to characters, narrator and, in many cases, reader.

Similar effects can be achieved with distance. There are moments in the novel
when Tess is pictured in the vast, sweeping Wessex countryside. Often in those
passages there isn't a corresponding emotional distance (literature can't be
expected to work in a neat, formulaic fashion); what interests Hardy is the place
that Tess has in the landscape and, on some occasions, the sense of her as part of
the universal sweep of living things. But there are moments when the physical
and emotional perspectives coincide. Our second example is the passage at the
close of the novel when Angel and Liza–Lou see Wintoncester Gaol on the day
of Tess's execution. They view it from a considerable distance:

Example

> Upon the cornice of the tower a tall staff was fixed. Their eyes were riveted
> on it. A few minutes after the hour had struck something moved slowly up
> the staff, and extended itself upon the breeze. It was a black flag.
>
> The emotional distance is in keeping with the physical distance. It's as if
> Hardy can't bear to look too closely so presents everything from the per-
> spective of the surrounding hills. The reader may well be grateful; there
> are some things that nobody wants to dwell on in painful detail.

6.7   Authors' attitudes, and irony

Authors' attitudes

It is one of the principles of literary study that what we call form and content
cannot be separated. This is as true in novels as it is in poetry. You can't split off
the sounds and rhythms of a poem from its meaning, and nor can you talk about
the way a novel is written in isolation from what it is about. In fact, the indivisi-
bility of these two things is present in the language we use about novels. The

word 'viewpoint' can mean both the angle from which something is looked at and the attitude of the one who does the looking. Therefore, whenever you think about how a novel is narrated, you will also be thinking about the attitude the author (and the reader) is taking up towards the characters and events. All you have to remember is that the attitude will emerge in and through the narration. The point may be made in the following way.

> *The reader thinks something about a character because the mode of narration has made such thinking possible.*

An author can take up virtually any attitude that he or she wants. For instance, in *The Mill on the Floss* George Eliot is understanding and sympathetic to everyone; no matter how disagreeable a character is, George Eliot (in all her novels) wants to present their behaviour as capable of being understood and therefore accepted and forgiven by the reader.

There is no point in going through all the attitudes authors and readers can take. But there is one particular attitude that is very important in narrative – irony.

Irony

Irony occurs when a reader sees that the author is showing that there is a gap between what is thought to be true and what actually is true. Whenever there is a gap (or discrepancy) of this kind, you can say that the writing is *ironic*. Because irony is about seeing the different kinds of gaps between what is thought and what really is so, there are many different kinds. Of these there are four with which you should be familiar.

(1)   A character can say something that the reader sees is mistaken. Here the gap is between *words* and *truth*.
(2)   A character may say something, the real meaning or implication of which is different from what the character supposes. Here the gap is between *words*, and *meaning*.
(3)   A character can expect certain events to happen or can set out to achieve something, but the reader can see that things won't work out as expected. Here the gap is between *intention* and *outcome*. This is sometimes called 'dramatic' irony.
(4)   A character can interpret the world in one way, but the reader will see that this interpretation is wrong. Here the gap is between *appearance* and *reality*.

What you should never overlook is the point of the irony. Because, as stated above, form and content are inseparable, there is always a meaning or a significance to irony. Let us, therefore, look at examples of those four sorts of irony in one novel – Jane Austen's *Emma* – and see how they contribute to the meaning of the book.

A gap between words and truth

Emma centres on the efforts of Emma Woodhouse to find suitable people for her friends to marry. She persuades Harriet Smith, a pleasant but not very bright girl, that the new vicar, Mr Elton, is in love with her. Harriet, rightly as it turns out, can hardly believe that this is true, but the confident Emma has no doubts: 'I cannot make a question, or listen to a question about that. It is a certainty.'

The reader, however, can see an ironic gap between Emma's smugly confident words and the truth. We can see that Mr Elton is actually interested in Emma, and that the certainty applies not to Harriet but to herself. That is its significance; the object of Mr Elton's attractions is Emma, and that echoes the fact that the centre of Emma's real interests is herself. She may present herself (and even think of herself) as someone who is helping her friends to find happiness, but her match-making is seen through this irony as being essentially an expression of her self-centredness.

A gap between words and meaning

As part of his courtship of Emma, Mr Elton gives Harriet a charade (a riddle in verse) for her collection. He intends it for Emma's eyes, but when she sees it she says: 'I never read one more to the purpose...'. She's right. There is purpose behind it, but not the one that she supposes. Because she thinks it means one thing and the reader can see that it means another, there is a gap between words and meaning. The use of the word 'read' indicates the importance of the episode; Emma is a *mis*reader of words and people. The novel is about true and false interpretation.

A gap between intention and outcome

The relationships between Emma, Harriet and Mr Elton prepare the reader for the discovery of the dramatic irony that there is a big gap between intention and outcome. Eventually Mr Elton proposes, but it is to Emma and not Harriet. In dramatic irony there is usually an element of the outcome rebounding upon the unsuspecting character, who is the object (or butt) of the irony. (I once heard a teacher describe this as the boomerang effect.) Emma is shocked and (a delightful touch) so is Mr Elton when he hears that Emma supposed he was pursuing Harriet. Both are offended. The irony has revealed their pride and even their snobbishness. He is upset that Emma thought Harriet good enough for him, and Emma feels the same about Mr Elton's hopes of her.

A gap between appearance and reality

The misunderstanding upon which the ironies are based is a case of one person – Emma – interpreting the world incorrectly. At one point she's actually warned by her brother-in-law of Mr Elton's intentions. She assures him that he is 'quite mistaken':

'Mr Elton and I are very good friends, and nothing more'; and she walked on, amusing herself in the consideration of the blunders which often arise from a partial knowledge of circumstance, or the mistakes which people of high pretensions to judgement are for ever falling into; and not very well pleased with her brother for imagining her blind and ignorant, and in want of counsel.

Emma here is confusing appearance with reality. She knows of 'the blunders which often arise from partial knowledge', but fails to see that this judgement applies to herself; she is a person of 'high pretensions to judgement' who is for ever falling into error. The irony here reveals two things that are very important in this novel – the necessity of knowing others and of knowing oneself. *Emma* (like other Jane Austen novels) is about the painful struggles of the heroine to see things properly. The irony exposes just how great the need for this is.

Some features of irony

In the light of those examples, we can point out some of the features of irony.

- **Irony is about seeing and not seeing.**

The reader must be *percipient* (able to see) and the character who is exposed must be *impercipient* (unable to see). Irony, therefore is about awareness and knowledge. When a reader sees and knows more than a character, irony is possible.

- **Irony is always against someone.**

It is, therefore, related to *power*. The one who is percipient is in a superior position to the one who is impercipient.

- **Irony is often a kind of alliance between author and reader.**

The author has led the reader to see what a character can't see. The reader, therefore, is close to the author and distant from the character.

- **Sometimes one irony undercuts another.**

This is sometimes called *double irony*. In this case the reader's position can be subverted. (*An example*: in Hardy's *Tess of the D'Urbervilles* there is a moment when Tess is described as a 'virginal daughter of Nature'. Two ironies are present here; Tess is not a virgin, and the one who says it, Angel Clare, will later reject her when he learns of her past. The reader can see the first and might anticipate Angel's disappointment when he discovers the second. But there is another undercutting both: Hardy presents Tess as a virginal daughter of nature in spite of what has happened to her. The irony rebounds on the reader; Angel speaks better than he knows.)

- **Irony is not always immediately apparent to the reader.**

The example above also brings out this feature of irony. The idea that in spite of everything, Tess is, as the sub-title indicates, a 'pure woman', is one that gradually emerges.

- **Ironies are often enjoyable when they are hinted at rather than baldly stated.**

If ironies are too obvious or heavy, the reader is likely to feel that he or she is being treated as a child.

Finally, because many ironies are subtle, it is not surprising that many readers (particularly new readers) are blind to them. All you can do is to ask yourself some questions. These may prove useful.

- Is what this character is saying true?

- Can I see more than the characters?

- Do these words mean more than the speakers think?

- Might events turn out differently from what the characters expect?

Exercises

6.1   Think about the novels you are reading from the point of view of how they are narrated. You may wish to think about such matters as the mode of narration, the knowledge we have of the characters and the viewpoint of the narrators.

6.2   Think about the attitudes of the authors in the books you are reading. If any of them are ironic, try to see how the irony works and what it contributes to the novel.

6.3   Read the following extract from Orwell's *1984* and answer the questions below.

The members of the department in which Winston Smith works are gathering for a daily ritual – the two minutes hate.

The other person was a man named O'Brien, a member of the Inner Party and holder of some post so important and remote that Winston had only a dim idea of its nature. A momentary hush passed over the group of people round the chairs as they saw the black overalls of an

Inner Party member approaching. O'Brien was a large, burly man with a thick neck and a coarse, humorous, brutal face. In spite of his formidable appearance he had a certain charm of manner. He had a trick of resettling his spectacles on his nose which was curiously disarming – in some indefinable way, curiously civilized. It was a gesture which, if anyone had still thought in such terms, might have recalled an eighteenth-century nobleman offering his snuffbox. Winston had seen O'Brien perhaps a dozen times in almost as many years. He felt deeply drawn to him, and not solely because he was intrigued by the contrast between O'Brien's urbane manner and his prizefighter's physique. Much more it was because of a secretly-held belief – or perhaps not even a belief, merely a hope – that O'Brien's political orthodoxy was not perfect. Something in his face suggested it irresistibly. And again, perhaps it was not even unorthodoxy that was written in his face, but simply intelligence. But at any rate he had the appearance of being a person that you could talk to if somehow you could cheat the telescreen and get him alone. Winston had never made the smallest effort to verify this guess: indeed, there was no way of doing so. At this moment O'Brien glanced at his wristwatch, saw that it was nearly eleven hundred and evidently decided to stay in the Records Department until the Two Minutes Hate was over. He took a chair in the same row as Winston, a couple of places away. A small, sandy-haired woman who worked in the next cubicle to Winston was between them. The girl with dark hair was sitting immediately behind.

(a) *1984* is largely written in the third person, but Orwell chooses to have access only to the mind of Winston Smith. What is the effect of this when Winston thinks about O'Brien?

(b) Since you, the reader, know no more about O'Brien than Winston does, write about the puzzles and problems that you have in understanding what O'Brien is like.

(c) When you read that Winston feels 'deeply drawn' to O'Brien and that he has 'a secretly-held belief' about him, what are your reactions to Winston?

(d) Winston feels that O'Brien has 'the appearance of being a person you could talk to'. What is Orwell inviting the reader to expect by writing this, and do you see any possibility that what is to come will cast an ironical light on these words?

6.4 Read the following passage from Dickens's *Little Dorrit* and answer the questions below. Mr Dorrit has spent many years of his life in the Marshalsea, a prison to which debtors are sent. It has been discovered that he is the heir to a fortune and, therefore, will be released. His daughter, Little Dorrit, is talking to Arthur Clennam. Mr Dorrit is asleep.

Little Dorrit had been thinking too. After softly putting his grey hair aside, and touching his forehead with her lips, she looked towards Arthur, who came nearer to her, and pursued in a low whisper the subject of her thoughts.

'Mr Clennam, will he pay all his debts before he leaves here?'
'No doubt, All.'
'All the debts for which he had been imprisoned here, all my life and longer?'
'No doubt'.

There was something of uncertainty and remonstrance in her look; something that was not all satisfaction. He wondered to detect it, and said:
'You are glad that he should do so?'
'Are you?' asked Little Dorrit, wistfully.
'Am I? Most heartily glad!'
'Then I know I ought to be.'
'And are you not?'
'It seems to me hard,' said Little Dorrit, 'that he should have lost so many years and suffered so much, and at last pay all the debts as well. It seems to me hard that he should pay in life and money both.'
'My dear child —' Clennam was beginning.
'Yes, I know I am wrong,' she pleaded timidly, 'don't think any worse of me; it has grown up with me here.'
The prison, which could spoil so many things, had tainted Little Dorrit's mind no more than this. Engendered as the confusion was, in compassion for the poor prisoner, her father, it was the first speck Clennam had ever seen, it was the last speck Clennam ever saw, of the prison atmosphere upon her.
He thought this, and forbore to say another word. With the thought, her purity and goodness came before him in their brightest light. The little spot made them the more beautiful.

(a)   Dickens chooses to have access to what Clennam thinks but he presents Little Dorrit through Clennam's impressions of her. What is the effect of this, and why do you think Dickens chose to write this way?

(b)   Look at the conversation from Clennam's 'You are glad that it should be so?' down to 'And are you not?' What clues does Dickens give to how we ought to understand the feelings of the two speakers?

(c)   How do you understand Little Dorrit's 'Yes, I know that I am wrong'? Is she wrong, or does Dickens intend us to see that it is not right for a man to 'pay in life and money both'?

(d)   Is there any irony in Arthur Clennam seeing 'a speck . . . of prison atmosphere upon her'. Is the speck on Little Dorrit, or is the reader invited to see that she is right and he is wrong?

7 Characters

7.1 Character and characterisation

There is an important distinction to be made between *character* and *characterisation.*

- *A character* is a person in a literary work.
- *Characterisation* is the way in which a character is created.

Since most readers are at home with the idea of character, comment on it can be brief. A character is someone in a literary work who has some sort of identity (it needn't be a strong one), an identity which is made up by appearance, conversation, action, name and (possibly) thoughts going on in the head. There's no reason why we should call these literary creations 'characters', but since it's become customary, it's wise to continue the practice.

Calling figures in literature 'characters' rather than, say, 'persons', is a way of reminding ourselves that a character is a literary creation. Characters in books may have all sorts of links with the people we meet everyday (in some cases we feel more strongly about them than real people) but we only meet them in books. A way of putting this is to say that characters are all the product of characterisation; that's to say, they've been made in a particular way. Much of what follows in this chapter is about how characters are created. The words an author uses are the means that make each character who he or she is. Characters are what they are like because of the way they've been made. The kind of conversations they have, the things they do, their appearances and so on are the particular ways in which the author has chosen to characterise his or her characters. We might remember the difference by saying that:

Characterisation is a method and character the product.

7.2 The creation of character

Characters in books are not real people but figures who have been specially created by the author. We may imagine an author looking at those aspects of people that make up their personalities and selecting some which are then put together. In this putting together, the author might play up some features and subdue others. The character so produced might be interesting, and we might react to him or her in ways similar to how we do to real people, but the fact remains that our reactions will be what they are because of the way the character has been made. Hence, of any character, you can ask this question:

- How is this character created?

This important question forms the basis of this chapter. What we shall do is think about the range of characters and then look at the number of ways in which characters are created and, therefore, our responses controlled.

7.3   The range of characters

One of the things that makes characters different from each other is the range and richness of their lives. Some characters are, so to speak, lightly sketched in, while others are very detailed. No reader can intelligently respond to the first kind in the same way as the second. How the character is created controls how we respond. Let's look at some examples.

Examples

Example 1

Our first example is a character who is very lightly sketched in.

In Dickens's *Little Dorrit* there is a character who is known as Mr F's aunt. This old lady has two characteristics: she does not like Arthur Clennam, the central character, and she utters inconsequential sayings. Whenever she appears she says something that has nothing at all to do with what everybody else is talking about. The following incident occurs during tea:

> A diversion was occasioned here, by Mr F's aunt making the following inexorable and awful statement:

> 'There's mile-stones on the Dover Road!'

There is very little else to Mr F's aunt; she is always very funny, and readers remember her with affection, because her remarks introduce a delightful note of absurdity into the novel. But she has no motives, no inner life, and she never grows, changes or develops.

Example 2

Some characters are fuller than Mr F's aunt but don't have a fully rounded quality. In Graham Greene's *Brighton Rock* there is a woman called Ida

Arnold. She is important in the plot; it is she who tracks down Pinkie, the boy who has taken over a Brighton gang. But whereas Pinkie is a deep and complex character, Greene treats Ida clearly but simply; she is friendly, worldly, good-natured, with a strong sense of justice. From the moment she decides to investigate Fred Hale's death (the incident with which the novel begins), Greene makes it clear that there's nothing complex about her:

> Somebody had made Fred unhappy, and somebody was going to be made unhappy in return. An eye for an eye. If you believed in God, you might leave vengeance to Him, but you couldn't trust the One, the universal spirit. Vengeance was Ida's, just as much as reward was Ida's, the soft gluey mouth affixed in taxis, the warm handclasp in cinemas, the only reward there was. And vengeance and reward – they were both fun.

That is clear but minimal. Greene tells us that Ida is bent on revenge, but we don't know any more than that, other than that it, like reward, is reduced to the simple word – 'fun'. No building up of resolution, no weighing of moral considerations; Ida doesn't have a developed inner life to allow her to do that.

Example 3

In complex, fully developed characters, we know a lot. George Eliot's *Middlemarch* begins with its central character, Dorothea Brooke.

> Miss Brooke had that kind of beauty which seems to be thrown into relief by poor dress. Her hand and wrist were so finely formed that she could wear sleeves not less bare of style than those in which the Blessed Virgin appeared to Italian painters; and her profile as well as her stature and bearing seemed to gain the more dignity from her plain garments, which by the side of provincial fashion gave her the impressiveness of a fine quotation from the Bible – or from one of our elder poets, – in a paragraph of to-day's newspaper.

Look at what we learn from just two sentences. She has social status (Miss Brooke), a special kind of beauty, a restrained taste in clothes, finely formed hands and wrists, dignity and a poise that makes her stand out from whatever is ordinary. And then there is the image of the Blessed Virgin; that tells us a lot about what Dorothea is like and how we should regard her – she has purity and yet the charitable and kind features of a mother.

And that is only the start. George Eliot explores Dorothea's rich inner life. We know a great deal about her – her innermost feelings, her wants, her hopes, her disappointments, her struggles and her aspirations. We know her through and through, yet not in such a way that we can safely predict what she will do. She lives and grows and has her own freedom to change.

7.4   Writing about characters

One way of writing about the range of characters is to employ pairs of words. For instance, simple characters can be called 'closed' and complex ones 'open'. The words indicate that one of the distinctions between the characters is their capacity to change. A closed one such as Mr F's aunt does not (and is not required to) change, whereas Dorothea is open to change. The novelist E. M. Forster, in *Aspects of the Novel*, distinguished between what he called flat characters and round characters. What he has in mind here is the degree of *fullness* a character possesses; a flat character has few characteristics, while a round one has several. Some make a similar distinction by calling some characters two-dimensional and others three-dimensional. Yet another distinction is that between caricature (a simple, stylised figure) and portraiture (a carefully drawn, complex figure). You might also use terms such as:

- inflexible or flexible
- surface and depth
- one-sided or multi-faceted.

There are three points you should bear in mind when writing about a character's range.

(1)   It's a mistake to think that even apparently closed characters have a fixed range throughout a novel.
(2)   A simple character can be as interesting and effective as a complex one.
(3)   Not all the characters in a book have a similar range.

Let's explore each of these ideas in turn by looking at some examples.

- **It's a mistake to think that even apparently closed characters have a fixed range throughout a novel.**

Some characters are closed and flat for most of the novel and then surprise the reader by displaying characteristics the reader did not think they had.

__ **Example** _____

Jane Austen surprises her readers in this way with Miss Bates – a pleasant, well-meaning but tiresomely talkative lady in *Emma*. Emma, through whom we see much of the novel, is understandably bored by her, and while we may think Emma is intolerant, Jane Austen makes it clear that Miss Bates is trying company. Then, towards the end of the novel, there is an outing to Box Hill, and it is there that we see another aspect to her. The day is not a success; it is hot, and the characters are bored and irritable. It is proposed that they play a game in which each person has the opportunity to say three very dull things. Miss Bates speaks:

> 'Oh! very well,' exclaimed Miss Bates, 'then I need not be uneasy. "Three things very dull indeed." That will just do for me, you know. I shall be sure to say three dull things as soon as ever I open my mouth, shan't I? – (looking round with the most good-humoured dependence on everybody's assent) – Do not you all think I shall?'
> Emma could not resist.
> 'Ah! ma'am, but there may be a difficulty. Pardon me – but you will be limited as to number – only three at once.'
> Miss Bates, deceived by the mock ceremony of her manner, did not immediately catch her meaning; but, when it burst on her, it could not anger, though a slight blush showed that it could pain her.
> 'Ah! – well – to be sure. Yes, I see what she means, (turning to Mr Knightley), and I will try to hold my tongue. I must make myself very disagreeable, or she would not have said such a thing to an old friend.'

At this point we adjust our view; she is not a closed or flat character, but someone with an inner life. Moreover, many readers find her admission that she must be very disagreeable to her friends touching and dignified.

- **A simple character can be as interesting and effective as a complex one.**

When we see more of a character it's understandable that we should judge that character as being more interesting than a closed and flat one. It's true that a fully realised character gives an author more opportunity, but this is a different matter from success. Dickens is a test case. I was brought up to think of his characters as cardboard cut-outs; the trouble with Dickens, I remember someone saying, is that his characters don't develop. But think how vigorous and entertaining they are.

___ **Example** _____

This is Mr Bounderby from *Hard Times*:

> He was a rich man; a banker, merchant, manufacturer and what not. A big, loud man, with a stare and a metallic laugh. A man made out of coarse material, which seemed to have stretched to make so much of him. A man with a great puffed head and forehead, swelled veins in his temples, and such a strained skin to his face that it seemed to hold his eyes open, and lift his eyebrows up.

The writing may be close to caricature with highly selective and exaggerated details; but he is monstrously funny. *Hard Times* is a novel about a manufacturing town; Mr Bounderby is a manufacturer who is presented as a factory-made article. He is 'made out of coarse material', which is 'stretched' and 'strained'. There is a point to this joke: Mr Bounderby's humanity is diminished – and so are the workers in his factory. Not only, then, is there a relish about the writing, but it also establishes a point about the novel as whole.

- **Not all the characters in a book have a similar range.**

A lot of English writing is mixed in style and approach. English art, unlike, say, French art, does not consciously stick to rules; it deliberately uses different styles and genre in single works. The word for this is *eclectic*; it means made up of things from a wide variety of sources. English novels can be eclectic in their approach to character; that is to say, it's possible to find in one novel characters who are presented in diverse ways.

Examples

Example 1

In Jane Austen's *Persuasion*, the central character, Anne Elliot, is presented in considerable depth and detail; she is aware, thoughtful and meditative. Yet the other characters, though they are engaging, interesting and lively, don't have the depth or richness of Anne.

Example 2

There are some novelists who give an equal depth of life to all the characters in their books. The most famous example is George Eliot, who seeks to present even some of her minor characters in sympathetic detail. *Middlemarch* is not only a triumph in its broad presentation of provincial life, but a masterpiece of characterisation in that the reader is intimately aware of the motivations of virtually every character.

Example 3

Things are different in Charlotte Brontë; *Jane Eyre* may be a novel that has a radical thrust in that it makes central a young woman who has neither beauty, riches nor social status, but no attentive reader can fail to see that there is only one really important character – Jane herself. All the other characters serve in one way or another the needs and desires of Jane.

Comparing and contrasting characters

Because in one novel there can be characters who differ in the way in which they have been created, it is a mistake to assume that they can easily be compared. This is something of a problem, because one of the things you are frequently asked to do in literature examinations is compare and contrast characters. It is possible to do this just as long as you remember that you are not comparing like with like.

__ **Example** _____

In Hardy's *Tess of the D'Urbervilles* the two men who court Tess – Alec and Angel – invite comparison, but they are, in terms of their characterisation (that is, in terms of how they've been created) very different.

We can see that they are different from the way in which they are introduced; all we are told of Alec's family is where they come from, whereas Angel has far more space and incident devoted to the life he lives apart from Tess. We hear, for instance, about his family life, his early ambitions, his education and his religious doubts. In short, Angel is a much rounder figure than Alec. He is also much more open; Angel is capable of change, whereas Alec, although not unchanging, is much closer in our expectations to the stock villain of Victorian melodrama

Hardy is not a consistent writer, but it would be true to say that most of the time all we know about Alec is external; he curls his moustache, smokes and addresses Tess in the clichés of the upper-class seducer: 'Well, my Beauty'. By contrast, Angel is said to be 'reserved, subtle, sad, differing'. There is a far stronger suggestion in those lines of an inner life. In view of their differences in characterisation, it's not surprising that they highlight different things in Tess; Alec draws attention to her spontaneity, while Angel appeals to her capacity for thought and reflection. These two characters can be compared, but the comparison cannot be a direct, point for point one. They differ because they are created in different ways. It's significant that they never meet.

7.5 Telling and showing

Broadly speaking, there are two ways in which novelists (and any other story-tellers) present characters. These are:

- telling
- showing.

The distinction is not a difficult one to grasp. In telling, the narrator directly informs the reader about a character; whereas in showing, the reader is left to gather what the character is like from what he or she sees.

- **Telling and showing are not exclusive of each other.**

A novelist can both tell and show. When, in *Mansfield Park*, Mary Crawford is introduced, the narrator tells us that she was 'remarkably pretty'. That is telling. Later, when she spends a long time riding (so long that Fanny, the central figure, is denied the opportunity of riding), we are shown that she is impulsive and self-centred.

- **Direct telling is often employed when a character first appears.**

For instance, Scott Fitzgerald opens *Tender is the Night* with a passage about Dr. Richard Diver, which tells us that he's twenty-six and is valued by those who know him. This is common practice among novelists; readers need to know what kind of a novel they are reading, and telling is the most efficient way of informing them.

There are, of course, problems. First-person narratives can't be treated in the same way. We have to be sure we can trust the narrator, so we must be on our guard lest we miss a note of irony. The other thing we must guard against is the assumption that telling is less important than showing. The point is that because telling is useful, novelists employ it a great deal.

- **Showing is a subtle mode of narration.**

That's why many readers like it. The novelist is treating them as intelligent in that they are trusted to see things. Humour and irony, for instance, can become tedious if the author insists on spelling out to the reader what is going on. Dickens and Hardy, for instance, sometimes overplay by pointing out what to the attentive reader is obvious. Such laboured, heavy-handed writing can become tedious. Jane Austen is far more subtle. When, as she frequently does, she relies on showing, she leaves her readers the freedom to see what's going on.

___ **Example** _____

In *Pride and Prejudice* there is a section towards the end when Elizabeth and Mr Darcy are beginning to come to a deeper understanding of each other. When they meet (always in company) they are, however, reticent; conversation is very difficult. She asks two polite questions, receives two polite answers, but there it stops:

> She could think of nothing more to say; but if he wished to converse
> with her, he might have better success. He stood by her, however, for

some minutes, in silence; and, at last, on the young lady's whispering to Elizabeth again, he walked away.

Jane Austen refrains from telling us what this all means; it's up to the reader to see that because what they have to say to each other is of a serious nature, neither has an inclination to engage in light conversation.

- **Some authors reserve showing for what matters most.**

For instance, one of the most important aspects of Harper Lee's *To Kill a Mocking Bird* is the way the central character, a young girl called Scout, grows up morally. In this first-person narration, she records how, as children, they used to play a game of running up to the Radley's house to touch the door. This was thought to be daring, because it was the home of Boo Radley, the strange and rarely seen son of the house who suffered from mental problems. Later, she says: 'I sometimes felt a twinge of remorse, when passing the old place ...'. Harper Lee tells us that, but she allows us to see its significance. Scout, we are shown, has grown up; her remorse is a sign that she can see the moral significance of her actions.

- **Telling and showing are not, of course, confined to matters of character.** Novelists can also show or tell us about settings and actions.

7.6 Questions about characters

So far we have been dealing broadly with the issue of characterisation. What follows is still concerned with that, because the focus will be on the kind of characters we find in novels. But the process of characterisation will be taken for granted in a good deal of what we say, and attention will be taken by what characters are like. We shall be looking at the various ways in which a character emerges. In particular, we shall be looking at how the identities of a character is present in the individual elements that make them what they are.

7.7 How characters speak

Authors frequently make characters distinctive by giving them recognisable and memorable ways of speaking, so it's important to ask:

- How do characters speak?

A character might, for instance, speak in a very complicated way, repeat certain words and phrases, use lots of illustrations, rely upon common sayings and proverbs, say a great deal or very little.

Example

George Eliot often gives a character such a distinctive way of speaking that a few sentences are all that is necessary for that character to be established. Listen to how Mr Casaubon, the scholarly clergyman from *Middlemarch*, speaks:

> Not immediately – no. In order to account for that wish I must mention – what it were otherwise needless to refer to – that my life, on all collateral accounts insignificant, derives a possible importance from the incompleteness of labours which have extended through all its best years. In short, I have long had on hand a work which I would fain leave behind me in such a state, at least, that it might be committed to the press by – others.

The style is the man; look how Mr Casaubon piles up the clauses of his sentences, and look how he says something and then stops to qualify what he has said by adding another remark. Even in the last sentence, when he begins by saying 'In short', he is not brief but wordily gropes his way to the end of his sentence. It is clear from those sentences that he is a dry, over-correct and lifeless man.

- You will not find every character is as carefully drawn as Mr Casaubon, but you should always look to see if a character speaks in a way which expresses his or her personality. Sometimes it is useful to point to the grammatical features which establish a particular speaking style. Mr Casaubon builds up clauses; other characters might use very short sentences, employ lots of adjectives, or use many personal pronouns that refer to themselves.

7.8   How characters think

Of course, when a character speaks, that character is thinking. A character might, for instance, use lots of vivid images (Mrs Poyser in George Eliot's *Adam Bede* is like this); or might be given a vocabulary which is laden with moral words (Fanny Price in Jane Austen's *Mansfield Park* is an instance of this).

Yet there is another way in which a character's thought can be evident to the reader. This is in their undeclared thoughts. If an author chooses to have access to the thoughts in a character's head, the reader can be aware not only of what he or she is thinking, but can be acquainted with the manner of thought – how the character's mind is made up, and how they approach problems and challenges.

This type of thinking is one that a number of early twentieth-century writers have tried to convey. Under the influence of psychological ideas, they regarded these private, undeclared thoughts as being particularly expressive of what a character is like. In the stories of Katherine Mansfield, for instance, these inner moments have the force of a revelation.

Example

Towards the end of 'The Daughters of the Late Colonel', there is a passage in which we follow the musings of Constantia:

> She remembered too, how, whenever they were at the seaside, she had gone off by herself and got as close to the sea as she could, and sung something, something she had made up, while she gazed all over that restless water. There had been this other life, running out, bringing things home in bags, getting things on approval, and arranging father's trays and trying not to annoy father. But it all seemed to have happened in a kind of tunnel.

That is the moment (there are a number like it in Katherine Mansfield), when a character comes to see her life more clearly. The 'other life' is her everyday one (all those errands), but her silent musing, her thought, shows us what really matters – that sense of freedom and even a kind of communion she enjoys on the edge of the sea. Compared to that openness, her 'other' or normal life is like a tunnel. It's fitting that when Katherine Mansfield tries to convey what a restricted life feels like she should go for an image. The life of the mind is so elusive, so difficult to recognise and tie down in words, that an image is often truer to the reality than a plainly stated idea.

Some twentieth-century novelists attempt to convey not just what a character is thinking to him or herself but the very flow of that thinking. If you try to recognise how thoughts pass through the mind, you will probably become aware of how fluid, fleeting and incomplete those thoughts are; they don't have the ordered neatness of a clearly reasoned argument but sometimes blend and blur with each other and sometimes jump from one point to another. It's this inner world that an author such as Virginia Woolf tries to convey in her novels.

Example

This is a passage from *To the Lighthouse*:

> What had happened she wondered, as she took up her knitting, since she had last seen him alone? She remembered dressing, and seeing the moon; Andrew holding his plate too high at dinner; being depressed by something William had said; the birds in the trees; the sofa on the landing; the children being awake …

The memories pass through her mind like images flashed on a cinema screen. Their importance is not to be found by seeing how one picture leads to another. That would be to turn it into a kind of argument. The point is that the memories briefly spring into luminous life before giving way to another. That's how minds work when they allow memories to well up.

- **In some writers the fluidity is even more pronounced:** James Joyce in *Ulysses* abandons punctuation to convey the rapid passage of thoughts through the mind.

7.9   The appearance of characters

A question you can ask about many characters is this:

- What does the author show or tell us about a character's appearance?

Of course, this question is more fruitful with some novelists than others. Dickens clearly enjoys painting verbal pictures of his characters, but Jane Austen is much less concerned about her characters' faces. She tells us, for instance, that Emma is pretty and looks healthy, but there is no hint as to which particular features make her pretty.

It's often useful to ask why an author seeks to convey a lot or a little about the appearance of characters. In the case of Jane Austen's *Emma* a number of questions spring to mind. If we don't know exactly what Emma looks like, we can enjoy the confusion as to whether Mr Elton's charade (which praises a woman) is intended for Harriet Smith (Emma's view) or, as it turns out, Emma herself. Also, there is the intriguing possibility that there is a symbolic or moral purpose behind the presentation of Emma. We are told that she's healthy-looking (several characters comment on this); could this be a preparation for one of the ironies of the book – the view that although her physical health is good, the health of her perceptions is questionable?

By presenting what a character looks like, the author is able to exercise a degree of control over the responses of the reader.

___ Example _____

Look at how D. H. Lawrence presents the central character of *Sons and Lovers*, Paul Morel:

Paul was now fourteen, and was looking for work. He was a rather small and rather finely-made boy, with dark brown hair and light blue eyes. His face had already lost its youthful chubbiness, and was becoming somewhat like William's – rough-featured, almost rugged – and it was extraordinarily mobile. Usually he looked as if he saw things, was full of life, and warm; then his smile, like his mother's, came suddenly and was very loveable; and then, when there was any clog in his soul's quick running, his face went stupid and ugly.

Lawrence tells us a great deal about Paul's appearance; he is 'small', 'finely-made', has 'dark brown hair', 'light blue eyes' and his face is becoming 'rough-featured' and 'rugged'. We are also told about the impression his looks give of his inner life. Throughout the passage Lawrence is directing us to see and feel; we are even told that his smile is loveable.

- **It is worth noticing that physical appearance is rarely described on its own.**

When an author writes about the appearance of a character, he or she is usually telling or showing the reader something about the inner world of the character's personality. It is not surprising in the Lawrence passage above that he goes on from saying that Paul's face was 'mobile' to tell us that he 'was full of life, and warm' – both of which are qualities of the inner self.

7.10 How characters dress

Closely related to the question of appearance is that of dress. Readers, therefore, may ask:

- Is there anything significant in the way in which this character dresses?

Clothes have several functions in novels.

- **Clothes as an expression of personality.**

If you look back to the passage about Dorothea Brooke from *Middlemarch* (p. 129), you'll see that her character in part emerges from the way she dresses. Her clothes are an extension or expression of her personality; their plainness not only sets off her beauty, but is also expressive of her seriousness.

- **Clothes are sometimes used to indicate social status.**

This is particularly true of nineteenth-century novels. In Hardy's *The Mayor of Casterbridge*, Elizabeth-Jane's clothes both establish her character and show the way she adjusts to her new social status. In a very different novel Margaret Atwood's *The Handmaid's Tale*, clothes distinguish the several strata of society. As a handmaid, the central character wears a headscarf. This, in fact, is a common ploy used by novelists who are imagining a different society.

- **Clothes can also help to create the atmosphere of a book.**

Graham Greene, for instance, presents a world of seedy characters, whose shabby, dirty and scruffy clothes enact the very strong feeling in his novels of corruption, decay and failure.

- **Clothes can sometimes be an essential element in the development of the plot.**

__ **Example** __

In L. P. Hartley's *The Go-Between*, the central character is Leo Colston, a boy on the verge of puberty, who spends the summer of 1900 with a wealthy school friend. The weather is very hot, and poor Leo is inappropriately dressed in warm, heavy clothes. A photograph records this:

> I am wearing an Eton collar and a bow tie; a Norfolk jacket cut very high across the chest, incised leather buttons, round as bullets, consciously done up, and a belt that I have drawn more tightly than I need have. My breeches were secured below the knee with a cloth strap and buckle, but these were hidden by thick black stockings, the garters of which, coming just below the straps, put a double strain on the circulation of my legs.

Leo, we are made to see, is enclosed, almost imprisoned, in his clothes: the jacket is cut very high, his buttons are done up, the belt tightly drawn, the breeches secured with a strap below the knee, and his legs covered with thick black stockings, held in place by garters.

His hosts see that he is uncomfortable, and he is taken into Norwich by Marian, the daughter of the house, to be bought something more suitable. The new clothes are lighter and freer, they remind him of Robin Hood, and he claims, though he admits it's not entirely true, that he feels 'quite another person'. The clothes are part of his transformation from a reserved boy to someone who is allowed freedom and is encouraged to indulge in fantasies. That is one of the themes of the book. Because he develops an increasingly high opinion of himself, symbolised by his new clothes, he suffers a terrible reversal of fortune, from which he never recovers.

7.11   The social standing of characters

As we have seen, the issue of clothes is related to that of social status. But there is more to social status than clothes. In many novels (again, particularly in nineteenth-century ones) the issue of social status is central. A question, therefore, that can often be asked is:

● What is the class of the character?

Class is not an easy term to handle. We use it with so many presuppositions in mind that we are always in danger of importing these into our thinking. Initially, it's best to take a simple line and view class as a kind of rank, a rank established by wealth, social standing and culture. With this in mind, there are a few questions that a reader can ask.

● **How is class evident?**

Obvious answers to this question are:

— in dress
— in employment
— (sometimes) in names.

Authors can also signify a character's class through *language*. For instance, the disdainful Estella in *Great Expectations* scornfully mocks the young Pip when, during a game of cards, he 'calls the knaves, jacks'. (Incidentally, she also criticises him for his clothes: 'And what thick boots!'

Class is also evident in other uses of language. For instance, many novelists show characters from what we would call the working class as speaking a lot of the time in proverbs and stories. It's notable, for instance, that the wonderful stories of rural life in Hardy's novels are all told by the rustics. A very good example is the chapter in *Far from the Madding Crowd* set in Warren's Malthouse.

● **What kind of class or classes is the novelist interested in?**

It's often said of Jane Austen that she only wrote about the classes with which she was familiar – the middle and upper ones. Lower-class characters do appear, but they are seen in the background as when, for instance, Emma visits the homes of the poor to dispense charity.

By contrast, a novelist such as George Eliot is interested in many strata of society. Her central figures come from many different levels; for instance, Silas Marner is a weaver, Adam Bede a carpenter, Dorothea Brooke the daughter of a gentleman and Maggie Tulliver the daughter of a miller. In each of the four novels from which those characters come there are rich families, what we might call the middle class, as well as labourers.

Dickens is similar. At the opening of *Our Mutual Friend* there is a scene in which a message is delivered by a working-class boy to the home of a man rising rapidly through the middle class. They don't meet (that's part of the point Dickens is establishing about the stratification of society) but the presence of representatives from both classes establishes the social dimensions of the book.

Yet there are differences in the way George Eliot and Dickens present the classes of their characters. This difference can best be seen by asking our third question about the class of characters.

- **What view of class and society emerges in the presentation of characters?**

As was hinted above, Dickens is aware of how class divides people. It is always, for instance, a problem for him when he wants to marry off two characters of very different classes. (He sometimes does this, as in *Our Mutual Friend*, by severely injuring the upper-class character, so that the lower-class one can't be said to have quite so good a bargain.) In Dickens class division sometimes gives rise to anger; because class divides, the characters can't see the essential thing – that we are all united in our common humanity. Sometimes the novels ironically highlight this; in *Hard Times*, the rich Mr Bounderby and the poor Stephen Blackpool both have problems with their marriages.

George Eliot is different. She is far more interested in the uniting bonds of social interests and rituals. Indeed, it might be said that one of the chief aims in the designs of her plots is to show how different levels of society belong together in what in *Middlemarch* she calls 'the great web'.

___ **Example** _____

Look at how George Eliot presents her characters going to church in *Adam Bede*. Church is important because it brings the whole rural community together:

> The women, indeed, usually entered the church at once, and the farmers' wives talked in an undertone to each other ... Meantime the men lingered outside, and hardly any of them except the singers, who had a humming and fragmentary rehearsal to go through, entered the church until Mr Irwine was in the desk.

George Eliot then writes about the congregation: the blacksmith, the farm labourers, the farmers, the landlord of the inn, the sexton and the Squire. By showing all these characters of different social standing gathering together, she suggests the strong ties and the unity of a country village.

7.12   The names of characters

It is useful to ask:

● Is there anything significant about a character's name?

Often the answer will be 'no', but there are novels in which the names suggest the nature of the characters.

Mr Rushworth in *Mansfield Park* is a silly man who rushes about the country and who rushes into the latest ideas.

In *1984* the central character is Winston Smith. His name is clearly symbolic. Smith is the commonest surname in England, so the character can be seen as standing for the ordinary man; and Winston is the name borne by the great war leader Winston Churchill. The novel was written in 1948, so the boldness and determination associated with the name Winston would be very much in readers' minds. The name is thus important for the meaning of the novel. Orwell intends readers to see the central character as one who fights tyranny just as Churchill fought it. The terrible irony of the name is that whereas Winston Churchill won, Winston Smith did not.

7.13   The company of characters

It is worth asking:

● In what company do characters appear?

One of the very many powerful aspects of the opening of *Jane Eyre* is the way in which the first event that is referred to is her banishment from the family circle. That establishes how we see Jane – a lonely character who has no real family. One way of reading that novel is to see it as a search (there are many journeys in it) for a place in which she can belong.

In that respect, *Great Expectations* is the very reverse of Jane Eyre. Pip wants to leave home and live the life of a gentleman in London, but the events of his life bring home to him that the place in which he most truly belongs is the place where he is loved, and that is his childhood home. That is why Dickens writes with such loving care about the way, as a child, Pip spent his evenings with Joe.

It's important to remember that what matters is not what we know about a character's family or society but how we actually see them in the novel.

___ **Example** _____

In George Eliot's *Adam Bede*, Hetty Sorrel lives with the Poysers, but, nevertheless, George Eliot often presents her alone. Later in the novel she leaves home, and her feelings of isolation grow:

> The horror of this cold, and darkness, and solitude – out of all human reach – became greater every long minute: it was almost as if she were dead already, and knew that she was dead, and longed to get back to life again.
>
> Hetty Sorrel appears to be a lonely character because she is frequently shown to be alone, and the most powerful writing about her, of which the above extract is an example, is concerned with her feelings of utter solitude.

7.14   What characters do

Finally, you can ask an important question:

● What does a character do?

The way in which a character is shown as acting or reacting is one of the chief ways in which authors establish personality. An author can make everything a character does important.

● **Even an action that is normally thought of as slight, can be made significant.**

Jane Austen is particularly skilful in showing how everyday events can express the moral standing of characters. Mary Crawford's habit of riding the horse usually reserved for Fanny Price shows that she is selfish. At another point in *Mansfield Park*, Mrs Norris's character is revealed through her insistence that she must have a spare room in her house and therefore can't accommodate Fanny.

● **Sometimes the action that reveals what a character is like is dramatic.**

Jane Eyre has to decide whether to live with a man whom she cannot marry, Hetty Sorrel must cope with an illegitimate child, and Winston Smith must revolt against the state.

● **You must be prepared to find some characters' actions to be complex.**

Not every character reacts in the same way throughout the novel. In the case of such characters you must look at everything they do and balance one action against another. Authors sometimes want to show tensions within characters and therefore show them acting in contrary ways.

Thus Tess *in Tess of the D'Urbervilles* is sometimes passive and sometimes forceful. She gives into Alec's desire to kiss her and eventually agrees to marry

Angel, yet she angrily shouts at the vicar who will not bury her child, strikes Alec, and, at the end, murders him. Although characters in books are not real people, they can be as puzzling. Therefore, you should be prepared to find their actions problematic.

Exercises

7.1 Write about the characters in the novels you are studying in terms of their range. You may ask whether some are fuller than others and question why the author has made them this way.

7.2 Look through the questions that have been set out in the second part of this section and see how many of them are helpful in showing you what the characters in your books are like.

7.3 Read the following extract from Jane Austen's *Pride and Prejudice* and answer the questions on it. Mr Collins is a clergyman who is visiting the Bennet family.

> Mr Collins was not a sensible man, and the deficiency of Nature had been but little assisted by education or society; the greatest part of his life having been spent under the guidance of an illiterate and miserly father; and though he belonged to one of the universities, he had merely kept the necessary terms, without forming at it any useful acquaintance. The subjection in which his father had brought him up had given him originally great humility of manner, but it was now a good deal counteracted by the self-conceit of a weak head, living in retirement, and the consequential feelings of early and unexpected prosperity. A fortunate chance had recommended him to Lady Catherine de Bourgh when the living of Hunsford was vacant; and the respect which he felt for her high rank, and his veneration for her as his patroness, mingling with a very good opinion of himself, of his authority as a clergyman, and his rights as a rector, made him altogether a mixture of pride and obsequiousness, self-importance and humility.
>
> Having now a good house and very sufficient income, he intended to marry; and in seeking a reconciliation with the Longbourn family he had a wife in view, as he meant to choose one of the daughters, if he found them as handsome and amiable as they were represented by common report. This was his plan of amends – of atonement – for inheriting their father's estate; and he thought it an excellent one, full of eligibility and suitableness, and excessively generous and disinterested on his own part.

    (a)   What is the effect of Jane Austen directly telling the reader that Mr Collins 'was not a sensible man'?

    (b)   How does what we are told about Mr Collins's background – his family, university, and position as vicar of Hunsford – help us to understand him?

    (c)   Write about the way in which Jane Austen is interested in his character rather than his appearance.

    (d)   What is your judgement of Mr Collins?

7.4   Read the following extract, which is the opening of Hardy's *Far From the Madding Crowd*.

When Farmer Oak smiled, the corners of his mouth spread till they were within an unimportant distance of his ears, his eyes were reduced to chinks, and diverging wrinkles appeared round them extending upon his countenance like the rays in a rudimentary sketch of the rising sun.

His Christian name was Gabriel, and on working days he was a young man of sound judgement, easy motions, proper dress, and general good character. On Sundays he was a man of misty views, rather given to postponing, and hampered by his best clothes and umbrella: upon the whole, one who felt himself to occupy morally that vast middle space of Laodicean neutrality which lay between the Communion people of the parish and the drunken section – that is, he went to church, but yawned privately by the time the congregation reached the Nicene creed, and thought of what there would be for dinner when he meant to be listening to the sermon. Or, to state his character as it stood in the scale of public opinion, when his friends and critics were in tantrums, he was considered rather a bad man; when they were pleased, he was rather a good man; when they were neither, he was a man whose moral colour was a kind of pepper-and-salt mixture.

Since he lived six times as many working days as Sundays, Oak's appearance in his old clothes was most peculiarly his own – the mental picture formed by his neighbours in imagining him being always dressed in that way. He wore a low-crowned felt hat, spread out at the base by tight jamming upon the head for security in high winds, and a coat like Dr Johnson's; his lower extremities being encased in ordinary leather leggings and boots emphatically large, affording to each foot a roomy apartment so constructed that any wearer might stand in a river all day long and know nothing of damp – their maker being a conscientious man who endeavoured to compensate for any weakness in his cut by unstinted dimension and solidity.

(a)   What do you think is the significance of the name Gabriel Oak?

(b)   What is the effect upon the reader of Hardy introducing Gabriel Oak's smile first?

(c)   Write about the importance of clothes in the passage.

(d)   What effects and expectations does Hardy create by the way in which he writes about Gabriel Oak in relation to church and 'public opinion'?

8 Setting

8.1 The importance of settings

It is the experience of many readers that the most memorable things about a novel are the scenes. Sometimes there are verbal pictures of a place, and sometimes a character is memorably presented as moving through a landscape or townscape. These places or locations are what in this chapter we shall call *settings*. They can be very important in novels. Novelists have learned to make them significant, so in their turn readers should try to understand the significances that the settings generate.

A word is necessary on just how broad a term 'setting' is. It can be used to cover:

- the places in which characters appear
- the social context of characters, such as their families, friends and class
- the customs, beliefs and rules of behaviour that give identity to a society
- the particular locations of events
- the atmosphere, mood and feel that all the above elements create.

This means that you might talk about the social setting of a novel by, say, D. H. Lawrence or the function of landscape in, for instance, Charlotte Brontë.

A setting can be memorable because it is in itself arresting, striking and beautiful. One of the delights of *Huckleberry Finn* is the long passages in which Huck talks about the river. Whatever else it signifies (and readers have felt that no other American novel conveys with such innocent, breathtaking wonder the astonishment and pleasure of living in an immense landscape), the writing in itself conveys a sense of just how beautiful the landscape is. An English example is Thomas Hardy; some of his most memorable scenes are just that – scenes in which the author shows the reader the subtle delights of the natural world.

Example

Look at this passage from *The Woodlanders*:

> Spring weather came on rather suddenly, the unsealing of buds that had long been swollen accomplishing itself in the space of one warm night. The rush of sap in the veins of the trees could almost be heard.

> The flowers of late April took up a position unseen, and looked as if they had been blooming a long while, though there had been no trace of them the day before yesterday; birds began not to mind getting wet.
>
> The minuteness of observation (some of it surprising) gives an accumulating richness to the scene. We move from the unsealing (a surprising yet accurate word) of the swollen buds, through the strange look of permanence that the newly opened flowers of April have, to that odd detail of the birds not minding about getting wet. Each vivid detail is pleasurable.

- But, as has been hinted, settings are not just enjoyable in themselves. They often have a striking appropriateness to other elements of the novel. The following sections explore different kinds of appropriateness. Settings can reflect the mood of a character in that they can become mental landscapes. They can also reveal the situation of a character and, by working symbolically, they can express personality.

8.2   Setting and the mood of characters

In *Tess of the D'Urbervilles* Hardy makes the landscape and the seasons appropriate to the mood of Tess. Not only are the scenes through which she moves striking in themselves, they also reveal a great deal about her feelings.

The section of the novel called 'The Rally' deals with her attempts to overcome the disasters of her earlier life. The opening words of the section establish the mood of the season:

> On a thyme-scented, bird-hatching morning in May, between two and three years after the return from Tantridge – silent reconstructive years for Tess Durbeyfield – she left her home for the second time.

These words are full of hope; there are sweet smells in the air, and new life is appearing. The words have a steady rhythm (you can scan them like poetry – 'Ŏn ă thýme-scěntĕd, bír̆d hătchĭng mórnĭng ĭn Máy') that carries the reader on in hopeful expectation. But the words are not just about the newness of life in the spring, for the new life reflects Tess's new start. She has spent 'silent reconstructive years' and now she has launched herself once again into life. A few paragraphs later Hardy makes it clear that we should see a relation between the season and Tess's mood:

> The irresistible, universal, automatic tendency to find sweet pleasure somewhere, which pervades all life, from the meanest to the highest, had at length mastered Tess.

The desire to find pleasure runs through the whole of nature; it's there in natural things, and now it has mastered Tess. That is Hardy's reason for the relation between her mood and the month of May.

But that is not the only time in the novel when the mood of Tess is reflected in the setting. Tess does find 'sweet pleasure' during the summer she works as a dairy-maid at Talbothays. There she meets Angel Clare. Hardy shows how they gradually come to love each other by placing them in appropriate settings. At one point they meet early in the morning: 'They met daily in that strange and solemn interval, the twilight of the morning, in the pink and violet dawn . . .' The 'strange and solemn interval' is not only Hardy's way of telling the reader when they met, it is also his way of indicating the growth of their love. For them, love, like the sun, has not fully dawned. They are in a strange, and wonderful, interval between the first light of affection and the full beams of love.

As the summer unfolds, their love matures. Setting matches mood. One chapter begins:

> Amid the oozing fatness and warm ferments of the Var Vale, at a season when the rush of juices could almost be heard below the hiss of fertilization, it was impossible that the most fanciful love should not grow passionate.

These words make clear the relation between setting and events. The seasons and the landscape are not pleasant, incidental decorations of the novel; they shape and reflect the feelings of the characters; as the juices of the season flow, love grows passionate. It is not surprising that, by the end of the chapter, Angel Clare has openly declared to Tess that he loves her.

Angel courts Tess throughtout the summer and autumn, eventually marrying her in December. On their wedding night he learns of her past and deserts her. From this point onwards both the weather and the landscape reflect Tess's sad mood; not only has Angel rejected her, but the whole of Nature seems to turn against her.

From the lush, fertile valley of the Great Dairies, where Angel courted her, Tess, in order to find work during a harsh winter, has to go to the bare hillsides of Flintcombe Ash. The name indicates the type of place it is – life there is as hard as flint, and nothing is left of pleasure but ashes. Hardy says of Flintcombe Ash that it is 'uncared for either by itself or its lord', and we see that in this it reflects Tess who is no longer cared for by her lord – her husband, Angel. The weather is also pictured as harsh and uncaring:

> Every leaf of the vegetable having already been consumed, the whole field was in colour a desolate drab; it was a complexion without features, as if a face, from chin to brow, should be only an expanse of skin. The sky wore, in another colour, the same likeness; a white vacuity of countenance with the lineaments gone.

Here the landscape reflects not only Tess's mood but also her situation. The drabness of the scene reflects the drabness of her world without love, and the anonymous nature of the land (there is something very disturbing about a face that only consists of skin) is Hardy's way of showing us that nobody is taking an interest in Tess – to the world she is faceless and anonymous.

8.3   Setting and the situation of characters

Hardy's scenes at Flintcombe Ash in *Tess of the D'Urbervilles* are examples of setting showing the situation of a character. (The fact that it also shows mood proves that a scene can have more than one function.) Dickens, like Hardy, uses setting to show how a character is situated.

___ **Examples** _____

Example 1

In *Hard Times* the factory worker, Stephen Blackpool, dies by falling down a disused mine shaft. The way he dies reflects his situation as a worker in a hard and unfeeling industrial society. Dickens shows how a society in which everything is calculated and run for profit is, to put it simply, a death-trap for its members. This is the moment when two women discover what has happened to Stephen:

> Before them, at their very feet, was the brink of a black ragged chasm hidden by the thick grass.

The mine (it has the dramatic name of 'the Old Hell Shaft') is a symbol of industrial society. Both are black ragged chasms that are ready to swallow up their victims, and both are dangerous because their danger is hidden from view.

Example 2

In *Great Expectations* Dickens also uses landscape to bring over the situation of Pip. In the third paragraph of the novel Pip realises who he is and how he is placed in the world. The bleakness of the landscape appropriately accompanies this realisation:

> … that the dark flat wilderness beyond the churchyard, intersected with dykes and mounds and gates, with scattered cattle feeding on it, was the marshes; and that the low leaden line beyond was the river; and that the distant savage lair from which the wind was rushing, was the sea; and that the small bundle of shivers growing afraid of it all and beginning to cry, was Pip.

The setting of the dark and oppressive landscape shows that Pip is a lonely and frightened child in a hostile world; the wilderness is 'dark' and 'flat', the sky 'low' and 'leaden', and the wind rushes at him from the 'distant savage lair' of the sea. Soon characters rush at Pip. He meets the convict who frightens him with ghastly threats, and then he returns home to meet his equally hostile sister.

8.4   Setting and the personality of characters

Settings can reveal the personality of characters. One of the features of *Jane Eyre* is that two men propose marriage to the heroine. One of the men, Mr Rochester, is loved deeply by Jane; the other, Mr Rivers, is admired but hardly loved in a romantic way. The settings in which the proposals occur reveal a great deal about Jane's impressions of these two men.

___ **Example** _____

Mr Rochester proposes in an orchard on a warm summer evening:

No nook in the grounds more sheltered and more Eden-like; a very high wall shut it out from the court on one side; on the other a beech avenue screened it from the lawn. At the bottom was a sunk fence, its sole separation from the lonely fields: a winding walk, bordered with laurels and terminating in a giant horse-chestnut, circled at the base by the seat, led down to the fence. Here one could wander unseen. While such honeydew fell, such silence reigned, such gloaming gathered, I felt as if I could haunt such shade for ever.

The landscape reflects what Jane (and therefore, to some extent, the reader) feels about Mr Rochester. She sees him as a romantic, mysterious, larger than life figure, who is quite unlike the ordinary run of people. Hence the setting: it is cut off from the world in romantic isolation – she even compares it to the Garden of Eden! Here, with Mr Rochester, Jane feels she 'could haunt such shade for ever'.

But Jane's view of Mr Rivers is very different; he is a man driven by a strong sense of duty, so will not allow himself to enjoy pleasures. Jane feels admiration, even awe, for his dedication to missionary work, but she finds him cold and aloof. There is a great contrast between the secluded, Eden-like orchard of Mr Rochester's proposal and the bleak, open moorland which Mr Rivers chooses for his offer of marriage.

Example

> One detail of this setting is very important: 'we reached the first strag-
> glers of the battalion of rocks, guarding a sort of pass, beyond which the
> beck rushed down a waterfall'.
>
> The landscape is spoken of in military terms – 'battalion', 'guarding a . . .
> pass' – with the river ('the beck') rushing as a waterfall. Military disci-
> pline, and cold water falling over hard rock: those are images that reveal
> Mr River's personality. He is a man of iron self-discipline, and, like the
> waterfall, he is cold and hard.
>
> Further on, Jane says he has 'no more of a husband's heart for me than
> that frowning giant of a rock, down which the stream is foaming in yonder
> gorge'. That makes it clear: Jane feels that Rivers is as hard as the rocks of
> the moor. The setting, in short, brings out what she feels he is like.

8.5   Setting and theme: the author's view

The points above have been about setting and character. We now move to another
area: what we might call setting and theme. It is sometimes useful to ask:

● Does the setting reveal anything about the author's views?

There are some novelists who create settings for the purpose of giving their
views about the world. Such a novelist creates landscapes, townscapes, interiors
of houses and the weather in order to convey his or her particular feelings and
views about life. A reader can look at these and see, to put it simply, what the
author thinks about things.

Graham Greene is an example. Not only do many of his novels establish a
similar atmosphere through their settings, but this atmosphere reveals how
Greene views the world. For Greene the world is a corrupt, seedy and oppressive
place, hence his novels are full of rotting houses, dirty towns, stiflingly hot
weather, dry, lifeless landscapes and grimy interiors. So distinctive are the settings of his novels that a word has been coined to characterise them –
Greeneland. No matter whether the setting is England, as in *Brighton Rock*,
Africa, as in *The Heart of the Matter*, or Latin America, as in *The Power and the
Glory*, an atmosphere of seedy corruption prevails.

But for Greene this is not just atmosphere; the settings show us something.
Greene is showing us that ours is a fallen world; that is, a world which is not at
peace with its maker, God, and so is given over to corruption. The settings of his
novels, then, present his religious view of the world. He fills his novels with
seedy settings as a way of showing that the world has been cut adrift from God.
People left to themselves will lead squalid lives is the basic point in Greene's
novels; this is borne out in the settings.

— **Example** ————————————————————————

There is a scene in *Brighton Rock* in which Pinkie marries Rose in order to prevent her from giving evidence against him. Both are catholics but they go to the registry office. Greene uses a civil wedding to show how squalid people can be when they fail to recognise God. This is evident in the setting.

> In the great institutional hall from which the corridors led off to deaths and births there was a smell of disinfectant. The walls were tiled like a public lavatory ... They sat down. A mop leant in a corner against a tiled wall. The footsteps of a clerk squealed on the icy paving down another passage. Presently a big brown door opened; they saw a row of clerks inside who didn't look up; a man and wife came out into the corridor. A woman followed them and took the mop.

Greene intends us to find these scenes very unpleasant. The setting shows us the squalid lives of people cut off from God. In such a world marriage is simply a civil arrangement carried out by council employees – 'a row of clerks inside who didn't look up'. Greene makes the scene seedy and corrupt by including details such as 'a smell of disinfectant', 'the walls . . . tiled like a public lavatory' and the mop leaning against the wall.

In that scene we have to make the link between the nastiness of the setting and the world adrift from God. Sometimes, though, Greene makes the connection clear. In *The Power and the Glory* he frequently uses the word 'abandoned' to sum up the condition of the world, and at one point – in an overcrowded jail – the priest realises that 'this place was very like the world: overcrowded with lust and crime and unhappy love, it stank to heaven . . .' That could be said of many of Greene's settings: as images of corruption they show his belief that the world is cut off from God.

- **You should not think that because Greene uses his settings to express a religious view of the world, other authors will do the same.**

Many of them use settings to give their views, but these views are not religious ones. For instance, in Conrad's *Heart of Darkness* the journey up an African river is expressive of his dark and pessimistic view of man; the oppressive heat, the huge tracts of jungle, and the squalid trading outposts create an overwhelming sense of evil. For Conrad, the world is a forbidding place, and to understand it properly is to take a journey into the heart of darkness.

8.6   Setting and theme: distinctive worlds

In both Greene and Conrad the settings have another function. They are so powerful and vivid that they take on a life of their own and thus create a distinctive world.

___ **Example** _____

Heart of Darkness works as a novel because it creates a special world. This is what Marlowe, the narrator, says of the journey up the river:

> Going up that river was like travelling back to the earliest beginnings of the world, when vegetation rioted on the earth and the big trees were kings. An empty stream, a great silence, an impenetrable forest.

The language makes the setting primitive. We are in a world where legends can begin, where vegetation can riot and trees can be kings. It is awesome; at once vacant – 'an empty stream' – and, at the same time, the forest is so thick that it's 'impenetrable'. This is not like the world we know (at least not obviously like it); it's a special and even mythical realm.

One of the experiences of reading *Heart of Darkness* is that of finding the setting the most important element in the whole book. The tale that Marlowe tells is a frightening and important one, yet it's the great jungle that so often sticks in the reader's mind.

_____

In some novels this can happen, even when the setting is not put in the foreground in quite the dramatic way in which it is in Conrad. D. H. Lawrence said of Hardy's *The Return of the Native* that the best character was Egdon Heath.

Distinctive worlds

Conrad's Africa and Hardy's Egdon Heath are literary re-creations of actual places. In some novels, however, there are settings that are distinctive and, in some respects, different from everyday actuality. Aldous Huxley in *Brave New World*, George Orwell in *1984* and Margaret Atwood in *The Handmaid's Tale* create distinct worlds.

In Huxley it is a world dominated by science and technology, and in Orwell there is the domination of a political regime. In both these novels it is the setting (the term is being used widely) which is the real achievement of the novelist. Huxley invents a world in which babies are born in bottles, and people bred to perform certain social functions and conditioned so they will be content. It's a world in which nobody ages, no lasting relationships are formed and in which worry and anxiety are banished by a drug called soma.

Orwell's world is even more inventive, because he sees that a world under totalitarian control has to have its own language. It is a thin functional language that is incapable of expressing deep feeling or profound thought. This narrow, inflexible language (called newspeak) empties life of all that makes it satisfying and human. And that is the point: *1984* is a world where what we would recognise as human has been banished. It is the same with *Brave New World*; we are supposed to recoil with horror from such an inhuman world.

What Margaret Atwood is doing is presenting a kind of allegory in which the only purpose of women is procreation. She therefore frames a whole social order, based upon the conception of the next generation. In these novels the distinctive world reflects what the authors think; if you reverse everything in them, you have a picture of what they value.

One thing that is clear about these books is that the chief imaginative efforts of the authors went into the creation of the settings; plots and characters are often less interesting. The setting embodies what the author wants to say, so it is worked on with considerable care and thought. In this sense Lawrence's comment on Hardy can be seen to be a useful one. There are books in which the setting, which we often think of as the background, is in fact in the foreground.

8.7   Setting and theme: the central feature

There are some books which are set in public examinations in which the setting is clearly intended to be the central feature.

In Flora Thompson's *Lark Rise* the focus is a north Oxfordshire village in the 1890s. There are events, but it's the change of seasons, the village institutions and the life of the land that are the book's chief subject matter.

In *Cider with Rosie* the pattern is similar; what is usually background – the setting – provides the chief interest.

Example

Look at this passage from *Cider with Rosie*; from his bedroom window Laurie is watching the lake:

> Then suddenly the whole picture would break into pieces, would be smashed like a molten mirror and run amok in tiny globules of gold, frantic and shivering; and I would hear the great slapping of wings on water, building up a steady crescendo, while across the ceiling passed the shadows of swans taking off into the heavy morning. I would hear the cries pass over the house and watch the chaos of light above me, till it slowly settled and re-collected its stars and resumed the lake's still image.
>
> Watching swans take off from my bedroom window was a regular summer awakening. So I woke and looked out through the open window to a morning of crows and cockerels. The beech trees framing the lake and valley seemed to call for a Royal Hunt; but they served equally well for climbing into, and even in June you could still eat their leaves, a tight-folded salad of juices.

What Laurie Lee is interested in here is the setting. He looks at the reflections on the ceiling, listens to the noises of the swans, gazes at the beech trees and thinks about how he climbed into them and even ate their juicy leaves. He uses words to convey the experience of looking and hearing. Hence the careful way he talks about 'a molten mirror', 'tiny globules of gold', 'the great slapping of wings' and 'the lake's still image'. He even talks about what he sees as a picture; the reflection of the lake on his ceiling is called 'the whole picture', and the beech trees are said to be 'framing' the lake. The passage is typical of the book; the sights and scenes of the countryside are what interests the author.

● **You should write about how settings express the themes of books in ways similar to those outlined above for writing about the relation between character and setting.**

You will need to show how the theme is evident in settings by looking at the words, and then write about the relation between the two in an appropriate way.

In order to do this, you will need to locate passages. Therefore, when you read you should look out for passages in which the setting expresses the book's theme. In doing this you will be acting upon the basic piece of advice this section offers:

Settings are not incidental but are a significant part of the novel as a whole.

___ **Exercises** ___

8.1   Look at the novels you are studying to see if there are any occasions when the settings reveal something about a character's mood, situation or personality. If there are, try to write in detail about those passages.

8.2   Look at the novels you are studying to see if any of the settings reveal the theme of the book. If you can find some, try to write in detail about how they do this.

8.3   Read the following passage from George Eliot's *Adam Bede*, and answer the questions below.
      Captain Donnithorne is visiting the dairy at the Old Hall Farm; there he meets Hetty Sorrel. A 'calenture' is a hallucination.

> The dairy was certainly worth looking at: it was a scene to sicken for with a sort of calenture in hot and dusty streets – such coolness, such purity, such fresh fragrance of new-pressed cheese, of firm butter, of wooden vessels perpetually bathed in pure water; such soft colouring of red earthenware and creamy surfaces, brown wood

and polished tin, grey limestone and rich orange-red rust on the iron weights and hooks and hinges. But one gets only a confused notion of these details when they surround a distractingly pretty girl of seventeen, standing on little pattens and rounding her dimpled arm to lift a pound of butter out of the scale.

Hetty blushed a deep rose-colour when Captain Donnithorne entered the dairy and spoke to her; but it was not at all a distressed blush, for it was inwreathed with smiles and dimples, and with sparkles from under long curled dark eyelashes; and while her aunt was discoursing to him about the limited amount of milk that was to be spared for butter and cheese so long as the calves were not all weaned, and the large quantity but inferior quality of milk yielded by the short-horn, which had been bought on experiment, together with other matters which must be interesting to a young gentleman who would one day be a landlord, Hetty tossed and patted her pound of butter with quite a self-possessed, coquettish air, slily conscious that no turn of her head was lost.

(a)   George Eliot is trying to create a special atmosphere in the opening paragraph. What is it, and what words does she use?
(b)   George Eliot speaks of 'these details' surrounding Hetty. What is she trying to tell us about Hetty by placing her in this setting?
(c)   Is Hetty's behaviour in the second paragraph in accordance with what was suggested about her in the first?
(d)   This is the first time Hetty Sorrel has been introduced: what do we expect from her in the rest of the novel, and what role does the setting play in our expectations?

8.4   Read the following passage from Dickens's *Little Dorrit*, and answer the questions below.

Arthur Clennam has returned to London, the scene of his childhood, after being abroad for many years. It is Sunday.

At such a happy time, so propitious to the interests of religion and morality, Mr. Arthur Clennam, newly arrived from Marseilles by way of Dover, and by Dover coach the Blue-eyed Maid, sat in the window of a coffee-house on Ludgate Hill. Ten thousand responsible houses surrounded him, frowning as heavily on the streets they composed, as if they were very one inhabited by the ten young men of the Calender's story, who blackened their faces and bemoaned their miseries every night. Fifty thousand lairs surrounded him where people lived so unwholesomely that fair water put into their crowded rooms on Saturday night, would be corrupt on Sunday morning; albeit my lord, their county member, was amazed that they failed to sleep in company with their butcher's meat. Miles of close wells and pits of houses, where the inhabitants gasped for air, stretched far away towards every point of the compass. Through the heart of the town a deadly sewer ebbed and flowed, in the place of a fine fresh river. What secular want could the million or so of human beings whose daily labour, six days in the week, lay among these Arcadian objects, from the sweet sameness of which they had no escape between the cradle and the grave – what secular want could they possibly have upon their seventh day? Clearly they could want nothing but a stringent policeman.

Mr Arthur Clennam sat in the window of the coffee-house on Ludgate Hill, counting one of the neighbouring bells, making sentences and burdens of songs out of it in spite of himself, and wondering how many sick people it might be the death of in the course of the year. As the hour approached, its changes of measure made it more and more exasperating. At the quarter, it went off into a condition of deadly-lively importunity, urging the populace in a voluble manner to Come to church, Come to church, Come to church! At the ten minutes, it became aware that the congregation would be scanty, and slowly hammered out in low spirits, They *won't* come, they *won't* come, they *won't* come! At the five minutes, it abandoned hope, and shook every house in the neighbourhood for three hundred seconds, with one dismal swing per second, as a groan of despair.

'Thank Heaven!' said Clennam, when the hour struck, and the bell stopped.

But its sound had revived a long train of miserable Sundays, and the procession would not stop with the bell, but continued to march on. 'Heaven forgive me,' said he, 'and those who trained me. How I have hated this day!'

(a) What impression of London is created by the first paragraph?
(b) Do phrases such as 'frowning as heavily' and 'the inhabitants gasped for air' suggest anything about the mind of Arthur Clennam?
(c) In the second paragraph Arthur Clennam thinks of 'sick people'; does this reveal anything about his feelings?
(d) From this passage, can you see how Dickens is going to treat life in London in the rest of the novel?

⬡ 9 Plot and story

9.1 Interest, expectation, surprise and relief

The easiest way to begin thinking about plots and stories is to start where all readers have to start – with reading. We know a story to be a story and a plot to be a plot only when we read. The first question to ask, then, is this:

● What happens when we read a novel?

The obvious answer (and sometimes it's very helpful to start with what's obvious) is that we encounter a sequence of events. In novels one thing happens after another. The next question to ask is:

● What happens to the reader as the events of a novel unfold?

The answer is that the events are likely to engage our interest in a number of ways. To read is to be aware of what has happened and to think about what, in the light of what we know, might happen in the future. The experience of stories and plots is of reading a book page by page and allowing the events to work upon us. The experience of most readers is that we respond in at least four ways:

● interest
● expectation
● surprise
● relief.

Interest

'Interest' means any way in which a reader responds to characters or events. It's not the same as liking or loathing (we can be interested in characters whom we loathe), and includes every possible kind of response except of indifference. This book has stressed that literature is not the same as actual living, but this is not to say that our concerns, values and judgements (three ways of describing 'interest') are to be left behind when we read. How could they be? If then, as in *The Lord of the Flies*, we read of children stranded on a desert island or, as in *The French Lieutenant's Woman*, we read of a mysterious figure standing forlornly on the end of a harbour entrance, it's likely that our interests are going to be engaged. And it needn't be a character that engages us; at the opening of *Our*

Mutual Friend it's the scene of a boat tacking against the tide of the River Thames that arouses our interest.

Expectation

But what is the nature of this interest? A very common form of interest is *expectation*.

___ **Example** _____

Look at the opening of Virginia Woolf's *To the Lighthouse*:

'Yes, of course, if it's fine tomorrow,' said Mrs Ramsay. 'But you'll have to be up with the lark,' she added.

That is the arousal of expectation: what can they do if the weather is fine? We learn within a couple of pages that the event in question is a visit to the lighthouse. Our next expectation is: will they go?

_____

Expectation occurs when an author leads a reader to think that something is going to happen. Expectation is not a matter of the reader being aware that almost anything might happen.

Expectation is the state in which certain specific things are entertained as a possibility. Expectation is always expectation of something.

___ **Example** _____

The theme of *Pride and Prejudice* is marriage. The famous opening paragraph establishes the theme of marriage in a delightfully playful tone when it says that 'a single man in possession of a good fortune, must be in want of a wife'. In the early chapters Jane is courted by Mr Bingley, but the attention of the reader, now and throughout the novel, is on her sister, Elizabeth. The reader sees that the man who might suit her is the quietly charismatic Mr Darcy, but when, at a ball, Bingley suggests he dances with her, Darcy is not complimentary:

> She is tolerable, but not handsome enough to tempt me; and I am in no humour at present to give consequence to young ladies who are slighted by other men.
>
> Elizabeth hears this and is, not surprisingly, angry. Nevertheless, our expectations are aroused. Why, we may ask, has the author shown us this scene? We can see that she is angry, but we might nevertheless be convinced that her agile intelligence is an interesting and appropriate contrast to his silent and reserved nature. Indeed, we may be convinced, as is often the case in comedy, that this pair will marry, in which case our expectation is on how, after such an unpromising start, they will find their way to what, we feel and expect, is the right ending.

Surprise

Not everything that happens in a novel is expected; sometimes we are surprised. In Thackeray's *Vanity Fair* the quite elderly Sir Pitt Crawley proposes to Becky Sharp and receives this reply: 'O sir – I – I'm married already.' Events such as that make us ask questions: is there something I missed, or have I misunderstood a character?

Surprise certainly makes us more attentive, and it can also make us review our judgements and expectations. For instance, most readers of *Middlemarch* are surprised when they discover that the upright and puritanical banker, Mr Bulstrode, is a man with a shady past. As soon as this is disclosed, our attitude to him changes; we think again about his character. Surprise also makes us do something else – it makes us revise our expectations. Will he be able to conceal it, how will he cope with the guilt? These are the questions that occur to us in the case of Bulstrode.

Relief

Sometimes our expectations are satisfied. This is what is meant by *relief*. This means that it doesn't matter whether what you're expecting is a happy or sad event; all that matters is that you have been led to think that something is going to happen, and that now it has. Relief is a simple experience; you know what you wanted to know or you hoped for something and now it has (or has not) happened. Throughout *Oliver Twist* the orphan Oliver has been exposed to the plots of a group of evil characters, but, at the close, it is revealed that Oliver does have a family, and with the finding of his family we are relieved because he will no longer be at the mercy of those who were out to corrupt him.

- **We must remember that expectation, interest, surprise and relief are generated in readers by authors.**   By placing events in certain orders and drawing characters into particular relationships, authors engage readers.

These things are a matter of what authors make us think. We should, there-fore, always try to read a novel so that we are following the 'directions' of the novelist. This will mean attending to the order of events, the access an author does or does not have into characters' minds, the kind of things char-acters say to each other and what we are shown or told about them. In other words, story and plot are closely related to narration.

9.2   Knowledge and events

By looking at how we read, we have put ourselves in the position of seeing a number of things about stories and plots.

The order of events

In a story or plot the order of events is always important. Stories and plots concern the unfolding of events, so when and how we learn about them is funda-mental. For instance, in *Huckleberry Finn* there are two vital things that we are not told about until the end of the novel. Had we known about them (they concern both Huck and Jim, the runaway slave), the novel would not have worked upon the reader the way it does. We would have had different expecta-tions and different perspectives.

The importance of knowledge

When we think about the order of events, we realise that plots and stories depend upon knowledge – the knowledge the characters have and the knowledge we have as readers. A plot exists in time, and so our knowledge of what has hap-pened is going to be a crucial element in our understanding. The same goes for what we don't know. In *The Woman in White* it's important that we know that Laura has promised her dying father that she will marry Sir Percival Glyde. No other knowledge could make it credible that she should marry a man when she is in love with someone else. In *Jane Eyre*, however, it's important that neither Jane nor the reader knows that Mr Rochester has a wife already. Neither of these plots would work the way they do if our knowledge were other than it is.

The linking of events

Because plots and stories are concerned with our knowledge of the order of events, we must take an interest in the relations those events have with each other. This is a way of pointing out something that is essential to the telling of stories and the making of plots. This is that the events are *linked*. This might seem too obvious to need comment, but those features of reading discussed above – interest, expectation, surprise and relief – are impossible without it. For example, when we read in *Wuthering Heights* that Heathcliff leaves, we want to know whether he will return.

Sometimes the links between the events are clear and public (Sir Thomas Bertram's return from the West Indies puts a stop to the amateur theatricals at Mansfield Park), and sometimes the linkage is the mind of a character (and hence the reader). We may not follow Emma in seeing a link between Mr Elton's attentions and Harriet Smith, but we may follow her in her suspicions about Jane Fairfax and Mr Dixon.

The link may arise out of:

- character
- the nature of the action (we expect certain outcomes from certain events)
- the shape and tone of the novel.

Whatever the reason, the reader sees the links, and those links, so to speak, bind a plot together.

9.3   Stories and plots: some distinctions

At this point it's useful to think about the two terms which, so far, we have used interchangeably – story and plot. Is there a difference?

This is not an easy question to answer. There are plenty of occasions when the two can be used interchangeably without causing confusion. If you were asked what the story of *Jane Eyre* was, your answer, in some circumstances, might not differ from an answer given to the question: what is the plot of *Jane Eyre*? In both cases you would relate the main events in order to bring out the nature of Jane's struggles.

One way in which people have tried to establish a difference between the two terms is by thinking about the issue of linkage between events. This was the approach of the novelist E. M. Forster. In *Aspects of the Novel* he wrote that 'the King died and then the Queen died' was a story, whereas 'the King died and then the Queen died of grief' was a plot. The 'of grief', according to Forster made a crucial difference, because a reason is given for what happened; we know why one event has followed another.

This approach sees the crucial difference in terms of *causes*: a story is just a set of events, whereas a plot is a set of events which the reader can see as related to each other.

There is something in this. We sometimes use the term 'plot' in two ways. We think of plots as the causes of the events in the novel. For instance, Dickens makes it clear in *Hard Times* that Mr Gradgrind's educational ideas (that education should only be concerned with what is practical and should root out anything imaginative) is the cause of his son's criminality and his daughter's misery in marriage. Somebody talking about the plot of *Hard Times* might say that it was about the stultifying effects of a utilitarian form of education.

The other way in which we talk about plots is to see them in relation to the *themes* of novels. To talk about underlying causes is to be aware of the chief issues in a work. Thus we might say that the plot of *Emma* is concerned with the mistakes that arise from false judgements. In saying that, we are not relating a series of events but summing up what importance the events have. In both those ways of talking about novels, we are recognising that to talk about plots is to talk about the causes of events.

But does this really help with making the distinction between stories and plots? Probably not. When a reader hears that the king has died and that the queen has died soon after, he or she is bound to ask why. Are stories a set of events without causes? Of course not. Unless there were some causes (either stated or inferred) we wouldn't see the events as a sequence or set. Is there then another way of approaching the problem?

Another way of treating the problem is to look at it from the point of view of the reader and ask about how and when the reader comes to know something. It's possible to draw a distinction in these terms between story and plot:

A story can be defined as the events in the order in which they happened.

and:

A plot can be defined as the order of events in which the reader learns of them.

This makes it clear that a plot is literary; that is to say, it is something that is made by the author arranging the events in a particular order. The author has done this so as to make the reader respond in very precise ways. If the author wants to arouse expectation or surprise a reader, he or she will hold certain things back.

For instance, if you think about the events of *Jane Eyre*, you will see that they did not happen in the same order in which the reader learns of them. Mr Rochester must have married Bertha Mason when Jane was a child (possibly before the first event that is recorded in the novel), but because Charlotte Brontë wants to arouse our expectation and then surprise us, she doesn't disclose this until over half way through.

This distinction may not always work. There might be no difference between the order of events in the novel and the actual order in time in which those events took place. Nevertheless, it still is a very useful idea. Anyone reading a book can ask:

● Why are the events told in this order?

Answering that can help us to see how the plot has been designed.

9.4   Plot elements

Two important but curious facts about plots are that they are central to the reader's pleasure yet difficult to talk about. One of the most basic (for many the most basic) pleasures of reading is the desire to know what is going to happen. Readers want to know what the outcome is going to be (I have read one writer who talks of the reader demanding to know how things will turn out), and their interest in character is usually inseparable from this desire.

This has always been the case: readers throughout history have longed to know whether David will kill Goliath or whether Odysseus will return safely to Ithaca. But in spite of this, there is very little literary talk on how plots work. Aristotle, the first person in the West to write a book about literature, said that plot was the most important element in tragedy, and he devoted a good deal of his *Poetics* to a discussion of it. The *Poetics* was probably written shortly before 322 BC (the year of Aristotle's death); readers might decide that little of real help has been written since.

The student, then, has something of a problem; plot is central, but it's not easy to talk about.

● **The best thing to do is to think about the way a plot is put together – its elements or parts – and to see in what ways the reader is engaged.**

In one sense, anyone who enjoys plots knows something about them. Thinking about literature is often a case of trying to state clearly what is gathered from the experience of reading.

The situation

Plots have to start somewhere. Usually they arise out of a network of aims, wants and desires. Certain characters have things they want to achieve, and in seeking to achieve them they encounter certain problems. Huckleberry Finn wants to escape from his father and the widow who looks after him, and Jay Gatsby wants to win back Daisy. What follows – the events of the novels – arises out of those wishes and aspirations. We may call this starting point the *situation* of the novel – certain characters with differing aims who engage with each other.

The point to remember about the situation of the plot is that the reader might not learn about it at the very start. In the case of *Huckleberry Finn*, there is some exceedingly funny writing about Tom Sawyer's gang before we reach the moment when Huck and Jim set off down the river. In the case of *The Great Gatsby*, we have to read a good deal of the novel before discovering why Gatsby feels the way he does about Daisy. It's as if the reader has to wait in order to understand how Gatsby has had to wait for her. What therefore we can say about the situation (or starting point) of the novel is closely related to the point about plot in general: what matters about it is the order in which it's revealed to the reader.

Disjunction

Novelists often start the main business of a plot by creating a situation and then causing a breach in it. There is, so to speak, a break or, as it is sometimes called, a disjunction in an established pattern of life, and this *disjunction* leads to the events with which the novel is chiefly concerned.

For instance, a careful reading of the opening of *Jane Eyre* reveals that although Jane has been badly treated at Gateshead, she does not retaliate until that moment in the first chapter when she turns on John Reed. The retrospective account she gives of the way she has been treated establishes the pattern of life at Gateshead, and her retaliation functions as the disjunction that launches the main events of the plot.

In *A Passage to India*, E. M. Forster makes the point that most of life is so boring that no one would turn it into literature. This points to the importance of disjunctions: it's not the ordinary patterns of life that make for plots but those occasions when the pattern is broken.

It's not surprising, therefore, that sudden death is often introduced by novelists to create a disjunction. Wilkie Collins's extraordinarily complex novel *No Name* opens with the deaths of both the parents of the Vanstone sisters. This allows him to create the problem upon which the entire novel turns: because the parents have never been married, the sisters have no status, no wealth and no name. The ingenious lengths to which Magdalen Vanstone goes in order to win back her own name is the central business of an exciting and provocative work.

In the first chapter of Angela Carter's *The Magic Toyshop* the central figure, a girl called Melanie, puts on her mother's wedding dress and, in a passage charged with symbolic pressures, goes out into the garden at night and climbs the fruit-laden apple tree. The opening chapter presents Melanie as someone at home in the world of the countryside, but with the disjunction of her parents' deaths she has to move to London. That disjunction brings Melanie into a different world.

Disjunction is usually how thrillers, mystery and detective fiction opens. There is a smooth pattern of life and then something disturbs it; it could be a murder, an inexplicable event or something out of the ordinary such as a coincidence. From that break in life's smooth patterns there spring the events that will puzzle, intrigue and entice the reader.

Example

An early example of the thriller/spy story is John Buchan's *The Thirty-Nine Steps*.

The first chapter opens with the hero, Richard Hannay, feeling rather fed up with his life. He says to himself: '. . . you have got into the wrong ditch, my friend, and you had better climb out.' Then one night there is a disjunction in the pattern of his life. He returns, as he always does, to his flat, and there he meets a man who is terrified. He offers the man shelter for the night, talks to him, and by the next morning the man is more cheerful. Hannay goes out, returns to find the flat in darkness. He switches on the light to discover:

> My guest was lying sprawled on his back. There was a long knife through his heart which skewered him to the floor.

That is how the first chapter ends. Sudden death is a disjunction that few readers can resist.

Trajectory

Once events start to occur, the plot takes on a shape. Because of the situation and the way events have happened, the plot can be seen to have a particular shape. Another way of putting this idea is to say that the plot is moving (plots move because they exist in time) in a certain direction. The direction is something the reader perceives, so the shape of the plot arouses expectation.

One way of discussing plot movement is to talk about its *trajectory*. A trajectory is the path taken by a moving object. Moreover, if one knows the direction and speed of the object, one can predict the path it's going to take. Plots are similar: if we know the plot elements – the characters' aims and the situation in which they find themselves – we can anticipate where it's going. We are often helped in this by our knowledge of other plots. For instance, many of us are used to the kind of plot in which a character appears briefly and then disappears. When this happens, experience of reading tells us that the character is likely to reappear and be important to the plot.

Some examples will help here.

___ **Example** _____

Example 1

When in *Mansfield Park* the Crawfords, fashionable young people from London, arrive, the novel acquires a new trajectory. There will be a clash between the traditional values of Mansfield Park and the pleasure-seeking Crawfords.

Example 2

The plot of *Wuthering Heights* is based on a parallel between the trajectories of the two Catherine plots. In both, mother and daughter have a relationship with a man who has been brutalised. Since we know what has happened to the mother, we are eager to know whether the trajectory of the daughter's plot will follow the same path.

Example 3

In *Sons and Lovers* the theme of the novel – a young man's quest to be both a son and someone with his own emotional life – is played out in repeating trajectories. First in the case of Miriam and then in the case of Clara, Paul tries to be true to his own needs and to the claims of his mother.

- **As you can see from these examples, you can't talk about trajectories without also discussing the expectations of the reader.**

Trajectories are a way of describing how the plots of novels oblige readers to think about the unfolding of events. And that is how you should think about a plot. From what you know you should ask yourself:

- How is the plot going to work out?

When in *The Mayor of Casterbridge* Michael Henchard's wife returns just as he is getting to know Lucetta, you can see that choices (and the consequences of those choices) are inevitable. Hardy, in fact, is the sort of novelist who sometimes draws attention to the trajectories of his plots; in *Tess of the D'Urbervilles* he says, when Tess meets Alec, that in him she encounters the one who is going to blight her life.

- **There are cases when a novel has two contrasting and even contradictory trajectories.**

This can make a novel very exciting, because the reader wonders how the author is going to reconcile the two movements.

___ **Example** ___

Jane Eyre has the trajectory of a romantic novel. When Jane falls in love with Mr Rochester it is her (and the reader's) hope that she will find happiness with him. The novel, therefore, is on the love/marriage trajectory.

But *Jane Eyre* also works another way. It is a novel about Jane seeking and finding independence. One of the ways in which this is expressed is through the rooms she lives in. Thus she moves from a dormitory at Lowood, to a shared room as a student teacher, to her own newly decorated and carpeted room at Thornfield and then to a share in the house near Moorton when she comes into her inheritance. (Charlotte Brontë might have anticipated Virginia Woolf and called her novel *A Room of One's Own*.)

How, the reader might ask, is Charlotte Brontë going to reconcile these two trajectories? Her answer is to make Jane marry Rochester from a position of strength (she's fitter and probably richer than he is) rather than dependency – something she suffered from at the start of the novel. It's up to the reader to decide whether this satisfies the claims of two very different trajectories.

- **Readers should not think of trajectories as working in a mechanical and therefore absolutely predictable way.**

A moving object will continue in its path, but the plot of a novel need not. Novels are full of surprises. Indeed, one of the pleasures of reading a novel is seeing how the trajectory is often diverted by the introduction of an unexpected element.

For example, readers are led to think that the secret in *The Woman in White* must concern the sexual misdemeanours of Sir Percival Glyde, but this is not the case. Anne Catherick and Laura Fairlie are still in danger from him, but the danger does not follow the pattern of the plot trajectory (so common in Gothic novels) in which young women are at the mercy of lustful aristocrats.

Proleptic events

As plots unfold, event follows event. Plots are, as has been emphasised, a sequence of linked events, each of which arises out of what has happened and, in its turn, makes possible a future event. The relation between a past and future event is what gives those events meaning. Sometimes, however, there are events that have a meaning which is only fully realised in the less immediate future. That is to say, the reader must wait in order to see what the real importance of the event was.

The technical word for an event the real meaning of which is only fully seen in later (sometimes quite distant) events is *proleptic*. When later in a book the reader sees the meaning of something that happened earlier, then the reader can see that the earlier event was a proleptic one. The word might seem unwieldy, but the idea it points to is an important one, particularly in thrillers and mystery stories.

In Conan Doyle's *The Hound of the Baskervilles* there is an apparently minor (and even pointless) occurrence early on when one of Sir Henry's boots goes missing. Only at the end is it revealed that the theft of the boot was a vital stage in the would-be murderer's plans.

Events, however, can be proleptic in other kinds of fiction. In William Golding's *The Spire* there is much emphasis upon the yawning pit the masons build for the foundation, but only towards the close is its grim, sacrificial purpose revealed. After that the reader can understand why the pit has such awesome significance.

Reversal and discovery – pivotal moments

One of the stages in a plot that Aristotle singled out as important was the moment which he called reversal. Closely connected to this was what he called discovery. These moments can be separate, but since it's discoveries that frequently bring about reversals, it's wise to think about them together. It's also wise to broaden the idea of reversal and speak of the moment as *pivotal* or even as the hinge of the plot.

Reversals and discoveries in novels are often crucial to the plot.

Example

In *Great Expectations*, the novel turns on the return of Magwitch, the convict who, in the novel's opening pages, was helped by the young Pip. His return is both the novel's pivot and a moment of discovery. Until this point Pip had believed that Miss Havisham was his benefactress, and from this he had the hope that the beautiful Estella would one day be his. When he discovers that it is Magwitch, a criminal, who has been supporting him, the whole of his life is changed.

Novels, of course, can have several turning points. In *Great Expectations* there is another, also the result of a discovery, when Pip learns who Estella's father is. This discovery further deepens the irony upon which the plot is based.

The place of recognition and reversal in a plot depends upon the nature of the narrative. Different kinds of stories have them in different places. Inevitably, the reversal in a short story is likely to come at the end. In Katherine Mansfield's 'Mr. and Mrs. Dove' it happens in the last line. Also, the recognitions and reversals in thrillers and detective stories are almost certainly going to occur in the final few pages. Even a sophisticated writer such as P. D. James has, because of the trajectory of her plot, to place them in the closing pages. In *Cover Her Face*, now set in public examinations, the recognition occurs at the end of the third section of the final chapter (there are only five sections in the chapter) when one character says to another: 'Then it was you!' The language shows how close detective fiction can be to the kind of plots that Aristotle wrote about. The novel opens with the words: 'Exactly three months before the killing at Martingale . . .', so the reader has two questions: who was killed? and who was the killer? The answer to the first question is supplied at the end of the third chapter, so for the rest of the novel the reader awaits the moment of recognition when he or she will be able to view one of the characters in the full knowledge of what has happened. When we do know who it is, it is as if we have never really seen the character before.

Recognitions and reversals occur at the close of other kinds of novels. To take just one example, J. L. Carr's *A Month in the Country* concerns two men bruised by the appalling experiences of the Great War who restore a medieval wall painting in a country church. Their month in the country becomes a period of healing for them. Towards the end it is discovered that the figure referred to in the wall painting was, like one of them, an outsider in his own society. The recognition of a parallel between the past and the present becomes part of the healing.

In novels, as we have seen, the pivotal discovery can happen much earlier; in *Great Expectations* it is just over half way. The reason for this is that usually at the close of a novel another element is the most important. This goes by a number of names: wind-up, resolution and denouement.

Wind-up, resolution and denouement

Each of those words expresses something of what happens as a novel closes.

• Wind-up

Wind-up gets at the idea that all the loose ends have to be tied up, so that the reader can be left with the satisfaction of perfect knowledge with regard to the individual destinies of the various characters. In Dickens's *Hard Times*, for instance, there are some brief yet informative sketches of the futures in store for all the leading characters.

• Resolution

Resolution is the experience we get when all the issues of a novel have been brought to a satisfactory state. This may be a matter of characters acquiring a suitable husband or wife or of the themes working themselves out so that the novelist's understanding of human life is seen clearly. At the close of Conrad's *Heart of Darkness* we are shown in the fate of Kurtz what happens when someone ventures into the heart of that darkness which is human evil. His fate resolves the themes of the novel.

• Denouement

Denouement is a word we have taken from the French. It means 'the untying of a knot'. It's a useful idea when trying to understand how a plot works out. Plots are like knots, in that several elements have become confusingly and unsatisfyingly intertwined.

For example, as *Middlemarch* draws to a close, there is much confusion about the relationships between Lydgate, his wife Rosamund, the central character Dorothea, and Ladislaw. The confusion is such that the happiness of the characters is in danger. Some candid conversations and moments of deep introspection lead to the satisfying unravelling of the twisted plot strands.

- **When thinking about how a novelist plots a novel, you can ask yourself a number of questions.**

Here are some based on the above discussion:

- Is there an important disjunction that gives rise to the plot?
- In what direction do the trajectories of the plot go?
- Are there any important diversions from the expected trajectory?
- Is the novelist asking us to notice events, the full meaning of which will only be revealed later?
- Are there crucial moments around which the plot pivots?
- Are the pivotal moments related to discoveries?
- How does the novelist wind-up, resolve or achieve the denouement of the plot?

There are other ways to think about how novels are plotted. One way is to look at the ideas upon which they are based. As you will see, these ideas (the word is being used broadly) are, in some cases, closely related to what has been discussed in this section.

9.5   Plots and past events

Nobody can change the past.

What's done is done.

Those two statements express what some novelists show – that characters can't escape from the past, be the past what they have done themselves or what other people have done.

Examples

Example 1

The plot of Hardy's *The Mayor of Casterbridge* can be summed up very simply as the failure of a man to live down his past. At the beginning of the novel Henchard gets drunk and in a grotesque auction sells his wife. As soon as he realises what he has done, he tries to find her, but when he fails to do so, he vows not to drink for twenty years and to lead a better life.

These events happen in the first two chapters. Chapter three shows that many years have passed, and Henchard is Mayor of Casterbridge – but then his wife returns. The rest of the novel is the record of his doomed attempts to escape from his past. He suffers disappointment and failure, usually as a consequence of his one foolish deed – the selling of his wife. Hardy shows that characters act the way they do because of the influence of past events.

Example 2

The weight of past events is not quite so heavy in Lawrence's *Sons and Lovers*, but, nevertheless, much of what happens later to the central character, Paul Morel, results from the unhappy marriage of his parents. When the romance of marriage has faded, Mrs Morel seeks her emotional companionship in her sons and not her husband. At first, William, the eldest son, is the object of her affection, but after his death she turns to Paul. Lawrence shows that the failure of his parents' marriage has a deep effect upon Paul. His relationships with Miriam and Clara are blighted by his mother, who resents him loving anybody but her. The past that affects him is not a specific event, as in *The Mayor of Casterbridge*, but a failed relationship.

You may have noticed that *The Mayor of Casterbridge* starts with a dramatic disjunction, while *Sons and Lovers* sees the past as a web of intertwined relationships. The point to observe in all this is that there are a number of ways in which the plot of a novel can be shaped by past events. In thrillers and murder stories it's usually a disjunction, whereas Lawrence, and many other authors, see a complex of social or psychological relationships as determining the trajectory of the plot.

In Arnold Bennett, for instance, there is a very strong sense of how the character's upbringing shapes his or her life. In *Anna of the Five Towns*, Anna loves one man but marries another whom she does not love. The narrator says: 'Nothing else was possible.' It is one of the functions of Bennett's plot to show how this comes about.

9.6   Plots and the aims of characters

When we read of characters who aim to do things, it is easy to see that what they hope to achieve will be a cause of the plot. No matter how different novels are in setting and tone, many of them share the common factor of a central character who attempts to achieve something.

For instance, Jocelin, the Dean of the Cathedral in William Golding's *The Spire*, wants to beautify the building by erecting a spire; Howard Kirk, the sociology lecturer who is the central character of Malcolm Bradbury's *The History Man*, wants more power and influence; and the hero of Sir Walter Scott's *Ivanhoe* wants to win back the affection of his father and his place in society.

- **You should be prepared to think about the aims of a character in a broad way.**

Jane Austen's *Emma* links the aims of the heroine to the more important, and unconscious, aim of self-knowledge. Emma, in her attempt to find suitable marriage partners for her friends, persuades, prompts and plans, but her efforts are all unsuccessful. The reader sees that the reason for this is Emma's lack of self-knowledge. Yet as she stumbles from one failure to another, it dawns upon her what she really wants for herself. Thus, it can be said that even if she were not aware of it, she was aiming at self-knowledge, and her actions can be said to lead to that end.

9.7 Plots based on journeys

A simple yet highly effective way of plotting a novel is by basing it on a journey. Such novels are often called *picaresque*, after the Spanish word for 'rogue'. In the original picaresque novels roguish servants embarked on a journey and enjoyed a number of adventures on the way. This pattern has persisted, although nowadays it's not required that the central characters are rogues. The plots of picaresque novels require two things:

(1)   a very simple outline (usually the need to go from one place to another)
(2)   a number of diverting and entertaining incidents.

Such plots are sometimes criticised for being episodic, and it's certainly true that plots based on journeys are very rarely complex. Their attraction lies in their incidents; it's often the case that what a reader remembers about a picaresque novel is not the outline but the individual events.
    This is true of two of the most famous picaresque novels – Defoe's *Moll Flanders* and Fielding's *Joseph Andrews*. There is a superb moment in *Moll Flanders* when Moll (the novel is written in the first person) tells of how she robbed a child. The writing is vivid and detailed, and the reader finds pleasure in seeing how Moll honestly comes to terms with the feelings the episode arouses in her. In *Joseph Andrews* there is a marvellously funny scene in which Joseph, having been robbed and left naked, meets a coach. Fielding uses the episode to satirise the occupants whose false ideas of good manners are stronger than their charity. Their reluctance to allow the coachman to pick him up is shown to be due to their distorted values.
    Although basing a plot on a journey is a simple idea, it is one that has shown itself to be durable. Mark Twain's *Huckleberry Finn* is still in the picaresque tradition, the new locations providing Twain with the opportunity for a series of hilarious yet significant incidents. His central character, it may be observed, is also quite close to the figure of the rogue.
    On a more sophisticated level both *Jane Eyre* and *Tess of the D'Urbervilles* are plotted around the journeyings of their heroines. It's probably not helpful to

call them picaresque, but they certainly share plot similarities with works of that type. What they do with the picaresque mode is turn it into a metaphor for the lives of their central characters – both Jane and Tess, in their different ways, are making journeys into womanhood and into the changing world of the nineteenth century.

Plots based on journeys often use characters of very specific kinds. A basic pattern is the contrast between the character who helps and the one who hinders. This is clearly seen in Bunyan's *The Pilgrim's Progress*, an allegory of the Christian life in which the protagonist, called Christian, undertakes a journey from the City of Destruction to the Celestial City. On his way he meets two companions, who accompany him, Faithful and Hopeful, as well as others who help him through their guidance and hospitality. But there are enemies. In Vanity Fair he is brought before a jury of antagonistic people, presided over by a man called Lord Hategood. Nor are the enemies only human; in the Valley of Humiliation he fights with a demon called Apollyon. The momentum of the book is sustained by these contrasting pairs.

9.8 Plots based on discoveries

Many novels show the central characters making discoveries about life. In some novels ideals are shattered, in others false ideas are recognised and replaced by truer ones. In most the connection between events is the growth in understanding that emerges from one event and then shapes the following one. Here are three examples.

(1) James Joyce's *Portrait of the Artist as a Young Man* tells how young Stephen Dedalus grows up in Ireland. As he moves from one stage in his life to another he learns to question Ireland's cultural and religious traditions.
(2) In Harper Lee's *To Kill a Mockingbird* the focus is on how Scout gradually becomes aware of the tensions and prejudices of the racially torn southern states of America.
(3) In L. P. Hartley's *The Go-Between* the plot concerns a boy, on the edge of adolescence, discovering the conflicts of adult sexuality.

There are some important things to look out for when you write about plots that deal with characters growing towards understanding.

● **You should bring out the pleasure the reader can feel when witnessing a character's development.**

Difficult as it is to explain, there is great pleasure in following through a plot which unfolds because the central character is gradually learning more about life. In *Great Expectations* wealth turns Pip into a snob. The reader can see that this snobbery leads Pip to neglect good and kind Joe. There may be pain in this for the reader, but this leads on to the pleasure of seeing him gradually wake up to the fact that, for all his wealth, he is not a true gentleman, and Joe is. The pleasure we feel is not just a case of being pleased when Pip sees things clearly; there is also a pleasure in recognising that that is how a mind might grow and respond to life.

- **You should also bring out the point that such plots can't be appreciated unless the reader responds in sympathy to the characters.**

George Eliot allows her readers to do this. In *The Mill on the Floss* she brings the reader very close to the wild and much misunderstood Maggie, who suffers a great deal from her unfeeling brother. But the novel is about how they both discover life, so when Tom is sent to school, George Eliot invites the reader to pity him in his life of grinding misery and to understand that this affects his later life.

- **A final point to bring out is the place of the reader in relation to events.**

One of the pleasures of these novels is seeing something before a character does. In *Emma* the reader sees that Mr Elton is courting Emma and not Harriet Smith long before the unseeing Emma does. There is, then, much humour leading up to her moment of discovery that she has been mistaken. This should help you to see that plots dealing with discovering life need not always be dark and sombre: *Emma* is a deep and serious book, but it is also an amusing one.

9.9 Plots based on the workings of society

Most plots deal with society in one way or another. There are, however, some novels in which one of the central concerns of the plot is to explore how a particular society works. Such plots might show:

- why some characters prosper while others do not
- how newcomers establish or fail to establish themselves in a society
- how societies gradually change
- why there are rivalries between families, institutions or classes

The point about plots based on the workings of society is that:

Characters behave as they do because of the way society runs.

The novel that achieves this in a quite outstanding way is *Middlemarch*, in which George Eliot presents the many social levels of a Midlands town in the early 1830s. She explores the relations between the rising middle class, the Vincy family, and the relative newcomer, the banker, Bulstrode. She shows how attempts to bring the railway affect the people, and how leading citizens differ in their politics. Individual events are looked upon in a social light. When the rich Peter Featherstone dies, his funeral is attended by his immediate family, but the upper classes only watch it from a distance.

Example

The young doctor, Lydgate, is a good example of a character whose actions are shaped by the way society runs. He is an intelligent, well-educated man of high ideals who wants to bring new medical ideas to the town. His interest in the new hospital is shared by Bulstrode, but because Bulstrode is not very popular in the town, Lydgate also arouses suspicion. This suspicion affects his day-to-day medical work. The people of Middlemarch are accustomed to old-fashioned ways of medicine, and when Lydgate, on what he thinks are good scientific grounds, refuses to prescribe pills, they become hostile. Lydgate is not a success, and the hostility he has aroused because of his new ideas does not help him when he is suspected of helping Bulstrode to kill off a blackmailer. Lydgate is a very interesting example of how a man with high ideals fails to bring improvement because he does not understand how society works.

- **When writing about plots that centre on the workings of society, you should try to show what attitude the author takes.**

In the case of Lydgate, George Eliot's is a very subtle one. She seems to admire his desire to improve health but she also likes the sensible, rather conservative townsfolk who don't like new ideas. There is a very interesting passage which shows Lydgate's keen thrill in discovering medicine, but against that are ones which show that he is naïve in expecting provincial people to respond readily to his ideas.

Above all, plots based upon the workings of society, or ones in which a picture of society is at least fairly central, give the feeling of the wholeness of life. In *Middlemarch* there are many different kinds of character and many human interests. In its wonderful sweep the novel deals with love, marriage, money, religion, social improvement, politics, the family, work, leisure, the arts and intellectual fashions.

9.10 Plots based on mysteries

There can be no denying that novels in which some things remain mysteriously hidden from the characters and the reader have an enormous popular appeal. The fact is that we like mysteries.

A simple case is the detective story – we want to know 'whodunnit'. It is true that detective stories need more than the mystery of who committed the crime if they are to maintain their appeal, but this is not to deny that there is pleasure in being held in suspense. In Sir Arthur Conan Doyle's Sherlock Holmes stories there are wonderfully atmospheric settings and an absorbing central character, but the problems and the intricate solutions they require generate a great deal of pleasure, simply because the reader wants the mystery to be solved. The same can be said about the novels of Wilkie Collins: the pleasure of *The Moonstone* and *The Woman in White* grows from the mystery created by crimes as well as atmosphere and characters.

There are, however, novels which are not detective stories, but which, nevertheless, have plots that depend upon mysteries. Dickens, for instance, enjoys enticing his readers with mysteries. Quite often readers find themselves asking:

- Who is this character?
- Why is he or she in this state?
- What is the relation between these characters?
- Why has this character appeared so suddenly in the novel?
- Why aren't we told anything about this character's past?

In *Little Dorrit*, for instance, there is a watch, which had belonged to Arthur Clennam's father, on which are engraved the initials D.N.F. They stand for 'Do Not Forget', but for much of the novel what it is that must not be forgotten remains a mystery. In addition, at the beginning of the novel Little Dorrit herself is employed by Arthur's mother, but nobody knows why. Arthur is puzzled – and so is the reader.

The point about such mysteries is that they depend upon the idea of plot as a sequence of events connected by a set of causes. The plot based upon a mystery works by allowing the reader to see that there must be a cause behind the events while keeping the cause concealed. The formula is: there must be a cause, but it is mysteriously hidden.

It is worthwhile asking yourself:

- Is the mystery central to the theme of the novel?

___ **Example** _____

Great Expectations has a plot which contains a good deal of mystery, as well as showing how the central character discovers about life. Quite often the reader is prompted to ask:

- Who is this character?

In the case of one character, the answer is very much to do with the theme of the book.

Pip wants to be a gentleman, but because of his early association with the criminal, Magwitch, he feels he is tainted by crime. This is particularly painful for him, because the beautiful Estella, whom he loves, is very scornful of criminals (at one point she calls them 'wretches') and he feels ashamed and unworthy of her because of this. But there is a mystery: who is Estella?

As the intricate plot unfolds, Pip feels Estella is increasingly superior to him, but then the truth emerges; Estella, far from being a character untainted by crime, is intimately associated with it – she is Magwitch's daughter. The identity of Estella, one of the mysteries of the plot, is thus part of the book's central theme – Pip's desire to be a gentleman.

9.11   Plots based on problems

One way of devising a plot is to create a problematic situation for the characters and explore how they cope with it. This form of plot construction is similar to using mysteries as a basis. In *The Woman in White*, Collins not only poses a mystery – who is the woman in white? – but also places the three central characters in a dilemma: how can Laura's true identity be established? Basing a plot on problems excites in the reader all the common expectations of a plot: will they succeed? how will they achieve it?

The word 'problem' can be used broadly to refer to any source of conflict from which a plot grows. Readers can always help themselves to see what is going on by putting this question:

● What is the nature of the problem from which this plot grows?

Asking this question can help a reader to see the thematic importance of the problem from which the plot grows.

___ **Example** ___

It's obvious to all readers that in Graham Greene's *The Power and the Glory* the priest has a problem because he's trying to be a priest in a country which has banned the practice of religion. But if you think further, you see that the reason he has this problem at all is to do with something much more fundamental to the book – the nature of the priesthood. As a priest he has to minister to his people, even though he is himself sinful and unworthy. Duty compels him to continue, and it emerges in the book that although he is weak and fallible, his role as a priest is unaffected by his personal shortcomings. A consideration, therefore, of the 'problem' from which the plot grows takes a reader into the heart of the book.

9.12   Short stories

What makes the short story distinctive is its length. Quite often a short story writer does what a novelist does – adopts narrative strategies, creates characters, plots, settings and makes these elements yield themes. A lot of what has been said above and will be said in the next chapter will therefore be relevant to the understanding of short stories. The difference is that in the case of the short story these occur within a few pages. Short stories are short.

Consequently, most short stories have few characters. Quite often the story concentrates on the dilemma of one character into whose mind the reader has access. For example, James Thurber's 'The Secret Life of Walter Mitty' depends for its success upon the reader understanding the gulf between Walter's pulp fiction dreams and his humdrum life – shopping for dog biscuits, problems with parking his car, waiting for his wife in hotels. The reader wouldn't see the gulf unless there were access to Walter's mind.

Another feature of the short story (and one not unrelated to small numbers of characters) is its economy. Whatever happens in a short story happens in a limited number of words. The writer of the short story knows that he or she has to make every word count. As a result of the necessity of making every word count, one of the features of a short story is that sentences sometimes have a number of different though related meanings.

___ **Example** _____

Katherine Mansfield's 'The Life of Ma Parker' is about an old lady who, as she says herself, has had 'a hard life'; her husband dies young, many of her children desert her, she has to look after an invalid and (the final blow) her grandson dies. The day after the funeral, she goes to clean the house of 'the literary gentleman' for whom she works. At one point she looks out of the kitchen window:

> Out of the smudgy little window you could see an immense expanse of sad-looking sky, and wherever there were clouds they looked very worn, old clouds, frayed at the edges, with holes in them, or dark stains like tea.

That sentence works in many ways: it evokes the atmosphere of a dreary day; it reflects Ma Parker's life (a life so narrow in scope that it seems as if it's viewed through a 'little window'); it reflects Ma Parker herself – old, frayed, stained with cares; it reflects the death of her grandson – the dark stain in her life; and it reflects what Ma Parker is feeling – the sad-looking sky reflects her own immense sadness. Such richness of meaning is something that is often associated with poetry. The comparison may be a helpful one: within the narrow scope of the short story an author has to compress many meanings, so, as in poetry, the words have multiple meanings.

Another feature of short stories is that their formal features are very prominent. In short stories the reader is often more aware of the importance of the opening and the close. Openings often draw attention to themselves and control the reader's expectations and reactions for the entire duration of the narrative.

Example

The first sentence of Katherine Mansfield's 'Mr. and Mrs. Dove' establishes the voice of the main character although, formally speaking, it's written in the third person:

> Of course he knew – no man better – that he hadn't the ghost of a chance, he hadn't an earthly.

The crucial words are the first two – 'Of course'; he knows all too well what the outcome will be and yet he's going to try. It's as if we hear him saying: 'Of course, I haven't an earthly' and recognise in the deliberately casual phrasing an attempt to disguise from others (and perhaps even himself) the truth of his hopeless plight. It soon emerges that this is a matter of love; he knows she won't have him, but he's going to ask her. Our expectations are aroused: what is he going to say? How will she react? How will it end? The frustration, hopelessness and desperation of that opening sentence control our expectations throughout the whole story.

Two further consequences of this heightening of the elements that make up a short story are the foregrounding of both the plot and the themes. Because a short story has to make every word count, its basic events and what it adds up to are, so to speak, pushed to the front of the picture.

Because a short story *is* short, the author has to establish the main elements of the plot rapidly. Within a few paragraphs (sometimes within a few lines), it is often clear to the reader what the story is going to be about. This is even true of those stories that depend upon surprise (quite a common way of closing a tale); a reader couldn't be surprised unless the plot had been clearly established, and a surprise is only a surprise within the terms established by a plot.

In Daphne du Maurier's story 'The Birds', the first paragraph deals with the sudden change to cold weather, and in the third the main character is aware of the unusual number of birds. That is the plot established. By the third page the birds are virtually attacking people.

— **Example** —————————————————————————

D. H. Lawrence's short stories often concentrate on one aspect of the turbulent relationships between people. They are often dramatic, and their themes, in the best of them, emerge with vivid clarity in the turning point (the recognitions and reversals) of the plots. In 'Tickets, Please', a story set on the Nottingham trams during the First World War, the Inspector flirts with one girl ticket collector after another until, in revenge, they join together and attack him. Compelled by the girls to choose one of them, he opts for Annie, the girl through whom much of the story has been mediated. She refuses him. Very pointedly the narrator shows how costly this rejection was: 'and something was broken in her'. The story explores the unresolvable tensions of belonging and not belonging to someone; of one person wanting to possess another and the other wanting to be free; and of the crippling rage that makes someone reject what she most desires. Those themes are present in her rejection of him, a rejection which is made clear by the way the narrator directly tells the reader about her reaction.

It would be a mistake to regard the foregrounding of both plot and theme as two completely distinct functions. Quite often they are inseparable. In Graham Greene's 'I Spy' the relationship between the father and the son is established very quickly – the boy doesn't like his father but loves his mother. Then through a number of plot devices, such as both of them saying and doing similar things, the story drives to the revelation of its theme: father and son are very similar. The foregrounding of the plot through parallels between father and son is the foregrounding of the theme.

Themes often emerge, as indicated above, in the turning point of a story. Many novels have turning points, but because of the formal clarity of short stories the turning point has a correspondingly greater impact. Indeed, many short stories can be defined as a plot that reaches its climax in a revelation, which re-orientates the lives of the characters and, sometimes, the perspectives of the reader. The turning point can be something that is said or an action. In many stories it's a moment of illumination experienced by one of the characters. A character sees something to which he or she had previously been blind or, for the first time, the shape of his or her life becomes clear. Such a moment is a turning point because, in the light of what is experienced, the character (and reader) can see things anew. It's because of this that short stories are often praised for being serious and profound; in the turning point something important about human life is brought home to us.

—— **Example** ——————————————————————————————

Lawrence's 'Odour of Chrysanthemums' closes with the wife finding in the dead body of her husband the wonder of his own independent existence – his being himself and nobody else – that she had been unable to recognise in his life. This is a devastating moment, but for her it's also a return to life:

> She had denied him what he was – she saw it now. She had refused him as himself. And this had been her life, and his life. She was grateful to death, which had restored the truth. And she knew she was not dead.

As with much Lawrence, the reader should recognise in the language what can only be called a religious dimension; contemplating the dead body of her husband, she is like the Virgin Mary cradling in her arms the dead body of Christ, and as with the death of Christ, his death brings her life.

——

Many writers of short stories choose childhood as a subject. It's not hard to see why: in childhood there are a number of occasions when we realise something for the first time, so the form of the short story with its emphasis on illumination is particularly apt. In Katherine Mansfield there are several children or young people who are faced with an experience that is new. In 'The Voyage' something of the mystery of time and the inevitability of loss is borne in upon the young Fenella, and in 'Her First Ball' Leila experiences the wonder of adulthood, the terrible realisation of how little time there is to be young in and the overwhelming pleasure of dance that, mercifully, obliterates all awareness of time and mortality.

—— **Example** ——————————————————————————————

Unlike Lawrence's telegraphed meanings (he frequently uses telling rather than showing), the moments of illumination in Katherine Mansfield are subtle and, in their language, appropriately elusive. How can an author capture the searing yet fleeting sense of life's promise and fragility? This is the subject of 'The Garden-Party'. On a day of celebration for her well-off family, Laura encounters death. Due to a misunderstanding, she is shown into the room of a cottage, where the body of a young man who has died in an accident is lying. The experience is unexpectedly consoling: 'He was wonderful, beautiful'. What Laura cannot put together in her mind is the sight of the young man – 'So remote, so peaceful' – with the merry bustle of the party. What can she say? How can she put it into words? She can't; but who can? She speaks to her elder brother, who asks whether the sight of the dead man was 'awful'.

'No,' sobbed Laura. 'It was simply marvellous. But, Laurie —' She stopped, she looked at her brother.
'Isn't life,' she stammered, 'isn't life —' But what life was she couldn't explain. No matter. He quite understood.
'Isn't it, darling?' said Laurie.

Katherine Mansfield uses her words to show just how inadequate words are. Laura can't say what she feels, and Laurie's response is both adequate and inadequate. Yet these attempts at speech say so much about the keen edge of an experience that eludes all expression. The silence at the end of the story is perhaps what it's about: how can we talk about these things?

We've used the term 'turning point' for the pivotal moment of a short story. Earlier in this book, the term 'revelatory moment' has also been used of the occasion when a character (and reader) sees something of importance. To those terms we might add 'disclosure'. James Joyce adopted the term 'epiphany' for such moments. The word's chief meaning is a religious one; it means the manifestation of God's presence. Joyce used it to refer to moments of spiritual insight. It can be broadened even further to refer to any moments when a character sees something or becomes aware of something in a new way. The boy in Greene's 'I Spy' is the subject of an epiphany when he realises how like his father he actually is. Likewise, Laura's inability to say anything adequate about the fulness of experience is epiphanous in its sense of something of extraordinary importance glimpsed in and through the events of her life.

An important variation upon the tale that ends with an epiphany is the ghost story. Tales about ghosts are well suited to the genre of the short story. Usually, there is not enough human interest to sustain a narrative of novel length. What is required of a ghost story is a plot which gives rise to mystery and foreboding and which climaxes in some uncanny occurrence. The design of the plot is therefore very similar to the tale ending in an epiphany. In the hands of a writer such as M. R. James, the ghost story is both engaging and suitably terrifying; a supernatural manifestation is darkly hinted at in the earlier parts of the narration but usually held back until the climax, when its appearance resolves the tension but creates further mystery. It can also be unnervingly nasty in a brilliantly unexpected way:

… and she turned and stared at seeing what at first she took to be a Fifth of November mask peeping out among the branches. She looked closer.
It was not a mask. It was a face – large, smooth and pink.

(from 'The Rose Garden')

It's surprising how uncomfortable the word 'pink' can be made to be.

Closely allied to the ghost story are detective and adventure stories. In both there are turning points; in the case of detective fiction a recognition – who did it? – and, usually, in the case of the adventure tale an escape or victory. Although Conan Doyle wrote four Sherlock Holmes novels, the short stories show the possibility of detective fiction far more clearly. In a story such as 'Silver Blaze' the very economy of the genre allows Doyle to puzzle the reader with a host of apparently unconnected details, which the eagle mind of Holmes sees as significant and revelatory. This includes the intriguing piece of evidence that doesn't exist – 'the curious incident of the dog in the night-time'. Perhaps the detective story, like the ghost story, is better suited to the genre of the short story than to a full-length novel; lots of clues in a few pages can intrigue readers, and many writers of detective fiction are far better on plot than character. P. D. James and Ruth Rendell are, however, able to sustain their plots and create interest in characters for a whole novel.

There are adventure novels, and they work just so long as the author can find a sufficient number of exciting incidents, but the short story is very well suited to such topics. Wilkie Collins's nightmarish tale 'A Terribly Strange Bed' succeeds in engaging the reader's interest in the fate of the hero as he lies in bed, watching the top slowly descend upon him. Many of Edgar Allan Poe's tales work by evoking a terrifying and grotesque situation from which the protagonists attempt (not always successfully) to escape.

An interesting twentieth-century variant upon the story that closes with an epiphany is the re-working of a traditional tale. By taking a well-known story, the author can expect the reader to keep the original plot trajectory in mind, so when a change occurs at the close, its impact will be all the greater. Angela Carter's collection *The Bloody Chamber and other Stories* either takes traditional fairy tales and gives them a different meaning or realises a meaning always latent in them by altering some of their features, particularly the close. Thus in her tales the wolf doesn't appear as savage and threatening, but the embodiment of a satisfying animality.

Of course, authors of short stories don't always write about moments of insight, supernatural visitation, criminal recognition or escape. Katherine Mansfield wrote what we might call 'mood pieces' – vivid accounts of scenes in which there is little unfolding of the plot and no moment of illumination. 'Bank Holiday' is an example; we are presented with a scene rendered with pin-point clarity, but though there are events, the interest of the story resides in the images she creates.

Much more like a story closing in a moment of insight is E. M. Forster's 'The Machine Stops'. This has most of the features of a short story – few characters, a clearly delineated plot, an unavoidable theme and a moment of illumination at the close. What, however, we take away from the story is the strong sense of the world Forster has created. The story is not unlike *Brave New World*, and, as in that novel, the imaginative effort of the writer has gone into fashioning a world which, in its abundant detailing, enacts its theme – the dehumanising effect of technology.

9.13 Construction and contrast

Most of what has been said in this chapter has been about the construction – or design – of plots. All that needs to be said now is to issue a warning about the word 'construction' and a remark about another way in which plots are put together.

The word 'construction' comes from architecture. As such it's useful. There is a similarity between how an architect plans a building and how an author plans a plot. Both, for instance, have (or ought to have) their 'users' in mind and both wish to achieve effects. So far so good. What, however, you should always remember is that a plot moves in time, whereas a building achieves its effects through space.

- **When writing about how plots work you should always keep in mind a memory of what has happened and your anticipations about the future.** If you do that, you'll be able to use construction without implying that a plot is something fixed and static.

- **Examiners are fond of the word 'contrast'.** A contrast is any structural device whereby elements in a novel, perhaps characters, perhaps setting, are drawn together so that the reader can see them as both different and linked. Authors do this to give shape to their novels and also to reveal how they judge the life they are presenting.

___ **Exercises** _____

9.1 Think about how the pleasure you find in a story is due to the way in which the author has created expectation, interest, surprise and relief.

9.2 Think about how the plots of novels commence and how they keep to or depart from their initial trajectories.

9.3 Think about what kind of plots the authors you are reading have created. You may wish to think about the ideas around which they are built and how they express the themes of the novels.

⬡10 Themes

10.1 The importance of themes

The previous chapter has been about how novels are made. It was, however, pointed out that how a novel is made is not something that can be separated from what it is about. As in all art, form (the 'how' of a work) can't be separated from content (what it is about).

One answer to the question: 'What is this book about?' would be a retelling of the story. It's sometimes very useful to do this for oneself, but it's no good in an essay or an examination. Teachers and examiners frequently say: 'Don't tell us the story; we've read the book!'

What they want to see is that you can appreciate the themes of the book. They might not put it exactly like that. They might ask any of the following questions:

- What is the author interested in?
- What are the author's concerns?
- How does the author view things?
- What is the author's vision of life and the world?

All of these questions come down to asking:

- What is important or signficant about the things that go on in the book?

The words 'important' and 'significant' are a way of getting at the point that authors lead readers to see that books add up to something, or say something, or show us something about human life. 'Themes' therefore is a very broad term for the way books make meanings.

____ Examples ____

Example 1

Alice Walker's *The Color Purple*, for all its harrowing events, ends on a note of thankfulness. In that thankfulness we can see the main business of the novel – that through compassion and sisterly companionship, Celie has won through. That is one of its themes.

Example 2

At the end of Conrad's *Heart of Darkness*, Kurtz, the figure to whom they have been journeying, is reported to have said before he died 'The horror!, the horror!' Since those words bring to full expression the different kinds of horror that the novel has been exploring, it can be said to be one of the themes of the book.

Example 3

One of the themes of *Hard Times* is the importance of imagination and compassion in education. Sissy Jupe, the girl brought up in the imaginative world of the circus, has an inner strength and a natural concern for others, whereas Tom Gradgrind and Bitzer, who have been subjected to a fact-based education in which everything is weighed and calculated, are weak when faced with temptation and heartless in their treatment of other characters.

- **Remember: a theme emerges in and through the development of characters, dialogue, settings and the movement of the plot.**

Themes are not (and should not be talked about as) separate strands that somehow exist independently of the other elements in the novel. They require the reader to recognise them and to see how the author has placed elements in the book so as to give rise to them. How an author does this is what the rest of this chapter is about. What we shall emphasise is the variety of ways in which the themes of a book emerge.

10.2 The titles of books

When you are thinking about the themes of a book, it is worth asking yourself:

- Why did the novelist give the book this name?

It could be that the novelist has chosen the title in order to tell the reader something important about the book. In some cases the central themes of the book are present in the title. This is the case with *Pride and Prejudice*, which is about Darcy's pride and Elizabeth Bennet's prejudice. *Middlemarch* is about life in a Midlands town; George Eliot provides a sub-title *A Study of Provincial Life*.

__ **Example** _____

A very interesting title is *Mansfield Park*. Why did Jane Austen name the book after the home of the Bertrams and not, as she might have done, after the heroine, Fanny Price, or the moral qualities the heroine displays – patience, sensitivity and loyalty?

> The fact that Jane Austen chose the name of the house indicates that one of her central interests is the whole way of life that is represented by Mansfield Park – a life based on tradition, a strict idea of manners, a demanding moral code, and an education that passes on such values to the next generation. This traditional way of life is shown to be under threat from people like the Crawfords, who seem to live for nothing but the pleasure of the moment, and, even more seriously, from the shallowness of those who have inherited it – the Bertram children. Jane Austen, then, gave the book its title as a way of indicating that what she was interested in was a tradition of country living rather than just the individual lives of the central characters.

- **It is worth noticing that examiners at both GCSE and A level do set questions in which they ask why a book was given the title it has.**

They could, for instance, set a question such as this: why did Dickens call his book *Great Expectations*? (You should note that this kind of question can also be set on drama: examiners might ask why plays such as *Measure for Measure*, *The Rivals* or *The Crucible* have these titles.)

10.3   How authors show their interests

It has already been stated that one way of saying that a book has themes is to say that the author takes an interest in certain aspects of life. But this raises the problem of how that interest is shown. Here are two suggestions: authors show their interest

- by writing in detail
- by devoting a great deal of space to some things.

To these a negative one can be added:

- authors' interests are sometimes evident in what they leave out

The detail in which George Eliot and Henry James write about how their characters change, grow and make up their minds shows that their interests include moral and psychological development. The point about space also applies to them; many pages of their novels are devoted to minute analysis of their characters' minds.

The space a novelist devotes to some topics is revealing also in the case of *1984*. Students are often puzzled by the lengthy section from 'the book' – a supposedly forbidden work that explains the workings of society. The space given to it shows Orwell's interest in political theory. Once you see that, you can ask whether elsewhere in the book Orwell is directing your attention to the political ideas that lie behind the way society runs.

It is, of course, difficult to be confident about whether the omission of something is important. It is, nevertheless, worth noticing. For instance, in Lawrence's *The Rainbow* there is very little about the kind of society in which the characters live. The characters are explored inwardly and they are written about with considerable emotional force, but the impression the reader is left with is of a world of individuals rather than a society. The fact that Lawrence has not stressed that factor shows that his interest lies in another direction.

10.4   Common themes

Some themes crop up in very many novels. There are, for instance, numerous novels that deal with love, growing up, or conflict. If a novel is clearly about one of these popular themes, the question you should ask is:

- What exactly is this author's approach to this theme?

It's not good enough to say 'this novel is about growing up'. What you must show is how an author handles that theme. When you come to write about the approach of a particular author, you must guard against assuming that the author treats a common theme in a similar way to other authors. You will have to look through all the relevant sections of the book and ask yourself whether the author has a particular viewpoint.

Example

Many books deal with love, but what exactly is the approach of Jane Austen to it?

In many books the author recognises that young men and women actively court each other. In fact, the way men court women is a central feature of a number of novels. If, however, you look at Jane Austen, you will see that she does not seem to approve of this. The men that actively and openly court women are seen to be untrustworthy and even wicked, whereas those couples who naturally grow together without any artificial plotting or planning are seen as being truly in love and capable of making lasting relationships.

Henry Crawford from Mansfield *Park* and Mr Knightley from *Emma* exhibit these differences. Henry Crawford sets out to woo Fanny as a game, but later, when he finds he does love her, he persuades his sister Mary to lend Fanny a necklace which, in fact, belongs to him. Fanny is quite unaware of this little plot, but when the truth is known, she is shocked. She speaks strongly to Mary about it:

Do you mean then that your brother knew of the necklace beforehand? Oh! Miss Crawford, *that* was not fair.

We can feel her anger in the 'Oh!', and 'fair' is a strong word; Fanny is accusing Henry of being deceitful. To deceive people into loving, Jane Austen suggests, is wrong. By contrast, Mr Knightley makes no attempts to court Emma; all he does is ask her, and since she has decided already that no one must marry Mr Knightley but she, he is accepted. In a conventional sense it is not like most proposals, yet we feel it is real love. Although it is not conventional, Jane Austen's view is deeply romantic: people need not plot and plan, because true love will grow naturally and will flower into marriage.

10.5   The function of symbols

Novels, as well as poems, employ symbols. A repeated symbol, or one used at an important moment, can give expression to a central theme of the novel. It is, therefore, a good idea to ask this question:

● Is there a repeated symbol in this novel, and what is its significance?

In asking such a question you should, of course, not ignore other elements in a novel. Symbols are important if they work alonside the characters and the settings. Here are some examples of the functions of symbols.

___ **Examples** ___

Example 1

L. P. Hartley's *The Go-Between* is a novel that employs symbols. The symbolism begins with a diary that Leo Colston is given in 1900. Young Leo is full of hope for the twentieth century, and he associates his hope with the figures of the zodiac that appear on the diary cover. When he goes to spend summer with a school friend of his in Norfolk, he interprets those whom he meets, and himself, in terms of the zodiac figures: the beautiful Marian, the elder sister of his friend, is the Virgin; the man she is to marry, a soldier called Hugh, is the archer; and the local farmer, Ted, is the water-carrier. Leo so looks up to them that he regards them as gods, and they call him Mercury – the messenger of the gods.

Leo is also fascinated by the temperature; each day he goes to see if the mercury in the thermometer has risen any higher. Seeing himself as the messenger of the gods and associating himself with the ever-rising temperature increases his hope and belief in the twentieth century. But without realising what is happening to him, he becomes the one who helps Marian and Ted to carry on a secret love affair by carrying messages between them. When they are discovered together, he suffers a nervous breakdown; his hopes for the century are destroyed, and he remains an emotional cripple for the rest of his life. Hartley, then, uses the symbols to express the theme of hope destroyed.

Example 2

You could not understand *The Go-Between* unless you saw the pattern of symbols. There are, however, some novels that don't depend upon such a highly developed scheme – and some people think they are all the better for it. For instance, the superb opening of Dickens's *Bleak House* presents London wrapped in a thick fog which penetrates every area of life. This fog that obscures and confuses is a symbol of the Court of Chancery, a maze with no exit, but, unlike the symbols in Hartley, it is not part of a rigid scheme of symbols running through the novel.

Example 3

The fog in *Bleak House* is near to being the case of a symbol used at an important moment. Another example of a moment that has a symbolic force is to be found in *Mansfield Park*, when Fanny Price is thinking about which necklace to wear with the little gold cross that her brother, William, has given her – the one that Edmund, whom she loves, has given her, or the one from Mary Crawford, which Edmund feels she ought to choose instead of his for the sake of politeness. But when she tries to thread Mary's necklace 'the one given her by Miss Crawford would by no means go through the ring of the cross'. It is an ordinary, everyday moment, but, nevertheless, it is charged with symbolic significance, for it is an indication that she is not fitted to the Crawfords' way of life. Her world, symbolised by the cross from her brother, won't fit in with the Crawford necklace, so she turns to the one from Edmund which, happily and symbolically, fits.

10.6 Important words

Authors can give expression to the themes of novels by stressing certain words. Words used carefully can focus the meaning of a novel and take the reader to the heart of the author's concerns. If the meaning of a novel is focused in a particular word, you will often find that it is used in the climax. When, therefore, you come to the climax of a novel you can ask:

- Is there an important word here that focuses the central theme of the book?

Example

Such a word is 'heart' in *Hard Times*. The novel has started with Mr Gradgrind saying, 'Now what I want is, Facts'. Education, he believes, should banish feeling and emotion and concentrate on nothing but facts. A model pupil in his school is Bitzer. Gradgrind brings his own children up this way, but the results are disastrous. Tom, his son, robs a bank and has to escape, but at the climax of the novel Bitzer prevents this. Gradgrind, who now sees that his ideas about education have been wrong, appeals to the very thing his method of education has neglected – feelings:

'Bitzer,' said Mr Gradgrind, broken down, and miserably submissive to him, 'have you a heart?' 'The circulation, Sir,' returned Bitzer, smiling at the oddity of the question, 'couldn't be carried on without it.'

What Mr Gradgrind means by 'heart' is sympathy, understanding, mercy and pity, but for Bitzer, 'heart' can only mean one thing – the organ that pumps blood round the body.

The word is the key to the book. Gradgrind's system of education ignored the heart by reducing the meanings of words to nothing but their factual content, but now that he can see the ghastly product of his own system he sees that feelings are important and the words shouldn't be reduced to a factual minimum. Dickens, therefore, focuses the theme of the book in the different way in which Bitzer and Gradgrind use the word 'heart'.

10.7   Moral words

Moral words work in a similar way. The point about a moral word is that it carries a judgement with it; that is to say:

We can tell whether we should approve or disapprove simply by attending to the meaning of the word.

For instance, we know that the word 'spiteful' means something which is bad, and the word 'generous' something which is good, because both words carry a judgement with them. Authors often invite us to judge characters by giving them moral words in their speech. A shallow character might be given rather trivial words, whereas a deep character would be given serious ones. Therefore, you can ask:

● Do the way characters use moral words indicate how the author is asking us to judge them?

___ **Example** _____

There is a very clear case of this in *Mansfield Park*. When Fanny learns that Henry Crawford has eloped with Maria she is deeply shocked. Her shock is expressed in very strong moral words:

> The horror of a mind like Fanny's, as it received the conviction of such guilt, and began to take in some part of the misery that must ensue, can hardly be described. At first, it was a sort of stupefaction; but every moment was quickening her perception of the horrible evil.

Look at the words used – 'horror', 'such guilt', 'misery', and 'horrible evil' – all of them very strong moral words, which show the depth of Fanny's character. But Jane Austen carefully shows that Mary Crawford's reaction is very different. Edmund reports them to Fanny:

> She said – 'I wanted to see you. Let us talk over this sad business. What can equal the folly of our two relations?'

Mary Crawford uses no stronger moral words than, 'sad business' (hardly a moral term at all) and 'folly', which is a very weak term, standing for no more than a silly mistake.

Throughout the novel Edmund has been captivated by the beauty of Mary Crawford, but these words make him see sense; nobody who talks like that can have any depth. From then on his affections for Mary cool. Thus one of the central themes of the book – Edmund's growth away from infatuation – is focused in the way he is shocked by Mary's use of the word 'folly'. Eventually he turns to Fanny, who, we have already seen, has judged the elopement as a 'horrible evil'.

10.8   The construction of plots

Since a novelist could write a novel in many different ways, the fact that a particular one has been chosen might tell you something about its appropriateness to the theme. You can ask of every novel:

- Does the fact that the novelist has chosen to write the novel this way tell me anything about its themes?

In the very best novels the way the novel is written, that is, the way it is constructed, plotted or ordered, is an expression of its themes. An example will make this clear.

— **Example** —

In *Middlemarch* the way the novel is written is an expression of one of its themes. Throughout, George Eliot tries to show us how characters think and feel, so that we will be sympathetic. No matter who the character is, George Eliot asks us to understand what it feels like to be that character. This way of writing the novel is, in fact, an expression of her belief that people should always consider what other people are feeling.

Take the case of Dorothea Brooke. The crisis of the novel occurs when Dorothea finds Will Ladislaw, the man she loves, holding hands with Rosamund, the wife of Lydgate. Will is not having an affair with Rosamund, but poor Dorothea does not know this. So hurt and shocked is she that she spends the night lying on the floor of her room, and it's only with the dawn, a symbolic moment, that she comes to this realisation:

> Was she alone in that scene? Was it her event only? She forced herself to think of it as bound up with another woman's life – a woman towards whom she had set out with a longing to carry some clearness and comfort into her beclouded youth.

What Dorothea sees is what George Eliot expresses in the way she writes the novel – that we should always consider what other people are feeling. Thus, it can be said that the way *Middlemarch* is written is an expression of one of its most important themes.

10.9   Important speeches

One of the clearest guides to the themes of a novel is what the characters say. Since some characters say a great deal, you will have to learn to detect those speeches that are particularly important. (This does not mean you should ignore the others.) You can only do this if you know a novel well, but when you are acquainted with a novel, you will be able to see that:

Particular speeches focus the main concerns of the plot.

— **Example** —

Throughout Emily Brontë's novel *Wuthering Heights* there is a deep yet very puzzling relation between Cathy and Heathcliff. They are together a great deal as children. Cathy can't bear to see Heathcliff beaten, and yet their relationship is very strange. For instance, it is not, in any conventional sense, a romantic one. They do use the word 'love', but it does not have its usual romantic and sexual meaning. It is because this relationship is puzzling that the reported speeches of Cathy are so important.

At one point she says this to Nelly, her nurse:

> My love for Heathcliff resembles the eternal rocks beneath: a source of little visible delight but necessary. Nelly, I *am* Heathcliff. He's always in my mind: not as a pleasure, any more than I am always a pleasure to myself, but as my own being.

That is the closest we ever come to understanding their relationship; Catherine says she *is* Heathcliff. The love she talks of, then, is for somebody who is herself – 'as my own being'. Of course, no reader can just take what Cathy says as true, but when that speech is seen alongside other aspects of their relation, it is difficult not to see it as expressing the truth. Her words, then, focus what goes on in the rest of the novel.

10.10   Important events

Novels are concerned with what happens as well as with what is said. Events, therefore, can express the themes of books. This is particularly the case with the climax of a novel. Many nineteenth-century novels contain what can be called 'big moments' in which, for instance, difficult decisions are taken, discoveries made, or mysteries revealed. One of the pleasures of reading such novels comes when the author handles the climax well. The reader enjoys the achievement of the author in making the events express the themes of the book. When, therefore, you reach a climax (or it could be a turning point) you can ask:

● Does this event express the themes of the book?

Dickens plans the climaxes of his novels very carefully. He handles them theatrically; that is to say, they have the vividness and impact of a play.

Examples

Example 1

At the end of *Little Dorrit* Mrs Clennam, who has sat in her room throughout the novel, dramatically rises from her chair and runs through London to the Marshalsea Prison to beg forgiveness from Little Dorrit.

This astonishing scene focuses on one of the main themes of the novel. Dickens has shown how difficult it is for characters to change their views and so escape from convention, habit or circumstances. For instance, Mr Dorrit physically escapes from the Marshalsea but mentally he lives in it for the rest of his life.

Nobody in the novel has been as fixed in views or physical position as Mrs Clennam. She is hard, unforgiving and self-righteous in her outlook and never leaves her room. The fact, then, that she rises to her feet and runs out of the house to beg forgiveness for what she has done wrong is not only a spectacular change, it is also very significant for the theme of the novel. If somebody as fixed in her views as Mrs Clennam can change, then the novel, while stressing how difficult change can be, is not entirely gloomy or without hope.

Example 2

An even more theatrical climax is the exposure of Mr Bounderby in *Hard Times*. He has always boasted that he is a self-made man who has risen from the very lowest level of society – a ditch.

Throughout the novel a mysterious lady of a neat and respectable appearance occasionally appears, looking at the buildings owned by Mr Bounderby. The climax of the novel occurs when it is discovered that this woman is his mother, and that his upbringing, far from being squalid, was a very comfortable one. Dickens sets this discovery in Bounderby's house. People crowd in from the street to see what is going on, and some of them, as in a theatre, stand on chairs 'to get the better of the people in front'.

This theatrical exposure of Bounderby is important because it shows that he is a hypocrite. Dickens uses it to hammer home the theme of his book – that the industrial world is run by hypocrites, who have beliefs about how to progress in society which are false.

10.11 The treatment of ordinary events

Not all the significant events in a book have to be dramatic. An author can write about an ordinary, everyday event in such a way as to bring out that it is very important. A book's theme can be present in the seemingly ordinary, and it is often the experience of readers that they enjoy the way an author brings out the depth of meaning that can be found in everyday doings.

Nobody handles the everyday better than Jane Austen. She can show the moral significance of events that seem very ordinary indeed.

Example

Take, for example, the outing to Sotherton, which happens in the first half of *Mansfield Park*. Sotherton is the home of Mr Rushworth, the silly young man to whom Maria Bertram is engaged. The visitors explore the extensive grounds of the house and arrive at a locked gate. Since most of them want to go through it, Mr Rushworth hurries back to the house to fetch the key, leaving, among others, Maria and Henry Crawford. Maria is impatient; the locked gate gives her, she says, 'a feeling of restraint and hardship'. They are significant words, and Henry Crawford understands what they really mean. What Maria is talking about is the restraint and hardship of being engaged to be married to the silly Mr Rushworth. The gate, therefore, to which only Mr Rushworth has the key, is a symbol for marriage. What Henry Crawford suggests is that she can avoid her feelings of 'restraint' by climbing round the side of it:

> And for the world you would not get out without the key and without Mr. Rushworth's authority and protection, or I think with little difficulty pass round the edge of the gate, here, with my assistance; I think it might be done, if you really wished to be more at large, and could allow your-self to think it not prohibited.

That is an invitation to adultery. To go round the gate with the 'assistance' of Henry would be to escape from 'the authority and protection' of Mr Rushworth. In addition, she could do so with 'little difficulty', and she is tempted with the thought that she would be 'more at large' if she could look upon what she was doing as 'not prohibited'. These words apply to the act of adultery – an adultery that becomes real when they elope – as well as they do to the perfectly ordinary event of finding a way round a locked gate. Jane Austen uses an ordinary incident to bring out the theme of marriage and adultery, which is central to the novel.

10.12 Writing about themes

Most examination questions ask you to show that you understand what the author is saying. Occasionally, however, your views are sought. These are not easy questions to prepare for, but here are some things you can do.

As you study, you can ask yourself:

● What view does the author take of this matter?

For instance, you might be struck about the view of love and marriage that emerges in Jane Austen or about what Lawrence thinks about the relationships between men and women. As you do this you can ask yourself whether or not you agree with what you are being shown. Is Jane Austen right in her apparent belief that true love will naturally emerge, and is Lawrence right about the inevitable conflict between men and women? Remember that only you can do this. You can talk to others, but when you are asked what you think, only you can answer. This is an area in which you have to be honest; if your view is wanted – give it.

Some students are worried that if they differ from their teacher, they'll be marked wrong. Of course, there are people who want to dictate to others. I once heard of a university student who had a piece of work returned with the comment on it: 're-write, stating departmental line'. But that is a very rare case. The majority of teachers will say that as long as you can support your views with reference to the text, you should, if invited, write what you think.

___ **Exercises** _____

10.1   Consider how appropriate are the titles of the novels you are studying.

10.2   By looking at what authors concentrate on and what they leave out, try to see what the central interests of their novels are.

10.3   Look at the novels you are studying to see if there are any symbols that express the theme of the book. If there are, write about them.

10.4   Can you see why the novelists you are studying have written the books the way they have?

10.5   Write about the central speeches and events of the novels you are studying, bringing out how they express their themes.

10.6   Try to sum up what are the themes of the novels you studying and work out in writing your reactions to what the novelists are saying.

Part III
Studying Drama

The conventions of drama

11.1　The importance of conventions

What would you make of a cowboy film if you'd never seen one before? A number of things might surprise you: when there was a fist fight there would be loud, cracking noises, and chairs would break in pieces if anyone was hit with one; the goodies would be handsome men who rode white horses, and the baddies ugly men on black ones; and when anyone rode a horse, you would see them starting, and then, in the next shot, arriving at their destination, the journey taking, so it seemed, a couple of seconds. If, however, you knew what to expect in a cowboy film, none of these things would surprise you. The reason for this is that you would recognise and accept the *conventions* of cowboy films. What is a convention?

> *A convention is an agreement between author and audience that a situation or idea will be presented in a particular way.*

Conventions need not mirror actual life in every detail; indeed, if they did they wouldn't be conventions. Their function is to be representative, so that the audience can accept what they see as real. For instance, in cowboy films fights are accompanied by loud cracking noises. Punches don't actually sound like this, but the noises are accepted as a convention indicating that the fighting is tough.

An audience is usually so used to most conventions that it hardly notices them. The stage itself is a convention; the audience see an open space over which actors move but know that it represents, and so treat it as, a living room, a battlefield, a court of law or a boat. The audience knows that actors are real people, yet it regards them as kings, generals, peasants and prime ministers. It knows, too, that a play is meant to portray the action of weeks, months or even years, and it accepts that a great deal of time has passed even if the performance only lasts two or three hours. When a character dies, the audience feels pity and sadness, yet knows the actor playing the part will come back at the end and take a bow.

―― **Example** ―――――――――――――――――――――――――――――――

Shakespeare jokes about conventions in *A Midsummer Night's Dream*. A group of humble working men rehearse a play, which they hope will be performed at the Duke's wedding, but they don't understand the basic conventions of drama. Moreover, they think the audience won't understand them either. Two of the things they don't expect the audience to understand are that actors aren't really dead when they die on stage, and that actors can represent animals. The well-meaning Bottom suggests that a prologue should explain these difficulties to the audience:

> Write me a prologue and let the prologue seem to say, we will do no harm with our swords, and that Pyramus is not killed indeed; and, for the more better assurance, that I, Pyramus, am not Pyramus, but Bottom the weaver.

His suggestion about the lion is even funnier; the actor should show half his face to show them he is a man and should say:

> Ladies, – or, fair ladies, – I would wish you, – or, I would request you, – or, I would entreat you, – not to fear, not to tremble: my life for yours. If you think I come hither as a lion, it were pity of my life: no, I am no such thing; I am a man as other men are.

Bottom stumbles across the point about conventions: audiences know the lion is not real in the same way that they *know* actors don't really die. They *know* because they understand conventions.

Understanding drama, then, includes understanding its conventions. Although you are not likely to be as badly off as Bottom, you will find that some things in plays, particularly Shakespearian ones, will puzzle you because you don't understand their conventions. In addition, you won't pick up the significance of what is going on unless you recognise the conventions that are being used. The aim of this chapter is to introduce you to some of these.

You may notice two aspects of how plays are constructed:

- they are divided into sections called acts and scenes
- time passes within them at different rates.

Both of these depend upon conventions.

11.2   Conventions of construction: acts and scenes

The longer divisions of a play are called *acts*, and acts are sometimes further divided into *scenes*. Modern plays are often divided into two or three acts, whereas the plays of Shakespeare and his contemporaries are usually divided into five. Modern plays can have many scenes or the acts can be undivided: Shakespearian plays usually have numerous scenes. *Antony and Cleopatra*, for instance, has thirty-eight.

In Shakespeare's plays all scenes start with the entrance of characters and close with the characters leaving the stage. When you read one of his plays, you will notice the 'Enter' at the beginning of the scene and the 'Exit' at the end, though you should remember that on stage the flow of action does not seem interrupted as it does on the page.

Can anything be learnt from these conventions? In the case of modern plays, it is a good idea to ask:

- Do the act divisions correspond to the important stages in the action of the play?

Peter Shaffer divides *The Royal Hunt of the Sun* into two acts, both of which have twelve scenes. The first act, called 'The Hunt', shows how Pizarro's army captures the Inca king and massacres the natives; the second, called 'The Kill', is concerned with the relation between Pizarro and the king and climaxes in the king's murder. Thus the convention of dividing a play into acts is made to serve the meaning of the play: Pizarro's army first hunts the Sun King and then it kills him. Of any modern play you can ask:

- Why has the playwright divided the acts and scenes in this way?

In answering that question you should see if the act divisions correspond to the development of the plot.

- **In Shakespeare, acts do not correspond to important stages in the action.**

There is, then, little point in studying how he divides his plays into five acts. Most of the plays consist not of an action in five sections but a two-fold movement: events gather pace till a crisis breaks, and from then on the play mounts to its conclusion.

What this does mean is that Act III – usually Scene 1 and/or Scene 2 – is the crisis of the play. Whenever you study a Shakespeare play, you should pay particular attention to these scenes. *Julius Caesar* has a two-fold movement: the growth of the plot to kill Caesar, and the campaign against those who killed him. The turning point – the crisis – is Act III, Scenes 1 and 2; in Scene 1 Caesar is killed and in Scene 2 Antony skilfully turns the crowd against the plotters.

11.3 Conventions of construction: the passing of time

It is a convention that a long period of time can be represented in a play that only takes two or three hours to perform. This means that the structure of a play – the way it is put together – must convey the passing of time. This is usually done in one or both of two ways:

(1)   time is assumed to have passed between scenes or acts
(2)   time can pass quickly within a scene.

In general, modern plays follow the first way, and Shakespeare – and his contemporaries – both.

Indications of time passing

It is now a convention that playwrights indicate the passage of time between acts and scenes by stating in the stage directions that so many days, say, have passed. In the theatre this information is printed in the programme. For instance Act 2 of Arthur Miller's *The Crucible* begins: *The Common room of Proctor's house, eight days later.*

Shakespeare does not employ that convention, so he indicates that time has passed between scenes by making characters refer to it. One of the most notable examples of this is in *The Winter's Tale*, when Shakespeare introduces the figure of Time, who announces that sixteen years have passed. In another play, *Twelfth Night*, Viola disguises herself as a man in order to join the court of Orsino. She states her intention to do this in Act 1 Scene 2, and at the beginning of Act 1 Scene 4 a courtier, Valentine, says that Orsino 'hath known you but three days', so we know that time has passed.

That convention rarely bothers anyone studying or watching a play, but time passing within a scene can seem strange.

Example

Christopher Marlowe's *Dr Faustus* closes with a scene in which Faustus waits in dread and horror for the Devil to take him off to hell. His speech lasts fifty-seven lines, and begins:

> Ah, Faustus,
> Now hast thou but one bare hour to live …

Fifty lines later, an hour has passed; the clock strikes, and Faustus despairingly cries:

> Oh, it strikes, it strikes! Now body turn to air,
> Or Lucifer will bear thee quick to hell.

When you read the scene, the quick passing of time might seem odd. It is a convention that you must accept: in plays time can be elastic. In the case of *Dr Faustus*, however, Marlowe creates such mental agony in the fifty-seven lines that enough emotion to last an hour has been generated. In other words, the emotional tension of the scene helps us to accept the convention.

Time devoted to important events

The convention that time is elastic in plays can be used by playwrights to indicate what is dramatically important. In general, a great deal of time is devoted to important events. For instance, although the action of *Julius Caesar* must take a few months, over half the action takes place in less than twenty-four hours – the night before and the morning of Caesar's death. By devoting so much time to the plot against Caesar, Shakespeare indicates the importance of that event and the issues it raises. Reading the play, we can see that we are meant to concentrate on Cassius's methods of organising the plot, Brutus's motives for joining in, and Caesar's attitude to danger.

The Flashback

There is one other way of indicating the passing of time that affects the structure of a play – the convention of the *flashback*. This convention has been used very effectively in modern plays. It allows the playwright to contrast past and present, and to show how the present is to be understood in the light of the past.

In *Death of a Salesman* Arthur Miller presents the pathetic contrast between the hopeful and confident young Willy Loman and the tired and defeated wreck he becomes. At the end of the play the audience are shown that Biff, the son upon whom Willy built his hopes, is hostile to his father because, in the past, he discovered that Willy was having an affair with a woman in Boston.

Playwrights use flashbacks because these devices can offer a psychological explanation for a character's behaviour. Therefore, it is worthwhile asking of any play in which flashbacks occur:

- What is the playwright showing about the characters by using the convention of the flashback?

11.4 Conventions of language: verse and prose

It is a convention in many plays that characters speak in verse and prose. Some characters always use one or the other, but many use both. Shakespeare, Marlowe, Jonson and Middleton write in both verse and prose, and though playwrights such as Congreve, Sheridan, Wilde and Shaw usually stick to prose, the convention has not died out. In this century T. S. Eliot, who is regularly set in public examinations, has written drama in verse. When you study a play that is written in both verse and prose, you should ask two questions:

(1) Why do some characters speak in verse and others in prose?
(2) What effects do verse and prose create?

- **Why do some characters speak in verse and others in prose?**

In Shakespeare and his contemporaries the important characters usually speak verse, whereas the minor ones use prose. Quite often an important character has a high social standing, whilst a minor one has not. The opening scene of *Julius Caesar* shows Marullus and Flavius dissuading a crowd from celebrating Caesar's triumphant return from war. They are tribunes (that is, representatives of the people), so they speak in verse. The citizens, however, are given prose, because they are both minor characters and members of the lower classes.

The distinction between prose and verse is, however, not always as clear as that. In *Julius Caesar* there is an important character of high social standing, called Casca, who speaks prose for much of the time. The reason for this is that he is a blunt, plain-speaking man. Prose, in other words, is given to him because it suits his down to earth character. Nevertheless, even the blunt Casca speaks in verse during the storm. Shakespeare has probably given him verse because it is better at producing the tense and frightening atmosphere of a terrible thunderstorm. Verse and prose, then, can be used to indicate character and produce atmosphere.

- **What effects do verse and prose create?**

Verse is usually more dramatically effective than prose because it uses all the resources of language – its figures of speech, rhythms, and sounds. Indeed, when you are writing about verse in plays, it is often appropriate to use the terms introduced in the poetry chapters of this book.

Examples ———————————————————————

Example 1

A very fine example of the different effects of verse and prose is Act III Scene 2 of *Julius Caesar*, when Brutus and Antony speak to the crowds about the death of Caesar.

Shakespeare has a problem in this scene: he must show that Antony is more impressive than Brutus, or else the audience will not believe that the crowd who supported Brutus at the beginning of the scene could be crying for his death at the end of it. Shakespeare solves the problem by giving Brutus dry prose and Antony eloquent verse. This is an extract from Brutus:

If there be any in this assembly, any dear friend of Caesar's, to him I say that Brutus's love to Caesar was no less than his. If then that friend demand why Brutus rose against Caesar, this is my answer: Not that I loved Caesar less, but that I loved Rome more.

Brutus offers cold, reasonable prose. He sounds as if he is conducting a hypothetical argument. Look, for instance, how both his sentences start with the word 'if'. His thoughtful, controlled prose, moving from question to answer, stirs very little emotion.

By contrast, look at Antony's verse about Caesar's robe:

> I remember
> The first time ever Caesar put it on;
> 'Twas on a summer's evening in his tent,
> That day he overcame the Nervii.
> Look, in this place ran Cassius' dagger through:
> See what a rent the envious Casca made:
> Through this the well-beloved Brutus stabbed;
> And as he plucked his cursed steel away,
> Mark how the blood of Caesar followed it,
> As rushing out of doors, to be resolved
> If Brutus so unkindly knocked or no;
> For Brutus, as you know, was Caesar's angel.

Look at the drama of the end-stopped lines; one begins with the arresting 'look' and ends with the grim picture of a dagger running through the robe. The horror of Caesar's death is thus dramatically expressed within one line. Look, too, at the image of Brutus knocking upon the door of Caesar's body, and, in a run-on line, Caesar's blood, eager to greet the friend, rushing out of doors. There is in that image a horrible contrast between what Brutus is doing (note how the word 'stabbed' forms the dramatic climax of the line) and the happy picture of a man gladly running to see his friend. Note, too, how the leisurely rhythms of the nostalgic opening – the lingering stresses on 'ever' and 'summer' – give way to the insistent monosyllables of the murder – 'look', 'rent', 'stabbed' and 'mark'. No wonder the crowd are moved to anger and revenge.

Example 2

T. S. Eliot uses the contrast between verse and prose in *Murder in the Cathedral*. When the knights have murdered Thomas, they explain why they have done it. Eliot, by giving them prose, shows that they are narrow, unimaginative and worldly men. They don't really understand what they have done, so all they can offer as explanations are unemotional, everyday reasons. One, for instance, tries to persuade the audience that Thomas was a psychological case, who, in effect, committed suicide. Eliot contrasts this lack of feeling with the words of the priest who mourns the death of Thomas. The priest, of course, is given verse to express his overwhelming grief and bewilderment.

11.5   Conventions of language: characters talking about themselves

Using the third person

If you look back to Brutus's speech quoted above, you will see that he refers to himself in the third person. This is a convention that often puzzles people who are new to Shakespeare. If you can recognise what is going on, you may be able to appreciate that it is a way of speaking that can make the occasion and the character impressive and grand.

Example

For instance, when Caesar refuses to listen to requests, he talks about his firmness in the third person:

> Be not fond,
> To think that Caesar bears such rebel blood
> That will be thawed from the true quality
> With that which melteth fools...

Caesar is saying that he will not give into the things that persuade fools to change their minds. Speaking of himself in the third person helps him to create an impressive and grand sense of firmness, because it presents the idea that even Caesar himself is looking on with admiration at such a determined decision.

Dramatic self-disclosure

Shakespeare often gives a character a speech which has the function of informing the audience who he or she is. This is sometimes called *dramatic self-disclosure* or *dramatic self-revelation*. Shakespeare often resorts to it when a character first appears.

Example

For instance, *The Taming of the Shrew* opens with the arrival in Padua of Lucentio and his servant Tranio. Shakespeare makes Lucentio deliver these lines to Tranio:

> Here let us breathe, and haply institute
> A course of learning and ingenious studies.

> Pisa, renowned for grave citizens,
> Gave me my being, and my father first —
> A merchant of great traffic through the world

There's no way in which these lines can be regarded as normal dialogue. Lucentio has no need to inform Tranio why they are in Padua and who Lucentio's father is.

But how then do the lines work? They are a statement, a public and objective one, of who Lucentio is and why he is in Padua. They are not made to further a relationship between the characters on the stage or to show us what and how the speaker thinks. They are spoken solely for the benefit of the audience; we need to know these things, so Shakespeare adopts the mode of dramatic self-disclosure to tell us.

What we mustn't do is try to understand this speech in terms of Lucentio's character, his mind, his feelings, his attitudes. It declares who he is and what he's doing; it's not a psychological but a theatrical use of language, and as such it forms one of the conventions that Shakespeare draws on when he needs to put the audience in the picture.

- **A useful thing can be learnt from this:**

Shakespeare does not try to be consistent about how he presents a character; he works in a number of different ways in order to make his plays vital and absorbing.

Kings referred to by name of country

Another convention that can confuse students is that of a ruler being referred to by the name of his country. These lines occur in King Lear:

> Call France. Who stirs?
> Call Burgundy.

It is the King of France and the Duke of Burgundy who are being called, not the lands of France and Burgundy. The convention is an important one, for it tells you something of the importance of a king. In a very important sense a king *is* his country. He is the representative of it, and his character affects it. Thus the victory of Henry V in the play of that name is celebrated as a victory of England over France. One of the things you must accept in Shakespeare is the important position of the king. The convention of referring to him by the name of his country is a way of establishing that importance.

11.6   Conventions of language: 'you' and 'thou'

The distinction between 'you' and 'thou' does not usually raise problems. It is, however, an important one to understand because it indicates the emotional tone of the scene. The distinction is that 'you' is used when the occasion is formal and a speaker wants to remind listeners of the social difference, but 'thou' when the speakers are equal and the mood is friendly and intimate.

Example

There is a striking example in the second scene of *Hamlet*, where the new king, Claudius, wants to be friendly to Laertes, the son of his chief minister. His speech to him is full of 'thees' and 'thous' and ends:

> Take thy fair hour, Laertes, time be thine,
> And thy best graces spend it at thy will.

'*Thy* fair', 'time be *thine*', '*thy* best graces' and '*thy* will'; we can feel that Claudius is going out of his way to appear friendly. When, however, he turns to Hamlet, the tone changes:

> How is it that the clouds still hang on you?

That is chilly. The way he holds back the word 'you' until the end of the line indicates that Claudius wants Hamlet to see that he is not going to treat him either as an equal or a friend. From the very start of the play, therefore, the tension between them has been established.

Whenever you come across a change from one form of address to the other, it is a good idea to ask:

● Is it important that the characters are using 'you' or 'thou'?

You will usually find that the change tells you something important about the attitudes of characters to each other.

11.7   Conventions of language: the soliloquy

A *soliloquy* occurs when a character is either alone or isolated upon the stage and speaks aloud his or her thoughts. It is a convention in Shakespeare to place soliloquies at the beginning or at the end of a scene, although he doesn't always do this. Macbeth begins Act I Scene 7 with his troubled thoughts about killing the king, and Viola ends Act II Scene 2 of *Twelfth Night* with her reflections on the tangle she has got herself in. An exception is Leontes, who, in *The Winter's Tale*, has two soliloquies in the middle of Act I Scene 2.

Soliloquies are usually of two kinds:

(1) public
(2) private.

Public soliloquies

In a public soliloquy a character openly addresses the audience. It is interesting that it is often the villain who does this. Iago in *Othello* and Richard III in the play of that name openly talk about what they are going to do. There is something rather disturbing about the way they buttonhole an audience and share their wicked plans with them. This is particularly disturbing in the case of Richard III, who is charmingly honest about what he wants to do:

Example

> Plots have I laid, inductions dangerous,
> By drunken prophecies, libels and dreams,
> To set my brother Clarence and the king
> In deadly hate the one against the other:
> And if King Edward be as true and just,
> As I am subtle, false, and treacherous,
> This day shall Clarence closely be mewed up.

Richard reveals everything: the plots he has laid, the goodness of King Edward, and his gleeful expectation that Clarence will soon be in jail. It is that glee, that relish, that audiences find charming.

- **This is something you should remember when you write about public soliloquies.** Because characters talk to us, and, in the case of Richard, reveal their delight in evil, it is easy to be taken in by them. Therefore, you should bring out in your writing that an audience can know that a character is wicked and yet find him or her attractive.

Private soliloquies

A private soliloquy creates a very different effect. The audience is not addressed but listens in to, or overhears, the innermost thoughts of a character. The audience does not share the thoughts but is aware of hearing the private questioning that is going on in a character's mind. You should, of course, write about such soliloquies in a different way from the public ones. Listen, for instance, to Hamlet angrily questioning himself:

> Am I a coward?
> Who calls me villain? breaks my pate across?
> Plucks off my beard, and blows it in my face?

Because you are not being addressed, it would be wrong to find answers to these questions. Hamlet is puzzled, and what you should do in your writing is reflect his bewilderment. You could point to the way question follows question with no pause for an answer, and to the way in which Hamlet feels himself to be attacked. Hamlet is a mystery to himself, and it is the purpose of the soliloquy to express that. You should respond to that mystery in your writing.

- **Public and private soliloquies create different effects and are appropriate to different dramatic situations.** Iago's public soliloquies in the early part of *Othello* show that he is a manipulator of other characters. The confident, controlled manner of these soliloquies is very different from the chaotic anguish of Othello's private soliloquies later in the play. In Miller's *Death of a Salesman* Willy's increasingly pathetic mental collapse is appropriately expressed towards the end of the play by a private soliloquy in which he talks to his brother, Ben, whom Willy wrongly imagines is present.

    Whenever you have to write about a soliloquy, then, you should ask:

- In what ways is it appropriate to the character's situation?

- What dramatic effect does it create?

11.8   Conventions of language: the aside

The *aside* is the convention in which a character momentarily turns away from the character to whom he or she is either listening or speaking and addresses the audience directly. Because it is always public, it establishes a relation between character and audience. Whenever you come across an aside, you should ask:

- What is the effect of this relation?

You will probably find that two effects are very common:

(1)   sympathy for the character
(2)   humour

Sympathy for the character

In the first scene of *King Lear* the old king divides his kingdom up between his daughters by asking them to declare their love for him. The youngest, Cordelia, refuses to please her father by playing what she sees as a hypocritical game. Her refusal is quite harsh, but it has also been the experience of audiences that they feel sympathy for her.

This is not just because she is honest. It is, in part, due to the fact that throughout the scene she speaks openly to the audience in a series of asides. After a particularly oily speech from one of her hypocritical sisters, Regan, she declares to the audience:

> Then poor Cordelia!
> And yet not so; since I am sure my love's
> More ponderous than my tongue.

Audiences, as we have seen in the section on public soliloquy, like being talked to. The spectacle of an anxious and honest girl opening her heart generates a sympathy which persists even when she speaks coldly to her father.

Humour

The aside has become an important convention in English comedies. Comedy is often built on misunderstanding, and audiences, who usually know what is going on, find it very funny when characters appeal to them about the confusion they are in. Audiences enjoy being in the know, so feel very superior when they are spoken to by a confused character.

Goldsmith frequently uses this device in his delightful play *She Stoops to Conquer*. At one point Marlow and Hastings arrive at their intended destination, the home of Mr Hardcastle, but, because of a trick, they believe it to be an inn. Hardcastle, of course, knows nothing of this, so can't understand why they treat him as little more than a servant, and they are puzzled by his over-friendly behaviour:

Hardcastle: ... Here, Mr Marlow, here is our better acquaintance!
Marlow [*aside*]: A very impudent fellow this! [*Drinks*] But he's a
   character, and I'll humour him a little. Sir, my services to you.

> *Hastings* [*aside*]: I see this fellow wants to give us his company, and
> forgets that he's an innkeeper, before he has learned to be a gentleman.

The asides allow us to laugh at all the characters. Hardcastle is trying to be
a genial host, but to Marlow he is 'a very impudent fellow'. But because we
know that they have been tricked, we knowingly laugh at their astonishment at his behaviour.

11.9   Conventions of action: the chorus

A *chorus* is an individual, or group, who speaks directly to the audience about the
action of the play. *Henry V* and *Dr Faustus* both start and end with chorus figures
talking about the play, and *Henry IV* part II begins with a chorus figure who is
called Rumour. The convention of the chorus seems strange because it makes
drama a mixed medium. On the stage are actors who are representing characters,
but they are joined by another figure who openly advertises the artificiality of the
stage by refusing to be a character like the others and talking directly to the audience about what is going on. Odd as this may seem, it is something that you will
have to accept. But not everything about a chorus is confusing:

- **Unlike many characters, the chorus can be believed**. When the chorus in
  Romeo and Juliet tells us that the play is about 'the fearful passage of their
  death-marked love', we have no reason for not believing him.

- **In addition, the chorus is openly helpful** – the one in *Henry V* is there to
  assist the audience to imagine the battlefield of Agincourt.

- **The most interesting chorus figures are those who serve the function of
  chorus and character.**
  This begins to happen in Shakespeare when a character, so to speak, steps
  out of his or her role to make a direct comment on the action of the play. It is
  as if Shakespeare decides that something needs to be said, so one character
  is made to change from his or her role to that of a public commentator on
  events. At the end of *Twelfth Night* the twins, Viola and Sebastian, appear
  on stage together. Since the whole play has depended upon the fact that they
  are identical, somebody must make this point to the characters and the audience. Shakespeare selects Orsino:

  > One face, one voice, one habit, and two persons,
  > A natural perspective, that is and is not.

What he says is not expressive of his character, but is a chorus-like comment
on what everybody can see.

It is, however, in a modern play, *A Man for all Seasons*, that the full development of the chorus figure who is also a character can be seen. Robert Bolt creates the Common Man, who opens and closes the play, as well as commenting on the action in between. But he is also a character, or, rather, a number of characters: steward, boatman, publican, jailer, foreman of the jury and, finally, executioner. He is both apart from and part of the action.

In so far as he is apart from it, he is close to the audience: an ordinary person who, like the audience, views the lives of kings and cardinals. Indeed, we are meant to see him as ourselves. At the end of the play he says: 'If we should bump into one another, recognise me.' In the play he becomes characters, and though the audience can't have the same relation with him, it might see in him the kind of roles its members might have played in history.

An interesting use of a figure who is close to being a chorus can be found in Arthur Miller's *A View from the Bridge*. What is interesting about him is that, unlike the Common Man, he is not presented in a symbolic way. What Miller does is create a character and then give him an overview of the action. His name is Alfieri; he is a lawyer of Italian extraction who understands the intense life of New York's Italian immigrants. His position in the design of the play, as well as what he says, makes him very close to a chorus. He opens the play with a long public soliloquy and talks of the position of the lawyer as one who watches. Alfieri also opens the second act (it is a two-act play) and he closes the play.

11.10   Conventions of action: disguise

Some students who are new to Shakespeare notice how much disguise is used. They also notice that characters hardly ever see through it. That is the convention that you will have to accept. What is important about disguise is the dramatic opportunities it presents. In Shakespeare it makes two effects possible. Characters can:

- say what they would otherwise be unable to say
- hear what they would otherwise be unable to hear.

--- **Examples** ---

Example 1

In *As You Like It* Orlando is too shy to court Rosalind openly, but when Rosalind has disguised herself as a man she playfully suggests to him that she will pretend to be Rosalind so he can court her. This Orlando feels able to do, so he can say what he never dared to say and she can hear what she never expected to hear. Their playful courtship is lively: he can be open and straightforward, and she can willingly accept his proposals.

Rosalind: But come, now I will be your Rosalind in a more coming-on
   disposition; and ask me what you will, I will grant it.
Orlando: Then love me, Rosalind.
Rosalind: Yes, faith, will I, Fridays and Saturdays and all.
Orlando: And wilt thou have me?
Rosalind: Ay, and twenty such.

Example 2

A more serious use of disguise comes in *Henry V*, when the king, on the
eve of the battle of Agincourt, disguises himself and wanders through his
camp, talking to his soldiers. Because he is disguised, he can hear what
otherwise he would never hear – what the soldiers really think of him. He
can also express what he feels his ordinary human emotions. He does this
in prose – the language of the soldiers:

   For, though I speak it to you, I think the king is but a man as I am. The
   violet smells to him as it doth to me; the element shows to him as it doth
   to me: all his senses have but human conditions.

A very important idea in the play is that of brotherhood. When, before the
battle, Henry speaks of the army as 'a band of brothers', he can do so
because they have spoken to him and he has spoken to them about what he
feels. This is made possible by the convention of disguise.

Whenever there is disguise, you should ask yourself:

• What does disguise allow the characters to say and hear?

11.11   Conventions of action: dance, music and songs

Shakespeare's plays are full of dance, music and song. They are not there just to
entertain, though they do, but to point to important meanings.

Dance

Dancing was thought of as very important in Elizabethan England because it
was an expression of peace and harmony between people, and even of the peace
and harmony of the universe. When, therefore, Shakespeare closes his comedies
with dancing he is using this convention to indicate that the characters are in
perfect harmony with one another. *As You Like It* and *Much Ado about Nothing*
both conclude with dances.

Music

Music in Shakespeare is an expression of harmony. Cordelia speaks of her father, the mad King Lear, in these words:

> O you kind Gods,
> Cure this great breach in his abused nature!
> Th'untuned and jarring senses, O! wind up
> Of this child-changed father.

His madness is seen as a lack of harmony – 'untuned' and 'jarring' – and hopes for his restoration are expressed as the tuning of a musical instrument – 'O wind up'. When he does come round from madness, it is to the accompaniment of music.

Songs

Many of Shakespeare's songs are very appropriate to the scene in which they occur and also to the meaning of the play as a whole.

Example

In one scene of *Twelfth Night* the drunken Sir Toby and Sir Andrew ask the clown, Feste, for a song. He sings a plaintive one about love, which includes these lines:

> In delay there lies no plenty,
> Then come kiss me, sweet and twenty.
> Youth's a stuff will not endure.

The words are sadly appropriate to the listeners; both are getting old, and Sir Andrew, in spite of his wooing of Olivia, is unlikely to find a wife. There is no 'plenty' at all in his 'delay'. And beyond this scene, the play enforces the idea that, because youth will not endure, happiness must be taken while it offers itself. When Olivia falls in love, she is determined to have the man whom she loves (she does not know it is Viola), and when Sebastian is approached by her, he seizes the opportunity to wed her. And even Feste, although he does not fall in love, takes every opportunity to earn money by his singing. The words of the song are thus deeply appropriate to the whole play.

- **Whenever you find dance, music or song in Shakespeare, you should ask yourself:**

● Does it tell us anything about the meaning of the scene or the play as a whole?

You will find that they are conventions that reveal to you the significance of the action.

11.12   Action within action

Occasionally, a playwright frames an action by placing it within another. In Shakespeare there is the example of *The Taming of the Shrew*, in which the two scenes of the Induction act as an introduction to the play of Kate the Shrew and Petruchio, the man who marries her. In the Induction, a Lord tricks a drunken tinker called Christopher Sly into believing that he is really a Lord. The play about Kate and Petruchio is performed to entertain Sly, but after a few exchanges, Sly is written out of the play, and we hear no more of him.

There are two things that need to be said about action within action.

(1)   **There is usually a link between the frame and the main action.**   In both the Induction and the main action in *The Taming of the Shrew*, there is an emphasis upon sport and trickery. This is clearly important in establishing the mood of the play. Also, the play turns on the issue of identity – is Sly a Lord and is Kate really a Shrew? – so there is a thematic link between the two parts.

(2)   **Action within action in Shakespeare tells us something about his dramatic art.**   Shakespeare is aware of his own art in virtually every play he wrote. It's interesting to observe that he frequently uses an image drawn from the theatre, even, as in *Macbeth*, at the climax of the play. He is also interested in scenes in which characters are entertained by plays; this happens in *Hamlet* and *The Tempest*. This discloses one of Shakespeare's central themes – the link between life and the stage. In his plays the men and women are, as Jaques says in *As You Like It*, 'players', and their actions can be likened to the acts that are seen upon a stage.

___ Exercises _____

11.1   Below is Act I Scene 4 of *Twelfth Night*. Read the scene carefully and answer the following questions on it.

Viola has disguised herself as a young man – Cesario – and is serving in the court of Orsino, the Duke. He is in love with Olivia, but she does not welcome his attentions because of the recent death of her brother.

A room in the Duke's palace
[*Enter Valentine, and Viola in man's attire*]

Valentine: If the Duke continue these favours towards you, Cesario, you are like to be much advanced. He hath known you but three days, and already you are no stranger.

Viola: You either fear his humour or my negligence, that you call in question the continuance of his love. Is he inconstant, sir, in his favours?

Valentine: No, believe me.

Viola: I thank you. Here comes the Count.

[*Enter Duke, Curio and attendants*]

Duke: Who saw Cesario, ho!   10

Viola: On your attendance, my lord, here.

Duke: Stand you awhile aloof ... [*Curio and attendants withdraw*]
    Cesario,
    Thou knowest no less but all: I have unclasped
    To thee the book even of my secret soul.
    Therefore, good youth, address thy gait unto her,
    Be not denied access, stand at her doors,
    And tell them, there thy fixed foot shall grow
    Till thou have audience.

Viola: Sure, my noble lord,
    If she be so abandoned to her sorrow
    As it is spoke, she never will admit me.   20

Duke: Be clamorous and leap all civil bounds
    Rather than make unprofited return.

Viola: Say I do speak with her, my lord, what then?

Duke: O, then unfold the passion of my love,
    Surprise her with discourse of my dear faith:
    It shall become thee well to act my woes;
    She will attend it better in thy youth
    Than in a nuncio's of more grave aspect.

Viola: I think not so, my lord.

Duke: Dear lad, believe it;
    For they shall yet belie thy happy years,   30
    That say thou art a man: Diana's lip
    Is not more smooth and rubious; thy small pipe
    Is as the maiden's organ, shrill and sound –
    And all is semblative a woman's part.
    I know thy constellation is right apt
    For this affair. Some four or five attend him,
    All if you will; for I myself am best
    When least in company. Prosper well in this,
    And thou shalt live as freely as thy lord,
    To call his fortunes thine.   40

Viola: I'll do my best,

> To woo your lady. [*aside*] Yet, a barful strife!
> Whoe'er I woo, myself would be his wife.

(a)   Why is the scene up to the entrance of the Duke in prose?
(b)   Try to account for why some characters use 'you' and others 'thou'.
(c)   Bearing in mind that the audience knows Viola is disguised as a man but that Orsino does not know this, write about the way Orsino speaks to Viola in the speech beginning 'Dear lad, believe it...' (line 29).
(d)   What is the effect of the aside at the end of the scene?

11.2   Look at the plays you are studying to see if their construction tells you anything about their meaning. If any of them are by Shakespeare, see if act three scene one or two is the turning point of a two-fold movement.

11.3   Look at how verse and prose are used in the plays you are studying. Can you say why the playwright has used one or the other?

11.4   Write about any conventions of action such as a chorus, disguise or music that are used in the plays you are studying.

12 The language of drama

12.1 Language and dramatic action

All literary works employ conventions; in this respect drama is no different from poetry or novels. All literary works also make meanings with words. But this raises a question:

● What is distinctive about the language of drama?

Poetry uses words in verse, and novels use them in prose. Since drama uses both, is it enough to say that an understanding of verse and prose is all that is needed to understand drama?

It is true that the poetry used in drama can be looked at in the way Part I suggests poetry can be studied, and some of the things said in Part II on novels apply to drama, but more is needed. Drama is not something just read or heard, it is acted out before an audience. It follows that there must be something about the language of drama that makes it different from non-dramatic poetry or prose. The difference can be put this way:

The language of drama suggests or invites action.

The words of a play should invite embodiment in action. When, therefore, you read a play you should ask this question:

● in what ways do these words invite us to act them out?

The answer to that question usually comes in three ways.

(1) They invite actors to make movements.
(2) They indicate the mood of the scene.
(3) They suggest grouping on stage.

12.2 Language and movement

Of any play you can always ask this question:

● Do these words invite movement?

Of course, most of them don't, but if no words at all do, the play will be undramatic.

- Sometimes the words of a play invite a specific gesture.

Example

In *Twelfth Night* Viola, disguised as Cesario, goes to see Olivia. Olivia is wearing a veil, but the bold Viola asks: 'Good Madam, let me see your face,' Olivia is a little shocked, but she agrees:

> . . . but we will draw the curtain, and show you the picture. Look you, sir, such a one I was this present: is't not well done?

Olivia employs the image of a curtain hanging before a picture; the picture is her face, and the curtain her veil. The words invite the actress to lift the veil. At the word 'draw' she could take hold of the veil, start to lift it at 'show', and by the time she says 'Look you' her face must be visible.

- **Sometimes the words make a wide range of actions possible.**

Most of the speeches that invite action are more complex in that, though it is clear the words need to be acted out, a wide range of actions carried out in a number of ways are possible. It is important for you to remember this. Shakespeare is not asking actors to behave mechanically; his words need to be given bodily expression, but in most cases a variety of movements and gestures are appropriate. This is why the plays act so well, and why new productions are always possible; the words ask to be acted out but leave the actor free as to exactly how it should be done.

Example

At the end of *Henry IV part II* Falstaff, the riotous companion of the youthful Prince Hal, hears that the old king is dead and that, consequently, Hal is the new monarch. Overjoyed with the news, he and Pistol rush to London to greet the new king in the expectation that their life of drunken merriment will continue. As Hal goes by, Falstaff confidently greets him from the crowd:

> *Falstaff*: God save thy grace, King Hal! my royal Hal!
> *Pistol*: The heavens thee guard and keep, most royal imp of fame!
> *Falstaff*: God save thee, my sweet boy!
> *King*: My lord chief justice, speak to that vain man.
> *Lord Chief Justice*: Have you your wits? Know you what 'tis you speak?
> *Falstaff*: My king! my Jove! I speak to thee, my heart!

King: I know thee not, old man. Fall to thy prayers.
How ill white hairs become a fool and jester!
I have long dreamed of such a kind of man,
So surfeit-swelled, so old, and so profane;
But, being awaked, I do despise my dream.
Make less thy body hence, and more thy grace,
Leave gormandizing, know the grave doth gape
For thee thrice wider than for other men.
Reply not to me with a fool-born jest,
Presume not that I am the thing I was,
For God doth know, so shall the world perceive,
That I have turned away my former self;
So will I those that kept me company.

The curt order 'Fall to thy prayers' tells the actor who is playing Falstaff what to do. The action is in the words – he must fall to the ground. It is as if a stage direction has been incorporated into the text of the play. It is, however, up to the actor as to *how* he falls. Does he immediately kneel, or does he stand in a state of shock and then slowly crumple, one knee at a time, to the ground? Does he fall to the ground himself, or does he need the help of Pistol? And how does Hal deliver the line? Does he point to the ground or does he move forward and force Falstaff to grovel before him?

There are other words that invite movement but don't specify what it should be. There could be a gesture in the words about Falstaff's 'white hairs'. Does the king gesture to the crowd to attend to him and then point to the head of the man who is pathetically kneeling before him? When he speaks of dreaming 'of such a kind of man', is he talking confidentially to the Chief Justice, publicly to the crowd, or reproachfully to the fallen Falstaff? Whichever way the actor chooses, there will be appropriate gestures; he could place his hand upon the Chief Justice's arm, extend his arm to the crowd, or point an accusing finger at his former friend.

The line 'Reply not to me with a fool-born jest' also offers interesting opportunities to the actor. Does the king see that Falstaff is about to speak? If so, does he make a dismissive gesture as he delivers the words, indicating that the humiliated Falstaff must not even open his mouth? Or does he angrily step forward and shout at Falstaff while gesturing towards himself at the words 'to me'?

The lines about God and all the world knowing and perceiving surely invite Hal to make gestures expansive enough to match the huge claim that he is making, and the words 'I have turn'd away my former self' could be accompanied by a sharp turn, a gesture of putting something behind him, or a movement to a different place on the stage.

12.3   Language and movement: the meaning of plays

Some of the actions suggested by the words have more than a particular importance. Words can invite actions which are significant for the whole meaning of the play. This, in fact, is true of the above scene. Throughout *Henry IV Parts 1 and 2* there is a tension between the need for order in society and the necessity – and pleasure – of games. Henry IV himself is worried that his son seems to spend all his time in the pursuit of pleasure and fears what the country will be like when Hal becomes king. The dismissive gestures which put Falstaff in his place are, therefore, central to the meaning of the play; when Falstaff falls to his knees, we know that Hal is a changed man, and that law, justice and order will not be neglected in England.

Another example of an action which reveals something central to the meaning of a play is to be found in *Macbeth*.

Example

Macbeth is given a soliloquy before he kills Duncan. Left alone, his mind starts to play tricks on him. In the air, or upon a table, he thinks that he sees a dagger. Aware that he might be having an hallucination, he questions its reality:

> Is this a dagger, which I see before me,
> The handle towards my hand? Come, let me clutch thee –
> I have thee not, and yet I see thee still.

Those words invite the actor to reach out for what Macbeth thinks is before him. It is a dramatic moment; Macbeth either grasps the air, or, if the director wishes, he can place his hand firmly on the table to find nothing but its hard surface.

But the moment has significance beyond the scene; Macbeth is a man who wants things. Earlier, when the witches have finished speaking, he demands to know more: 'Stay, you imperfect speakers, tell me more.' And later, when he has become king, he longs to know more about the future. Above all, Macbeth wants the throne. Just as he clutches desperately at the imaginary dagger so he burns with desire for the throne of Scotland. In short, the dramatic gesture of reaching out reveals the very nature of the man and the central theme of the play – Macbeth is a bold, ambitious and ruthless man who clutches at those things he wants.

12.4   Language and movement in non-Shakespearian drama

It is one of the very important features of Shakespeare's dramatic writing that there are movements in the words. What, however, of the other plays you are likely to find in public examinations?

If you look at post-Shakespearian drama, you will find the words dramatists use still invite action, although it might not be quite so striking. Let us look at some examples.

Examples

Example 1

In the opening scene of Congreve's *The Way of the World*, Mirabell and Fainall are rising from the card table. Fainall has been winning but he does not take up Mirabell's suggestion to 'play on to entertain you'. This is part of what Fainall says:

> No, I'll give you your revenge another time, when you are not so indifferent; you are thinking of something else now, and play too negligently; the coldness of a losing gamester lessens the pleasure of a winner.

Is there a light, dismissive gesture in the opening 'No', and could the words 'when you are not so indifferent' suggest that Fainall either leans forward or points his finger for emphasis? His remark that Mirabell is 'thinking of something else now' could be accompanied by a pointed finger or a wide sweep of the arm to suggest that thoughts are elsewhere. The final remark about 'the coldness of a losing gamester' might be said with a small flourish associated with words which have the self-evident truth of a proverb – the kind of gesture that is made when the speaker is effectively saying, 'we all know that'.

Congreve's words, then, do suggest movement, although it is not dramatic or even immediately obvious. Yet that is appropriate; Congreve is writing about characters who are rich and leisured, but who do not lead momentous lives like kings and queens.

Example 2

The second example is from a modern play, *A Man for all Seasons*. At one point Sir Thomas More deliberately picks a quarrel with the Duke of Norfolk. He shows that the nobility of England, because they have given in to the king, are men without honour. More, however, will not give in. This is part of the speech, including Robert Bolt's stage direction:

> Well, as a spaniel is to water so is a man to his own self. I will not give in because I oppose it – *I* do – not my pride, not my spleen, nor any other of my appetites but *I* do – *I*. [*He goes up to him and feels him up and down like an animal*]. Is there no single sinew in the midst of this that serves no appetite of Norfolk's but is, just, Norfolk? There is! Give *that* some exercise my lord!

> Bolt's stage direction is unnecessary; it is clear from the words that More
> must feel, or playfully thump, Norfolk as he speaks these lines. And in the
> words before it is clear that the emphasised 'I's must be accompanied by a
> gesture indicating More's true, inner self; perhaps he points towards his
> heart with both hands, or places one of his hands, palm down, in the centre
> of his chest.

The gestures in Congreve and Bolt are much weaker than in Shakespeare, yet
they are there. In some plays, however, the words don't suggest action. In Tom
Stoppard's *Rosencrantz and Guildenstern are Dead* some actions are given in
stage directions, and one character, the player, is given words that invite sweeping, theatrical gestures, but the two main characters entertain the audience not by
embodying words in actions but by the rapid and witty nature of their dialogue.

Example

Near the end of the play they discover that Hamlet, whom they are taking
to England, will be executed on arrival. This is what Guildenstern says
about this:

> Let us keep things in proportion. Assume, if you like, that they're going
> to kill him. Well, he is a man, he is mortal, death comes to us all,
> etcetera, and consequently he would have died anyway, sooner or later.
> Or to look at it from the social point of view – he's just one man among
> many, the loss would be well within reason and convenience. And then
> again, what is so terrible about death?

It is difficult to see that those words are dramatic in the sense defined
above. Of course, it is possible for an actor to invent accompanying actions,
but that is different from the words suggesting or inviting movement. The
words are entertaining, because a man trying to be rational about death is
likely to sound absurd, but it is hard to see them requiring performance.
Some think this is a fault; others say that an audience should just enjoy the
wit of the words. You should make up your own mind, remembering that
the theatre offers a variety of pleasures – big actions and clever dialogue –
but bearing in mind that unless dramatic language is in some way distinctive it fails to be dramatic at all.

12.5   Language and mood

An important characteristic of dramatic language is the way it indicates the
mood of a scene. It does this, so to speak, by incorporating stage directions into
the dialogue.

Quite often in Shakespeare at moments of high tension a character will remark upon how a speech has been delivered. Such remarks, of course, direct the actor to deliver the lines in a particular way. Let us look at two examples.

Examples

Example 1

In *Much Ado about Nothing*, the young soldier, Claudio, who is to marry Hero, has been deceived into believing that she has been unfaithful to him before marriage. Claudio decides to denounce her at the wedding. This is from the speech he delivers before he leaves the church:

> O Hero, what a hero hadst thou been,
> If half thy outward graces had been placed
> About thy thoughts and counsels of thy heart!
> But fare thee well, most foul, most fair! farewell,
> Thou pure impiety and impious purity!

Claudio, who is deeply puzzled and angry, delivers these emotional words to the girl whom he once loved. Many readers have been shocked by their unfeeling harshness. He accuses her of being utterly deceitful and goes so far as to use the word 'foul' of her. If, however, the reader looks at the later part of the scene, something interesting emerges. Leonato, who is heartbroken, speaks of *how* the lines were delivered:

> speaking of her foulness
> Washed it with tears.

That indicates both how the lines should be delivered and how distressed Claudio is. The reader, therefore, should remember that though the words are harsh, they come from a man who weeps as he speaks. The emotional mood is one of distress and regret, as well as outrage.

Example 2

In *Othello* there is a highly dramatic scene in which Othello, convinced that his wife has been unfaithful, enters her bedroom with the intention of killing her. But, like Claudio, his mood is not a simple one. He is outraged by her imagined adultery but, at the same time, he is overwhelmed by her beauty and his love for her. The actor playing Othello must portray a man suffering the terrible tension between loathing and love. In order to indicate the mood of the scene and manner in which the actor should deliver the lines, Shakespeare gives these lines to Desdemona:

> And yet I fear you, for you are fatal then,
> When your eyes roll so . . .
>
> Alas, why gnaw you so your nether lip?
> Some bloody passion shakes your very frame.

These lines are directions to the actor built into the text; he must roll his eyes, gnaw his bottom lip and shake. Those are the outward expressions of the terrible emotional conflict that is consuming Othello.

12.6   Language and grouping

A very important characteristic of dramatic language is its ability to indicate how actors should be grouped upon stage. If the above point about language and mood can be looked upon as instruction to actors, this point can be seen as advice to directors.

In Shakespeare there are no detailed stage directions telling a director where to place and group actors. All the director has – and all you have – is the text of the play. Once a play is looked at in detail, it is apparent that Shakespeare built into the language of his plays directions on where to stand. You will find that these directions do much more than tell you where actors might stand, they bring out the significance of the action. Let us look at two examples.

___ Examples _____

Example 1

Richard II is about the fall of one king, Richard, and the rise of another, Henry IV. At the start of the play Richard banishes Henry, but after Richard has seized the property of Henry's dead father, Henry returns to England with an army. They meet first at Flint Castle; Richard is inside, Henry outside with his army. The text of the play makes it clear that Henry and his army should be placed on the stage, whilst Richard should be on a balcony above it. This is what Henry says:

> See, see, King Richard doth himself appear,
> As doth the blushing discontented sun
> From out the fiery portals of the east ...

The gesture in the words 'See, see' and the image of the sun both point to Richard being in a physically higher position than Henry. The picture is at once glorious and troubled. The rising sun is a majestic image expressive of hope, yet the sun is blushing and discontented.

As the scene develops, it is the troubled aspect of the image that dominates. Richard, the sun king, sees that he can't resist Henry so he agrees to descend. Using the image of the mythical Phaeton, who guided the sun across the sky, Richard descends to the level of Henry. The words 'Down, down I come' express one of the central actions of the play. Richard's fortunes are declining, so his descent from a higher to a lower level is symbolic of his fall. The words not only indicate position on stage but also invite the actor to perform an action which is central to the meaning of the play.

Example 2

In Act II, Scene 1 of *The Winter's Tale* Shakespeare indicates how characters should group themselves. This grouping, as we shall see, is expressive of the mood of the scene. Hermione, the Queen, is shortly to have a baby. It is, therefore, not surprising that she does not want to play with her lively son, Mamillius. The grouping of the scene is immediately suggested in the first words from Hermione:

> Take the boy to you: he so troubles me,
> 'Tis past enduring.

She is speaking to her attendant ladies. One of them replies by inviting Mamillius to join them:

> Come my gracious Lord,
> Shall I be your playfellow.

The conversation that follows shows that Mamillius has left his mother and is sitting with the ladies. There are, thus, two groups: Hermione, and the ladies. When Hermione feels she is ready to play with Mamillius again she calls him from the ladies:

> Come, sir, now
> I am for you again: pray you, sit by us,
> And tell's a tale.

There follows a delightful dialogue between Hermione and her son. He says he will tell a tale of 'sprites and goblins', but from his mother's next remark, 'Nay, come, sit down, then on', it is clear that he is not sitting next to her. Then he says he doesn't want the ladies to hear the tale, so Hermione says:

> Come on, then
> And give't me in mine ear.

It may be assumed that after that line there are two groups on the stage: Hermione with her son, and the ladies. But Mamillius's story gets no further. Leontes, believing that Hermione has committed adultery with Polixenes, bursts into the room with a group of lords. This creates a third group. He demands the boy and tells the lords to

> Bear the boy hence, he shall not come about her;
> Away with him!

It is clear from the dialogue that follows that there are three groups on stage: the angry Leontes and his lords, the ladies, and the now isolated Hermione. The loneliness of Hermione is brought out in the language of Leontes. There is surely a condemnatory gesture in these lines spoken to the lords:

> You, my lords,
> Look on her, mark her well . . .

All eyes are directed at her lonely figure. The women are of no comfort to her; indeed, so overcome are they that it is Hermione who has to comfort them:

> Do not weep, good fools,
> There is no cause . . .

Her words are moving. In spite of her increasing loneliness, she comforts her weeping attendants. Soon they are all dismissed.

The sudden change from light-hearted merriment to anger and the increasing isolation of Hermione are all expressed in the groupings suggested by the words. The grouping, therefore, can be said to express the emotional mood of the scene.

Whenever you have to write in detail about a scene from Shakespeare (there are questions on individual scenes at both GCSE/A level), you should follow the practice outlined above of seeing how Shakespeare groups characters by indicating their positions in the words of the play.

A good question to ask of any scene is:

- Are there indications in the words of where characters stand?

It is not sufficient just to mention groups. You should go on to show that the grouping suggested by the words is expressive of the mood and meaning of the scene, or even the play as a whole.

___ **Exercises** _____

12.1   Read the following extract from Act II Scene 3 of *Twelfth Night* and
       answer the questions below. Sir Toby Belch, Sir Andrew Aguecheek
       and the Clown (Feste) are drinking and singing until late into the
       night. Maria, a servant, has been trying to stop them making so
       much noise, but the din they have been making has awoken the stern
       steward, Malvolio. At this moment, a song has just finished, and Sir
       Toby addresses the outraged Malvolio.

   Sir Toby: . . . Art any more than a steward? Dost thou think because
      thou art virtuous, there shall be no more cakes and ale?
   Clown: Yes, by Saint Anne, and ginger shall be hot i'th' mouth too.
   Sir Toby: Th'art i'th' right. Go, sir, rub you chain with crumbs. A
      stoup of wine, Maria!
   Malvolio: Mistress Mary, if you prized my lady's favour at any
      thing more than contempt, you would not give means for this
      uncivil rule; she shall know of it, by this hand.

                                                                  [*Exit*]

   Maria: Go shake your ears.

   What actions and groupings do these words suggest? You might like
   to think about how the following lines could be acted:

   (a)   'Art any more than a steward?'
   (b)   'Th'art i'th' right. Go, sir, rub your chain with crumbs.'
   (c)   ' . . . she shall know of it, by this hand.'
   (d)   'Go shake your ears.'

12.2   Read these two extracts from Goldsmith's *She Stoops to Conquer* and
       answer the questions below. In the first, Mrs Hardcastle is complain-
       ing about the life they lead in their old mansion and Mr Hardcastle is
       defending it. In the second, Mr Hardcastle is talking to his servant
       about how they should serve at table when their important guests dine.

   Mrs Hardcastle: Ay, your times were fine times, indeed; you have
      been telling us of them for many a year. Here we live in an old
      rambling mansion, that looks for all the world like an inn, but that
      we never see company. Our best visitors are old Mrs Oddfish, the
      curate's wife, and little Cripplegate, the lame dancing-master: and
      all our entertainment your old stories of Prince Eugene and the
      Duke of Marlborough. I hate such old-fashioned trumpery.
   Mr Hardcastle: And I love it. I love everything that's old: old friends,
      old times, old manners, old books, old wine; and, I believe,
      Dorothy, you'll own I have been pretty fond of an old wife.

> *Mr Hardcastle*: You, Diggory, whom I have taken from the barn, are to make a shew at the side-table; and you, Roger, whom I have advanced from the plough, are to place yourself behind my chair. But you're not to stand so, with your hands in your pockets, Roger; and from your head, you blockhead, you. See how Diggory carries his hands. They're little too stiff, indeed, but that's no great matter.

What actions and groupings do these words suggest? In the first extract, you might like to think about how the following lines could be acted:

(a) 'Here we live in an old rambling mansion …'
(b) '… and all our entertainment your old stories of Prince Eugene and the Duke of Marlborough.'
(c) 'And I love it.'

In the second extract, you might like to think about how the following lines could be acted:

(a) 'You, Diggory, whom I have taken from the barn …'
(b) '… are to place yourself behind my chair.'
(c) 'But you're not to stand so . . .'
(d) 'See how Diggory carries his hands.'

13 Character and plot

13.1 Characters and words

Many of the questions on drama in public examinations deal with character. They ask you to:

- say what a character is like
- show how he or she changes
- discuss the way one character differs from another
- judge the importance of a character in the plays as a whole

What, then, can you say about characters?
The most important thing to remember is this:

You can only learn about a character from the words of the play.

This means that your sources of information are dialogue, soliloquy and, in certain special cases, stage directions. A playwright, unlike a novelist, can't tell you things directly. When we look at the words of a play we see four ways in which characters are created:

(1) the way they speak
(2) what they say about themselves
(3) what they say about each other
(4) how they are contrasted.

13.2 Characters and speech

The most important point about character in drama is this:

What makes a character distinctive is the way in which he or she speaks.

This means that you can always ask:

- Do these characters speak in an individual way?

For instance, characters might speak in very short sentences, they might repeat words, they might speak formally, they might say a lot or a little, and so on. Let's look at some examples.

— **Example** ———————————————————————————

In Bernard Shaw's *St. Joan*, Joan goes to see Charles, the Dauphin, to tell him that she has a mission to drive the English from France and have him crowned in Rheims Cathedral:

> *Joan:* Gentle little Dauphin, I am sent to you to drive the English away from Orleans and from France, and to crown you in the cathedral at Rheims, where all true kings of France are crowned.
>
> *Charles:* [*triumphant to the court*] You see, all of you! She knew the blood royal. Who dare say now that I am not my father's son? [*To Joan*] But if you want me to be crowned at Rheims, you must talk to the Archbishop, not to me. There he is [*he is standing behind her*]!
>
> *Joan:* [*turning quickly, overwhelmed with emotion*] Oh, my lord! [*She falls on both knees before him, with bowed head, not daring to look up.*] My lord: I am only a poor country girl; and you are filled with the blessedness and glory of God himself; but you will touch me with your hands, and give me your blessing, won't you?

How does Joan's speech reveal her character? Look at her first words: 'Gentle little Dauphin'. There is kindness and simplicity in that expression. There is also simplicity in the rest of that speech, yet it is a simplicity which is direct and purposeful. Look, for instance, at the way in which one difficult task directly leads to another; she will drive the English from France *and* (the task is as simple as uttering that ordinary word) crown him at Rheims. Her directness and simplicity are also evident when she speaks to the Archbishop. Look at the confidence behind her request for a blessing. In a few lines, then, Shaw has shown Joan to be kind, simple, direct and purposeful.

He also gives the Dauphin words that reveal his character. Look at the childish glee with which he says: 'You see, all of you! She knew the blood royal.' Those are the words of a man who feels he has to assert himself. But he is also something of a coward. After that outburst, he pathetically tells her she should speak to the Archbishop about the coronation. From his one speech we can see that he lacks confidence and is cowardly.

——

The second example is from Shakespeare. Alexander Pope, the eighteenth-century poet, said that even if all the names of Shakespeare's characters were to be lost, it would still be possible to work out who said what. His point was that Shakespeare gives each of his characters a unique way of speaking. Although there are some servants and messengers who don't seem to have any individuality, the point is generally true. If you want to know what a character in Shakespeare is like, look at the words he or she speaks.

Example

In *Hamlet* there is a character called Polonius. He is the chief minister of
state, who claims that he is very good at finding things out. At one point he
explains to the king and queen that he has found out why Hamlet is behaving strangely:

> My liege and madam, to expostulate
> What majesty should be, what duty is,
> Why day is day, night night, and time time,
> Were nothing but to waste night, day and time.
> Therefore, since brevity is the soul of wit,
> And tediousness the limbs and outward flourishes,
> I will be brief. Your noble son is mad.
> Mad I call it, for to define true madness,
> What is't but to be nothing else but mad?

What do these lines reveal about Polonius? It is clear he is a busy man,
whose mind overflows with ideas. Look at the examples he gives: majesty,
duty, day, night and time. Notice, too, that he is liable to become confused.
The order changes from day, night and time to night, day and time.

When he comes to the point he says he will be brief, but here another
characteristic emerges: his practice contradicts his intention. Instead of
coming to the point he elaborates the metaphor. He moves from 'wit' (it
means intelligence) to talk of 'limbs'. At last, he makes his point: 'Your
noble son is mad'. But he feels that needs elaborating, so in two further
lines he explains that to be mad means to be mad! We can see, then, what
Polonius is like. He is busy, energetic, and his mind is full of ideas, but he
is easily confused, frequently contradicts himself, and is given to repetition.

13.3   Characters on themselves

Occasionally, a character says something about him or herself. It is therefore
useful to ask:

• Do any of the characters comment on themselves?

Clearly, there are cases when a character is deceived or is trying to deceive
others, so you will have to be careful. The easiest thing to do is compare what
they say with how they act. A character such as Willy Loman can be quickly
seen to be inconsistent and lacking in self-knowledge, but Shakespeare's
Richard III announces in his opening soliloquy that he's going to be a villain,
and that's exactly what he proves to be. Shakespeare, in fact, makes good use of
the convention of dramatic self-disclosure.

Example

For instance, in *The Winter's Tale*, Hermione says this of herself:

> I am not prone to weeping, as our sex
> Commonly are; the want of which vain dew,
> Perchance shall dry your pities: but I have
> That honourable grief lodged here, which burns
> Worse than tears drown.

The speech reveals a great deal about her. She has been accused of adultery and treason but she remains calm. She is aware the onlookers might judge her harshly, so she tells them it is not in her character to weep, although deep within her there is the terrible, burning pain of grief. The lines are important; Hermione is noble, self-controlled and strong yet she seems to lack warmth. Her speech helps us to see that though outwardly rather cold she is someone who can be deeply hurt.

13.4   Characters speaking about each other

This is the third way of establishing character – what one character says about another. You can ask:

- Do characters make comments upon other characters?

When the Common Man in *A Man for all Seasons* speaks directly to the audience about Sir Thomas More, we believe him because he is acting as a chorus. When Biff in *Death of a Salesman* says that Willy was 'never anything but a hard-working drummer who landed in the ash-can', we believe him, because everything in the play points to the sad truth of that statement. In *King Lear* a gentleman says of Cordelia that she

> redeems nature from the general curse
> Which twain have brought her to.

Although it is only one view, everything in the play confirms the truth of his words.

However, one character's speech about another can express no more than an individual point of view. One of the problems in *Antony and Cleopatra* is whether Antony is a great lover or a once great man infatuated by a wily woman. This view is given right at the beginning of the play when Philo calls him:

> The triple pillar of the world transformed
> Into a strumpet's fool. . .

To Philo he was a great soldier and statesman who is reduced to playing around with a woman who is no more than a prostitute ('strumpet'). It would be foolish both to accept or reject that view until the play has been studied in great detail.

● You should, then, attend to what one character says about another, but always ask whether or not it is true.

13.5 Characters contrasted

Examination questions are often built around the fact that some playwrights deliberately contrast one character with another in order to bring out what each is like. It's always worthwhile asking:

● Are any of the characters in this play contrasted?

The contrasts can be of different kinds. Some characters are contrasted because they have a lot in common, others because they are very different. For all their differences, Brutus and Cassius share many ideals, whereas, to pick an extreme example, Ariel and Caliban in *The Tempest* are opposite to each other in almost every way.

It is important to understand why the playwright contrasts characters. Usually a contrast brings out something important about the meaning of the play as a whole.

Example

The vivid contrast between 'Captain' Jack Boyle and Juno Boyle in Sean O'Casey's *Juno and the Paycock* brings out the difference between those who never face tragedy and those who do. Jack is idle, irresponsible and concerned with little else but drink, whereas Juno is sensible, determined and sensitive to the terrible times through which they are living. The contrast between them is brought out in their attitudes to the 'political' killings. Jack dismisses them as nothing to do with him:

'That's the Government's business, an' let them do what we're payin' them for doin'.

But Juno thinks otherwise: 'Sure, if it's not our business, I don't know whose business it is.' The contrast in their attitudes is focused in the difference between Jack's 'them' and Juno's 'us'; he shuffles off responsibility, she sees it as theirs.

● **Whenever you write about contrasts between characters, you should examine how their language creates differences.**

You should then be able to show that these differences, as in the case of *Juno and the Paycock*, are central to the play's meaning. O'Casey is concerned with how people react to the troubles of the civil war: Jack ignores them, whereas Juno chooses to face the horror and recognise her responsibility.

13.6   Characters without distinctive personalities

The discussion above has shown that the four ways of creating character can be used as approaches to the study of character. Sometimes, however, you may not be able to discover characters who have distinctive personalities. There may be three reasons for this.

(1)   They could be 'stock' characters
(2)   They may change to serve the plot
(3)   The playwright may not be interested in them as personalities at all.

Let us examine each of these.

The stock character

A stock character in a play is like a flat character in a novel; that is, someone who has only one or two features rather than being fully rounded. One of the conventions of English drama is that there are a number of stock characters whom the audience can recognise. Here are some:

- the bashful lover
- the domineering wife
- the henpecked husband
- the lovesick young man
- the bold girl who will go to any lengths to get a husband
- the stern father who will not allow his daughter to marry
- the clever servant who gets his dim-witted master out of trouble
- the revenger who seeks to right wrong by murder
- the malcontent who shuns and is shunned by society
- the fop who follows fashion
- the rake who leads a riotous life
- the fool
- the jester who is clever and witty
- the soldier who boasts about his deeds
- the melancholy man who is never cheerful
- the priest who thinks up a clever plan to put everything right.

Let us look at an example.

─ **Example** ───────────────────────────

The plot of *She Stoops to Conquer* requires that Marlow is a bashful lover, who is overcome with shyness when he meets the girl he wishes to court. Hardcastle says that he is 'one of the most bashful and reserved young fellows in the world'. That is Goldsmith's way of preparing the audience. When Marlow is left with Kate Hardcastle, he never looks up, and speaks hesitantly. But it is also part of the convention of the bashful lover that he is bold with serving women. Kate, therefore, has to dress as one in order to attract his attentions. She is not disappointed. Marlow never does anything unexpected; Goldsmith makes him conform to the stock figure of the bashful lover. There is, then, no need to say anything about his character other than that he conforms to the convention of a stock theatrical type.

───

● **In the case of Shakespeare, you will have to be careful:** many of his characters have, as it were, grown from stock types, but in their growing they have developed an individuality that makes them distinctive.

Orlando in *As You Like It* is a bashful lover but he also vigorously defends Rosalind to others, is quick-witted when talking to Jaques, has a strong sense of family loyalty, is kind to his old servant, and, when roused, has a temper. None of these qualities are part of the conventional bashful lover.

Even a character such as Brabantio in *Othello*, who comes very close to the stock figure of the angry father who won't let his daughter marry, is given an unexpected depth of feeling. At the end of the play it is revealed that he was so distressed by his daughter's marriage that he died of grief. When the audience knows that, it sees him not just as the conventionally angry father but as a man of deep feeling.

Characters who change to serve the plot

Sometimes characters are made to do a number of things in order to help the progress of the plot. The result is that when you study them, you find they don't make sense as individuals. The phrase that is often used of them is 'psychological inconsistency'. The point, however, is that they are consistent in a *dramatic* sense, not a psychological one. Quite often such characters don't cause problems in the theatre; it's only when the play is studied that their psychological inconsistency is noticed.

─ **Example** ───────────────────────────

Shakespeare uses the Duke in *Measure for Measure* to do a number of things: he leaves Vienna, gives power to a young lawyer called Angelo, returns in disguise, prepares for death a man who has been condemned by Angelo, works out a plan to save the young man from death, helps Mariana to take the place in bed of Isabella, a young nun with whom Angelo wishes to sleep, and, at the end, stages his return, exposes Angelo and marries Isabella.

It is difficult to make consistent psychological sense of the Duke. (For instance, since the Duke knew that Angelo had refused to marry Mariana because her dowry was too low, why did he leave such an untrustworthy person in charge?) But we don't have to. Shakespeare is using the Duke to serve the demands of the plot. His interest in him can be said to be opportunist; that is, he uses him to do very many different jobs as the opportunities arise. Without him the plot would not work.

Symbolic figures

The third reason why you may not be able to find characters in a play is that there aren't any! Instead of characters a dramatist may create symbolic figures or mouthpieces for ideas.

___ **Example** ___

Marlowe's Dr Faustus is more of a symbolic figure than a character. It is true that he is proud, adventurous and self-centred, but these don't give him a personality. Rather, they are symbolic of human pride, discontent and selfishness. At the end of the play the chorus invites the audience to see him not as a particular character but as an example from which to learn:

> Regard his hellish fall,
> Whose fiendful fortune may exhort the wise
> Only to wonder at unlawful things,
> Whose deepness does entice such forward wits,
> To practise more than heavenly power permits.

The language sets him forward as an example. The audience is to 'regard' his fall, which will 'exhort the wise' to only 'wonder' rather than 'practise' 'unlawful things'. Faustus is a warning to those who don't take that advice.

Oscar Wilde was interested in clever dialogue. Therefore, his 'characters' are mouthpieces for it. In *The Importance of being Earnest* the young men and women can hardly be said to have personalities. What matters about them is their dialogue.

For instance, Gwendolen says: 'I never travel without my diary. One should always have something sensational to read in the train.' That is delightfully funny because it combines a primness of manner – 'one should always ...' – with an open admission about the sensational nature of her diary.

Likewise, Jack Worthing's remark, 'It is a very ungentlemanly thing to read a private cigarette case', is funny because it links what is socially important – being a gentleman – with something as trivial as looking at the initials inside a cigarette case.

In neither case does the remark express the personality of the speaker. Wilde is interested in the wit of the dialogue not the creation of individual characters.

If you are unsure whether or not a character is a rounded individual or a stock figure, you can ask this question:

- Is it important that we know in some detail why this character does what he or she does?

If the answer is 'Yes', then the character is an individual; if 'No', then he or she is best described in terms of dramatic function.

Of course, you will have to be careful; Hamlet puzzles people about the reasons for his delay, but that's not to suggest that he's only a functional character.

13.7 Dramatic plots

As soon as you ask what a character does in a play, you are asking a question about *plot*. The plot of a play can be defined as all the actions of all the characters, and the reasons for them. But since plot has already been discussed in Chapter 9 when looking at the novel, and since many of the things said there apply to plays, there is no point in repeating them. What you should pay attention to are the different parts of dramatic plots. But before they are discussed, a question must be asked:

- Is there anything distinctive about dramatic plots?

The answer is yes. It can be put this way:

The plot must act out, or embody, what the play is about.

What makes a play a play is not its ideas, but the fact that these are presented to the audience in the words and actions of the characters. In drama, audiences not only hear about issues, they see them acted out before them.

--- **Example** ---

One of the ideas in J. M. Synge's *The Playboy of the Western World* is the Irish people's love of heroes. Synge presents a young man, Christy Mahon, who arrives in a remote part of Ireland with the story that he has murdered his father. The people regard him as a hero when they hear what he has done, because he has done what few dare to do. But Synge has to *show* the audience that this is an important element in the plot. He does this by introducing a group of girls who bring him gifts:

> *Sara:* And asking your pardon, is it you's the man killed his father?
> *Christy:* I am, God help me!
> *Sara:* Then my thousand welcomes to you, and I've run up with a brace of duck's eggs for your food to-day. Pegeen's ducks is no use, but these are a real rich sort. Hold out your hand and you'll see it's no lie I'm telling you.

Handing over gifts acts out the theme of the play. Honouring a hero is not a mere idea, it is publicly acted out in Sara's words and actions.

You can always ask this question:

- Are there moments in this play when the basic issues of the plot are acted out?

One way of thinking about this issue is to stand back, so to speak, and think of what the action of the play adds up to. Then you may be able to locate that idea in a detail of the play.

13.8   How plots begin

Drama is the most immediate and intense form of literature. It is immediate because it is performed and intense because, in most cases, it is short. At the beginning of a play, therefore, the playwright must bring the issues of the plot quickly and clearly into focus. A good question to ask about the opening of a play is:

- Can I see the plot emerging in the opening words and actions?

Terence Rattigan's *The Winslow Boy* is a good example.

Example

The play begins with Ronnie Winslow alone on the stage. He looks nervous and is very worried when he hears someone coming into the room. It is Violet, the elderly maid, who enters. She is surprised, though pleased, to see him. She sees that he is anxious, so asks: 'What's the matter with you? What have they been doing to you at Osborne?' Ronnie replies sharply: 'What do you mean?' An attentive audience will see from that that his worries are connected with the Osborne naval college, and when, a few lines later, he hears his parents and rushes into the garden, the audience will guess that he is ashamed of something. Later the entire plot of the play is brought to light – Ronnie has been expelled for stealing a postal order – but already Rattigan has made the audience aware that it must be something like that. The plot, then, emerges in the opening lines of the play.

13.9 Scenes, sub-plots

A natural question to ask of any play is:

- Why has the playwright made one particular scene follow another?

The most useful general answers to that question are these.

(1) The playwright is inviting the audience to see links between the two scenes.
(2) One scene has raised expectations that the following scene might fulfil.

Some examples will help.

Playwrights often invite audiences to see the connection between two scenes when plays have sub-plots. A *sub-plot* is a separate piece of action which is less important than the main plot; it might use a different set of characters though it could also use some from the main plot. In many cases sub-plots echo the themes of main plots, which is why playwrights invite audiences to see the connection between scenes.

___ **Examples** ___

Example 1

Dr Faustus starts with three scenes in which Faustus decides to practise black magic, summons Mephistopheles, and agrees to sell his soul in exchange for twenty-four years of pleasure. And then in the fourth scene the sub-plot is introduced: Faustus's servant, Wagner, asks a clown to wait on him and summons two devils.

The fourth scene reflects the preceding three. Both Faustus and Wagner want power and both want an assistant, and though Faustus is learned and Wagner only a servant, there is a disturbing relation between the two. The sub-plot is an ironical reflection on the main one, because although Faustus dreams of power he fritters his power away, like Wagner, on playing tricks. The two scenes show that they are not very different from each other.

Example 2

There is an interesting case of one scene raising expectations which the next fulfils in *Twelfth Night*.

At one point Viola is in a dilemma because she loves Orsino, who, in turn, loves Olivia, who, because she is misled by disguise, loves Viola. Viola can't see a way out of the problem, but in the very next scene Shakespeare introduces her twin-brother, Sebastian. When the audience learns that Sebastian, whom Viola thought was dead, looks just like her, it realises that there is somebody for Olivia to marry. The fact that Shakespeare moves so quickly from one scene to another indicates that he wants the audience to see the possibility of a happy ending; hence the quick fulfilment of expectation.

13.10   The pace of plots

If you have to answer a question on a play's hold over an audience (these questions are usually put in terms of a play's *tension* or *dramatic interest*), one of the issues you must discuss is pace.

Pace is the speed of events, and the point about it is that it always varies throughout a play. Even in Samuel Beckett's *Waiting for Godot*, a play in which two tramps wait for Godot, there are marked variations of pace, and though Godot never comes, the action changes from being quiet and leisurely to quite hectic.

There are two things to think about when considering pace:

- why pace changes
- the appropriateness of pace to action and atmosphere.

Here are two examples.

___ **Examples** _____

Example 1

In the fourth act of *Antony and Cleopatra* there are many short scenes: within the space of 280 lines soldiers hear strange noises, which they interpret as bad luck for Antony, both armies prepare for battle, the deserter Enobarbus becomes convinced of Antony's generosity and dies, a battle takes place, another battle takes place, Antony turns on Cleopatra, and Cleopatra tells her servants to inform Antony that she is dead.

After such hectic activity, the pace slows dramatically; in a scene of 140 lines Antony attempts suicide, and in another of 90 lines Antony and

Cleopatra meet for the last time, and he dies. In other words, instead of seven separate pieces of action in 280 lines, there are two in 230.

Why does Shakespeare slow down the pace? The answer is that he wants to concentrate on the death of Antony. The change from hectic activity to the simple gravity of death focuses the audience's mind and makes it see Antony's death as both touching and grand.

Example 2

The pace of the opening scenes of *Macbeth* is in keeping with the action and atmosphere of the play. Once Macbeth has met the witches, he desires the crown. Scene then follows scene at a quite relentless pace until Duncan is murdered. The pace of the play is deeply appropriate to its action and atmosphere. The Macbeths desire power, and their desire is enacted in the swift succession of short scenes. The speed of events creates a tense, concentrated atmosphere.

13.11 Expectation and surprise

Playwrights hold audiences by arousing expectations. At any point in a play, it's possible to ask:

- What expectations is the action of the play raising?

Drama appeals to something very primitive in us: we want to know what will happen next. Moreover, we want to know how it will all work out.

Expectation

That 'how' is important; not only do we want to know *what* will happen to the characters, we also want to know *how* the playwright will make it happen.

This is particularly the case in comedies. In *The Importance of being Earnest* there are two young men, neither of whom is called Ernest, who love two young women, both of whom want to marry someone called Ernest. Wilde has raised expectations that this problem will be resolved, but it is not until, at the end, he focuses attention on the governess, Miss Prism, that he sorts it out. The audience will be relieved that the problem has been resolved and will admire the skill with which Wilde has handled the plot to produce a satisfying end.

In more serious plays expectation arouses foreboding. We know that *Death of a Salesman* is not likely to end happily (the title tells us that), so as the plot unfolds, our expectations are touched with sense of oncoming disaster.

Surprise

Most plays raise expectation, but sometimes a playwright works another way –
by surprise – which, of course, is the failure to fulfil expectation. It can happen
both in the middle and at the end of a play.

Example

The first act of *The Winslow Boy* (it is a two-act play) closes with Sir
Robert Morton, a famous lawyer, interviewing Ronnie about the alleged
theft of the postal order. The Winslows hope he will agree to act as their
barrister. The pace increases as Sir Robert asks him about every detail of
the case. Ronnie becomes increasingly confused, and Sir Robert concludes
by saying he should stop wasting everybody's time and confess that he is a
liar and a thief. Ronnie runs to his mother and bursts into tears, and his
father says Sir Robert's treatment of the boy is 'outrageous'. Then, very
casually, Sir Robert asks that all the papers be sent round to his office in the
morning. Everyone is surprised (including the audience), because it had
looked as if Sir Robert believed Ronnie had stolen the postal order. But
Rattigan has a further surprise – it is the last line of the act: 'Oh, yes. The
boy is plainly innocent. I accept the brief'.

Surprises are often sprung on an audience at the end of a play. An audience
watching *The Playboy of the Western World* is surprised at the beginning of the
third act by the appearance of Christy's father, whom Christy claims to have
killed. But Synge provides more surprises. When father and son meet, Christy
again attacks his father, but this time, instead of looking upon him as a hero, the
people of the village are horrified and want to turn him over to the law. And then,
in the last minutes of the play, father appears again – battered but still alive!

13.12   Climax

A successful climax to a play should do two things:

- fulfil expectations (or overturn them by surprise)
- embody the fulfilment in dramatic action.

Example

The climax of *Measure for Measure* does both. The returned Duke
stages a kind of trial in which the crimes of Angelo are exposed.
This fulfils the expectations of the audience; throughout the play it
has seen his moral decline, and, like Isabella, demands justice.

But the play is also about mercy. The Duke insists that Angelo should die, but Isabella, although she believes Angelo has executed her brother, is persuaded to beg for mercy. In the words of the play, she lends 'a knee'; that is, she kneels and begs for the life of the man whom she thinks has wrongly condemned her brother. The point is that Shakespeare does not simply make her ask for mercy, he makes her kneel. That dramatic action embodies the theme of the play – the relation between justice and mercy. That is what all good climaxes should be like.

13.13   How plots end

There are two questions to ask about the close of a play:

- Does the close finish off the action?
- Does the end reflect the beginning?

Does the close finish off the action?

Some plays leave no questions to puzzle an audience. At the end of *The Importance of being Earnest*, for instance, it never occurs to anyone in the audience to ask whether the young couples will be happy. The play has fulfilled all its expectations so nothing is left to puzzle or intrigue the audience.

But at the end of *The Playboy of the Western World* questions remain. Christy returns with his father, though their relationship has changed, with the son now dominating. The last words of the play, like the first, are given to Pegeen, the daughter of the landlord, who has grown to love Christy:

'Oh, my grief, I've lost him surely. I've lost the only Playboy of the Western World'.

These words raise questions: will she marry the weak Shawn to whom she was engaged at the start, and if she does, will she be happy with him?

It is a good exercise to ask yourself:

- Does the end of a play finish the action completely or does it leave questions?

You will find that the more serious a play is, the more questions are left to worry you. It is usually only in the happiest, lightest and most artificial plots that the action is neatly and smoothly finished off at the end.

Does the end reflect the beginning?

Shakespeare makes the ends of his plays mirror the beginnings. He seems to do this for two reasons:

- to make the audience aware of the form of his art and so find pleasure in the symmetry of beginnings and ends
- to show the audience how much, or how little, things have changed in the course of the play.

For instance, *Romeo and Juliet* begins with a street quarrel between the servants of the Montagues and the Capulets, the leading families of Verona. The play ends with both families reconciled and united in grief for their dead children. Thus, although there is personal tragedy, there is a change in atmosphere from the beginning to the end.

But it is more difficult to see change in *Macbeth*. The play begins and ends with a battle. Moreover, in both battles the cause of the trouble is the Thane of Cawdor. At the beginning he is a rebel helping Norway; at the end Macbeth, as well as being a tyrannical king, is also the Thane of Cawdor. Peace is restored and the play ends with rejoicing, but the end mirrors the beginning so clearly that it is not wrong to wonder whether anything has really changed.

Exercises

13.1   Write about how the playwrights you are studying create characters. You can ask yourself whether the major characters are given a special way of speaking.

13.2   Bearing in mind the point about what makes a plot dramatic, write about the plots of the plays you are studying.

13.3   In the light of what has been said about how characters are created through the way they speak, read the following extract from Shakespeare's *Richard III* and then answer the questions below. Two murderers have been sent to kill the Duke of Clarence.

Second Murderer: What, shall we stab him as he sleeps?
First Murderer: No, he'll say 'twas done cowardly when he wakes.
Second Murderer: Why, he shall never wake until the great Judgement Day.
First Murderer: Why, then he'll say we stabbed him sleeping.
Second Murderer: The urging of that word 'judgement' hath bred a kind of remorse in me.
First Murderer: What, art thou afraid?
Second Murderer: Not to kill him, having a warrant; but to be damned for killing him, from the which no warrant can defend me.
First Murderer: I thought thou hadst been resolute.
Second Murderer: So I am – to let him live.
First Murderer: I'll back to the Duke of Gloucester and tell him so.

Second Murderer: Nay, I prithee stay a little. I hope this holy humour of mine will change; it was wont to hold me but while one tells twenty.

First Murderer: How dost thou feel thyself now?

Second Murderer: Faith, some certain dregs of conscience are yet within me.

First Murderer: Remember our reward when the deed's done.

Second Murderer: Zounds, he dies! I had forgot the reward.

First Murderer: Where's thy conscience now?

Second Murderer: O, in the Duke of Gloucester's purse.

First Murderer: When he opens his purse to give us our reward, thy conscience files out.

Second Murderer: 'Tis no matter, let it go. There's few or none will entertain it.

First Murderer: What if it come to thee again?

Second Murderer: I'll not meddle with it; it makes a man a coward. A man cannot steal, but it accuseth him; a man cannot swear, but it checks him; a man cannot lie with his neighbour's wife, but it detects him. 'Tis a blushing shamefaced spirit that mutinies in a man's bosom. It fills a man full of obstacles. It made me once restore a purse of gold that, by chance, I found. It beggars any man that keeps it. It is turned out of towns and cities for a dangerous thing, and every man that means to live well endeavours to trust to himself and live without it.

First Murderer: Zounds, 'tis even now at my elbow, persuading me not to kill the Duke.

Second Murderer: Take the devil in thy mind, and believe him not. He would insinuate with thee but to make thee sigh.

First Murderer: I am strong-framed; he cannot prevail with me.

Second Murderer: Spoke like a tall man that respects thy reputation. Come, shall we fall to work?

First Murderer: Take him on the costard with the hilts of thy sword, and then throw him into the Malmsey butt in the next room.

Second Murderer: O excellent device: And make a sop of him.

By looking very closely at the way the two murderers speak, what do you learn about the character of each? (You might like to think about the significance of the second murderer's use of 'judgement' and 'damned', and about how the first murderer speaks of 'reward' and 'purse'. You might also ask yourself why the second murderer is given a long speech, and why it is the first murderer who suggests the manner of killing Clarence.)

13.4   Here is the closing scene of Arthur Miller's *The Crucible*. Read it carefully and then answer the questions below. The play is about the trials for witchcraft in Salem. John Proctor has falsely signed a confession that he has served the devil. The Judge, Danforth, intends to display the confession publicly, but Proctor refuses because he does not want his name to be ruined. Parris and Hale are clergymen, Elizabeth is Proctor's wife.

Danforth: Then explain to me, Mr Proctor, why you will not let –
Proctor [*with a cry of his soul*]*:* Because it is my name! Because I cannot have another in my life! Because I lie and sign myself to lies! Because I am not worth the dust on the feet of them that hang! How may I live without my name? I have given you my soul; leave me my name!
Danforth [*pointing at the confession in Proctor's hand*]: Is that document a lie? If it is a lie I will not accept it! What say you? I will not deal in lies, Mister! [*Proctor is motionless.*] You will give me your honest confession in my hand, or I cannot keep you from the rope. [*Proctor does not reply.*] Which way do you go, Mister? [*His breast heaving, his eyes staring, Proctor tears the paper and crumples it, and he is weeping in fury, but erect.*]
Danforth: Marshal!
Parris [*hysterically, as though the tearing paper were his life*]: Proctor, Proctor!
Hale: Man, you will hang! You cannot!
Proctor [*his eyes full of tears*]*:* I can. And there's your first marvel, that I can. You have made your magic now, for now I do think I see some shred of goodness in John Proctor. Not enough to weave a banner with, but white enough to keep it from such dogs. [*Elizabeth, in a burst of terror, rushes to him and weeps against his hand.*] Give them no tear! Tears pleasure them! Show honour now, show a stony heart and sink them with it! [*He has lifted her, and kisses her now with great passion.*]
Rebecca: Let you fear nothing! Another judgement waits for us all!
Danforth: Hang them high over the town! Who weeps for these, weeps for corruption! [*He sweeps out past them. Herrick starts to lead Rebecca, who almost collapses, but Proctor catches her, and she glances up at him apologetically.*]
Rebecca: I've had no breakfast.
Herrick: Come, man. [*Herrick escorts them out, Hathorne and Cheever behind them. Elizabeth stands staring at the empty doorway.*]
Parris [*in deadly fear, to Elizabeth*]: Go to him, Goody Proctor! There is yet time! [*From outside a drumroll strikes the air. Parris is startled. Elizabeth jerks about toward the window.*]
Parris: Go to him! [*He rushes out the door, as though to hold back his fate.*] Proctor, Proctor! [*Again, a short burst of drums.*]

Hale: Woman, plead with him! [*He starts to rush out the door, and then goes back to her.*] Woman! It is pride, it is vanity. [*She avoids his eyes, and moves to the window. He drops to his knees.*] Be his helper! – What profit him to bleed? Shall the dust praise him? Shall the worms declare his truth? Go to him, take his shame away!

Elizabeth [*supporting herself against collapse, grips the bars of the window, and with a cry*]: He has his goodness now. God forbid I take if from him! [*The final drumroll crashes, then heightens violently. Hale weeps in frantic prayer, and the new sun is pouring in upon her face, and the drums rattle like bones in the morning air.*]

(a) What is the significance of Proctor tearing the paper which bears his signed confession?

(b) Write about the dramatic significance of Proctor saying that he can hang.

(c) Write about the dramatic impact of Elizabeth not preventing her husband going to the gallows.

(d) Do you think this is a successful conclusion? (You might like to think about the relation between Proctor's concern for his name and his willingness to be hanged.)

⬡14 Tragedy and comedy

14.1 The terms

Many of the plays set in public examinations are described as tragedies or comedies, and many of the questions ask candidates to discuss the tragic or comic qualities of a play. You must, therefore, understand what these terms mean.

The word, 'tragic', for instance, means a certain kind of literary art and not, as it does in the newspapers and television, any kind of disaster. (Snooker players failing to pot the black, as well as serious accidents, are called 'tragic', by journalists and commentators.) In understanding the terms, you will see that they are broad. This means that it is sometimes difficult to say whether a play is tragic or comic. Hence, you must learn to use the terms flexibly and avoid treating them as laws to which plays must conform.

Nevertheless, tragic and comic plays do have certain recognisable features. Let us look at them in turn.

14.2 Tragedy, chaos and death

Tragic plots offer a bleak vision of life; they concentrate on failure, conflict and disaster. In most tragedies two aspects of this vision are stressed:

- chaos
- death

Chaos

Chaos (it could also be called disorder) is both personal and communal; in some plays the central character goes to pieces, in others society disintegrates, while in many both fall apart.

___ **Examples** ___

Example 1

Othello descends into a personal chaos when he is misled into believing that his wife is unfaithful.

254

At one point he actually uses the word, though the tone is a loving one. His wife, Desdemona, has just exited, and, looking after her, he playfully says:

> I do love thee, and when I love thee not
> Chaos is come again.

The terrible irony is that it does. When Othello is misled, he becomes a psychological wreck who, at one point, collapses in helpless rage. Nobility and dignity give way to the chaos of an inhuman thirst for revenge.

Example 2

In *Macbeth* the nation is thrown into disorder. Shakespeare presents this by showing the murders of Lady Macduff and her family, and through the imagery. Look at the following lines about Scotland:

> It cannot
> Be called our mother, but our grave.

> Good men's lives
> Expire before the flowers in their caps. . .

> Meet we the medicine of the sickly weal. . .

These images are of death and disease. They show the state into which Scotland has fallen under the tyranny of Macbeth. There are many other lines. Shakespeare shows Scotland howling in pain, fearful and becoming accustomed to death.

Example 3

In *King Lear* the chaos is both personal and communal. Lear gradually loses control of himself and, as he descends into madness, first his family, then the nation, and finally nature plunge into chaos. The central third act shows a mad Lear (personal chaos), having been shut out of his daughter's home (communal chaos), raving in a storm (universal chaos).

Death

Chaos usually ends in death – the great shadow that hangs over all tragedy. At the end of Shakespeare's tragedies there is often a stark comment on the triumph of death. *Hamlet* closes with the entry of Fortinbras, who sees the bodies of Hamlet, Laertes, Claudius and Gertrude. He solemnly addresses death:

> O proud Death
> What feast is toward in thine eternal cell,
> That so many princes at a shot
> So bloodily hast struck.

The image is horrific; death is pictured as a hungry hunter, who, in order to have a feast, has struck down princes.

Shakespeare uses such a horrible image in order to bring home the power and presence of death. At the end of many tragedies the audience is left staring the reality of death in the face. Indeed, some people say that the tragic vision of life arises from the fact that all life ends in death.

14.3   Tragic heroes and heroines

Tragedies usually centre on one character – a man of exceptional qualities in a high position. Lear is King of Britain, Coriolanus the greatest soldier of Rome, Hamlet a prince. These men inspire wonder and awe in others, so whatever happens to them has grandeur and significance. Because they are both remarkable and occupy high positions, it is understandable that their tragedy will affect the whole nation.

This central character is called the 'hero'. The title indicates the character's importance: a hero is larger than life, almost god-like, and is at the centre of myths and legends. At this point two questions arise.

- **Can the central character be a woman?**

Though tragedy is dominated by men, this does not mean there are no tragic women. In Shakespeare, Juliet and Cleopatra are clearly tragic, and so, too, is Lady Macbeth. Moreover, there are minor characters such as Portia in *Julius Caesar*. Though she says little, she is a remarkable woman, whose bravery and anguish mark her out as potentially tragic. The question that hangs over her, however, is whether she is fully developed enough to be tragic. That, generally speaking, is often the case with tragic women: although there are tragic heroines, they do not attract playwrights so often as do tragic heroes.

- **Can the character occupy a low position in society?**

This question can be answered in a similar way. There are tragedies centred round ordinary characters (they are often called *domestic tragedies*), but there are very few.

A popular question about *Death of a Salesman* is whether or not Willy Loman is tragic. There is no reason why a salesman should not be tragic (remember that tragedy is a broad term), but Willy Loman is so stupid that he fails to qualify as one. It should be possible to admire or stand in awe of a tragic hero, and, of course, 'ordinary', characters can be admirable. The fact remains, however, that domestic or everyday tragedy is a very rare thing.

14.4 The fall of the hero

The main action of tragedy is the fall of the hero. This fall is both external and internal: externally the hero falls from power and respect and internally from peace of mind.

For instance, King Lear starts the play as a king, and, though stubborn and wilful, he has personal authority and confidence. By the third act he is wandering, crazed and half-naked, across a heath in a terrible storm. There could hardly be such a striking fall: from riches to rags, from sanity to madness.

- **When you write about the fall of a tragic hero, you should explore the way his language changes.**

Example

Consider the case of Othello. At first he speaks simply yet eloquently, the verse moving with the steady grandeur of great music. This is part of what he says to the Senate (the parliament of Venice) in the third act of the play:

> Most potent, grave and reverend signiors,
> My very noble and approved good masters:
> That I have ta'en away this old man's daughter,
> It is most true...

Othello is in control of his language. Look at the solemn, measured rhythm of the opening line, the dark cadences with which the lines close, and the grave honesty of the admission that he has 'ta'en away this old man's daughter', which culminates in the openness of 'It is most true'.

The tragedy of Othello is enacted in the change from that speech to the rambling incoherence into which he later falls. Later on he speaks in disjointed prose about a handkerchief which he believes provides evidence for Desdemona's unfaithfulness:

Handkerchief – confession – handkerchief! To confess, and be hanged for his labour. First, to be hanged, and then to confess: I tremble at it. Nature herself would not invest herself in such shadowing passion without some instruction. It is not words which shake me thus. Pish! Noses, ears and lips. Is't possible? – Confess? – Handkerchief? – O devil!

Othello's control has gone. What he says is close to nonsense; he wildly jumps from one point to another, obsessively repeating 'handkerchief'. The fall of Othello is a fall in his language from noble coherence to ranting nonsense.

- **When you study a tragedy, you should ask yourself this question:**

- Why does the tragic hero fall?

Many reasons have been offered, and, though none of them are completely satis-fying, they are worth thinking about. The two most popular are:

- the hero has a fatal flaw
- the hero wilfully goes against the fixed moral laws of life.

The fatal flaw

The idea of the flaw is that the hero has a fault, which, under pressure, brings disaster. It is common to think of this flaw in terms of *excess*. Dr Faustus longs for learning too much, Hamlet is too thoughtful, and Othello *too* willing to believe rumour. For all their great qualities, a flaw makes them unstable.

However, the idea has two disadvantages.

- **It seems too weak to account for the terrible consequences of tragedy.**

The first disadvantage can be seen in *Macbeth*. The flaw of over-ambitiousness might explain why Macbeth wanted to become king, but can it explain why Macbeth plunges Scotland into a bloodbath?

Here the second point comes in. What is tragic about Macbeth is not that he has a flaw but that a man with such a huge poetic imagination should *willingly* pursue evil. There is no point in killing Lady MacDuff and her children, and, what is more, Macbeth realises this. Nevertheless, he goes ahead with the murder. There is tragedy in that. If Macbeth were not free to act (even if he chose evil), there could be no tragedy at all.

The second reason for the fall of a hero – that of going against the fixed moral law of life – does take account of freedom. The word that is often used is *hubris* – an arrogant and extensive pride and confidence in oneself. The *hubris* of a tragic hero is seen when he decides to go against the fundamental moral and religious laws of life. The hero either believes that he is right or that his task is more important than morality. As a result, he falls foul of the moral laws of the universe. In other words, the *hubris* of the hero is always shown to be *wrong*.

This idea does do justice to the significance audiences find in tragedy. It also does justice to the mixed feelings an audience might have. For instance, Hamlet might seem justified in revenging his father's death, but when his revenge destroys Ophelia and Polonius, an audience might not be so sure. But in that lies the difficulty of the idea: audiences often find themselves approving of, or at least being interested in, action that they know is wrong. Tragedy, then, can't just work on a moral level.

- **Whenever you write about the fall of a tragic hero, you should remember that there is always an element of mystery.**

Fatal flaws and the moral laws of the universe are simply ways of trying to account for the terrible mystery of tragedy. But though they go some way in explaining it, they never explain it away. At the end of a tragedy both the characters and the audience (and probably the playwright) wonder why the terrifying events took place. Even when reasons are given for a fall, the strange mystery of it persists.

14.5 The sense of inevitability

The fall of a hero is often inevitable. The harrowing thing about *Romeo and Juliet* is that the young lovers seem powerless to avoid the catastrophe that overwhelms them. It is very painful for an audience to witness events which it sees as inevitable, particularly when the tragic hero can't see this.

The inevitability of tragedy raises two closely related problems:

- the extent to which the characters are free or controlled
- whether the outcome of the events could have been avoided at all.

- **The tension between freedom and control**

The tension between freedom and control is certainly there in tragedy. In some plays there is tension between the fact that characters make free choices and the feeling that there are unseen forces controlling them. This is evident in the opening chorus of *Dr Faustus*.

> Till swollen with cunning of self-conceit,
> His waxen wings did mount above his reach,
> And melting, heavens conspired his overthrow.

Marlowe compares Faustus with Icarus, who, in the Greek myth, flew too near the sun. His *hubris* – 'did mount above his reach' – comes from free will, but his fall – 'heavens conspired his overthrow' – suggests that he was controlled.

Macbeth is a similar case; it is never clear whether Macbeth freely chooses or is controlled by the witches. The point about tension is that it can't be neatly sorted out one way or the other. The extent to which heroes are free or controlled, like the reasons for their fall, is a mystery.

- **Could the outcome have been avoided?**

The question of whether or not the outcome of events is inevitable is related to the idea that tragedy recognises moral, or religious, values. If there are no values, there can be no tragedy. But since tragedy recognises moral laws, it is clearly why the fall of a hero is inevitable. A hero falls because he tries to break the unchanging, and unchangeable, moral order. This is why there can't be social tragedy; that is, tragedy based on the customs of the society. Customs change from age to age, so a hero who tries to break them and fails in one age would not inevitably fail in another.

There is, then, the feeling in tragedy that events are always going to turn out disastrously, because characters have broken unchangeable moral laws. It will, for instance, always be wrong for someone to take upon himself the role of a revenger. If we ever came to believe that revenge *was* right, *Hamlet*, for example, would not be seen as tragic.

14.6   Suffering

In tragedies there is suffering as well as death. Suffering can be both physical and mental.

For example, in *King Lear* Gloucester suffers when his eyes are gouged out and when he is told, immediately afterwards, that the son whom he loved, Edmund, has betrayed him. Gloucester's suffering is like that of many tragic characters in that it is excessive. This is another terrible mystery:

> *the tragic hero not only suffers, he suffers excessively.*

Lear, for instance, has been foolish and blind, but what he undergoes physically and mentally is far in excess of his crimes. He is, as he says, a 'man more sinned against than sinning'.

Some people point out that though the suffering of heroes is excessive it does lead to greater self-knowledge. This is only partly true. Hamlet suffers intellectual, moral and emotional anguish, yet at the end of the play he is, if not happy, more composed and settled. But Lear gains no insight from his suffering because he is simply too old to learn. His suffering is appalling, and nothing can be said to lighten its terrible weight.

14.7   The sense of waste

Because tragedy shows the fall, excessive suffering and death of a great man, audiences are likely to experience a sense of waste. A great man has come to nothing. At the end of a play, therefore, there must be the feeling that a great human being has passed away.

At the end of *Antony and Cleopatra* the cold and unfeeling Octavius is victorious, but his victory does not diminish the stature of the two lovers. Even the death of Macbeth leaves the audience with the feeling that greatness has passed away, because the new king, Malcom, is not as impressive as the tyrant whom he replaces.

● **There is something massive and universal about tragedy.**

Tragic action involves individuals, nations and even the whole realm of nature. In *Antony and Cleopatra* two nations – Rome and Egypt – are locked in battle;

in *King Lear* Britain is at war with France, and nature and the gods, it seems, are at war with mankind.

● **The vastness of tragedy is moral and religious as well as physical.**

In tragedies audiences see the central issues of human life explored. In *Macbeth* there is good and evil, love and hate, and loyalty and rebellion. These are universal; hence the sense of vastness.

The fear that tragedy arouses is not that of being frightened or shocked, but the feeling of being in the presence of forces that are strange and terrible.

For example, *King Lear* shows what a fearful thing hatred is. Lear responds in hatred when Cordelia won't say she loves him, and when the other daughters refuse to do as he wants, he launches into horrible curses. Likewise, *Macbeth* shows how one man can plunge his country into a bloodbath, and *Antony and Cleopatra* shows that love can be destructive. These themes don't frighten as a horror film does but they are fearful in their power to disturb.

14.8   Tragedy, ambiguity and ambivalence

'Ambiguity' and 'ambivalence' are words often used when talking about literature, and because they are, the words have come to have a number of meanings. In this section we shall mainly consider ambiguity, though in the matter of audience reaction, ambivalence is a very useful word.

Ambiguity

Tragic ambiguity is present in the moral status of characters.

Tragedy requires an audience to make moral judgements. The fear, loathing and even horror that is felt in the presence of tragedy depends upon the audience knowing what is right and what is wrong. What a character such as Iago does can only be regarded as evil, and whatever an audience thinks of the folly and the immorality of King Lear, it can't endorse the behaviour of his daughters, who are not only content to let him out in the storm but ensure that he won't return by shutting the door on him. But as with so much art nothing is ever quite as simple as that. We have to make those kind of judgements, but we also have to recognise many other factors. It is this that makes tragedy ambiguous.

Example

Let's look in more detail at *King Lear*. It is customary to talk about, and for examiners to set questions on, the clash in the play between the good and evil characters.

This is not an untrue statement, but it's best understood as a structural statement rather than a moral one. The experience of seeing *King Lear* certainly makes us focus on the opposition between Edgar, Kent and Cordelia on the one hand and Edmund, Cornwall, Goneril and Regan on the other. As far as the design of the plays goes, one can see the two groups giving the action shape and, in the various trajectories of the plots, showing how their various values work out in their own and in other's lives.

Yet the actual moral experience of the play is more complex than that. Certainly Cordelia and Kent are good, but in their striving to be good they cause Lear almost as much pain (in Cordelia's case possibly more) than the evil group.

That is ambiguity – characters who strive to do good often end up doing harm. That's the way it works out, and the inextricable fusion of good and evil, of pleasure and suffering, is what we call tragedy.

Sometimes this blend of good and evil becomes the central business of tragedy in that it's seen as constituting the very life of the central figure.

Example

Take the case of Brutus in *Julius Caesar*. He is undoubtedly noble and, unlike those on his side and those who oppose him, he has a conscience. Antony, Lepidus and Octavius plan the murder of those who oppose them in frighteningly clinical terms – 'These many then shall die', – whereas Brutus recognises Antony's right to speak to the crowd at Caesar's funeral.

It can, however, be argued that it's his conscience which is his moral downfall. What Brutus agrees to do is join a conspiracy to kill Caesar. He thinks there are good reasons why Caesar should be killed, but what he screens from himself is what actually killing a man involves. Listen to what he says:

> And, gentle friends,
> Let's kill him boldly, but not wrathfully.
> Let's carve him as a dish fit for the gods,
> Not hew him as a carcase fit for hounds.

Brutus fails to see that neither of those alternatives is appropriate. Certainly no one should be treated as a carcase thrown to the dogs, but killing a man (a man who is or has been your friend) can't be like a religious sacrifice. The image of sacrifice, an image born of Brutus's conscience, veils from him the terrible reality of what killing a fellow human being is.

The audience might observe that those who drew up the list of the 'many' who shall die were at least, for all their cold-blooded efficiency, aware of what they were doing. That dilemma is central to the play; we know that Brutus is a good man and yet his actions are tragically ambiguous.

- **It is often the case in Shakespeare that what brings a character down are his or her good as well as bad qualities.**

In the case of *Othello* the ambiguity is painful. Othello has, as Iago perceptively observes, 'a free and open nature', and it's this attractive feature that makes him a victim of Iago's devastating insinuations about his wife's infidelity. Othello falls not because he has a fault or fatal flaw, but because his is a rare, trusting, open and receptive nature. It's what's best about him that brings him down, not what's worst.

Ambivalence

It's a short step from this to consider the reactions of the audience. It's been the experience of countless theatre goers that seeing tragedy is never a simple experience.

For example, audiences are both attracted and repelled by the actions of the tragic protagonist. This is so with Macbeth; he is a brave and loving man (at times he speaks to his wife like Romeo) yet he kills an old man in his bed. We are drawn to him and we are also repelled. Even if, as some people do, we admire his terrible purposefulness, we still have to recognise his unfeeling brutality.

This is where the word 'ambivalent' is required. Ambivalence is an uncertainty in the reactions of an audience or reader. We don't know what to make of something or how to judge it. Ambivalence is the experience of being divided in our thoughts and feelings. Most tragic characters stir this feeling in us. We admire and are even daunted by their courage, imagination, dedication, zeal and vibrancy but we are also appalled and horrified. This isn't a state we can resolve by drawing up a kind of balance sheet; our ambivalence can't be allayed, because the characters are irreducibly ambiguous.

14.9   Shakespeare and the theatricality of tragedy

Shakespeare's tragic figures are ambiguous in another way: in the attitude they take and want us to take to what they have done.

What Shakespeare shows in his characters is something very close to a love of display. It's as if they know they are on the stage and they revel in their tragic dilemma in such as way as to call the audience's attention to it. They implicitly admit that they are in the wrong, and we cannot help admiring their blend of honesty and self-knowledge as well as their sheer daring; but there is something very corrupt about the way they revel in their own plight, drawing attention (the attention of other characters and the audience) to the enormity of what they have done and to the depth of their suffering.

Audiences find this very difficult to cope with; there is something both magnificent and reprehensible about these tragic figures. They are ambiguous and we are ambivalent about them.

__ **Example** _____

Consider Macbeth. He speaks about what he has done as his 'deed':

> This deed I'll do before this purpose cool.

'Deed' is a word usually used of the actions of an epic hero, but here Macbeth is talking about killing children.

Also, there is a grisly relish in his resolution to persist in evil:

> I am in blood
> Stepped in so far that, should I wade no more,
> Returning were as tedious as go o'er

That's the kind of thing someone says to justify wading further into a river; but what Macbeth is drawing our attention to is a river of blood.

What is characteristically Shakespearian about Macbeth's language is the way this display is seen in theatrical terms. At one point, a moment of appalling suffering for Macbeth, he uses the image of an actor:

> a poor player
> That struts and frets his hour upon the stage

Macbeth is that 'poor player'; as he says the words the audience can see the actor upon the stage, strutting (perhaps proudly) as he delivers the lines.

The theatricality of the tragic plight is not confined to Macbeth; it can also be found in Lear, Hamlet and Othello, and it is one of the major characteristics of both Antony and Cleopatra.

Two words are associated with this tragic ambiguity.

- hubris
- bravado

Hubris

'Hubris' has already been used. The pride – the overweening pride – of tragic figures is seen in the way they regard their own fall as a spectacle that all should watch. Hubris, as implied earlier, is always an ambiguous quality.

Bravado

Bravado means the swaggering and ostentatious display of courage. It is always a noisy and public way of calling attention to one's own qualities.

In the tragic context it carries with it an implication of pleasure – the tragic figure enjoys acting out his or her downfall; and a measure of positive judgement – tragic heroes and heroines show bravado when they strongly suggest that what they are doing is magnetic and deeply interesting. We see bravado in the way in which they summon us to witness their acting out of the tragic role and find it a stirring spectacle.

14.10 The involvement of the audience

One of the distinctive things about tragedy is that the audience is invited to understand what the hero is undergoing; it is not an external observer but feels what the hero is feeling. (This is why the soliloquy is so important in tragedy.)

The response the audience makes is one of pity. It is pity because terrible things are happening, which the audience sees as inevitable and is consequently powerless to prevent. As it sits and witnesses the terrible decline of a character, its heart can go out to him or her, but it knows there is nothing that it, or any other character, can do.

In *Othello* the pity and the sense of powerlessness are so great that members of the audience have been known to shout, in frustrated desperation, at the doomed and misguided hero.

An audience can even come to pity a character whom it did not like at first. Such a case is Richard II. In the early part of the play he is vain, proud and foolish, but when he falls from power, the audience shares his grief and pities the lonely figure in the prison cell who tries to imagine that his prison is like the world over which he once ruled.

14.11 How the audience responds to the end of tragedies

Although tragedy brings suffering and ends with death, it is the experience of audiences that it is moving but not depressing. It has puzzled many people that audiences don't leave the theatre in a gloomy frame of mind but with a feeling of uplift, and, strange as it may seem, even joy. Nobody has satisfactorily explained why this is so, but three important ideas have been advanced:

- the idea of catharsis
- the idea of seriousness
- the idea of human dignity.

Catharsis

Catharsis is an idea that goes back to the Greek philosopher Aristotle. He said that tragedy aroused and then drove from the audience feelings of pity, so that, by the end, they felt relieved. Catharsis is the act of being relieved, or purged, of those feelings.

As an explanation of tragedy it has a number of difficulties.

- It was thought out to explain *Greek* plays, so it is not necessarily applicable to later ones.
- It is based upon ancient ideas of medicine that few people accept nowadays.
- Aristotle did not elaborate on the idea, so it is not clear *exactly* what he meant.

Nevertheless, it is quite useful not as an explanation but as a *description* of what happens to an audience. Audiences *do* feel uplifted after a tragedy and leave the theatre calm and serene. Milton put the idea this way in *Samson Agonistes*: 'And calm of mind, all passion spent.' That, for many theatre-goers, is what catharsis means.

Seriousness

Tragedy reminds the audience that life is serious. At the end of a play the audience might feel that they have been reminded of the depths of life, of the fact that things *matter*. It could be they have been reminded that life is vast and wonderful, or that human relationships are both wonderful and very difficult.

For instance, an audience coming out of *Hamlet* might realise very powerfully that friendship matters, because it would have seen a play in which, for all its darkness, confusion and doubt, Hamlet is sustained by the loyalty and friendship of Horatio.

Human dignity

Finally, tragedy reminds an audience that people can be dignified and noble. It is not always easy to believe or remember this in everyday life. Wars and starvation suggest that human life is cheap and in many industrialised societies people feel small and anonymous – like cogs in a machine. But in tragedy we see heroism, nobility, courage, patience and love. And we see these things in spite of flaws, wilful evil and appalling suffering. It is said of Othello that he is 'great of heart'. The same can be said of most tragic characters, and of human beings in general.

14.12   Comic plots and conventions

The plots of tragedies are often simple. The fall of the central figure must be the chief experience, so playwrights rarely complicate the plot by including other elements. In comedy, however, plot is primary. What delights and intrigues audiences is the complex interweaving of a number of characters with a different set of (often contrary) ambitions. The audience will certainly anticipate that all will end well, but they are frequently both perplexed and fascinated to see how the playwright will achieve this.

- **More than any other kind of drama, comedy is dependent upon its conventions.**

An audience faced with the dazzling tumult of events in, say, a Joe Orton comedy needs to have something it can rely upon. This is where conventions come in. Conventions – agreements between audience and playwright that certain pieces of action will have a particular significance and will summon up a particular response – are the chief way in which an audience can enjoy the welter of events and still know what to make of what is going on. This is even the case when conventions are subverted. In *Loot*, for instance, there's a thoroughly corrupt policeman. Audiences can cope with this because the character is a subversion (one might say inversion) of the conventionally honest and reliable stage bobby.

- **Conventions are of different types.**

- *Conventions of subject matter*   As we shall see, one of the central topics of comedy is love. Here there are many conventions: characters fall in love at first sight, their parents object, there is misunderstanding between the lovers, they run away, their love has to be tested and marriage is regarded as a reward.
- *Conventions associated with the way in which characters go about seeking for happiness*   Disguise is a good example; virtually everything that happens when characters are disguised is controlled by a highly developed set of conventions.
- *Conventions about characters*   Twins are popular in comedies (just think of the confusion that they can bring) and so are lovers, clever servants and characters who have no self-knowledge.

It's a good idea to look through any comedy you are studying and try to identify the conventions the playwright deploys. In *Twelfth Night*, for instance, there are, among others, characters who fall in love at first sight, a character who adopts disguise, a set of twins and a sort of servant who is more successful in the pursuit of love than the master.

- **There are two important points to make about comic plots and conventions.**

- *They are traditional.*   We laugh at the same jokes on television that have amused generations of readers and audiences. In Jeeves and Wooster, P. G. Wodehouse created a splendidly conventional comic pair – a dim-witted master helped out of scrapes by a clever servant. It's the same joke (the crazy yet heartening disparity between brains and status) that amused Shakespeare's audience in *The Taming of the Shrew* (Tranio the servant has to do most of the thinking for his master Lucentio); Chaucer's audience in his portrait of the Manciple, who was wiser than a heap of learned men; and, if we go back further, Greek and Roman audiences.

  The point to remember is that there's nothing wrong with this – comedy is above all a traditional art.

- *Because plots and conventions are so central to comedy they are virtually coterminous with its theme.*   Tragedy is often about the big issues in life, whereas comedy is usually about its own processes. This can be easily seen in the sort of questions that are set about comedy. Very frequently examiners ask students to write about the importance of disguise and deception in *Twelfth Night* or *As You Like It* or *Much Ado About Nothing*. These can be said to be the themes of those plays, but equally importantly they are also their conventions.

  When talking or writing about comedies you will often find that the words you use to talk about the themes and the words you use to talk about the conventions of the plot are the same.

14.13   How comedies begin

There are conventions in Shakespeare, and other comic writers, about the opening of plots. Shakespeare regularly deploys two:

- the arrival of strangers
- the authority of the older generation unjustly exercised against the young, often by means of the revival of an ancient law.

The arrival of strangers

A number of Shakespeare's plays begin either with characters making a journey to an unfamiliar location (as in *The Tempest*) or the life of a community being interrupted by the arrival of strangers (as in *Much Ado About Nothing*). These plot devices reveal something of the nature of comedy – it's concerned with the impact of change upon a settled and often stultified way of life. Strangers disrupt the patterns of life and in doing so they create new problems.

--- **Examples** ---

Example 1

Consider the opening of *Twelfth Night*.

There is something fixed, almost unhealthy, about the life of Illyria – the country upon whose shores the twins, Viola and Sebastian, are ship-wrecked. Orsino is content to play the role of the love-sick young man, who vainly strives to woo an indifferent but beautiful woman, and the object of his love, the Lady Olivia, has decided to mourn seven years for the death of her brother. The audience surely feel that these people need to be woken up from such self-imposed lethargy; and they are. Viola creates a problem when she adopts the disguise of a young man, and since she looks like her brother (she actually imitates him), other characters encounter considerable problems when they mistake the one for the other.

Example 2

The comic pattern of a community with a problem playing host to strangers is very clearly seen in *The Taming of the Shrew*.

Life in Padua has clearly reached an impasse; Bianca, daughter of Baptista, has at least two men wanting to marry her, but her father refuses permission until a husband has been found for Katherina. This, however, seem unlikely to happen, because she has the reputation for being sharp-tongued, quarrelsome and belligerent.

Then the strangers arrive: the love-sick Lucentio who also falls for Bianca, and the rumbustious Petruchio who, for financial reasons, is willing to court Kate. What happens initially is further confusion: three characters adopt disguise, Petruchio woos Kate in a wildly unconventional manner and ludicrous claims are advanced (which later have to be supported) about the status and wealth of Lucentio. Yet the end result of this confusion is a plot in which all the elements are neatly resolved.

- The pattern, then, is a difficult situation made more difficult by the arrival of strangers but one which, because there are new characters, works itself out.

Not every comedy follows such a pattern, but in many there is a similar kind of arrangement. *The Playboy of the Western World* opens with the arrival of a stranger; *The Importance of being Earnest* really gets under way when the characters go to the countryside; and Jonson's *The Alchemist* starts with the departure of the real Alchemist and the arrival of the clever imposters, Face and Subtle.

The oppression of the young by the old

This way of opening a comedy is often used in plots dealing with love.

For instance, in *A Midsummer Night's Dream* the love of Hermia and Theseus, already in being when the play opens, is threatened when her father claims his right, under an ancient law, to order his daughter to marry whomsoever he wishes. (The penalty for disobedience is death.) In *Measure for Measure* the newly appointed governor, Angelo, revives a law which punishes by death anyone who has sexual relationships before marriage.

What both these examples highlight is the extent to which one of the favourite topics of comedy is the trials lovers undergo. The famous line 'The course of true love never did run smooth' comes from *A Midsummer Night's Dream*. The revival of the ancient law is there to provide such a trial. In both cases it's forgotten or quickly overruled when the playwright has extracted the necessary tension and excitement from the plot.

Again, similar conventions are found in non-Shakespearian comedies. For instance, dotty rules affecting the young are common in Gilbert and Sullivan's operas. In *The Importance of being Earnest* there is a delicious variation on this theme whereby the young girls themselves impose the unreasonable rule, namely that the men they marry must each be called Ernest. Sometimes, the plot is simply the old denying the aspirations of the young, as in Aphra Behn's *The Rover*, where it is clear from the opening scene that Florinda wants to marry one man but her father (typically) wants to marry her off to an old rich man and her brother to his friend.

14.14   Comic devices

Falling in love with someone with whom marriage seems impossible, or the revival of an ancient law threatening the happiness of lovers, makes characters (particularly the women) enterprising and inventive. Those in love (in Shakespeare always the young) are not going to be thwarted, so plans and schemes are invented in order to enable their desires and longings to be fulfilled. In comedy, lovers are very often energetic and inventive – as inventive, we might say, as Shakespeare himself. He, after all, is a kind of wooer, only in his case it's the audience and not a beloved he has to please.

There are two words that Shakespeare uses for the stratagems or ruses his characters deploy:

- device
- practice.

For instance, in the scene in *The Merchant of Venice* in which Portia plans to disguise herself as a man, she says to Nerissa that she has 'a thousand raw tricks... Which I will practise' and when questioned by Nerissa says: 'I'll tell thee all my whole device'. A practice or device is any trick or plan one character or set of characters adopts against another. The aim is always to create an advantage. In *The Taming of the Shrew* Tranio, speaking of his devices says he will 'watch our vantage in this business'.

Advantage consists in knowing. The currency of Shakespearian comedy is knowledge. To know more than those whom one is trying to outwit is the aim of implementing devices and practices.

- When watching or reading a comedy you should always remind yourself of who knows what.

Moreover, you should remember the position in which you find yourself; usually in comedy the audience knows more than any single character. In *Much Ado About Nothing* the audience knows that neither Beatrice nor Benedick is aware that they are being practised upon by those who are leading them to fall in love with each other. However, when they declare their love and plan revenge for Claudio's 'exposure' of Hero, only the audience knows what has passed, so we enjoy the shock the plotters experience when they discover that Benedick is wholly serious in his challenge to Claudio.

- **There are three popular devices in Shakespeare:**

- disguise
- overhearing
- misinformation.

Disguise

We have already discussed how disguise works in drama, so little more need be added.

In addition to disguise allowing characters to speak and hear that which they normally would be barred from, it gives characters a freedom and raises the issue of identity.

Examples

Example 1

Rosalind finds that her disguise allows Orlando to say to her that which he is too bashful to utter, but it also bestows upon her an enjoyable freedom to joke and, when necessary, speak her mind firmly.

Example 2

In *Twelfth Night* Viola, disguised as a male servant, reflects at one point upon her identity and her unhappy situation in which she finds herself loving her master yet the object of love of Olivia, the woman whom her master is courting:

> As I am a man
> My state is desperate for my master's love.
> As I am a woman, now, alas the day,
> What thriftless sighs shall poor Olivia breathe!

Viola knows what it is to be both man and woman, a knowledge that touches on the intriguing question of human identity, its nature and causes. This is given further spice by the fact that in Shakespeare's day, all the women's parts were played by boys, so we have a boy dressed as a woman dressed as a man pondering his/her own identity.

Overhearing

A sure way of gaining an advantage over another character is overhearing what he or she is saying. That way the character who knows is at an advantage because he/she not only knows but knows that the other character doesn't know that he/she knows. Thus neither Beatrice nor Benedick is aware that they are being deceived into loving each other. In that respect the 'plotters' have the advantage over them.

Sometimes Shakespeare implicitly jokes about theatrical conventions. In *A Midsummer Night's Dream*, Oberon, because he is a fairy, can assume invisibility, so when the lovers enter, Shakespeare has him say: 'I am invisible/And I will overhear their confidence', thereby creating the comedy of a character plainly visible yet still in the position of the overhearer. Overhearing, it should be noted, is not only found in comedies. In *Othello* (a play which in its design resembles a comedy) Iago uses it to dupe Othello.

Misinformation

One of the conventions of comedy is that in which a clever rogue deceives a gullible fool, usually by conveying false information. This is called 'gulling', and the one who does it is the 'shark' and the victim is the 'gull'. Ben Jonson's plays are built around this convention.

In *Twelfth Night* Sir Toby, Sir Andrew, Fabian and the enterprising Maria gull Malvolio into believing that Olivia, his employer, is in love with him. This misinforming occurs in the form of a letter, supposedly from Olivia but actually penned by Maria. Her intention is to 'gull him into a nayword', and throughout the escapade they refer to their stratagem as a 'device'. As in other devices, they know the truth, whereas Malvolio is at a disadvantage because he doesn't.

● In a number of plays there is a character who is the chief deviser or practiser. In many of the comedies this is a role performed by the woman. They are clever, resourceful and inventive, whereas the men are slow-witted and easily led. Maria is the chief practiser in *Twelfth Night*, even though it's Sir Toby who puts her plans into action.

Occasionally, a character has few distinguishing features but is just there to implement plans. Don Pedro in *Much Ado about Nothing* has often puzzled readers because of his lack of personality; the truth is that he's a character who exists to perform a function – that of chief practiser. In at least one play Shakespeare appears to have fun at the expense of the practiser. The Duke in *Measure for Measure* tries to organise everything while disguised as a friar, but unlike many practisers, he's not altogether competent. He doesn't anticipate what Angelo will do, and some of the other characters, in particular Lucio and Barnadine, are less than co-operative. The Duke is funny, but he only appears to be if the audience can see that he's a chief practiser who is failing to fulfil his role.

14.15 Confusion, recognition and closure

Unlike tragedy, it's not possible to talk in general terms about the main business of comedy. Tragedy, in one way or another, is about fall, but the plots of comedy are more varied. For instance, in *Twelfth Night* several plot elements are interwoven: the deception of Malvolio, the Duke's attempts at wooing Olivia, Olivia's attempts to attract 'Cesario' and Sebastian's exploration of the town. If generalisations are to made about the central actions of comedy, we have to turn to the kind of experiences that comic plots give rise to.

Confusion

Of these one of the most important is confusion. An audience watching a comedy sees a set of characters who, to a greater or lesser degree, are in doubt as to what is happening to them. This is in a large part due to disparities in knowledge; some characters know more than others, and (usually) all characters know less than the audience. The experience, then, of such characters is of a world that is out of control, and possibly even slightly mad. It's notable that the word 'mad' appears in *Twelfth Night* more than in any other of Shakespeare's plays.

This feeling of a world that has departed from the trustworthy patterns of normality can be pleasant and disturbing. Beatrice and Benedick and the young men in *The Importance of Being Earnest* appear to enjoy the merry confusions of love; they certainly launch into the mode of loving with enthusiasm. On the other hand, there is anguish for the lovers in *A Midsummer Night's Dream*, and Antonio, of course, is threatened with almost certain death in *The Merchant of Venice*. It's not an accident that one of those plays contains the word 'dream' in its title. There is something dreamlike about the confusions created by comic plots. Characters sometimes compare their experience to dreams, as in *The Two Gentlemen of Verona*, where one character remarks:

How like a dream is this!

Recognition

Perhaps the most important feature of confusion in comedy is that it doesn't last. Like other plots, there is usually a moment of recognition when characters see what has been happening to them. These moments come towards the end of a play, though not necessarily at its very close.

- **The essential point about comic recognitions is that they come about when characters acquire knowledge.**

Comic plots are set in motion by characters who deliberately create disparities in knowledge and they draw to a close when those disparities are eliminated. In *Twelfth Night* there is an inkling of approaching harmony when Antonio meets Viola and treats her as Sebastian, and when Sebastian himself enters the initial shock of seeing the twins soon gives way to the joy of understanding and of re-uniting. In Shakespeare's late plays – *The Winter's Tale* and *The Tempest* – recognition becomes the central event, largely because people have either been separated for a very long time or are convinced that people dear to them are dead.

Closure

Several things happen when a comedy ends. The elimination of disparities in knowledge is, as we have said above, a very important ingredient. Each charac-ter who has been in some measure confused by what has gone on has to under-stand what has happened to him or her and why it has happened. Shakespeare is enough of a realist to see that neither audiences nor characters could be satisfied with a situation in which some people are still in the dark. Therefore Beatrice and Benedick have to know that their love, real and even tough as it is, has been brought about through trickery.

Hence at the end of comedies there are often speeches in which explanations are given of what has gone on. This is important. The experience of comedy is, as has been said above, one in which life is changed into a kind of dream. But if characters are to take back into their 'ordinary' life the transforming vision of a dream, they need to be able to understand something of what has happened to them. Hence the explanations.

Yet it would be a mistake to assume that the atmosphere at the close of a comedy is a dry one, chock full of reasons. The note on which many comedies close is that of wonder and amazement. Look, for instance, at these lines from the ends of some of Shakespeare's comedies:

> Here is a wonder, if you talk of wonders
> (*The Taming of the Shrew*)

> But wonder on, till truth make all things plain.
> (*A Midsummer Night's Dream*)

> You are all amazed
> (*The Merchant of Venice*)

> I'll tell you as we pass along
> That you will wonder what hath fortuned
> (*The Two Gentlemen of Verona*)

Whether the subject is an action, a set of extraordinary events, a revelation or puzzlement, the reaction that Shakespeare directs us to is astonishment. This is interestingly at odds with the impulse to explain, and it shows Shakespeare carefully matching the desire to know with the equally strong desire to stand back in awe.

Sometimes these two feelings appear together. At the close of *Much Ado About Nothing* the Friar, a very able practiser, sees the astonishment of the characters and assures them that he can explain ('qualify') all that has happened but that until then they should regard their state of wonder as normal:

> All this amazement can I qualify
> When after that the holy rites are ended
> I'll tell you largely of fair Hero's death.
> Meantime, let wonder seem familiar

It's as if Shakespeare is saying that both reactions must have a place at the close of a comedy.

The feelings of wonder and amazement are close to happiness, and happiness is the note on which comedies end. A very old definition of comedy is that

it starts in adversity and ends in felicity.

It's not always true that comedies have to start with problems (though some do), but it's essential that the note on which they close is one of joy, love and understanding. Comedies are not tragedies in disguise; the audience must feel throughout that the two kinds of plays have different trajectories: tragedy moves towards death and comedy towards a renewed happiness. Happy endings, particularly in Shakespeare, are often created by two events:

- the finding of the lost
- marriage.

- The finding of the lost

The plot of the lost being found is present in Shakespeare from the start of his career. What is probably his first play, *The Comedy of Errors*, closes with two sets of twins re-united and the re-union of a long-parted husband and wife. Later, in *Twelfth Night* the plot element that becomes increasingly important is that of the two twins, Viola and Sebastian. When they are restored to each other in the final scene of the play, Shakespeare devotes a good deal of space to the moving passage in which they gradually come to recognise who they are. In *A Midsummer Night's Dream* finding is accompanied by the emergence from delusion into a full knowledge of whom it is that one really loves. The lovers awake (both literally and metaphorically), and one of them, Helena, says:

> And I have found Demetrius like a jewel.

The one whom one loves is like a jewel – precious, valuable and the cause of endless delight and wonder.

Finding is also present in *The Importance of Being Earnest*; Jack Worthing has been lost by his governess as a child, but at the end he finds out who he is and, to his delight, discovers that his name is really Ernest. The finding can be metaphoric.

This is the theme of many of Shakespeare's late plays. At the close of *The Tempest*, Gonzalo sums up the different kinds of finding in the play when he says:

> In one voyage
> Did Claribel her husband find at Tunis,
> And Ferdinand her brother found a wife
> Where he himself was lost; Prospero his dukedom
> In a poor isle; and all of us ourselves,
> When no man was his own.

- The fact that this idea is one that appears throughout Shakespeare from what is probably his first to his last plays may indicate that it was a theme that held a particular fascination for him.

- Marriage

The ending of many comedies is marriage. The plots are largely taken up with the heady business of falling in love – its pranks, pains and pastimes – and it's significant that the play closes before we see what married life is like. (Often the married couples in comedies are there merely to provide problems for the young, or to be laughed at.) Yet in a comedy marriage is to be seen as the fulfilment of what the young most desire. In comedy marriage is seen as the proper conclusion of falling in love and as a promise for the future. Marriage unites the lovers and is the means by which the next generation will be conceived and nurtured. There is therefore in comedy the hope for the renewal of society.

Example

At the close of *As You Like It*, the god of marriage, Hymen, enters and speaks and sings of marriage. There is a stress upon the harmony of marriage:

> Then is there mirth in heaven
> When earthly things made even
> Atone together.

'Made even' means reconciled and 'Atone together' means brought together as one. That is what marriage does in comedies; because it is a social institution, characters are given a place in human society. Marriage is so important that Hymen says he wants the last word:

> Peace, ho, I bar confusion
> 'Tis I must make conclusion

And he points to the purpose of marriage – the birth of children:

> Wedding is great Juno's crown
> O blessed bond of board and bed.
> 'Tis Hymen peoples every town
> High wedlock then be honoured.

Whatever the individual reader or the members of an audience think of such language, they have to accept that this is the way in which comedy has traditionally worked. It is a convention that marriage is a 'blessed bond' in which husband and wife enjoy the companionship of the meal (board) and the marriage bed.

The stage filled with characters

What usually happens at the end of a comedy is that the stage is filled with all the characters. How a playwright engineers this is often a matter for admiration.

The fact that the stage is full gives expression to the idea that characters are given their place in society and that with marriage society is being renewed. One of the patterns of comedy is that a character is isolated from society and subjected to an ordeal or test; the happy ending of a comedy is the re-admission of that character. (In tragedy there is a similar pattern but the conclusion is one of the permanent exclusion of death.) Therefore it is particularly poignant when a character refuses the fellowship of society; Jaques in *As You Like It* stays in the forest instead of returning home, and Malvolio rushes off the stage in a rage.

Comedy can seem to be a very conservative art; its aim appears to be the endorsement of the status quo – society is renewed but it's not materially changed. A country girl may have been discovered to be a princess and is rewarded with a prince and a palace to live in, but her fellow milkmaids remain in the drudgery of the farmyard. But the experience of comedy is more complex than that. The stage full of people suggests that everyone does belong, no matter what their social status is, and if the currency of comedy is knowledge what we see at the end is an equal sharing of that commodity. Comedy may be conservative in its stress on the continuation of society but it's quite radical in its insistence upon the equality of those who participate. And remember:

- **the most important thing about a comic plot is that it ends happily.**

The audience, therefore, must be able to think of a society in which each has a place but in which all share the same knowledge as a happy one.

The Audience

Finally, a word must be said about the feelings of the audience. Unlike tragedy, the audience doesn't usually get deeply involved in the inner lives of comic characters. The audience always retains a slightly distant view of all the elements of the play. They are delighted and filled with wonder and they are also aware of how the complex plot has been worked out.

14.16   Comic characters

Characters in comedies are much more ordinary than those in tragedies. Although there is a king and a queen in *Love's Labour's Lost* and a duke in *Twelfth Night*, the audience never feels that the fate of their country rests upon them. In comedy even kings and queens are human and pleasantly ordinary. Consequently, comedies are not dominated by towering, heroic figures.

The names of plays confirm this: *Hamlet* and *Othello* are tragedies, whereas *The Taming of the Shrew* and *A Midsummer Night's Dream* are comedies.

Tragic titles focus on individuals, comic ones on the nature of the action.

The central characters of comedies come in pairs or groups. In *Much Ado about Nothing* there is the pair of Beatrice and Benedick, and in *As You Like It* Rosalind and Orlando. In a play such as *She Stoops to Conquer* there are a group of important characters: Hardcastle, Kate Hardcastle, Tony Lumpkin and Marlow. Two very important aspects of comic characters should be discussed at greater length:

- the centrality of women
- the importance of stock characters.

The centrality of women

Comedy, particularly Shakespearian comedy, is dominated by women. Men are tongue-tied or over-romantic, but the girls are witty, sensible and enterprising.

Rosalind is a splendid example. When she is turned out of her uncle's court, she disguises herself as a man and with her cousin, another enterprising girl called Celia, she goes off into the Forest of Arden. When she finds the man she loves, she proposes to him that she will pretend to be Rosalind so he can woo her to gain confidence. At the end she organises the marriages.

The idea of the enterprising girls is also present in Goldsmith. When Kate Hardcastle discovers that Marlow is too shy to marry her, she disguises herself as a serving maid.

Even in Wilde's *The Importance of being Earnest* the girls are more decisive than the men: both Gwendolen and Cecily decide they must marry a man who is called Ernest.

The idea of enterprising women getting their men is present in modern films and plays. In Bill Forsyth's *Gregory's Girl* (a play with a truly Shakespearian understanding of men and women) the awkward Gregory thinks he's going to have a date with one girl, but finds himself with another. When he innocently asks what's going on, he's told: 'It's just the way girls work. They help each other.'

The importance of stock characters

We have already seen (p.241) that Marlow in *She Stoops to Conquer* is a conventional character. There are many more in comedies. One reason for this is that stock figures are amusing.

Ben Jonson was aware of this. In *The Alchemist* Subtle and Face take over an alchemist's premises and let it be known that they have discovered what all alchemists were searching for – how to turn ordinary metal into gold. This news brings many visitors, all of whom are stock characters. For instance, there is the worldly man, Sir Epicure Mammon, who wants to satisfy his appetite for wealth, women and food; and a puritan called Tribulation Wholesome, who, although he is as greedy as the other visitors, solemnly claims he wants the money for the members of his religious congregation. One of the reasons why they amuse is that they conform to conventions; the audience can say of them, 'How typical!'

The other reason why there are more stock characters in comedy than tragedy is that in comedy the action is very important. Many of the things that entertain in comedy do so because of what is done rather than who is doing it. The stuff of comedy is mistaken identity, deception, and disguise, and those things are amusing in themselves. For instance, the trick Tony Lumpkin plays on Hastings and Marlow in *She Stoops to Conquer* is funny, because there is something basically amusing about two men thinking they are in a hotel when they are really in a private house. Because that idea is amusing in itself, there is no special need for the characters of Marlow and Hastings to be very full because their being full wouldn't add to the humour.

Whenever you meet a stock character in a comedy, you should ask:

- Why does the playwright introduce a stock character?

Two answers have been offered:

- stock characters are funny,
- stock characters can show that what is important is action.

There is a third reason which particularly applies to Shakespeare:

- they serve as a contrast to the more fully developed and original characters.

In *As You Like It* there are two very conventional characters – the love-sick Silvius and the girl he loves, the proud and disdainful Phoebe. In one scene Rosalind, a highly original character, overhears their conversation. She becomes so angry with Phoebe that she joins in. This has a comic result, for Phoebe falls in love with her (remember, she is dressed as a man), but the scene is important in another way. It shows how different Rosalind is from a stock character, and, consequently, the audience is led to see that her love is more real.

14.17   Love

If the central action of tragedy is the fall of the hero, the central action of comedy is another sort of fall – falling in love. Because love is very important, several aspects of it need to be explored:

- its suddenness
- the ways in which characters speak about it
- how it can be planned and the kind of plots it produces.

Love's suddenness

In comedies falling in love is often sudden and surprising. In *As You Like It* Rosalind and Orlando fall in love, if not quite, 'at first sight', after a very brief conversation. They meet at the wrestling match, and after Rosalind and Celia have failed to persuade him not to wrestle, Orlando overcomes the Duke's champion. Then he is overcome by her. When she gives him a chain as a token of his success, he stands in speechless admiration. Rosalind, as always, is never lost for a word, but even when she goes back to talk to him, he remains dumb. When she has gone he simply says: 'O poor Orlando, thou art overthrown!' He is – that is what love does.

In *The Importance of being Earnest* love is at first hearing rather than first sight. Cecily says that the moment she heard about Ernest she fell in love with him!

How characters speak about love

Because love is sudden, it is spoken about in dramatic ways. Love is said to be

- a madness
- a plague
- a game.

The thing that these three have in common is *transformation*. When characters are in love, they are transformed, and their picture of the world is transformed too.

Examples

Example 1

When Malvolio is deceived into believing that Olivia loves him, he transforms himself. The letter that has deceived him has spoken of yellow stockings and cross-gartering. These he willingly wears when he comes to woo her. The scene is both very funny and painfully embarrassing. He is in love with her, but she is only thinking of Cesario. Her attendants say that Malvolio has gone mad, to which she says:

> I'm as mad as he,
> If sad and merry madness equal be.

Example 2

In *A Midsummer Night's Dream* the Duke sums up the strange events that have happened to the lovers by saying:

> Lovers and madman have such seething brains,
> Such shaping fantasies, that apprehend
> More than cool reason ever comprehends.

That speech touches on two things: the 'seething' brains of both lovers and madmen, and the fact that they both see the world in quite strange ways. Their minds – 'fantasies' – are, 'shaping'; that is, they create in their minds the world they experience.

Love can be as sudden and devastating as the plague. When Olivia first falls in love she says:

> How now!
> Even so quickly may one catch the plague?

Two ideas are expressed in these lines. The idea of the suddenness of love and the comparison with disease. In the section on tragedy much stress was laid upon the mysteriousness of tragic action. The likeness between love and disease points to a similar mysteriousness in love. Love strikes suddenly and for no reason, as does the plague.

Love is compared to games, because games, or holidays, are joyful transformations of the ordinary working world. Throughout *As You Like It* there are frequent references to games, sports and holidays. At the beginning of the play Rosalind says to Celia: 'From henceforth I will, coz, and devise sports. Let me see, what think you of falling in love?' Later in the Forest of Arden (a place where life is transformed by love into a dream-like holiday) Rosalind playfully says to Orlando: 'Come, woo me, woo me; for now I am in a holiday humour and like enough to consent.' The image of games is deeply appropriate: love is playful, enjoyable and, above all, *not* like ordinary life.

How love is planned

You will remember that Jane Austen shows that love should be allowed to grow naturally, and that those who try to plan and plot are wrong (see pp. 191–2). That idea is not found in Shakespeare's comedies; in his plays characters can be brought to love each other.

The plot of *Much Ado about Nothing* turns on the attempts of Don Pedro and his friends to make Beatrice and Benedick fall in love. They succeed. Even in *As You Like It* plotting has a place. Although Rosalind and Orlando are in love, Rosalind needs to plot and plan in order to get the shy Orlando to declare his love. Comedy, then, shows that characters can be brought to love each other by trickery. The tricks that are used most are disguise and deception. Rosalind dresses up as a man and uses this disguise to get Orlando to court her, and Beatrice and Benedick are deceived into loving each other.

There is something comical about being in love. When cupid's arrows strike even the most staid and calm person can become wild, unpredictable and unstable. Watching people in love can, therefore, be very entertaining. This is why love has always been one of the major subjects of comedy. Of course, to the character in love, the experience can be frustrating, puzzling and confusing; to the audience, however, the antics of lovers can be very amusing. Take the case of Willis Hall's *Billy Liar*. This has a standard comic plot: Billy gets involved with too many girls and has to invent stories to wriggle out of difficult situations. If the audience allowed itself to imagine what it would be like to be in Billy's situation, they might well be horrified, but comedy does not work like that. We enjoy the attempts Billy makes to get himself out of tight situations and we laugh at how frantic the action becomes when he's close to being exposed. In one sense it's very Shakespearian (think of the confusions of *A Midsummer Night's Dream*), but in another it's not, because it doesn't close with marriage.

14.18 Laughter

The detachment of an audience makes laughter possible. Because many of the situations an audience laughs at are painful for the participants, a detachment from the feelings of characters is necessary. It has been stressed that comedy need not be funny, but the fact remains that it often is. Although it is very difficult to explain why something is amusing (a joke that has to be explained ceases to be funny), you should, when you write about comedies, be prepared to indicate how laughter arises. To help you to do this, three ideas about what makes people laugh will be discussed:

- expectation
- characters behaving like machines.
- a sense of proportion.

Expectation

Expectation can be funny both when it's fulfilled and when it's denied. When Tony Lumpkin directs Marlow and Hastings to Hardcastle's by telling them it's an inn, the audience expects to be amused by the misunderstanding and it is not disappointed; but when, towards the end of *The Playboy of the Western World* Christy Mahon's father turns up, the audience laughs because what has been expected has not occurred. Two common reactions to expectation are:

- I could see it coming

and

- I never expected that.

Characters behaving like machines

An audience also laughs when it sees characters being beaten or humiliated. The reason for this is that it sees characters' bodies simply as bodies. The more the human body approximates to a machine, that is, to something lacking personality, the funnier the actions become. It is possible to see bodies as machines because of the detachment of the audience.

In *The Comedy of Errors* there is much confusion between the two twin sons and the two twin servants that results in the servants being beaten. In *Twelfth Night* Sir Toby and Sir Andrew enter, bleeding and sore, after a beating they have received from Sebastian. Because the audience is detached, it laughs at the sight of characters reduced to little more than puppets.

When this kind of action is the major point of a play's humour, the result is farce rather than comedy. Farce can be a strangely disturbing experience:

characters are reduced to types, and bodies become machines, so that action is both frantic and absurd.

A sense of proportion

What usually saves comedy from being farce is a strong sense of proportion. Because we have a sense of proportion, we have an idea of how characters should and do, behave. When that sense of proportion is not reflected in behaviour, we laugh. When Malvolio woos Olivia, he offends our sense of proportion. When he appears in his yellow stockings, Olivia thinks he is ill, so suggests he goes to bed. Malvolio takes this in quite another way: 'To bed! ay, sweet-heart, and I'll come to thee.' That is funny, because people don't say that kind of thing when they start to woo; Malvolio outrages our sense of proportion. From this you can see that what counts as funny often depends upon the manners of society.

Exercises

14.1   Read the last scene in Shakespeare's *Julius Caesar* and then answer the questions below. Those who have killed Caesar, led by Brutus and Cassius, have been defeated by Mark Antony and Octavius. Cassius has committed suicide.

> *Brutus:* Come poor remains of friends, rest on this rock.
> *Clitus:* Statilius showed the torch-light, but my lord,
>   He came not back; he is or ta'en or slain.
> *Brutus:* Sit thee down, Clitus. Slaying is the word;
>   It is a deed in fashion. Hark thee, Clitus. (*Whispers*)
> *Clitus:* What I, my lord? No, not for all the world.
> *Brutus:* Peace then, no words.
> *Clitus:* I'll rather kill myself.
> *Brutus:* Hark thee, Dardanius. (*Whispers*)
> *Dardanius:* Shall I do such a deed?
> *Clitus:* O Dardanius!
> *Dardanius:* O Clitus!
> *Clitus:* What ill request did Brutus make to thee?
> *Dardanius:* To kill him Clitus. Look, he meditates.
> *Clitus:* Now is that noble vessel full of grief,
>   That it runs over even at his eyes.
> *Brutus:* Come hither, good Volumnius, list a word.
> *Volumnius:* What says my lord?
> *Brutus:* Why this, Volumnius,
>   The ghost of Caesar hath appeared to me
>   Two several times by night; at Sardis once,

And this last night, here in Philippi fields.
I know my hour is come.
Volumnius: Not so, my lord.
Brutus: Nay, I am sure it is, Volumnius.
Thou seest the world, Volumnius, how it goes;
Our enemies have beat us to the pit. [*Low alarums*]
It is more worthy to leap in ourselves,
Than tarry till they push us. Good Volumnius,
Thou know'st that we two went to school together;
Even for that our love of old, I prithee
Hold thou my sword-hilts, whilst I run on it.
Volumnius: That's not an office for a friend, my lord.

[*Alarum still*]

Clitus: Fly, fly my lord, there is no tarrying here.
Brutus: Farewell to you; and you; and you, Volumnius.
Strato, thou has been all this while asleep;
Farewell to thee too, Strato. Countrymen,
My heart doth joy that yet in all my life
I found no man but he was true to me.
I shall have glory by this losing day,
More than Octavius and Mark Antony
By this vile conquest shall attain unto.
So fare you well at once, for Brutus' tongue
Hath almost ended his life's history.
Night hangs upon mine eyes; my bones would rest,
That have but laboured to attain his hour.

[*Alarum. Cry within, 'Fly, fly, fly!'*]

Clitus: Fly, my lord, fly.
Brutus: Hence! I will follow.

[*Exeunt Clitus, Dardanius and Volumnius*]

I prithee Strato, stay thou by thy lord.
Thou art a fellow of a good respect;
Thy life hath had some smatch of honour in it.
Hold then my sword, and turn away thy face,
While I do run upon it. Wilt thou Strato?
Strato: Give me your hand first. Fare you well my lord.
Brutus: Farewell good Strato. [*Runs on his sword*] Caesar, now be still;
I killed not thee with half so good a will. [*Dies*]

[*Alarum. Retreat, Enter Octavius, Antony, Messala, Lucilius, and the Army*]

Octavius: What man is that?
Messala: My master's man. Strato, where is thy master?
Strato: Free from the bondage you are in Messala;
　　The conquerors can but make a fire of him.
　　For Brutus only overcame himself,
　　And no man else hath honour by his death.
Lucilius: So Brutus should be found. I thank thee Brutus,
　　That thou hast proved Lucilius' saying true.
Octavius: All that served Brutus, I will entertain them.
　　Fellow, wilt thou bestow thy time with me?
Strato: Ay, if Messala will prefer me to you.
Octavius: Do so, good Messala.
Messala: How died my master, Strato?
Strato: I held the sword, and he did run on it.
Messala: Octavius, then take him to follow thee,
　　That did the latest service to my master.
Antony: This was the noblest Roman of them all.
　　All the conspirators save only he
　　Did what they did in envy of great Caesar;
　　He only, in a general honest thought
　　And common good to all, made one of them.
　　His life was gentle, and the elements
　　So mixed in him that Nature might stand up
　　And say to all the world 'This was a man.'
Octavius: According to his virtue let us use him,
　　With all respect, and rites of burial.
　　Within my tent his bones tonight shall lie,
　　Most like a soldier, ordered honourably.
　　So call the field to rest, and let's away.
　　To part the glories of this happy day.　　　　[*Exeunt*]

(a)　Look for all the mentions of suicide and death in the scene and think about the effect this has on the atmosphere of the scene.

(b)　Even in death, Brutus stands out from the rest of the characters; how does Shakespeare make him such an outstanding figure? (You should look at how the others talk about him.)

(c)　Try to describe the feelings of the characters and your own feelings at the death of Brutus.

(d)　What is the effect of the two closing speeches from Mark Antony and Octavius?

14.2　Read the following passage from the end of *Twelfth Night*. The twins, Viola and Sebastian, are recognising each other. Sebastian has already married Olivia, the lady whom Orsino had courted by sending Viola to court for him. Viola is still dressed as Cesario, the name she assumed when she served Orsino and whom Olivia mistakenly loved.

Viola: If nothing lets to make us happy both
    But this my masculine usurped attire,
    Do not embrace me till each circumstance
    Of place, time, fortune do cohere and jump
    That I am Viola, which to confirm
    I'll bring you to a captain in this town
    Where lie my maiden weeds, by whose gentle help
    I was preserved to serve this noble count.
    All the occurrence of my fortune since
    Hath been between this lady and this lord.
Sebastian [*to Olivia*]: So comes it, lady, you have been mistook.
    But nature to her bias drew in that.
    You would have been contracted to a maid,
    Nor are you therein, by my life, deceived,
    You are betrothed both to a maid and man.
Orsino [*to Olivia*]: Be not amazed. Right noble is his blood.
    If this be so, as yet the glass seems true,
    I shall have share in this most happy wreck.
    (*To Viola*) Boy, thou has said to me a thousand times
    Thou never shouldst love woman like to me.
Viola: And all those sayings will I overswear,
    And all those swearings keep as true in soul
    As doth that orbed continent the fire
    That severs day from night.
Orsino: Give me your hand,
    And let me see thee in thy woman's weeds.

a)   Think about the extent to which explanation is important in the passage.
b)   Look through the passage for moments of wonder and amazement.
c)   Consider the importance of disguise in the passage.
d)   Think about the importance of love in the passage.

⬡15 The theatre of the imagination

15.1 A performing art

Drama is what is called a performing art. As a result, plays are the most immediate, the most intense and the most communal of all literary works. They are immediate because they are acted out in front of an audience, intense because what is said is concentrated into a few hours, and communal because they are enjoyed and judged by a group of people who have specially gathered to view them.

Examiners frequently complain that candidates hardly ever convey the *dramatic* nature of what they are writing about. This is often because they have never seen plays performed. You should, therefore, try to see a performance of your set plays, or, failing that, see any plays, so that you will understand the kind of impact drama can have.

The fact remains, however, that most candidates for public examinations get to know plays from books rather than theatres. Instead of the immediate, intense and communal experience of the theatre, you will be faced with words printed on paper.

● What can you do to make these words live as drama?

The answer is that you will have to learn to act out a play in the theatre of your imagination; that is, you will have to picture for yourself all the elements that go to make up a theatrical performance. The aim of this chapter is to suggest ways in which you can do this. Four areas of the theatre will be examined:

● atmosphere
● staging
● actors
● performance

15.2 Atmosphere

When you see a play in the theatre, you are aware of its atmosphere. The play creates a particular mood or feeling. On the page a play often seems to lack atmosphere. What you must do in order to appreciate the play is look at three aspects which create atmosphere:

- the characters
- the actions
- (in the case of Shakespeare) the imagery.

The characters

You can sometimes tell what the atmosphere of a play is by looking at the characters:

- if there are a number of stock characters, the play is likely to be light-hearted
- if it concerns kings and soldiers, the atmosphere is likely to be grave and serious.

Of course, characters are only a guide to what a play *might* be like. It is possible to have light-hearted plays about matters of state, and disturbing plays, such as Joe Orton's *Loot*, which contain stock characters. But as a guide it can be useful.

For instance, if you look at the characters of *She Stoops to Conquer*, you will expect the atmosphere to be a happy, domestic one. The major characters are the Hardcastles, their children, a family friend, Sir Charles Marlow, and his son and friend. When you see the social status of the characters – comfortable, upper middle-class – you may anticipate that much of the humour will revolve around manners. In both cases you will be right. Goldsmith presents a happy, domestic play in which the misunderstandings which cause the laughter are social in character.

The actions

The actions of a play create atmosphere:

- plays containing murders and battles are likely to be serious and even tragic
- eavesdropping, disguise and trickery produce an atmosphere of light-hearted merriment.

There are, of course, exceptions. *Othello*, one of the most harrowing tragedies, depends upon dramatic action associated with comedy – deception and eavesdropping. *Othello*, however, *is* an exception.

A play such as *The Importance of being Earnest* follows the general rule. There is a case of impersonation, the very funny requests of both Jack and Algernon that Canon Chasuble baptise them with the name of Ernest, and, at the end, a discovery which stems from Miss Prism recalling that, in a moment of absent-mindedness, she mistook the manuscript of the novel she had written for the baby she was looking after! Actions such as those are almost bound to produce a light-hearted atmosphere.

The imagery

It is often remarked of Shakespeare that each of his plays has its own distinctive atmosphere. Each play is, as it were, a separate world. This is in large measure due to the way in which each play has its own set of images.

In Part I on poetry it was pointed out that some poems are built around a single image. In Shakespeare, plays are built around a family of images, which are repeated as the action unfolds. Readers and theatre-goers often notice the recurrence of a word or image which gives a play a particular mood or colour.

Example

Consider *Macbeth*, which is full of recurring images: blood, clothes, darkness and night. Imagery of night occurs throughout.

When Lady Macbeth hears that King Duncan is to stay with them, she calls upon 'thick night' to hide her proposed crime. She later speaks of Duncan's murder as 'this night's great business', and after the murder there are a number of references to the terrible storm: 'the night has been unruly', 'the obscure bird / Clamoured the live long night', and 'a rough night'.

When Macbeth is eagerly looking forward to the murder of Banquo, he mentions night three times within ten lines: 'night's yawning peal', 'seeling night', and 'night's black agents'. The effect of these and other images is to create an atmosphere which is dark, threatening and 'thick' (a favourite word in the play) with evil.

15.3   Staging: the stage itself

You can always ask:

- What kind of stage would be most appropriate for this play?

Three types are used in the modern theatre.

The traditional stage

The traditional stage is that of an acting space behind the proscenium arch, from which hangs the curtain. The audience, as it were, see the action of the play through the 'window' formed by the proscenium arch. This type of stage is appropriate to plays that have realistic settings and deal with the manners and social habits of everyday living. It would, for instance, be appropriate to perform *The Importance of being Earnest* on such a stage.

The apron stage

A second type is the apron stage, which projects out into the body of the theatre, so that the audience sit on the three sides of the acting area. Some theatres that have apron stages have no proscenium arch, but others retain this feature. Apron stages bring the audience in and emphasise the *theatricality* of the theatre. When someone in the audience can look across the stage to another part of the audience, he or she will be very much aware of being in a theatre. As a result, plays that are deliberately theatrical work very well on apron stages. *A Man for all Seasons* is an example. The Common Man, who acts as a chorus as well as taking a number of parts, could talk to the audience and then join in the action of the play.

Theatre in the round

The third type is a variation of the apron stage – theatre in the round. This is a stage which, rather like a circus ring, is surrounded by the audience except for the entrance and exit point. This type of stage works very well for small-scale works. Harold Pinter's plays *The Homecoming* and *The Caretaker* can be effective in the round.

- **When you think about staging Shakespeare, it is useful to bear in mind the kind of stage for which he wrote.**

It was a very large apron stage with two doors for entrances and exits. In addition, between the two doors there was probably an inner stage which was screened off by a curtain, and, above the main acting area, a gallery or balcony. A number of scenes are understandable in the light of these conditions.

- Because the stage projected a long way into a circular, tiered theatre, the soliloquy would be very effective. The actor would not be very far away from the audience, so could either address them directly or could allow them to overhear his or her innermost thoughts.
- The two doors would be useful for opposing armies. Towards the end of *Julius Caesar* Antony's army could enter at one door and Brutus's and Cassius's at the other.
- The inner stage could be used for eavesdropping, as in the scenes in which Beatrice and Benedick overhear the other characters talking about them,
- The inner stage could also be used for discoveries, as at the end of *The Tempest*, when Miranda and Ferdinand are discovered playing chess.
- The balcony could be used as the ramparts of a castle. Richard II could appear on the balcony to Bolingbroke at Flint Castle.

Shakespeare's plays work well on most stages, though, of course, the effects are different with the type of stage used. It is certainly not the case that his plays only work on the kind of stage described above. Nevertheless, it is a good idea to imagine how Shakespeare's plays would have worked in the theatres of his day.

When you study one of his plays, you can try reconstructing such a performance in your imagination, paying attention to the effects made possible by the size of the stage, the proximity of the audience, the two entrances, the inner stage and the balcony. When you do this, certain features of a play become evident. For instance, *Macbeth* is a lonely play in which, for much of the time, two isolated, mentally tortured characters occupy a vast stage. Messengers come and go, but the lonely and anguished Macbeth and Lady Macbeth remain in stark isolation.

15.4   Staging: scenery

Stage scenery is usually the responsibility of the designer. If you like art, it is a useful exercise designing your own scenery for a play, but if not, you should still try to imagine what kind of sets would be appropriate. In some plays a specific set is required. For instance, it would be impossible to produce *The Caretaker* without two beds and a pile of junk.

Other plays are not quite so specific, but their words make it clear that a particular kind of setting is necessary. *She Stoops to Conquer*, for instance, needs a rambling domestic set, and *The Royal Hunt of the Sun* should have rich, exotic settings. Shakespeare can be produced with elaborate or plain sets, with sets that change each scene, or one that remains throughout the performance.

- **The question you should always have in mind is that of appropriateness.**   For instance, in *The Winter's Tale* the scenes in Sicilia need to be very different from those in Bohemia, and in *Antony and Cleopatra* the Roman scenes must look different from the Egyptian ones. Whenever, then, you study a play, you should ask yourself:

- What kind of scenery would be appropriate to the atmosphere of the play?

15.5   Staging: costume

Costume, like scenery, should be appropriate to the play. It should express the particular character of an individual and contribute to the atmosphere of the play. It is, therefore, a useful exercise to ask yourself how you imagine the characters to be dressed.

For example, at the beginning of the play, Hamlet must look different from everyone else. He is still in mourning for his father (he talks of his 'customary suits of solemn black') whilst the rest are celebrating a royal wedding. You should try to picture the contrast and understand how it shows the difference between the brooding, inward-looking Prince and the practical, busy nature of the new king's court.

In the case of Shakespeare, it is interesting to ask about the period of the play. With the exception of the histories, Shakespeare's plays lend themselves to being costumed in a number of historical periods. There have been eighteenth-century, Victorian, Edwardian, 1920s and 1960s productions of tragedies and comedies. When you are thinking about costumes, you can ask yourself:

• Would a particular historical period be appropriate to this play?

For instance, a 1930s setting of *Julius Caesar* would emphasise the threat of dictatorship and highlight Brutus's dilemma: should Caesar be killed in case he becomes a tyrant?

15.6   Staging: lighting

Although lighting is a recent introduction to the theatre, it is a very powerful way of creating atmosphere. You should always ask yourself:

• How should this scene should be lit?

The tense, mysterious opening to *Hamlet* requires subdued lighting, while the wonderful sunrise scene in *A Midsummer Night's Dream*, when the lovers wake up and find that their confusing nightmare is over, would be very effective if the light gradually grew stronger and stronger, signifying the return of sanity and harmony. The point to remember about lighting – and also about scenery and costume – is that particular effects can interpret the play. *Twelfth Night*, for instance, can be played as a happy comedy and also as a rather melancholy play. Bright, clear light would help the former interpretation, and subdued light the latter.

15.7   Actors: age

The third major area to think about is that of the actors. When you stage a play in the theatre of your imagination, you will have some idea of what kind of actors would be suitable, and how you think they should perform their parts. Here the matters discussed in Chapter 12, 'The Language of Drama', are important. You are free to imagine the kind of movements an actor makes and the kind of groupings that would be suitable on the stage.

In doing this, you must remember that in many plays you are offered a *number* of opportunities. It is very rare that a play needs to be acted in one particular way. You should also remember that actors bring their own particular personality to bear upon a part. When, therefore, you think about actors, you should remember that the words of a play are a starting point for a number of different performances. With those qualifications in mind, you can think about three things:

- age
- size
- voice.

To ask about the age an actor needs to be to play a part is to ask about how old a character is. This question only really arises in Shakespeare, because in most of the plays since his time the playwright makes the ages of characters clear. The point to remember in Shakespeare is that the age of a character has a bearing upon the interpretation of the play.

Example

Take the case of Malvolio. He is often presented as quite an old man, although there is no real support in the text for such an interpretation.

If he is played as old, the scene in which he tries to stop the drunken riot caused by Sir Toby, Sir Andrew and Feste becomes a case of age rebuking youth. But how would the wooing of Olivia be played? If the actor is old, or just plays the part as an old man, the scene in which he approaches Olivia in his yellow stockings would be grotesque as well as funny.

This scene would work very differently if the actor were young. The actor then could play Malvolio as someone deeply in love with Olivia but sadly inept in his courtship. Instead of the grotesqueness of age the audience would be presented with the pathos of love-sick youth.

Both scenes could be moving but in quite different ways.

- **The question of age can be usefully applied to other characters:**

- Are the Macbeths old or young?
- How much older is Claudius than Hamlet?
- Is Don Pedro much older than Benedick and Claudio?
- Should Antonio be played as a mature man, or as someone very much in decline?

15.8   Actors: size

It is worthwhile asking what contribution an actor's size makes to a performance.

- Lady Bracknell is a domineering figure in *The Importance of being Earnest* but if she were played by someone who was small there would be the added comedy of the smallest person on stage ordering everybody else about.
- Likewise, O'Casey's *Juno and the Paycock* would have a comic opening if the Captain were a big lumbering man and Juno were short. The size of the actors would reflect the farcical elements in the play – a wife violently angry

with her husband – but might cause problems when, towards the end, the action becomes more tragic.

- It is worth asking about the size of actors playing Shakespeare. It would, for instance, be very poignant if Othello were played by a big man and Iago by a small man, because the spectacle of a big, heroic figure of evident nobility brought to a state of inhuman jealousy by a slight, spare man would show how vulnerable Othello was.

15.9   Actors: voice

Voice should be appropriate to character.

- The man who plays Sir Thomas More in *A Man for all Seasons* should speak in a quiet, thoughtful manner, so an actor with a voice that is either deep or soft would be most suitable.
- In comedies it is very important for voices to match parts. It would, for instance, be difficult to imagine Lady Bracknell with a high-pitched voice or Sir Andrew Aguecheek with a hearty, deep one.
- In other parts, particularly tragedies, the quality of voice matters less. However, it is important to ask yourself how you imagine Hamlet or Macbeth to sound. A Hamlet with a slow, heavy voice might bring out the brooding elements but would be less suited to the playful aspects of the character. Likewise, an actor with a rich, romantic voice could do justice to the poetic side of Macbeth but might be less suited to portraying the character's ruthless side.

15.10   Performance: the presence of actors

When you have thought about the kind of actors that would be suitable, you can go on to consider the last area – how the play is performed. There are a number of points you should consider:

- the effect of an actor's presence
- the use of the pause
- the contribution of music and dance
- the effect of spectacle, ghosts and fights.

When you see a play, you realise that a character can be very effective even if he or she says little or nothing. The mere fact of a character's presence can be dramatically telling. When you read a play, you will have to remind yourself that though a character is not saying anything his or her very presence might be effective.

Pinter's *The Caretaker* begins with an intriguing scene. A man stands all alone in a room, he looks about him, turns and exits. Although he says nothing, the audience will find itself asking a number of questions. Who is he? What is he doing? Where is he going? Will he be seen again? When you read a play with a scene such as that in it, you will have to imagine the strange and intriguing presence of a silent character.

In the scene from *The Winter's Tale* discussed above in Chapter 12, 'The Language of Drama', the boy Mamillius remains on stage after the violent entry of his father, Leontes. While his parents argue, he stands silent. This could be played so as to be very moving, because before Leontes's entry he was very talkative. His silent presence, no doubt the result of sheer bewilderment, could be touching and effective.

15.11   Performance: the pause

In a theatre the audience is very much aware of pauses. When an actor stops speaking, the audience feels that the pause indicates that either something important has or will happen.

In modern plays pauses are part of the text. Pinter and Beckett clearly give a great deal of thought to where they are placed. When, therefore, you can act out a play in the theatre of your imagination, you have to imagine the expectation and the tension caused by pauses.

__ **Example** _____

Pinter's *The Homecoming* starts with Max asking Lennie whether or not he has finished with the scissors:

> *Max*: What have you done with the scissors? [*Pause*] I said I'm looking for the scissors. What have you done with them? [*Pause*] Did you hear me? I want to cut something out of the paper.
> *Lenny*: I'm reading the paper.
> *Max*: Not that paper. I haven't even read that paper. I'm talking about last Sunday's paper. I was just having a look at it in the kitchen. [*Pause*] Do you hear what I'm saying? I'm talking to you! Where's the scissors?

The pauses bring home the annoyance of Max, who wants attention, and the frustration of Lenny, who wants to get on with his newspaper. They also give the audience time to see that these are the emotions that are present, and time, too, to see that the situation is tense and also slightly comical. In other words, the pauses direct the audience's attention to what Pinter thinks is significant in the relation between Max and Lenny.

In the case of Shakespeare, there are no pauses in the text. Therefore, when you study a play you have to ask:

- Would pauses be suitable in this scene, and, if so, where?

Example

When in *Macbeth* the body of Duncan is discovered, there is confusion and panic. It emerges that the grooms (attendants) appear to have been responsible for the murder, and Macbeth admits that he has killed them:

Lennox: ... they stared, and were distracted;
  No man's life was to be trusted with them.
Macbeth: O! yet I do repent me of my fury,
  That I did kill them.
Macduff: Wherefore did you so?
Macbeth: Who can be wise, amazed, temperate and furious,
  Loyal and neutral, in a moment ...

It is a very tense moment: will the real murderer – Macbeth – be discovered, or will everyone believe that the grooms were responsible?

If there were a pause after Macbeth's 'That I did kill them', Macduff's question would sound very threatening. If, too, there were a pause before Macbeth answered Macduff's question, it would seem as if he were searching for an explanation to hide his guilt.

You should not only imagine where pauses come in order to realise the dramatic tension of the scene. A lack of a pause can also interpret a scene in a particular way. If, for instance, there were *no* pause before Macbeth's reply, it would indicate that Macbeth had already anticipated the question and had thought out a reply. Macbeth would then be interpreted as a ruthless schemer rather than a man learning painfully how to be evil.

15.12 Performance: the contribution of music and dance

The effects of music and dance are very difficult to imagine. On stage music can have a transforming effect upon a scene, and dance adds a physical excitement that is very difficult to convey in words. Hard as it is to imagine their impact, you can approach the contribution of music and dance by reminding yourself of certain things.

Song

You can recall what was said in Chapter 11, 'The Conventions of Drama', that a successful song should echo and contribute to the mood of the scene, and that dances were understood by the audience as an expression of harmony and concord.

You can also ask yourself what kind of tune would be suitable. When you come across a song (and remember, it is not only Shakespeare who includes them), you should look very closely at the words in order to judge their tone and then decide what kind of tune would match them. You can be quite free in thinking about suitable kinds of tune; there have been successful productions of Shakespeare that used the rhythms of pop music.

Dance

In the case of dance you can always write about the impact it makes. Drama is not just a matter or words; the vigorous physical movements of dance can be a very impressive contribution to a play.

If you have to write about a scene that includes dance, you should remember that drama is a performing art, and so point to the way in which the play comes over through words, action and dance. You can do this by asking what kind of dance would be suitable: rapid and lively, slow and languid, smooth and graceful? The dance in *Romeo and Juliet*, for instance, will be different from the one in *The Winter's Tale*; in the former the dance is a courtly affair, in the latter it is part of rustic celebrations.

15.13   Performance: spectacle

When you want to talk about the total impact of words, action and dance, a useful word to use is 'spectacle'. Some scenes in plays demand the colour of settings and costume, the stylised gestures of actors, the accompaniment of music, and the excitement of dance.

Such a scene is the wedding masque in *The Tempest*. The allegorical figures speak in elaborate, lyrical verse. It would be appropriate to imagine them richly costumed, moving with delicate, stylised steps, and being accompanied by mysterious music. Other plays also present opportunities for spectacle.

In Shakespeare the Egyptian scenes of *Antony and Cleopatra* require to be performed in a lush and spectacular fashion, and in the modern theatre a play such as *The Royal Hunt of the Sun* requires a colourful and dramatic production.

● **When you read a play, you should look out for moments of potential spectacle and try to imagine the impact they make.**

15.14   Performance: ghosts and fights

Ghosts

Ghosts are often a problem, particularly in Shakespeare. All you are given in the text of a play is 'Enter a ghost'; it is up to you to do the rest. You could think how a ghost could be presented. Eerie music, weird lights and a hollow, sepulchral voice present a popular solution, but some audiences get so used to that kind of presentation that ghosts cease to arouse feelings of strangeness and mystery. Alternatively, the ghost could be played by someone who was very tall or very thin. The actor could move in a very stylised way, and speak slowly, dreamily or in a monotone.

You could also ask yourself what the impact would be if there were no ghost physically present. In some plays the absence of an actor playing a ghost would have a considerable effect. Macbeth is the only one who sees Banquo's ghost. If the audience can also see him, it looks upon Macbeth as a man who is either especially sensitive or especially guilty. But if there is no ghost for the audience to see, it views Macbeth as the guests at the banquet do – as a strange and rather terrible man who is troubled by hallucinations.

Fights

The main difficulty you will have with stage fights is to imagine the impact they have upon the audience. Stage fights, in order to be effective, must appear to be savage and violent. You will have to imagine that. You can think of the noises – the clash of swords, the gasps for breath, the sounds of bodies crashing onto the stage – and picture the fear in the faces, the desperate movements and the sight of blood. Recalling fights you have seen on television may help you, but they are often tame in comparison with the sight of real people wielding real weapons.

Fights bring home the immediacy of drama. The best thing you can do, as with all matters relating to the acting out of a play in the theatre of your imagination, is to try to realise the impact, which is basic to all theatre, of seeing real people performing in front of you.

Exercises

15.1   The following passage is the close of the first act of Peter Shaffer's *The Royal Hunt of the Sun*. Atahuallpa is the Inca king who is thought by himself and his people to be divine; Valverde is the priest of the invading Spanish army, and Pizarro is their leader. Read the passage carefully and then answer the questions below.

[*The music crashes over the stage as the Indian procession enters in an astonishing explosion of colour. The King's attendants – many of them playing musical instruments: reed pipes, cymbals, and giant marraccas – are as gay as parrots. They wear costumes of orange and yellow, and fantastic head-dresses of gold and feathers, with eyes embossed on them in staring black enamel. By contrast, Atahuallpa Inca presents a picture of utter simplicity. He is dressed from head to foot in white: across his eyes is a mask of jade mosaic, and round his head a circlet of plain gold. Silence falls. The King glares about him.*]

Atahuallpa [*haughtily*]: Where is the god?

Valverde [*through Felipillo*]: I am a Priest of God.

Atahuallpa: I do not want the priest. I want the god. Where is he? He sent me greeting.

Valverde: That was our General. Our God cannot be seen.

Atahuallpa: I may see him.

Valverde: No. He was killed by men and went into the sky.

Atahuallpa: A god cannot be killed. See my father! You cannot kill him. He lives for ever and looks over his children every day.

Valverde: I am the answer to all mysteries. Hark, pagan, and I will expound.

Old Martin: And so he did, from the Creation to Our Lord's ascension. [*He goes off*]

Valverde [*walking among the Indians to the right*]:   And when he went he left the Pope as Regent for him.

De Nizza [*walking among the Indians to the left*]: And when he went he left the Pope as Regent for him.

Valverde: He has commanded our King to bring all men to belief in the true God.

De Nizza: He has commanded our King to bring all men to belief in the true God.

Valverde and De Nizza [*together*]: In Christ's name therefore I charge you: yield yourself his willing vassal.

Atahuallpa: I am the vassal of no man! I am the greatest prince on earth. Your King is great. He has sent you far across the water. So he is my brother. But your Pope is mad. He gives away countries that are not his. His faith also is mad.

Valverde: Beware!

Atahuallpa: Ware you! You kill my people; you make them slaves. By what power?

Valverde: By this. [*He offers a Bible*] The Word of God.

[*Atahuallpa holds it to his ear. He listens intently. He shakes it.*]

Atahuallpa: No word. [*He smells the book, and then licks it. Finally he throws it down impatiently.*] God is angry with your insults.

Valverde: Blasphemy!

Atahuallpa: God is angry!

Valverde [*calling*]: Francisco Pizarro, do you stay your hand when Christ is insulted? Let this pagan feel the power of your arm. I absolve you all! San Jago!

[*Pizarro appears above with drawn sword, and in a great voice sings out his battle-cry.*]

Pizarro: SAN JAGO Y CIERRA ESPANA!

[*Instantly from all sides the soldiers rush in, echoing the great cry.*]

Soldiers: SAN JAGO!
　[*There is a tense pause. The Indians look at this ring of armed men in terror. A violent drumming begins, and there ensues:*

　　　THE MIME OF THE GREAT MASSACRE
　To a savage music, wave upon wave of Indians are slaughtered and rise again to protect their lord who stands bewildered in their midst. It is all in vain. Relentlessly the Spanish soldiers hew their way through the ranks of feathered attendants towards their quarry. They surround him. Salinas snatches the crown off his head and tosses it up to Pizarro, who catches it and to a great shout crowns himself. All the Indians cry out in horror. The drum hammers on relentlessly while Atahuallpa is led off at sword-point by the whole band of Spaniards. At the same time, dragged from the middle of the sun by howling Indians, a vast bloodstained cloth bellies out over the stage. All rush off; their screams fill the theatre. The lights fade out slowly on the rippling cloth of blood.]

(a)　Would you include any other pauses in the dialogue, and where and why would you place them?

(b)　How do you imagine the Incas and the Spaniards are dressed?

(c)　The music is said to be 'savage'. Try to imagine what kind of music would be suitable and what effect it would have.

(d)　Read very carefully the stage directions for THE MIME OF THE GREAT MASSACRE. Try to imagine how you would stage it. You could think about such matters as the grouping of the actors, the lighting, the actions of the killers (stylised or realistic?) and the kind of stage that would be suitable.

15.2　Read the following extract from Act IV Scene 4 of *The Winter's Tale* and answer the questions below. Perdita is dressed in a special way for the feast, and so, you may imagine, are the rest of the characters. The atmosphere is one of celebration.

　　[*Enter Shepherd, with Polixenes and Camillo disguised; Clown, Mopsa, Dorcas, and others*]
　Shepherd: Fie, daughter! when my old wife lived, upon
　　This day she was both pantler, butler, cook;
　　Both dame and servant; welcomed all, served all,
　　Would sing her song and dance her turn; now here,
　　At upper end o' th'table, now i' th' middle;
　　On his shoulder, and his; her face o'fire
　　With labour, and the thing she took to quench it
　　She would to each one sip. You are retired,

As if you were a feasted one and not
The hostess of the meeting: pray you, bid
These unknown friends to's welcome; for it is
A way to make us better friends, more known.
Come, quench your blushes and present yourself
That which you are, mistress o' th' feast; come on,
And bid us welcome to your sheep-shearing,
As your good flock shall prosper.

Perdita: [*To Polixenes*] Sir, welcome:
It is my father's will I should take on me
The hostess-ship o' th' day: – [*To Camillo*] You're welcome, sir.
For you there's rosemary and rue; these keep
Seeming and savour all the winter long:
Grace and remembrance be to you both,
And welcome to our shearing!

Polixenes: Shepherdess, –
A fair one are you, – well you fit our ages
With flowers of winter.

Perdita: Sir, the year growing ancient,
Not yet on summer's death, nor on the birth
Of trembling winter, the fairest flowers o' th' season
Are our carnations, and streaked gillyvors,
Which some call nature's bastards: of that kind
Our rustic garden's barren, and I care not
To get slips of them.

Polixenes: Wherefore, gentle maiden,
Do you neglect them?

Perdita: For I have heard it said
There is an art which in their piedness shares
With great creating nature.

Polixenes: Say there be;
Yet nature is made better by no mean
But nature makes that mean: so, over that art,
Which you say adds to nature, is an art
That nature makes. You see, sweet maid, we marry
A gentler scion to the wildest stock,
And make conceive a bark of baser kind
By bud of nobler race: this is an art
Which does mend nature, change it rather, but
The art itself is nature.

Perdita: So it is.

Polixenes: Then make your garden rich in gillyvors,
And do not call them bastards.

Perdita: I'll not put
The dibble in earth to set one slip of them;
No more than, were I painted, I would wish

This youth should say, 'twere well, and only therefore
Desire to breed by me. Here's flowers for you;
Hot lavender, mints, savory, marjoram;
The marigold, that goes to bed with' sun,
And with him rises weeping: these are flowers
Of middle summer, and I think they are given
To men of middle age. Y'are very welcome.

(a)   How would you design costumes for the play? Would you clothe Polixenes and Camillo, who have come to spy on the gathering, in a different way from the shepherd and his son, the clown?

(b)   How would you imagine the shepherd delivers his speech? What actions and gestures would he use, and how should the actors be grouped on the stage?

(c)   What is the impact of Perdita giving flowers to the characters? How do you imagine it should be staged?

(d)   There is tension between Polixenes and Perdita: how would you like it to be acted out on stage?

Part IV
As You Study

16 Reading, notes, preparation

16.1 Reading

If you are taking an examination in English Literature, you should aim to know the books you are studying thoroughly, more thoroughly, in fact, than either your teacher or your examiner. They are not taking the examination!

But what does it mean to know a book thoroughly? It can't just be a matter of knowing the names of all the characters and remembering all the lines. What you should aim at is *understanding*. In fact, the title of this chapter could be extended to

'Reading and *re-reading – with understanding*'.

If you don't understand what you are reading, you are not really reading.

The question to ask yourself, then, is.

- How can I read a book with understanding? Before advice on that question can be given, three preliminary points must be made.

- **You should read the *whole* book.**

There is no place in proper reading for skipping passages. Since a book, be it a novel, play or poems, is something that an author intended to write, you can only grasp that intention by reading all of it.

- **You should try to read in a place that is quiet.**

Nowadays, many people find this difficult because they are so used to having background music; some even say that without it they feel distracted. Nevertheless, if you are to do justice to a book you *need* silence. This is particularly important in the case of poetry, or drama written in verse. Background music, particularly if it has a strong rhythm, is bound to clash with the rhythms of the lines you are reading. The result will be that you do not fully take in what is before you.

- **You should read frequently.**

If you read a novel over a very long period of time, you will miss the shape of the plot and the development of characters. With poetry, frequent reading is necessary because poetry is an unusual form of literature. In order to appreciate the way, for instance, rhythm enacts meaning or the ambiguity of words is exploited, you need to read frequently in order to accustom yourself to the way poets use words.

16.2   Reading with understanding

Now for the question: how can I read a book with understanding? The best advice that can be given is to bear in mind a number of questions as you read. If you find you are losing the thread of the book, or your concentration is slackening, you can bring the book sharply into focus again by putting a question to yourself. Of course, some questions are more appropriate to one book than another, and the list that follows is not exhaustive. You can always look back through the separate chapters on poetry, novels and drama to find further questions to ask. The point to remember, however, is that the questions you put to yourself are intended to help you read with understanding. Therefore, the basic one that can apply to any book is this:

● **Do I understand what I am reading?**

The questions that follow are all aspects of that one.

● **Am I following what is happening?**

This can apply to the argument of a poem, the developing relation between characters in a novel, and the growth of a plot in a play. A simple way of answering the question is by looking back through the preceding lines or pages and trying to understand how arguments or events have developed. It is usually worthwhile doing this. If you miss a connection in the argument or story, you may find yourself increasingly puzzled as you read further.

● **You can ask this: why are the characters behaving in this way?**

In the case of novels, plays and, in some cases, narrative poems this question turns on the motives of characters. In most literature the author is interested not only in what characters do but in *why* they do it. If you feel you are not in touch with the characters of a book, you can always stop and think about their reason for behaving as they do. If you cannot find a satisfactory reason, it may be that the author is not bothered about motivation but merely wants to establish a new situation in the plot.

● **Am I in touch with the mood?**

When you are reading a book for the first time, it is easy to misinterpret its mood. Mood is usually two-fold:

(i)   atmosphere – you can think hard about how the settings build up the atmosphere of a book in a way that is appropriate to its meaning.

(ii) tone – this comes down to asking about the attitude of the author, and considering such matters as how he or she views the characters and passes judgement upon them.

When you question the motives of characters and inquire about the mood of a book, you are thinking about the way the author is writing the book. This, of course, is central to understanding what a book is about. There is another question directly concerning authorship.

- **Can I see how the plot is being constructed?**

It is a good idea to ask yourself this question, because many students, to put it simply, fail to see the wood for the trees. They understand individual incidents but can't see the book as a whole. Therefore, as you read, you can ask yourself whether you can see the problem from which the plot grows and whether it is built on parallels and contrasts – in other words, whether you can see the plot and not just a sequence of events.

The above questions are more applicable to novels and plays than to poetry. In the case of a number of poems by one author or an anthology based on a common period or theme, you can ask the next question.

- **How similar is this poem to the others?**

This is very important. One of the hardest things at GCSE and A Level is seeing connections between a number of short poems. If, as you read, you can bear in mind the other poems, you can begin to see them as a group rather than as separate pieces.

- **How am I being invited to respond?**

This is one question that applies to any work of literature. It is a particularly good idea to ask this question if you find that your concentration is slackening. Reading a book is a collaboration between you and the author. The author is inviting you to feel, to think, and to judge as you read. If you are not paying proper attention, you will take the book in as a set of facts but no more. It is, then, a good idea to stop and ask yourself what you are feeling about the characters. As you do so, you must remember that your feelings will be appropriate if they arise out of a response to what the author is trying to do.

- There is a final point that must be made about reading and understanding:

If you read a book attentively, you will be studying it. Sometimes, it is thought that reading and study are two entirely different activities. They are not.

Studying is reading done with an awareness of what it is you are looking at and of what is going on in your mind.

16.3   Making notes

Although reading and study are not separate activities, there is one thing you should do when you are studying that you are unlikely to do if you are just reading for pleasure – make notes. There are two ways of making notes, and if you are wise you will do both.

(i)   If you own the book you are studying (and if you don't, it is a good idea to buy one) you can make brief notes in the margin. Because margins are not very broad, you will not be able to write very much. All you will be able to do is underline important parts or make the briefest of comments on what is happening. Nevertheless, this is very valuable. If you mark your book in this way, you have a guide to the important parts and some notes that will help you interpret what is happening.

(ii)   But notes in the margins of books are not enough. You are foolish if you try to rely solely upon them. What you need as well is a notebook in which you can write at greater length about the ideas that occur to you. Sometimes notes in the margin of a book are so brief that you forget what you mean by them. If you have a notebook in which you can write down your ideas at length, you will not fall into this trap.

But what should you put into your notebook? Here are a few ideas.

(1)   A brief summary of the plots of novels and plays

Some students find this helpful. It can take a number of forms.

●   You can summarise the bare bones of the plot in one or two paragraphs. The advantage of this is that it helps you see what problems the plot is based on and what issues it raises.

●   You can give a brief summary of what happens in each chapter or scene. This has the advantage of ensuring that you don't get the order of events confused.

●   You can draw up a chart of characters and scenes, noting who appears in which. (This is more appropriate to drama than novels.) This can be helpful in seeing who the major characters are and estimating the extent to which they dominate the stage.

●   When making notes on poetry, you can briefly record the issue with which each poem deals.

(2) Make detailed notes

To know a book well you must think about it in detail. You should, therefore, make detailed notes about chapters, scenes, lines, and words. You can do this in a number of ways.

- You should try to recognise anything that puzzles you and frame it as a question. Sometimes the question yields more writing; you could, for instance, briefly explore two ways of answering it. But some questions are simply useful on their own and can be left to prompt more thought when you read through your notes.
- Many of the notes you will want to make will be on the significance of something. That is to say, you will want to express *why* an event is important. This could be because

  — it shows a character developing
  — it focuses on the main theme of the book
  — it parallels another part of the work.

When you note down that an event is significant, you will be interpreting the book's *meaning*. (More will be said about this in Chapters 17 and 19.)

- Your notes will also be about your reactions. It is a good idea to record how you feel about a word, a line or what a character does, particularly when you are reading the book for the first time. The impressions you receive from a first reading are especially valuable, because you don't know what to expect. Among your impressions you will want to say something about the quality of the book. You should note whether you think a scene is handled well, and also remark upon it if you think it is done badly. If you can see a reason for this, you should, of course, give it.

Avoiding problems

- Notes can easily get out of hand. Some students make too many. This is unwise; you should remember that examinations test your thinking about works and not your notes on those works!
- Another difficulty is that notes can become jumbled. You can avoid this by remembering to take four precautions

  — You should make it clear what the notes on the page are about by writing clear headings.
  — You should work out a convenient form of abbreviations and stick to it: for instance, you can call Shakespeare 'Sh.'

— You should leave a line between each remark. You will find it is much easier revising if each point appears separately on the page.

— You should find a method of distinguishing between particular and general points. Particular points are about the immediate words or lines of a stanza, chapter or scene; general points are about what the author is doing in the book as a whole. As you read and make notes about particular points, you will find that ideas start to occur to you about the whole book. You can keep a separate section for these notes, or you can put them in with the others, but distinguish them by putting them in brackets or writing them with a different coloured pen. Either way you will have a fund of ideas for thinking about the work as a whole.

16.4   Re-reading

Many people who don't take examinations re-read their favourite books. They do so because they find the books rich and rewarding. It is to be hoped that the books on your syllabuses are like that, because when you study for an examination, you will have to re-read your set works. Indeed, some teachers say that reading only really begins with re-reading, that is to say, you can only really think about a book when you are familiar with its plot and characters.

That view may be an extreme one, but it does point to the fact that in order to get to know a book well, re-reading, or, in the case of plays, re-viewing is essential. And when you re-read a book, you will be surprised to see what you have missed or forgotten. To re-read a book is to see new aspects of a character, to respond more deeply to the atmosphere, to understand its themes more deeply, and to appreciate more keenly how it is written. Sometimes a line that you ignored will jump at you from the page, and on other occasions you will find that what you didn't like because it seemed far-fetched is now quite credible. Furthermore, you will find that as your experience of life grows, your response to literature will grow too.

Since, then, re-reading is essential to study, what can be said about reading a book with an examination in mind? You will find that you have to do three kinds of work:

● preparation
● classwork
● follow-up notes

If you are taking an examination on your own, preparation and class-work will not apply to you, but follow-up notes will.

16.5   Preparation

If you know that a poem, chapter or scene is to be discussed in class, you will have to read or re-read it to prepare yourself. You should remember that the more familiar you are with the work under discussion, the more you will be able to contribute to and gain from the class. Preparation, if it is done properly, can be a lengthy business. First, you must read the sections that are going to be discussed. It is always helpful if you can read them more than once, particularly with poetry.

But reading is not all you should do. The discussion of literature usually centres on an examination of the meaning of a book, on appreciation of how the author establishes that meaning, and the thinking through of the pleasures, questions and judgements that occur to you in the act of reading.

In order to prepare yourself for this you should make notes that you can use in class. These need not be extensive. The best thing to do is read the sections to be discussed and notice what you notice. In other words:

- Try to be aware of the impressions and thoughts that are forming in your mind.

It is these that you should commit to paper. You will usually find they are of three kinds:

- notes on the meanings of a passage
- questions arising from the passage
- difficulties you have had in understanding.

You should try to write these down in as clear a form as you can and then bring them to the lesson for discussion.

16.6 Classwork

In class you should do three things:

- listen
- make notes
- talk.

Listening

You should listen not only to what your teacher says but also to the contributions of your fellow students. Teachers don't have a monopoly of wisdom, and quite often the questions and puzzlements of other students can suggest new and interesting lines of thought.

Making notes

When you hear something of interest, you should, of course, make a note of it. As with ordinary notes, you can do this by jotting a remark down in the margin of your book and putting a slightly more developed version of that idea in your notebook. In order to avoid confusion, you should try to take notes in class in the way in which you have been advised to take them in your own time. And remember: in many classes you will be left to make notes yourself, so don't wait to be told – get on with it!

Talking

Talking can be as important as writing because it is a way in which you can master the ideas of a book. When you make a point that has arisen from your preparation, ask a question about what someone has said, or disagree with a remark, you are finding words to express your understanding of the book.

As soon as you speak, you will realise that there is a great difference between having a hunch in your mind and having the appropriate words to express it. Talking in class will help you bridge the gap between the two, because the more you speak, the more you will learn to master the necessary words.

16.7   Follow-up work

But the place where you must master words is on paper. This is where follow-up work comes in. When the lesson is over, *your* work begins. It is up to you to understand and master what has been said in class.

- **The best way to do this is by more reading and writing.**

You should:

(i)   re-read the passage under discussion
(ii)   try to write about the ideas that emerged in the lesson.

What you will be left with in the way of notes will be jottings in your book and slightly longer remarks on paper.

- You should look through these in the light of the passages discussed and see if any of them can be taken further.
- You may find that there are one or two important ideas in your notes. You should try to master these.
- Given that there is a great difference between understanding an idea when it is explained to you and finding the right words to express that idea yourself, you should attempt to write as clearly as you can about the ideas that have emerged.
- Sometimes all you will need to do is explain the idea, while on other occasions you will find that the idea leads you to explore other issues. If you can do one or two pieces of follow-up writing of between half a page and a page

in length, then you will be working satisfactorily.

- **The more re-reading and writing you can do, the easier you will find revision.**

In fact, the most useful revision is not the intense work done in the weeks leading up to the examination but the steady, week-by-week business of reading, re-reading and writing. If at the end of every week you can look through what you have studied, what you have learned from your reading and re-reading will become part of the way in which you think about books. It is obvious that you will want to work harder when you are faced with examinations, but you will find that revision much easier if re-reading is a regular feature of your work.

⟨17⟩ Interpretation

17.1 The importance of interpretation

There is no need to be frightened of the word 'interpretation'. What you should remember is that all readers are interpreters. Whenever you think about the meaning of a work, of what's important about it or what it adds up to, you are interpreting it. If, for instance, you say that Alice Walker's *The Color Purple* shows how the central character has to struggle, you are offering an interpretation. When you do this you are not exactly telling the story; rather you are drawing out what you think matters. That is interpretation.

Of every work therefore you can ask:

- What is its meaning or significance?

Sometimes this is easy. If a feature of the work attracts your attention (remember: puzzlement, interest and pleasure) you can set to work by thinking about it. There are times, however, when you are stuck; times, that is, when you say to yourself: 'I don't know what to make of this!' At such times, it's useful to think about the book from a number of different angles. There is more to interpretation than this; after all, you should remember that what you see will be determined by the angle you are looking from. But it's often a good way of getting started and, sometimes, a good way of eliminating an approach.

Before, however, we consider some approaches, there are two points that need to be made about interpretation.

- **Interpretation only comes into play when there is a real doubt about what something means.**

What you know for certain can't be a matter of interpretation. It's not, for instance, a matter of interpretation that Mrs Reed in *Jane Eyre* is a widow. We know that. If, however, we raise the issue of whether she is simply a wicked woman, we have to pause and think. What do we make of the treatment of her own children, of the fact that she summons Jane to her death bed, of the fact that she confesses to lying about Jane's whereabouts? All these are matters to ponder, and when we ponder them we will be interpreting. Interpretation starts when there isn't a clear answer to our questions.

316

● **Interpretation is at the moment a hotly disputed issue.**

Some of the matters that are argued about are rather abstract and don't directly impinge on the reading of books. You are, however, likely to come across some of the others. Therefore in what follows we shall sketch out a traditional pattern of interpretation, using one book – Jane Austen's *Emma* – as a guide to interpretation. This will be followed up by a glance at some of the more recent ways in which books have been interpreted.

17.2   Interpretation through characters

The approach through characters is very popular. It finds the meaning of works in what they show about characters' thoughts and feelings, the views they have of themselves, the way they change and grow, and the way they establish, maintain or break relationships. If you interpret a work in this way, you will have to consider:

● the effect characters have on you
● the feelings they arouse in you
● the judgements you make about them.

You will know it is worthwhile taking a psychological approach to a novel if the author takes an interest in the motives and reactions of characters. Therefore, if you find, as you do in George Eliot, long passages exploring characters' minds, you will know that this approach will be fruitful.

--- **Example** ---

There are many passages in *Emma* in which Jane Austen either says what Emma is thinking or recounts events from Emma's point of view. Emma has definite views of herself (she says she will never marry), and equally definite views of others (she does not think, for instance, that Robert Martin is socially good enough to marry Harriet Smith).

Jane Austen, however, makes it quite clear that Emma does not know herself, and consequently misjudges other characters. For much of the time she tries to find a suitable marriage partner for Harriet Smith. She has no difficulty in persuading herself that Harriet would be happy with Mr Elton and even the romantic Frank Churchill, and no difficulty either in persuading herself that each of them takes an interest in Harriet.

But it is not until Harriet thinks that Mr Knightley is in love with her that Emma wakes up to the reality of the world about her and the reality of herself. She realises she has been blind (the word is very important) in encouraging Harriet to hope for marriage from the Eltons and Churchills of the world, and, even more important, she wakes up to her own true feelings: 'It darted through her, with the speed of an arrow, that Mr Knightley must marry no one but herself!'

That metaphor (a very rare thing in the book) enacts her awakening, an awakening which is both painful and yet wonderful. It is also the moment when an approach through character makes sense: *Emma* is about growth towards understanding, about the painful (and funny) path Emma treads from blindness to real sight and, in her own case, *insight*.

Once the approach through character has made sense with Emma, it can make sense of other characters. Mr Knightley, too, is someone who has not really known himself. Throughout the novel he has played the role of father and guide to Emma (her real father, Mr Woodhouse, never advises or guides her) but, at the end, he recognises that he loves her. In his case, too, the novel is about how he grows towards a clear vision of life and himself.

17.3   Interpretation through society

The social approach to literature emphasises not so much the personality or inner feelings of characters as the relations they have with each other. A social interpretation of literature sees these relations in terms of the traditions and customs of society. There is, therefore, much stress in a social interpretation on the classes to which characters belong. For instance, it is important to see:

- who is rich and who poor
- who is rising in society and who falling
- who earn their living from trade, a profession, family land.

A social approach also looks at the institutions of society. One of the most important of these is marriage. It is important to ask:

- who marries whom
- whether they come from the same class
- the extent to which it is a marriage of love or a means of social improvement.

___ **Example** ___

A social approach to *Emma* is profitable in a number of ways. Although all the characters are middle class, some are professional like the lawyer John Knightley, some in trade (there is an important scene in a shop), and Mr Knightley runs the family estate.

The question of marriage is very important. At the beginning of the novel (it starts and ends with a marriage) Mr Weston, a man who by trade in London has made enough money to buy a small estate, marries Miss Taylor, a governess. Socially it is not an equal marriage. The marriage between Mr Elton, the vicar, and Augusta Hawkins is not equal either. He has a social position but her family, though wealthy, are not quite as respectable. For Augusta Hawkins, then, marriage is socially advantageous. Frank Churchill is wealthy but he marries the poor but educated Jane Fairfax. Socially, then, they are not equals.

It is interesting that the only marriage that is an equal one is the most important – Emma's to Mr Knightley. She is the daughter of a highly respected family and he owns the big estate. In addition, though this is a point about character, they are intellectual equals.

What do such marriages tell us? Jane Austen recognises that marriage – the basic institution of society – can, even within one class, be entered into for different reasons and can, therefore, be very different from one case to another. It is interesting, however, that the most important marriage is an equal one. This probably indicates that although Jane Austen recognises the variety of marriages that do occur, her ideal is one in which the partners are socially and intellectually equal. A social interpretation, therefore, reveals that her view of marriage is that it should maintain the stability of society by being, as near as possible, between characters of the same social positions.

17.4 Interpretation through ideas

The approach through ideas is not very different from the approaches through characters or society. It sees works of literature as being about attitudes and concepts. It is a philosophical approach. Literature is seen to be about such ideas as:

- honesty
- ambition
- freedom of choice
- guilt

(This list is not complete!)

You can tell whether the approach through ideas will be fruitful if the book contains passages in which ideas are either discussed or scenes which are the expression of ideas occur.

For instance, in *1984* there are long discussions of political ideas, and the scenes in which Winston rewrites history are examples of the idea that the ruling party can even change the past. The aim of the approach through ideas is to be able to say that the book deals with such-and-such an idea. These ideas can, of course, be psychological or social.

Example

Emma can be said to be about self-deception and true self-knowledge, and about marriage. For much of the time Emma is deceived. Her deception is wilful. She *wants* to believe that Mr Elton loves Harriet, so everything that happens is interpreted in that light. As we have seen, she eventually wakes up. She realises that she has been misleading herself and Harriet, and consequently feels foolish and guilty. (The morality of manipulating other people is also one of the ideas of the book.) This awakening leads her to self-knowledge. *Emma*, thus, is about the psychological ideas of deception and self-knowledge.

It is also about the social idea of marriage. Jane Austen is interested in the idea of marriage. She observes why people marry and also leads the reader to ask whether some marriages are more suitable and satisfying than others.

In short, *Emma* is about ideas that are both psychological and social.

17.5   Interpretation through literary forms

The approach through form opens up a different set of problems. It asks:

- how plots are constructed
- what place the narrator has in relation to events
- whether or not the author is deliberately trying to write a particular kind of book (say, an allegory, comedy or tragedy)
- (in the case of poetry) how the stanza form, rhythm or sounds contribute to the meaning of a work.

A formal approach stresses the importance of parallels, balances and contrasts. These can be:

- events
- images
- individual words or lines

Of course formal interpretations are never complete because they can't tell you what is *significant* about a work. They can, however, help you in making other interpretations because, for example, a psychological understanding of characters must be given formal expression in a book.

Example

We have already touched on two formal aspects of *Emma*. Parts of *Emma* are written in the third person, yet it is quite clear that it is Emma's thoughts and not Jane Austen's that are being given. To put the point formally, you could say that the narrative is effectively first-person although grammatically it is in the third. Thus Emma on the future Mrs Elton:

She was good enough for Mr. Elton, no doubt; accomplished enough for Highbury – handsome enough – to look plain, probably, by Harriet's side.

That is in the third person yet it is not direct speech. It is narrative express-ing Emma's view point. Note the grudging use of 'enough'. The reason why Jane Austen writes in this form is because the novel is about how Emma imagines and interprets the world. Third-person narrative that gives a first person view is the formal expression of that. Emma *thinks* she is seeing the world clearly but, in fact, she is interpreting it as she would like it to be.

The second formal feature already touched upon is the way the novel starts and ends with a marriage. The marriages, as it were, serve as a frame for the novel, giving it a neat and satisfying shape. But the formal device of framing the book in this way helps to draw attention to marriage. In itself it can do no more, but a reader can be alerted by this to think about the mar-riages of the book. He or she will then see that marriage is important and will be able to appreciate the start and finish of the book as the formal expression of the importance of marriage in the novel.

17.6 Interpretation through history

The starting point of historical interpretation is that a work will reflect the thoughts, feelings and customs of the age in which it was written. It follows from this that knowledge about the period will help a reader understand books. A knowledge of manners, for instance, will help a reader judge the relations between characters. It is also useful to know what the society valued. This includes such things as:

- the books they read
- the games they played
- the ideas they discussed
- the things they took for granted
- the clothes they wore.

In some cases it is useful to know:

- what they thought.

It is difficult to read Shakespeare without a knowledge of how important the monarch was in Elizabethan England and also of how religion played a very important part in people's lives. You can see from this that historical interpreta-tions can be close to ones concerned with society and ideas. You can't interpret the society of a book unless you have some idea of what society was like in the period in which it was written, and the ideas in a book are bound to reflect those that were held at the time. It is not, however, *just* a case of books reflecting their time. What matters is what an author *makes* of the thoughts, feelings and customs of his or her age.

___ **Example** _____

In order to understand *Emma*, you should know about the importance of large estates in early nineteenth-century England, the position of governesses, the difficulties of travel and the position of the church. Let us, however, look at how a knowledge of the period helps in two areas – manners and reading. Manners are important in the novel, and it is also important to note what Jane Austen makes of them. The fact that Emma commends Mr Elton for his manners indicates that they were highly regarded at the time. This is what she says about them:

> In one respect, perhaps, Mr. Elton's manners are superior to Mr. Knightley's or Mr. Weston's. They have more gentleness. They might be more safely held up as a pattern. There is an openness, a quickness, almost a bluntness in Mr. Weston, which everybody likes in *him* because there is so much good humour with it but that would not do to be copied.

The fact that Emma draws attention to manners in this way shows the importance they have, but the passage also indicates Jane Austen's attitude. Emma assumes that manners are a matter of copying a model; Mr Elton's, she says, could be held up 'as a pattern', whereas Mr Weston's 'would not do to be copied'. When, however, we learn that Mr Elton is only putting on a show to impress Emma and when we see that, after his marriage, he is calculatingly rude to Harriet, we see that Jane Austen is using a current interest in manners to indicate her belief that the best manners are those, like Mr Weston's, that are a genuine expression of his character and not copied like Mr Elton's.

She also uses the matter of reading to indicate her judgements. Emma likes popular novels, as does Harriet Smith. In the late eighteenth and early nineteenth centuries there were many books written for ladies. They were romantic, shallow and cheap. If a reader knows this, the following passage will be of particular significance. Emma has asked Harriet whether Mr Martin, a young farmer who has taken an interest in Harriet, reads. This is part of Harriet's answer:

> And I know he has read *The Vicar of Wakefield*. He never read the *Romance of the Forest*, nor the *Children of the Abbey*. He had never heard of such books before I mentioned them, but he is determined to get them now as soon as ever he can.

Unknown to Harriet, those words are a judgement on her and Emma. The *Romance of the Forest* and *Children of the Abbey* are cheap and sentimental, whereas *The Vicar of Wakefield* is a masterpiece. Robert Martin's reading is unfashionable but shows real taste. The reader who knows about fashions in reading will be able to appreciate that point.

- **There is a final point that should be made about historical interpretation.**

It is helpful to study an edition that has some explanatory notes. Such editions usually explain the historical background and sometimes go on to indicate how the author handles the ideas of his or her time. If you don't own an edition with notes, it is a good idea to buy one. There are many available in the shops, and some of them are quite cheap.

17.7 Interpretation today

In the last twenty to thirty years there has been a great deal of interest in what has come to be called literary theory. In fact, literary theory is now a vast industry. If you look on the shelves of the literary criticism section of any large bookshop, you are likely to find a lot of books on the topic. The point about it is that a good deal of it is concerned with what it is for a book to be a book, not so much with literature in the sense of this or that book but with the literariness of literature. Now this is an interesting question, but it's a different one from the matter of reading books. To think about what makes a book a literary work is different from saying what you think a book is about. When therefore it comes to interpretation, a good deal of literary theory is not much help.

There are, however, aspects of it that are concerned with the reading of books. It is these approaches that sometimes prove to be helpful.

The approach through structure

One approach is concerned with the structure of the book. It is therefore a form of what was discussed under 17.5 above. The basic point about the structuralist approach is that any literary work is designed, and therefore if we wish to understand it and appreciate how it works on us, we should attend to its elements and how they are arranged. There's nothing surprising about this. What makes a literary work the thing that it is is the way it's been put together. We have seen this at work in our discussion of comedy. A comedy is not necessarily a story that makes us laugh but a particular kind of plot.

Common patterns

Those who interest themselves in structure like to see common patterns in books. For instance, there is often a hero and, opposite to him, a villain. The hero often has a task to perform. In this task there are those who help and those who hinder him. The hero has to undergo various trials to show the reader he is fit to marry the heroine. At the end of the book the villain is exposed and the hero is vindicated and rewarded in a number of ways. It is often useful to look at the book you are reading from the point of view of how the plot has been put together. Often this can tell you something significant about the book as a whole.

—— **Example** ——

Take, for instance, the case of *The Woman in White*. Several important things emerge from a consideration of the structure of the plot. The hero is Walter Hartright, but the plot is puzzling as to who the heroine is. There are two candidates: Laura and her half-sister, Marion. He marries one of them, but, at the close, all three are living in the same house, so there is the feeling that he's actually married both. What, however, is curious is that neither of these women is the woman in white of the title, though structurally she is close to Walter in that he helps her, and, even more interestingly, she is a kind of double of Laura. So in terms of characters, there is an interesting asymmetry: one man but three woman dependent, in one way or another, upon him.

Here the other two male characters come in; Sir Percival is the opposite to Walter – the villain – and Count Fosco, who is and is not the villain. Sir Percival plays the part the reader expects the villain to play: he is smooth-talking but cruel and he imprisons the women who cross him. There is no doubt that Sir Percival is a villain; one sure sign is that the dog growls at him! But Fosco is different. He is interesting because he departs from the conventional plot structure. Yes, he is evil, but all readers are drawn to him, not least because he alone appreciates the true qualities of Marion. In fact, one of the interesting aspects of the plot is the plot that isn't there – the love story of Fosco and Marion.

The matter of narrative

Also of concern to those who take an interest in the structure of literature is the matter of narrative. What they particularly stress is the matter of *knowledge* and *perspective*. It's become fashionable to emphasise what we don't know about a book. Characters, for instance, only exist on the page, and therefore if the narrator doesn't show or tell the reader, and if the reader can't legitimately infer (work out) something, then this can't be known. For instance, in *The Woman in White*, Walter falls in love with Laura, but since we are merely informed of this we can never know how he came to love her. That remains what some critics call *a silence in the text*.

Limitations of this approach

Looking at the structure of a book can help us to see a good deal about it, but there is a limitation to this approach. When we talk about the design of a plot we are talking in broad generalisations. What actually makes one book different from another is the words it uses, and no structuralist approach, precisely because it has to work with generalisations, can do justice to the differences that emerge through the words. An approach through structure, therefore, is helpful just so long as you remember that you are dealing with general ideas rather than specific ones.

- **The emphasis in structuralist approaches is always on the created or made aspects of art.** Art, that is, as artifice, as something that doesn't exist naturally but is brought into existence. One way of understanding the current approaches to interpretation is to see them as concerned with the artiness of art.

The approach through society

In line with this there is a development of the approach through structure, which links up with the approach through society. This approach stresses the 'made' nature of literature, but sees the making as something that is shaped by the society in which the writer lives. For instance, think about those terms 'hero' and 'heroine' used to discuss *The Woman in White*. What makes a hero a hero is not just the author but the constellation of ideas and attitudes that the author encounters in his or her day-to-day world. This is not to say that an author merely transcribes these ideas and attitudes, for that would be to deny the power of arrangement and the capacity of the author to work variations upon his or her material. What it does insist upon is that the elements of literature are, in an important sense, made (a favourite term is 'constructed') by the culture of the artist's society. Note, for instance, that Sir Percival can be violent, whereas the heroic Walter defends women, only fights when attacked and even tries to save his enemy. Walter is obviously the product of the mid-Victorian age, an age when notions of heroism and the code of the gentleman were particularly strong.

Reflexivity

Another aspect of the concern for the 'made' nature of art is one that sees the making of art as an aspect of the work of art itself. There is, therefore, an emphasis upon the processes of the work of art. This, in fact, is not a new thing at all. Writers have often been fascinated by the nature of artistic inspiration and composition, so those concerns have often become the subject matter of art.

In the early nineteenth century, for instance, many poets wrote about the problems of writing poetry. Coleridge makes lack of inspiration the central issue of 'Dejection'. In our own century Yeats makes the issue the subject of 'The Circus Animals' Desertion', and T. S. Eliot weaves thought about the nature of poetry into those meditative poems called *Four Quartets*.

Modern criticism has added to this the useful term 'reflexivity'. This is a word derived from grammer. In French there are reflexive verbs, the function of which is to denote actions which a person does to him or herself. To wash is an example; the object of the verb's action is the one who does the action. The word has come to be used of the way in which literature draws attention to its own literary nature. This is sometimes called 'literariness'.

Reflexivity is present in a number of ways. It can be the theme of a work, as in the Coleridge and Yeats poems or it can appear in such minor conventions as the writer addressing the reader directly. It's present in Shakespeare: sometimes he draws attention to the theatricality of the scene by having characters point to the stage and their own acting. In *Twelfth Night* one character, speaking of the hugely entertaining events taking place on the stage, says that if this were to be acted on a stage no one would believe it. Well, do we? You could argue that this remark makes us see that these things can only happen on a stage and that therefore we are having our attention drawn to the artificiality of art. On the other hand, this is something that people do say, so it could be that we are being reminded of a feature of everyday life. What talk about reflexivity draws attention to is the extraordinary thing that art is: it's not real life but we often value it because it shows us what real life is like.

The Marxist approach

An approach to literature that owes a good deal to the idea that all we think and say is rooted in our social conditions is the Marxist one. What it sets out to argue is that everything in a literary work must be understood in terms of social and economic factors. This is OK if you are a follower of Karl Marx, but willing adherents to his philosophy are not numerous at the moment.

What the Marxist believes is that all that people think and do is the product of their social and economic conditions; there are no other factors influencing us. The only use this can have is that of drawing attention to the economic factors that are present in works of fiction. Dickens shows that the bogus code of the gentleman that Pip lives by in *Great Expectations* is made possible by his inheriting his 'expectations'. To that extent, economics is important. But, as in nearly all authors, Dickens is not making a Marxist point; what chiefly interests him is the *moral* question of who is the real gentleman.

The feminist approach

A much more useful approach to interpretation is provided by what is called feminism. This is an extension of the social approach and of the approach through character. Its basic starting point is that all thinking is a kind of making. This goes for people just as much as it goes for ideas. Men and women are who they are because they have been thought of (and that means spoken of) in a number of very particular ways. Feminism at its broadest concerns itself with the literary presentation of women, but there's no reason why readers shouldn't also look at how the men in a work of fiction are created. Like a lot of currently fashionable critical talk, there's a lot of theorising in feminism, and sometimes it has to be said that it works with a barely concealed set of presuppositions. Nevertheless, it's often very illuminating to see how authors present women and to see in that presentation a whole set of unstated attitudes.

Hardy, for instance, is very interesting on women. Unlike many Victorian novelists (Dickens, for instance) his women are interesting characters. Think, for instance, of Sue Bridehead in *Jude the Obscure* – the female counterpart to the hero in her efforts to live her own life. Sue is both interesting and intrepid, but sometimes Hardy's women are both those things but are also coquettish. Bathsheba Everdene in *Far from the Madding Crowd* is forceful in many ways, but Hardy also draws our attention to her vanity, her irresponsibility (sending a valentine to Boldwood) and her weakness for a rogue such as Sergeant Troy. She shows just how ambiguous Hardy is.

Hardy's ideal woman – Tess – is a very revealing figure. She is a dream woman, whom, one feels, nobody either fully understands or really loves – apart, that is, from the author. Yet Hardy wants to control her: for instance, he sometimes reports what she says instead of allowing her to speak for herself, and for certain crucial passages he presents her as attractively half-asleep. Does he kill her off, one wonders, so that he alone will be able to own her?

There are, of course, works written which deliberately explore the situation of women. *Jane Eyre* can be read this way; it is a kind of female *Pilgrim's Progress*, in which Charlotte Brontë explores the opportunities and challenges facing young women in the nineteenth century. (Charlotte Brontë doesn't put it in those terms.)

In this century there has been Virginia Woolf's *A Room Of One's Own*, in one respect a book not unlike Jane Eyre in that what Jane wants from the very start is her own space. Margaret Atwood's *The Handmaid's Tale* is clearly an allegory of how women are viewed and what is expected of them.

No reader is obliged to take a feminist approach to every book, but you can't understand writers such as Virginia Woolf, Margaret Atwood, Alice Walker, Toni Morrison or Maya Angelou unless you do.

The place of the reader

The final emphasis that is helpful in modern interpretation is the place of the reader. One of the current stresses is on how the reader collaborates with the writer to come to an understanding of the book. This is not to say that the reader makes up the meaning but that meaning isn't really meaning until a reader has responded to what an author has written. Those who emphasise the role of the reader go further by stressing that sometimes the author offers clues and leaves the reader to respond to them in his or her way. In other words, the position of the reader becomes important when the book itself is what people call indeterminate; that's to say, when its meaning has been left open rather than being closed down or fixed.

There is a strange poem by Browning called "'Childe Roland to the Dark Tower Came'". It's vivid and even surreal in its writing, but it's not very clear what it's about. In such a case the role of the reader becomes crucial, because it's up to him or her to make links and see patterns. The Browning case is an extreme example, but quite frequently in reading you see that you are being asked to see something or make up your mind. That is when your response becomes important.

17.8   Interpretation and the reader

It would be a mistake to give the impression that interpretation is just a matter of approaching every poem, novel or play in all the ways discussed above. Some works of literature, for example, only require to be looked at from one or two viewpoints.

Furthermore, interpretation is always personal. This means that one reader is not going to stress the same points as another. You will find that the way you interpret a book reflects your general interests and beliefs. If, for instance, you are interested in politics, you will tend to take a social approach, and if your interests are historical, you will find pleasure in studying how the work is related to the period in which it was written.

You should, however, remember that interpretation is not just a matter of saying what you enjoy about a work. One of the points about *Emma* is that it is dangerous to read your own wants and prejudices into a situation. That is something you should avoid doing with books.

There are three things you should remember, which should prevent you from looking at books from a merely personal viewpoint. These are:

- the words
- the views of others
- the idea of intention.

The words

Because it is all too easy to imagine that a book says something, you should look at its words very closely to see what it is they are really saying. Quite often we form general ideas about books which, whilst they are not exactly false, are still too sweeping. The remedy for general ideas is to study the words closely to see if they qualify, or even deny, the impression you have received.

Example

An example is the way Jane Austen presents Emma's treatment of Harriet Smith. It is very easy to see Emma as a selfish manipulator of Harriet's feelings. This is not entirely untrue, but it does need qualifying. In one chapter Emma persuades Harriet to reject Robert Martin's proposal of marriage. Emma's behaviour is not commendable, but Jane Austen does show that Harriet is a rather shallow person. She is not happy about rejecting Robert Martin, but when Emma speaks of Mr Elton she brightens up. Jane Austen, therefore, shows that although Emma was wrong to manipulate her, Harriet is a weak and foolish girl whose feelings for Robert Martin are not very strong.

The views of others

The second thing you should do is make yourself aware of other people's interpretations, by listening to what other people say and reading books of criticism.
If you are in class, you should listen to and, of course, take notes on, what your
teacher and fellow students say. You should listen particularly hard to views
with which you *don't* agree.

Literary criticism is the phrase given to the business of interpreting and
judging literature. School, college and public libraries, as well as bookshops,
usually have a large selection of critical works. You should read them to find
new ideas, new questions to ask and new lines of interpretation, though it is
important to remember that literary criticism is most helpful when you know
the books you are studying well and when you already have views about them.
You will then be able to appreciate the fact that it is possible to interpret books
in a number of ways and will be in a position to judge the value of the ideas
given to you by literary criticism.

The author's intentions

Finally, it is not easy to think about interpretation without discussing the intentions of the author. If a work has a particular meaning, it is difficult to escape the
idea that that meaning is there because the author intended it. Literary works are
specially designed by authors, so to interpret a work is to follow the creative
mind of the author. This means that when you write about the meaning of a
work, you should remember to mention the author. You can write about how the
author presents the psychology of the characters, or explores ideas in the writing
of a book.

Exercises

17.1.   Try interpreting your set books from the psychological, social and
        ideas points of view. Which do you find the most helpful?

17.2.   Examine the forms of all the books you are studying. Do their forms
        help you to interpret them?

17.3.   Try to find out as much as you can about the historical period in
        which your books are written, and try to see how the authors have
        used the ideas and customs of their time.

17.4.   Select one or two passages from your set books and examine the
        words closely. To what extent do the words modify the general
        interpretations of these works you have made?

18 Effectiveness

18.1 The issue of effectiveness

In examinations there are often questions of the following kind:

- How successful is Shakespeare in combining the two plots in *King Lear*?
- Do Wordsworth's poems achieve the quality of experience recollected in tranquillity?
- Discuss the effectiveness of Hardy's presentation of rural life in *Far From The Madding Crowd*.

Those questions are all getting at the same thing – how well an author has written.

It's usually difficult trying to answer such questions. What they are doing is asking you to evaluate (place a value upon) literature. Some people think this is impossible and therefore stick to description and interpretation. But however hard evaluation is (and few people pretend that it's easy) it's difficult to avoid. Why do we read one book rather than another? Why do we prefer certain effects to others? Why are some books on examination syllabuses whereas others are not? Whenever we ask these questions we are, whether we recognise it or not, making judgements. Judgements, in other words, may be hard but they are very difficult to get away from.

Judgements about literature are varied, but there are a few points that can be made about how it's wise to go about making them.

Positive and negative reactions

The first thing that needs to be said is that whenever we take an interest in anything, there is a judgement implicitly present. That's to say, we may not be intending to make a judgement, but a judgement, even if it's not a fully formed one, is present in the interest. (The same can be said about any other positive reaction – pleasure, the feeling of being intrigued, the experience of meeting a teasing problem and so on.)

First impressions can't be ignored but they mustn't be taken as the sole guide. When your first impression is one of enjoyment (you may be struck by a line of verse or intrigued by a character), you should certainly regard your response as significant. You will certainly need to think about it. (Why, for instance, do you feel as you do? Can you trace this to anything in the words?) A strong initial reaction is often something that will grow into an appreciation of how the book works and an understanding of why it's to be valued.

On the other hand, a negative reaction doesn't necessarily mean that the book is no good. Much literature, for all sorts of reasons, is difficult, so first reactions may be of puzzlement, incomprehension and even boredom. I've known classes who didn't like Donne on first acquaintance but, with study, came to consider him as the most interesting author they studied. You might use as a guide the suggestion that:

First impressions are more to be trusted when they are positive than when they are negative.

Evaluation (like interpretation) is not a once-for-all exercise

Readers go on making judgements about a work; they may completely change their minds about it or, more usually, they modify or refine what they previously thought. Any judgement should be capable of modification, and so every judgement should be made tentatively. Here, again, we are in a situation similar to interpretation. Neither interpretation nor judgements about effectiveness are the sort of thing that can be done to a formula. All readers can do is try to practise (that is, put into action) interpreting and judging in the hope that experience will provide some guidelines. What follows are some suggestions as to what happens when we judge. They may help you start thinking about why works are said to be effective.

18.2   Questions about the effectiveness of poetry

When you are thinking about the effectiveness of a poem, you ask about:

- how interesting the words are
- their appropriateness to the subject
- the function of the imagery
- rhythm and form
- whether the words enact the meaning.

Let us examine these questions in more detail

Are the words interesting?

When asking this question, you should remember that words can be used in very many ways. If you look back to Chapter 2, 'Words and Meanings', you will see the different effects that are created by metaphors, similes, images, symbols, and so on. Yet the effectiveness of words does not depend upon their being a figure of speech. Words can interest a reader by summoning associations or by being direct and simple.

Example

Take the end of the first stanza of W. B. Yeats's 'The Wild Swans at Coole':

> Upon the brimming water among the stones
> Are nine-and-fifty swans.

Those words are effective although they are direct and simple. 'Brimming' is a strangely impressive word which suggests fullness and the marvellous shimmering quality of water in lakes. 'Water' and 'stones' are simple words, yet their very simplicity impresses because they point to the plain, unadorned yet wonderful reality of natural things. There is a stately, measured exactness about the phrase, 'nine-and-fifty'. 'Fifty-nine' would sound horribly trite, but 'nine-and-fifty', because the phrase is built up steadily, sounds serene and poised. Of course, it is unlikely that those words will impress you upon first reading (though they might). In most cases you have to read a poem a number of times in order to recognise which are the interesting words.

Are the words appropriate to the subject?

This is a more specific question. Readers have long felt that an effective poem is one in which the words match the subject matter. A poem that deals with important subjects such as religion, morality or important events should, it is felt, use elevated words, whereas one that deals with ordinary things should use everyday ones. Two modern examples will make this clear.

Examples

Example 1

In the fourth section of *Little Gidding* Eliot writes about the descent of the Holy Spirit. In order to bring out the momentous character of the event, he uses elevated words:

> The dove descending breaks the air
> With flame of incandescent terror
> Of which the tongues declare
> The one discharge from sin and error.

You will see that the 'tongues' don't merely speak, they 'declare'; and what they 'declare' is not a let-off or even a pardon but a 'discharge'. Those elevated and powerful words indicate that the subject matter is weighty.

Example 2

By contrast, look at these lines from John Betjeman's 'In Westminster Abbey'. Betjeman beautifully captures the tones of a well-meaning, honest but rather shallow lady who has gone into the Abbey to say her somewhat self-centred prayers:

> Now I feel a little better
> What a treat to hear Thy Word.

The ordinary, everyday phrases – 'a little better' and, 'what a treat' – are delightfully appropriate to the subject. The words Betjeman has chosen are effective because they match his speaker – a pleasant, middle-class lady who fails to appreciate that prayer is not quite the same as a nice chat over afternoon tea.

The function of the imagery

A similar kind of question can be asked about the imagery:

● Is the imagery appropriate to the subject?

One of the pleasures of imagery is that of finding it expressing in its own concrete yet imaginative way the theme of the poem.

--- **Example** ---

Tennyson does this in 'Mariana'. It is a bleak poem in which the speaker, a woman, hopelessly waits for her estranged lover to return to her. The imagery of the poem beautifully enacts the desolation, boredom and frustration she feels. This is the first stanza:

> With blackest moss the flower-plots
>   Were thickly crusted, one and all:
> The rusted nails fell from the knots
>   That held the pear to the gable wall.
> The broken sheds looked sad and strange:
>   Unlifted was the clinking latch;
> Weeded and worn the ancient thatch
>   Upon the lonely moated grange;
> She only said, 'My life is dreary,
>   He cometh not,' she said;
> She said, 'I am aweary, aweary,
>   I would that I were dead!'

The imagery is of things overgrown or broken down: the 'flower-plots' are 'thickly crusted' with 'blackest moss', and the 'ancient thatch' is 'weeded'; 'rusted nails' fall from knots, sheds are 'broken' and look 'sad and strange' and the 'unlifted latch' clinks. Such imagery prepares us for her lamenting refrain. We can see from the imagery that her life is 'dreary' and understand, so near to death is everything, that she, too, wishes she 'were dead'. The imagery of the poem is no mere afterthought or decoration; it both creates and expresses the resigned hopelessness of the abandoned Mariana in her. 'lonely moated grange'.

Rhythm and form

Since the rhythm of a poem should be appropriate, you can ask:

• Is the rhythm appropriate to the meaning?

An effective rhythm is not one that is regular (good rhythms are very rarely exactly regular) but one in which the stresses, and the weight of the stresses, fall on the crucial words. Indeed, in the best poems the rhythm of the words and the meaning of the words appear as *one* and not two things.

Example

For instance, when you read the opening lines of Donne's 'The Good-Morrow', are you not simply aware of the awakened astonishment of the poet:

> I wonder, by my troth, what thou and I
> Did, till we loved?

Yet those lines read as an expression of awakened astonishment because the rhythm so perfectly expresses the meaning. The rhythm is roughly iambic, but 'wonder' is stressed heavily, and the pace of 'thou and I' (note that the important words are stressed) is a steady crescendo leading to the achievement of 'Did'. That 'Did' breaks the rhythm, yet its urgency and ardour, so close to everyday speech, is felt by the reader to be emotionally right. The reader has the experience of listening to one thing, not an easily separable meaning and rhythm.

The question that can be asked about form is similar to the ones already given:

• Is the stanza form appropriate to the subject of the poem?

The test of a successful stanza form is close to the one used of rhythm: if you get the feeling that the idea could not have been said so effectively had it been in another form, then you can judge the stanza successful.

Another way of putting the point is to say that the length of line and the rhyme scheme have an inevitable sense of rightness. For example, are not heroic couplets deeply appropriate to the strict, disciplined and deft turn of Pope's mind?

Example

Look at this couplet from his *Essay on Man*:

> Know then thyself, presume not God to scan;
> The proper study of mankind is Man.

The first line is an instruction (in grammatical terms it contains imperatives), and the second completes it by firmly supplying a reason. What makes the couplet deft is the rhyme 'scan/Man', but this deftness is not just that of pleasing harmony of sound that delights the ear. The rhyme sums up the meaning of the couplet – 'man' should study, that is 'scan', himself. In short, the instruction is: scan man.

Does the poem enact its meaning?

This final question sums up all the questions above. Enactment is a matter of all the aspects of words – associations, rhythms, sounds – combining to express the meaning. And meaning, of course, should be understood widely to include emotions as well as ideas.

Enactment can be understood to apply to a poem as a whole and to individual parts. Blake's 'The Tyger', for instance, enacts throughout its six verses the attractive energy and fearful terror of the creature. Those impressions are enacted by the whole of the poem.

An example of an individual line enacting its meaning can be found in Philip Larkin's 'The Whitsun Weddings'. In one delicately beautiful line – 'Thence the river's level drifting breadth began' – Larkin enacts the sense of peace and spaciousness felt by a railway traveller who sees the landscape broaden out over and beyond a wide, gently flowing river.

18.3 Questions about the effectiveness of novels

Characters

When you are thinking about the effectiveness of novels, it is good to start where examination questions do – with characters. There are three main questions that can be asked about them.

● Can the characters in a novel be understood?

The word, 'understood' must cover all the ways in which a reader can appreciate what it is a character is feeling and why he or she is feeling it. If a character has feelings that are utterly contradictory, then no understanding is possible. However, it is important to remember that a reader can understand a character whom he or she does not like.

__ **Example** __

Mrs Elton from *Emma* is quite awful – showy, interfering, bossy and affected. Yet it is clear to the reader *why* she is like that – she wants to be accepted by the society into which she has married. This is what she says to Emma about her first meeting with Mr Knightley, whom she has met at the Westons:

'Knightley!' continued Mrs Elton; – 'Knightley himself! – Was not it lucky? – for, not being within when he called the other day, I had never seen him before; and of course, as so particular a friend of Mr E's, I had a great curiosity. "My Friend Knightley" had so often been mentioned, that I was really impatient to see him; and I must do my caro sposo the justice to say that he need not be ashamed of his friend. Knightley is quite the gentleman. I like him very much. Decidedly, I think, a very gentleman-like man.

Mrs Elton offends Emma and the reader, yet, awful as she is, Jane Austen makes it possible for us to understand her. She wants to feel at home so she boldly talks of 'Knightley', when everybody else (including Jane Austen – and the reader!) refers to him as '*Mr* Knightley'. She also tries to impress by talking in a fashionable way. Her husband she affectedly calls 'Mr E.' and 'my caro sposa'. Awful as she is, we understand her. It is because we see that she is putting on a show that we find her an effective character.

● **Does the author use access to a character's mind to good effect?**

The answers to this question will be different, depending upon whether the novel is written in the first or third person.

In the case of first-person narratives the mind of the narrator must either be interesting in itself or must undergo a series of interesting experiences. Jane Eyre is interesting in herself. There is a very remarkable tension in her between passion and duty. She is a girl who desires love and yet also someone who strictly adheres to her moral code. For instance, she passionately loves Mr Rochester but feels she must not live with him while his first wife is still alive. Pip in *Great Expectations* undergoes very interesting experiences – fear, dread, guilt, ambition, love, disappointment, sickness, remorse and self-realisation.

In the case of third-person narratives access into the mind of a character must show why that character acts as he or she does. Winston Smith in *1984* is effective, because Orwell vividly shows why he seeks to rebel against society.

Jane Austen is particularly interesting in this respect. She usually has a single, central character into whose mind she chooses to have almost constant access: we know, for example, the twists and turns of Emma's mind and are familiar with how Elizabeth Bennet changes her mind. An effective way in which Jane Austen achieves this is by making the narration very close to a first-person one. The form (the grammar of the sentences) is third-person, but the viewpoint is entirely that of the central character. The effectiveness of this is that we learn what the character is thinking in such an intimate way that we have sympathy, but at the same time we never forget that this is just the view of one character and may not, therefore, be the view the reader should take.

Nothing that has been written above should imply that novels are only good if everything a character does is plain and simple. Far from it; novels often fascinate because readers don't come to clear and universal agreements. A novel that can be sorted and, so to speak, 'closed down', is one to which readers will not often wish to return. Often what we value about a character is whether we are left with questions. Is Paul Morel in *Sons and Lovers* deserving of our sympathy? In *Mansfield Park* do we really prefer Fanny Price to Mary Crawford? Should we be pleased at the end of *Middlemarch* that Dorothea has married Will? I have answers to these questions, but I've changed my mind on some of them and am uncertain about whether I'm right. I will probably change my mind again.

But this uncertainty points to the power and effectiveness of these works. They present us with unavoidable moral dilemmas, and there is no way in which we can escape them. Books that don't yield simple answers are often great for this very reason; they unflinchingly present the moral and emotional tangles of living. That is why we keep reading them.

- **Has the author been fair to his or her characters?**

It is quite clear that authors create characters whom they invite readers to like or dislike. When, however, an author's feelings get out of hand and a character is praised or condemned too much, a novel is made less effective. Successful novels, by contrast, contain characters who are unattractive yet presented fairly.

— **Example** —————————————————————

Such a character is Mr Casaubon in *Middlemarch*. He is not a man for whom the reader is likely to feel affection, and it is equally clear that George Eliot judges him a failure who has a damaging effect upon Dorothea, his young wife. Yet George Eliot is never unfair to him. She presents him as a sad, disappointed man who is all too painfully aware that he is a failure. Moreover, she knows that her readers find him cold. At one point she directs her readers' attention away from Dorothea towards him. One chapter begins in this way:

> One morning, some weeks after her arrival at Lowick, Dorothea – but why always Dorothea? Was her point of view the only possible one with regard to this marriage? I protect against all our interest, all our effort at understanding being given to the young skins that look blooming in spite of trouble; for those too will get faded, and will know the older and more eating griefs which we are helping to neglect. In spite of the blinking eyes and white moles objectionable to Celia, and the want of muscular curve which was morally painful to Sir James, Mr. Casaubon had an intense consciousness within him, and was spiritually a-hungered like the rest of us.

That is George Eliot being fair. She protests against always seeing life from the point of view of the young. Mr Casaubon, she insists, and insists strongly, had 'an intense consciousness within him, and was spiritually a-hungered'. We are turned away from Dorothea and asked to consider what it must be like to be Mr Casaubon.

Narrative

A question that can be asked about narrative is:

- **Does the narrative mode help to engage the reader?**

The point about narration is that it establishes the relationship between the reader and the events of the novel. A narration is effective if it helps to establish an appropriate and interesting distance. For instance, in *The Woman in White* there is a set of events that ends in the 'death' of the heroine. *The Woman in White* is a multiple narration, and Collins deliberately frustrates the reader by giving the narration to characters who are emotionally distant from the central business of the plot. The characters relate what has happened faithfully but coldly (the final narration in this section is not a character at all, but the words on the gravestone), so the reader feels increasingly impotent because nothing can be done and increasingly angry because Laura is not being accorded the concern we know she deserves.

Plot

You can ask questions about the plot of a novel. A good one is:

- **Is the problem from which the plot grows an interesting or important one?**

Of course, what is thought to be important will differ from reader to reader, but it is generally held that problems such as a failed marriage, the struggle to overcome an unhappy childhood or the fight to resist evil are ones that engage people deeply. Yet it is not good enough simply to base a novel round an important problem. The novelist must really present the complexity of the situation if the plot is to be effective. Again, it is George Eliot that succeeds in doing this.

Example

Middlemarch presents, among other things, the failed marriage of Casaubon and Dorothea. But George Eliot never simplifies their relationship. She shows that whilst they grow further apart they remain sensitive to each other's needs. At one point Dorothea agonisingly asks: 'What have I done – what am I – that he should treat me so?' Yet, at the end of the very same chapter there is this touching moment:

> When her husband stood opposite to her, she saw that his face was more haggard. He started slightly on seeing her, and she looked up at him beseechingly, without speaking.
> 'Dorothea!' he said, with a gentle surprise in his tone. 'Were you waiting for me?'
> 'Yes, I did not like to disturb you.'
> 'Come, my dear, come. You are young, and need not to extend your life by watching.'

Neither understands the other, so in that sense their marriage is a failure, yet they are understanding and sensitive in this scene. She sees that he is 'haggard', and he speaks in a tone of 'gentle surprise'. By refusing to simplify the marriage, George Eliot makes the novel effective and increases its poignancy.

Setting

It is important to ask about the effectiveness of the setting. The most direct question is

- **Does the setting reinforce the theme of the novel?**

You must remember that setting can be the society depicted, or the landscape and townscape. In *1984* the theme of the book – the destruction of humanity by an oppressive society – is expressed in the settings. What we learn of the people in general and what we see of rotting London houses show how life is narrow and brutalised.

Likewise in *Tess of the D'Urbervilles* the scenes in Talbothays are effective because the society and landscape reflect Tess's joy in finding love. The society at the farm is a happy communal one in which the owner eats with his workers. The landscape is rich and overflowing with life. Both these settings show that Tess is at home in a rich and wonderful world.

Themes

The last question you can ask about novels is concerned with their themes or issues.

- **Does the novelist have something interesting and important to say about human life?**

Novels that either say nothing or are confused in what they say are ineffective, so the first thing you must be sure about is that a view of life does emerge in a book. But you don't have to agree with the view in order to find the book effective. Effectiveness depends upon the force and complexity with which a view is presented.

Take, for example, William Golding's *The Spire*. The book is very forceful; it concentrates intensely on the dean's attempts to build a spire on his cathedral. It is also complex; the spire stands for so many things – prayer, ambition, sexuality, art and pride. Yet it is a book that divides readers. Some agree with the negative judgement passed on human ambition, whilst others do not. Both groups, however, can agree upon the effectiveness with which the important themes are communicated.

18.4   Questions about the effectiveness of drama

All the questions you can ask about the effectiveness of drama turn upon whether or not a play is *dramatic*. A basic one is about language:

- **Do the words of the play invite action?**

In order to answer that question you will have to think hard about whether the words invite gestures, movements and groupings. Plays that in no way invite action can't be called dramatic. The point about plays that do, is that the actions invited by words are various.

___ **Example** _____

Look at this passage from *Macbeth* in which Macbeth is persuading the murderers to kill Banquo by showing that Banquo is the enemy of all of them:

> So is he mine; and in such bloody distance,
> That every minute of his being thrusts

> Against my nearest of life: and though I could
> With bare-faced power sweep him from my sight,
> And bid my will avouch it, yet I must not.

The words 'thrusts / Against' and 'sweep him from my sight' cry out for accompanying gestures, but there could be a number of appropriate ones. Does 'thrusts / Against' invite the actor to point to his heart or his head, and does the word 'sweep' indicate that the dramatic gesture (it must be that) should be with one or both arms? The words, then, provide different opportunities for dramatic expression.

A similar question can be asked about the theme of a play:

- **Is the theme acted out in the words of the play?**

A play will be effective if its central issues are both spoken about and acted out.

___ **Example** _____

In *King Lear* there is a great deal of talk about seeing and blindness. When Lear foolishly decides to disown his youngest daughter, he is told to 'see better'. In the sub-plot Gloucester can't see that Edgar is a good son and that Edmund is plotting against him.

But there are also actions. In one of the most terrible scenes in the whole of Shakespeare Gloucester has his eyes put out. His moral blindness (blindness to people, that is) has become physical blindness. The terrible irony of the play, however, is that once he is physically blind, he begins to 'see' clearly what has happened to him. At a crucial moment he 'sees' that he was 'blind': 'I stumbled when I saw.' What makes the word effective is the fact that the audience can see they come from a blind man. The theme of seeing and blindness is in the action as well as in the words.

As drama is a literary form that very obviously depends upon conventions, you can ask:

- **Are the conventions used in an interesting way?**

Plays can't be understood unless the audience recognises dramatic conventions, but unless those conventions are extended, the play will not be enjoyable. What Shakespeare often does is allow a character to grow beyond the conventions of the role he or she is playing. He often does this with villains.

Example

Take, for instance, Oliver in *As You Like It*. The first scene presents him as unnaturally cruel to his brother, Orlando, and viciously scheming. However, when he is left alone at the end of the scene, his soliloquy is not what convention would lead us to expect:

> Now will I stir this gamester: I hope I shall see an end of him; for my soul, yet I know not why, hates nothing more than he. Yet he's gentle; never schooled and yet learned; full of noble device; of all sorts enchantingly beloved; and, indeed, so much in the heart of the world, and especially of my own people, who best know him, that I am altogether misprized...

The only thing there that convention would lead us to expect is the hope that he will 'see an end of' Orlando. But what follows is an enlargement of character beyond the convention of the villian. He virtually praises Orlando, and stands in wonder at his qualities. Moreover, he admits (painfully?) that he has no idea why he hates him, and there could be sadness in the thought that everyone loves Orlando and looks down on him. What Shakespeare is doing is making a character grow out of a convention. This helps to make the play effective.

● **Are the characters distinctive?**

Of course, if a dramatist has decided that some characters need only be stock ones, it is foolish to say that they should have been fuller. However, unless the play is a farce, characters of some individuality are needed. You should also see if there is a balance in a play between those who are fairly fully drawn and those who are not.

In Bolt's *A Man for all Seasons*, for instance, the Common Man plays a number of stock roles. This is appropriate, because detailed characterisation could not add anything of importance. But the play is a serious one, so characters who are distinctive are required. Sir Thomas More, of course, is created in some detail, as is Cromwell, Rich and Margaret. The balance between the stock and the distinctive characters is good, because the play moves from lightness to seriousness, depending upon who is on stage. This gives the play variety and makes it effective.

● **Does the play create a vigorous and immediate sense of life?**

This question depends not so much upon the personality of one or two characters but the *impression* the actions of characters make upon the audience. The action of the play need not be striking.

<hr>

Example

Beckett's *Waiting for Godot* is a play in which actions are few but the dialogue is varied and lively, so an immediate sense of life is created. In this passage the two tramps, Estragon and Vladimir, are wondering what Godot will offer them:

Estragon: What exactly did we ask him for?
Vladimir: Were you not there?
Estragon: I can't have been listening.
Vladimir: Oh nothing very definite.
Estragon: A kind of prayer.
Vladimir: Precisely.
Estragon: A vague supplication.
Vladimir: Exactly.
Estragon: And what did he reply?
Vladimir: That he'd see.

That is lively, quick-fire dialogue in which there are remarkable changes of mood. Vladimir is cautious in reply to Estragon's first question and then sadly vague ('Oh nothing very definite') in his answer. However, when Estragon makes some suggestions he is much more assured – 'Precisely', 'Exactly'. It would be right to say that the characters create a vigorous and immediate sense of life.

<hr>

The final question that can be asked about drama concerns the plot.

● **Is the plot well handled?**

In order to answer that, you will have to see whether all the elements of a plot are held harmoniously together and whether they naturally grow to produce a credible conclusion.

The question is more likely to be asked about comedies than tragedies, for comedies demand complex, well-made plots.

<hr>

Example

Take, for instance, the plot of *Twelfth Night*. Shakespeare has several elements that he has to hold together. One of the ways in which he does this is by drawing the audience's attention to the similarities and differences between those elements.

At the beginning of the play we hear of Olivia who, because of the death of her brother, has withdrawn from the world. In the second scene, however, we are shown Viola, who believes her brother is drowned. Instead of withdrawing from the world she adopts a disguise and seeks employment at court.

That is not the only case of similarity and difference in the plot. Orsino, who loves Olivia, adopts a very romantic attitude in loving. Olivia, however, when she falls in love, is very practical. She asks questions such as: 'How shall I feast him?' That is very sensible and down to earth. She is thinking about what she will give Cesario (Viola in disguise) to eat.

The plot ends when Orsino goes to visit Olivia and, although it is not seen, Sir Toby pursues his idea of challenging Cesario to a duel. This brings the twins on to the stage together, and enables Shakespeare to close the play effectively. He can allow all the characters to see what has confused them and also stage the beautiful and touching reconciliation between Viola and her brother, Sebastian.

18.5   Two general questions about effectiveness

There are two questions that you can ask of any literary work, whether it be a poem, novel or play.

Has the author fulfilled his or her intentions?

If you decide that the author had a particular intention in mind when the work was written, a way of judging its effectiveness is by asking whether that intention has, in fact, been fulfilled.

You can often decide what the intention of the author was by looking at the events of the plot as a whole. The plot shows you how the author intends a character to be interpreted and judged. You then have to look at the work closely to see if what was intended has been achieved. You must prepare yourself for disagreements with your fellow students.

What, for instance, was Jane Austen's intention with regard to Fanny Price in *Mansfield Park*? Some readers would say she is meant to be a quiet and reserved heroine, whom readers will both like and judge as being good. Many readers find her to be that, but others agree that though that was Jane Austen's intention, the character actually created does not fulfil it, because she is cold and self-righteous.

Lawrence's *Sons and Lovers* presents another problem. What were Lawrence's intentions? Should a reader approve of Paul Morel and think that Miriam was a bad influence on him? That might be what Lawrence intended, but many readers both like her and feel she is treated unfairly by Paul *and Lawrence*.

In some cases, however, the intentions of an author are clearly and marvellously fulfilled. Bulstrode in *Middlemarch* is intended to be an unattractive character for whom the reader has increasing sympathy. He is that, and we do.

Does the work hang together as a whole?

One of the pleasures of reading literature is of finding works in which every part contributes to the general effect. This is very clearly the case with short poems, but is also true of longer works. However, bulky and rambling some of Shakespeare's plays appear to be on first acquaintance, you may find that close study shows you that each element blends in with the others to make a satisfying whole. Sometimes even a single line can take you into the heart of a play. When the mad Ophelia enters, she asks: 'Where is the beauteous majesty of Denmark?', that poignant question takes you to the heart of *Hamlet*. The 'beauteous majesty of Denmark' – the late king – is dead, and his son, Prince Hamlet, has been (possibly) driven out of his wits and (certainly) driven out of the country. When the question is asked, there is no beauty nor majesty left. And that is one of the themes of the play – the whole society is corrupted and rotten.

● **Talking about effectiveness is not easy.**

There are times when we feel that something is effective but can't say why. There are also occasions when someone produces what seems like a devastating argument against a book that we like. Perhaps even more disturbing are those arguments that suggest that there are no such things as evaluative judgements about literature. For instance, some people think that the idea of intention is so difficult that it can't be used.

In the face of all these problems it's good to remember two things.

(i)   People have always made judgements about books. That is a fact of life. It's difficult to believe that something as deeply rooted as that is going to go away just because some people have problems in framing successful arguments about why a book is good.

(ii) Although it's interesting, it's not really the job of a reader to produce arguments of a philosophical kind about why we should (or for that matter should not) judge books. The starting point (and for most us the finishing point) for the reader can only be the experience of finding something in a book effective. As long as that is the case, the issue of effectiveness is still alive.

___ **Exercises** _____

18.1   Recall your first impressions of a book. How helpful do you now find them in judging whether or not a book is effective.

18.2   Try to say why you think a poem, novel or play is effective.

18.3   Look at the poems, novels or plays you are studying in the light of each of the above questions examined. Do they make you change your mind about the effectiveness of your set works?

18.4   Try to say what you think the intentions of the authors were in writing the books you are studying. Do you think the authors have fulfilled these intentions?

18.5   Try to say how the books you are studying hang together as a whole. If you think they don't, try to say why not and whether you think they are less effective because of that.

19 Questions

19.1 Answering questions

Let's start with the obvious:

- whatever question you are asked, you should try to answer it.

As a matter of fact, this is easier said than done. The experience of most (I suspect all) examiners is that the majority of students don't answer questions. The three most common errors are retelling the story, reproducing notes they've made in class and reframing the question so that it means something different from what is actually being asked.

There are two things you can do about this. They are very closely related.

- Practise looking at and thinking about questions.
- Concentrate on the actual words of each question.

By looking at a lot of questions you will get used to their 'language'. All examiners use a set of phrases, so students would be wise to recognise them. For instance, when you are asked to 'Discuss the view that …', they mean that the idea they are going to introduce is one that is important but about which there is not necessarily agreement. Sometimes they indicate this by using a phrase such as 'To what extent…'. That is a clear indication that they expect different answers about an aspect of the book that is important but (usually) not one about which everybody thinks the same. Sometimes, the invitation is an open one; some questions end: '… what do you think?' Here you are plainly asked to give your views.

You should remember two things about this 'language'.

(i) **You are still expected to write about the issue.** It's no good setting about a question that asks you to discuss the importance of, say, the past in Seamus Heaney by saying you think the present is far more important, so you are going to write about that instead. That is not answering the question.

(ii) **There isn't a 'right' answer in the mind of the examiner.** It can't be said too strongly that if you address the issue in the question in the terms in which you asked to do so and if you produce a reasoned argument supported by details from the text, you will be rewarded by the examiner.

347

- It always pays off to look in detail at what a question is asking.

Too many candidates see a few phrases and imagine they know from that what the question requires them to do. Consider this question on Hamlet:

Hamlet often speaks of his delay and inactivity, and yet the play is full of action. Try to account for this.

A student who has done a lot of work on the teasing problem of why Hamlet, so apparently eager to carry out revenge, fails to do anything about it for most of the play might be tempted to seize upon that part of the question and turn it into one about delay. But this would be wrong. What the question is asking the candidate to do is think about why a play which in one sense is about delay is also one in which there is a great deal of stage action – Hamlet may not kill the King immediately but he does mock and then murder Polonius and have fraught scenes with his mother and Ophelia. Only by looking at all the words of the question will a student be able to answer this question properly.

- **It's important to remember that two questions may involve the same material but require a different focus.**

Consider, for instance, these two questions on *Death of a Salesman:*

(1)   Trace the breakdown of Willy Loman in *Death of a Salesman*.

(2)   Trace Arthur Miller's treatment of Willy Loman's breakdown in *Death of a Salesman*.

The first requires you to map out the events that lead to Willy's disintegration and death, whilst the second is about Miller's treatment of this. You will probably refer to the same events, but in an answer to the second question you will focus on how Miller puts these events on the stage. This will require discussion of the 'flashbacks', his conversations with Charlie and Willy's capacity for glamorising the past.

19.2   The form of questions

Another thing that it's useful to be aware of is the form in which questions come. They are usually of five kinds:

(1)   the direct question
(2)   the question based on a quotation
(3)   the question in the form of a list
(4)   the question based upon an extract
(5)   the empathy question.

(1)   The direct question

This is the one that asks the candidate to think through an issue. Most questions in a literary examination come in this form. These questions differ according to their focus; they may be about

- what the book is saying (the interpretation question)
- how it's done (the form or technique question)
- whether or not it succeeds (the effectiveness or evaluation question).

It is, of course, possible to combine these in one question.

- **Interpretation questions**

These use phrases and words such as 'subject matter', 'the themes of the book', 'the author's concerns', 'issues', 'preoccupations'; what they all point to is the matter of what the book is about.

Example: Do you agree that in *Sons and Lovers* Paul Morel finds it harder to be a lover than a son?

- Form questions

These are about plots, narrative methods, the design of a play, the contribution (a favourite examiner's word) of imagery and stanza forms, the pace of a book, the use of contrast, the presence of variety and the importance of settings. They are often related to matters of interpretation and evaluation.

Example: How does George Eliot sustain our interest in all the strands of plot in *Middlemarch*?

- Evaluative questions

These are concerned with such matters as the enjoyment of the reader, the way a book holds the reader's interest, the contrast between the important and the less important areas of a book, the place of details in the design of a whole work, the popularity of a work on stage and the issue of whether or not an author has produced a convincing picture of life.

Example: Discuss the kind of pleasures the reader might experience when reading Donne's poetry.

(2)   The quotation question

This usually invites the candidate to range widely over an area of the book. Quotation questions are composed by finding, or more usually inventing, a quotation about a central aspect of a work, and inviting the candidate to discuss the idea framed in the quotation.

Examples: (i)   'Wilfred Owen has only one subject – War – so his poetry is of limited interested to the reader.' Discuss.

(ii)   'William Golding has a gloomy view of people.' Do you agree that Golding's view of people in *The Lord of the Flies* is a gloomy one?

You should remember that the examiner is not expecting you to agree with every word of the question. You can agree with one part and not with another. What the examiner is expecting, however, is that you will write about the issue expressed in the quotation.

One way of preparing for quotation questions is to think through the important issues of a book; that way you may be familiar with the kind of thinking the question requires you to do. But in such cases beware of offering the prepared answer.

(3)   List question

These are questions in which you are given a series of items from which you have to make a selection.

Example: Discuss Shakespeare's treatment in *The Winter's Tale* of two of the following: song and dance, the court and the country, children and young people, disguise, the passing of time.

The point about these questions is that they are usually a general invitation to write what you like about the items. If you are at a loss as to what to say, you can always treat them as interpretation, form and evaluation questions and discuss what the item means, how it's presented and whether or not it makes a valuable contribution.

(4)   The question based upon an extract

Increasingly, examiners are setting extract or passage questions. (Another word to describe them is gobbets – the word means lumps). These questions have become popular with the growth of what is called 'open book' examinations – examinations in which the candidates are allowed to take the books into the examination with them.

The most important thing to remember about these questions is that you are expected to write in detail about the passage. Extract questions are more like practical criticism exercises than essays in which an argument is advanced.

Often the passage has a specific focus. For instance, an examiner might ask a candidate to look at the passage in *The Mayor of Casterbridge* in which

Henchard speaks disparagingly about the new piece of farm machinery on display in the Market Place. The question might ask candidates to write about how the passage brings out the difference between Henchard and Farfrae or about the clash in the novel between the old and the new.

What an extract question never asks you to do is show that you know the book well; it's chiefly interested in your understanding. Of course, open book questions require you to know the book (in fact, you need to know it very well), but you will never gain many marks merely for knowing something.

One of the most popular kinds of extract question is the passage from a Shakespeare play. These usually ask you to write about the dramatic aspect of the language. When you are faced with this kind of question, there are some general points about Shakespeare's dramatic language that you should bear in mind.

- The dramatic success of Shakespeare depends upon the way the dialogue is always alive with human interest. Characters demand attention from each other, so the emotional force of the dialogue constantly shifts from one character to another.
- Shakespeare's language is dramatic because it invites gesture, movement and grouping on stage.
- The meaning of Shakespeare emerges not only through ideas but through imagery.
- The plays have their own distinctive atmosphere, mood and world of ideas. These are often present in words (particularly images) that are repeated throughout the play.
- The plays are designed in such a way that scenes echo and anticipate each other.
- The plays work by engaging the interest of the audience. The relationship we have to characters creates the special emotional world of each play.
- The plays often work by encouraging the audience to hope for or fear certain outcomes. What the audience knows and what individual characters know is essential for expectation.
- The kind of language given to characters creates their individuality and their status in the society of the play. Whether a speech is in verse or prose and whether the language is studded with imagery or plain is an important contribution.

The above points are not to be taken as an infallible guide to what the questions are going to ask, but they can be used as a guide when revising extract questions.

(5) Empathy questions

These are questions in which you are invited to imagine yourself as a character in a book and write from this perspective. Questions often start with the words: 'Imagine you are ...' They come in varied forms; you may be asked to write a letter, an imaginary diary, to write about what a character might be thinking or to reminisce about events

What they are testing is your appreciation of characters and the situations in which they find themselves. They can only be successfully answered if you have a firm grasp of what the character is like, and that requires you to know the text of the book. Knowing the text means at least two things:

- seeing what is directly revealed about a character
- being able to deduce what is not explicitly stated.

For instance, you might be asked to imagine what Macbeth might be thinking as he rode home to his castle, having met the witches and knowing that the King is going to stay with them that night. Because Macbeth has asked the witches to stay and tell him more, you could present him as a man who wants to know what his destiny is.

You can also deduce things from what he has said. Up to this point Macbeth has not said he intends to murder the King, but because murder is in his mind (he says: 'My thought, whose murder yet is but fantastical'), you may deduce that his thoughts are tending that way. It would therefore be appropriate to imagine him being led, perhaps even against his will, to the idea that it would be possible to kill the King.

19.3   Questions about poetry

Questions about poetry are usually about

(1)   style
(2)   theme
(3)   the problems readers have encountered in a poet's work.

You can also expect

(4)   passage questions.

(1)   Style questions

What lies behind questions about poetic style is the insight that each poet has an individual way of handling language. This individuality will be evident in the choice of words, the stanza forms, the rhymes and the rhythms. Questions about style usually ask you to identify the features that make a poet distinctive.

Example: What features of Milton's poetic style are present in the first two books of *Paradise Lost*?

The examiners are expecting in your answer a discussion of such matters as blank verse, epic similes, classical allusions, latinate diction and complex syntax. Often there is an addition, asking you to comment on how these stylistic elements are effective. For instance, you might be asked to write about what contribution Donne's conceits make to his love and religious poetry.

Sometimes the questions specify what aspects of poetic style are to be discussed. For instance, you might find the following kind of questions.

Examples: (i) Discuss Christina Rossetti's narrative gifts.
    (ii) Discuss Browning's use of the dramatic monologue.
    (iii) What does Emily Dickinson's imagery contribute to the success of her poems?
    (iii) Write an essay on the variety of verse forms in the poetry of W. B. Yeats.
    (iv) Discuss the power of Dylan Thomas's voice as it is heard in the rhythms of his poems.

● Preparing for style questions
In all the above cases, the questions fix on a central feature of the poet's work. To that extent, you can prepare for the possibility of such questions by working out what you think about the chief formal characteristics of the poet's verse. When you do this you should make notes on the important elements of style and find one or two good examples.

A variation of this is to ask what aspects of a poet's style make it appropriate to call him or her a poet of a particular group. The following questions do this.

Examples: (i) What aspects of Andrew Marvell would you call metaphysical?

    (ii) Why have readers called Blake a romantic poet?

    (iii) In what ways can Sylvia Plath be said to be a feminist poet?

Those questions are wider than some of the formal ones, but they will require a candidate to consider elements of style.

(2) Theme questions

Questions about themes are as varied as the diverse subjects and personalities of poets. You could, for instance, be asked about how a poet treats

● love
● the passing of time
● changes in the seasons
● war
● the life of the city

- failure
- death
- the future
- childhood
- old age
- work

That is not a complete list!

A variant of this is to quote a couple of lines and ask how characteristic they are of the poet's outlook. Where such preoccupations are prominent, you can prepare for them. In so doing, you will have to do more than say that such and such a poet is interested in, say, love. The real question is exactly what the poet thinks. In Yeats, for instance, love is often anguished and painful, and the beloved is often compared to literary figures such as Helen of Troy. In other words: try to be specific.

Sometimes theme questions are more general. You might, for instance, be asked about the emotional or intellectual character of a poet's work.

Examples: (i)   Is Donne too intellectual in his love poetry?
             (ii) Discuss the view that although he was not a religious person, Dylan Thomas's poetry is filled with religious feeling.
             (iii) Do you find that Hopkins's zest and energy are the most appealing things about his poetry?

- Preparing for theme questions

Such questions can be prepared for by thinking about the exact nature of a poet's outlook and by selecting a few examples that bear out the points you want to make. You should, of course, remember that very few poets are either emotionally or intellectually simple, so be prepared to write about range and variety.

(3)   Questions about the problematic nature of a poet's work

These are more likely to be set at A-level and beyond rather than at GCSE. The starting point for such questions is the realisation that there is something odd, difficult, controversial or even apparently contradictory about a poet's work. It has, for instance, seemed odd to some (but not all) readers that Donne wrote passionate (and sexually explicit) love poetry and religious poetry.

Another 'problem' is that a poet such as Wordsworth talks a good deal about nature and yet there aren't many detailed passages about natural things such as birds or flowers in his poetry. Another problem with Wordsworth is his capacity for responding very warmly to very ordinary things. Most people remember his (very fine) poem about daffodils.

Some of the problems attached to a poet have been debated for generations. Milton's *Paradise Lost* is a work of great power, but for centuries readers have been divided as to whether Satan is the villain or a very unusual kind of hero. Also, some readers find the work thrilling, while others find it austere and cold.

A special form of this type of question is the harsh words that one writer has said of another. For instance, the following question might be set on Wilfred Owen:

Do you think that Owen's poetry can be defended from Yeats's view that it is 'all blood, dirt and sucked sugar-stick'?

- Preparing for 'problem' questions
  'Problem' questions can be prepared for in two ways.

(i) *You should read them with an eye for what might be strange.* A good question to work with is:

- Do I find anything strange about this poet's work?

This question can be backed up by a little knowledge of what has been said about the poet.

(ii) *Make use of literary criticism.*

Generally speaking, it's not necessary to read a lot of what is called literary criticism (writing about the interpretation and evaluation of literature), but when you are asking about the problems a poet presents, such writing can come in useful. Sometimes these ideas can be picked up in the classroom, but failing that there are plenty of books where famous literary criticism can be found.

- **When preparing for such questions, the most important point to bear in mind is this:** you must try to show *why* a poet is problematic. This will involve locating examples.

(4) *Passage questions*

These either come in the form of practical criticism (see p. 96) or extracts from the body of work you've been studying, usually with a focused question. Sometimes there is an invitation to write about any aspect of the work, while at others you might be asked to write about particular aspects. Quite often, these questions tell you to concentrate upon the printed passages, though you are told that other poems, relevant to the argument, could be mentioned in your essay.

There are a few general 'dos' and 'don'ts' that candidates should remember when tackling these questions.

- Make sure that the bulk of your essay is on the words printed on the paper.
- Always try to be detailed; that is, try to show how individual words and phrases work.

- Never identify a figure of speech, for example a metaphor, and leave it at that. You should always try to show how poetic features enact the meanings.
- Always try to look at the meaning of the poem in detail. The meaning, of course, is inseparable from the words of the poem.
- Don't be misled by subject matter into thinking that you know what the tone of a poem is going to be. Poets have written merry poems about death and gloomy ones about love.
- Try to convey how the poem grows and develops. It's a good idea thinking of the poem as a kind of emotional and intellectual journey that you have to trace.
- Don't leave the poem as 'bits'; try to see what it adds up to as a whole.

19.4   Questions about novels

The most common questions on novels are about

(1)   characters
(2)   themes
(3)   style
(4)   the attitudes of authors

(1)   Questions on characters

These often focus on what they are like, how they change, how they contrast with other characters and how the author has created them.

- Questions about what a character is like

These are numerous at GCSE, A-level and beyond. It's not unusual to find questions such as these.

Examples: (i) Do you think Gatsby is great?

(ii) Discuss how George Eliot presents Maggie Tulliver as both rebellious and dutiful.

(iii) What qualities do we find to admire in Moll Flanders?

Because everything in literature has been made, to ask what a character is like is to think about how the author has presented him or her. Therefore when you are faced with such a question, the first thing you should think about is the mode of narration. You might ask these questions.

- Do we know this character as part of a first-person or a third-person narration?

- Do we have access to the character's thoughts?

- What does the author tell or show us about the character?

In the light of the narratorial mode, you can go on to think about the following matters:

- what the characters say and do
- the motives of their actions
- their background and the settings in which they appear
- what other characters say about them

When thinking through these issues, it's a good idea to locate passages which exemplify what a character is like. For instance, when, in *Jane Eyre*, Jane refuses to live with Mr Rochester because his wife is still alive, she reveals herself to be strong-minded, disciplined and upright.

- Questions on growth and change.

These are of course, a variant upon those about character. You may encounter questions of the following kind.

Examples: (i) Trace Dorothea's moral growth in *Middlemarch*.

(ii) How and why does Elizabeth Bennet change?

What you need to look out for are those crucial moments when characters are seen to be different. The difference may be a matter of personal realisation (Pip at the end of *Great Expectations* sees that the convict is a better man than he is) or a publicly observed change, as in the climax of Evelyn Waugh's *Brideshead Revisited*, when Lord Marchmain signifies on his deathbed that he has repented.

In order to do this you will have to think about character in relation to plot; quite often a plot turns on whether a character will be able to act differently from how he or she has done in the past. Conrad plots *Lord Jim* around this problem. In questions about change, you will often find that character, plot and theme all need to be discussed.

- Questions about how characters are contrasted.

These also build on the issues discussed above. You may find questions such as these.

Examples: (i) What do the differences between the Bertrams and the Crawfords contribute to *Mansfield Park*?

(ii) How important are the differences between the two Cathys in *Wuthering Heights*?

The specific contribution of contrast is that it helps a reader to see more clearly what a character is like. *Jane Eyre*, for instance, is designed around a number of doubles. Throughout the novel there are characters whose function it is to reveal by way of contrast an aspect of Jane's character: Helen Burns is resigned, whereas Jane is rebellious; Celine Varens is the unfaithful mistress, whereas Jane refuses to be a mistress but is loyal; Bertha Rochester is the incarcerated wife who cannot control her passion, whereas Jane, who is also incarcerated, has won the battle over her powerful feelings.

As in the case of questions about change, questions about contrast usually require candidates to write about the plot and the theme of the novel. One of the themes of *Great Expectations* is Pip's snobbery, so Dickens designs a plot that makes the reader (and Pip the narrator) ponder the nature of this unpleasant feature. Pip is therefore contrasted with Joe – a man quite without that taint – and with the convict, who, (a richly ironic feature), is probably more of a snob than Pip.

- Questions about characterisation

At A-level you may find questions about characterisation.

Examples: (i) How does Emily Brontë make Heathcliff both evil and attractive?

(ii) Write about how Scott Fitzgerald makes Jay Gatsby a mysterious character.

Questions such as this can be prepared for by looking through the sections in Chapter 7. Sometimes a question focuses on the fact that characters are often created in different ways. It's often said that in Jane Austen's novels some characters are fully rounded – Elizabeth Bennet, Emma Woodhouse – whereas others approach caricature in that they are composed of a small number of (usually exaggerated) features – the snobbery and lack of self-awareness in Lady Catherine de Bourgh and the chatty inanities of Miss Bates. When considering such differences it is, of course, important to ask why the author has done this. The answer to that question is usually something to do with maintaining the reader's attention clearly focused on the main business of the plot.

(2)   Thematic questions

These come in a number of different forms.

- The development of a relationship which is central to the novel

Example: Discuss how Paul Morel's relationship with his mother is present in all his other relationships.

● The examination of a central idea

Example: Discuss the view that the main theme of *A Passage to India* is India itself.

● The tension between two ideas, often posed in the form of which is the more important or successful

Example: Is it more important to regard Tess as a child of nature than as a victim of the modern world?

● The thematic importance of the title

Example: Why is the novel called *Mansfield Park*?

The point always to bear in mind is *how* the themes are present. It's not usual for books to announce their themes (though some do), so readers must be alert to how they emerge in and through the dialogue, the thoughts, the actions, situations and settings of the novel. Therefore when preparing for such questions, your notes must include actual incidents in the novel when the themes, so to speak, become transparent.

(3) Questions about style

Questions about style – about how a novel is written – are usually only set at A-level and beyond. They cover a number of issues.

● The mode of narration

Example: Discuss multiple narration in *Wuthering Heights*.

● The point of view of the narration

Example: What does Mark Twain want us to think about Huck's account of his life on the river?

● The construction, development and pace of the plot

Example: Discuss how Wilkie Collins creates and sustains interest in the plot of *The Woman in White*.

● The function of settings

Example: What do the detailed pictures of rural life add to *Far from the Madding Crowd*?

Candidates are often wary of these questions, but there is no need to be. It's clear, for instance, that the intense first-person narration of a novel such as *Jane Eyre* is very different from a George Eliot novel in which we are given the point of view of virtually every character. Once you see this, it's not difficult to find examples of where the characteristic narrative mode is evident. If you want some ideas to work with as you prepare for style questions, you can ask yourself these questions.

- What is the author telling or showing me?

- What do I know that other characters don't?

- In what direction is the author developing the plot?

- Is the setting important?

One of the pleasures of the style question is that it allows candidates to write about the control an author exercises over the plot. It never does any harm to let your admiration for what an author has done surface in your writing: you may, for instance, admire how the plot produces ironies, creates tension, shifts our attention at crucial points or arouses our expectations.

(4)   Questions about authors' attitudes

Most of the questions discussed above are also about the attitudes of authors, in that it's only through those elements – character, theme, style – that what an author thinks can emerge. Questions are often presented in the following ways.

- A question about what an author thinks

Example: What is Huxley's view of the society he has created in *Brave New World*?

- A quotation or comment from the author about what he or she was attempting in the novel

Example: How helpful is Hardy's remark that *Tess of the D'Urbervilles* is more often charged with impressions than convictions

- An invitation to discuss what the author approves or disapproves of

Example: Where in *A Passage to India* do Forster's sympathies lie?

- An invitation to discuss the author's view in terms of a particular idea

Example: To what extent is it helpful to describe Charlotte Brontë's attitudes in *Jane Eyre* as feminist?

These questions can be approached by thinking about how the author's attitudes are present.

(i) *Attitudes seen through tone* No one can miss Dickens's anger in *Hard Times* or can fail to see that the novel is giving us his thinking about education. It's there in the pointed contrasts in the opening scene between the model pupil who is unnaturally pale and the fresh, healthy-looking girl, who is persecuted because she can't give the required answers.

(ii) *Attitudes seen in the pattern of events.* It's George Eliot's belief in *The Mill on the Floss* that we can never escape the influences of our childhood; those whom we've grown up with are always going to mean more to us than anyone else. Hence Maggie is always prepared to do what her brother demands.

(iii) *Attitudes seen through how the novel ends.* Novelists with strong views often use the close as a way of showing the reader what their understanding of life is. At the end of Golding's novels there is often an ambiguity: characters see the evil in their own and other people's lives, but the act of seeing brings relief and even a kind of joy. We see that human life is both glorious and terrible.

19.5 Questions about drama

Questions about drama usually focus on

(1) characters
(2) themes
(3) dramatic effectiveness
(4) genre.

(1) Character questions

Some character questions are almost the same as those set on novels – they deal with:

● what characters are like
● how they change
● their relationships with others
● how they contrast with each other.

What is sometimes distinctive about a character question on drama is the invitation to write about your reactions to a character. For instance, examiners may set questions of the following kind.

Examples: (i)   Discuss the extent to which Shakespeare invites the audience to sympathise with King Lear.

(ii)   'Coriolanus is too cold to be the object of our pity.' Discuss.

Questions such as this are in keeping with the nature of drama as a performing art. Drama works by playing upon the immediate reactions of the audience. When therefore you come to write about your reactions you must do what was discussed in Chapter 15 – act out the play in the theatre of your imagination. If, for instance, you are writing about what you feel about Malvolio in *Twelfth Night*, you must imagine those scenes that have the biggest impact on the audience – his disruption of the late-night drinking, his reading of the letter, his strutting before Olivia in yellow stockings and his incarceration on alleged grounds of lunacy. When you imagine these scenes you will have to balance the pomposity of the law-enforcing steward against the pathetic figure locked in a dark room, pleading to be treated as sane.

(2)   Questions about themes

These are also similar to the questions on novels. You may be asked to do the following.

● Trace the presence of a theme throughout a play

Example: Discuss the theme of justice in *Measure for Measure*.

● Decide which of two themes is the more important

Example: Is love or the finding of the lost more important at the close of *Twelfth Night*?

● Defend or attack the suggestion that a particular theme is central to the play

Example: To what extent do you agree that the main theme of *Hamlet* is revenge?

In preparing for these questions, you may find it helpful to think about the following points.

● Examiners don't like vagueness, so try to find scenes in which the themes of the play are fully present.

- Always think about how a theme emerges; this will help you with the point above.
- Try to bear in mind how the play works as a whole; themes often emerge in the total action of the play.
- Pay attention to how the theme emerges in the imagery, the dialogue, repeated words and actions.

One last point should be made about themes in plays.

- **Because the theatre is both immediate and communal, playwrights often use it as a vehicle for their own ideas.**

For instance, John Arden uses some of his plays to voice his political beliefs. The problem with this is that audiences and readers can feel that they are being got at. The plays sometimes become too didactic; that is, the play's aim is to teach rather than to entertain. When you write about plays that very clearly press home a particular belief, you can think about how the plot is being controlled by the beliefs of the author.

It should be added that this is not true of the works of Arden studied at A-level. *Sergeant Musgrave's Dance* is an exceptionally interesting play that opens up the issue of how, in spite of someone's passion and sincerity, people can fail to respond to a belief that has been dramatically presented to them. In fact, it can be read as a parable of the failure of didactic drama.

(3) Questions about dramatic effectiveness

Questions about how effective a play is on stage are, of course, special to drama. They are of various kinds, of which the following are popular.

- Questions that ask candidates to write about the effectiveness of a play as a whole

Example: Is *The Tempest* too static to be a success on stage?

- Questions which focus on particular elements such as dialogue and action

Example: To what extent do you agree that the chief interest in *Rosencrantz and Guildenstern are Dead* is Stoppard's dialogue?

- Questions about how the audience might react

Example: Do you think an audience will respond sympathetically to the society presented in *The Playboy of the Western World*?

- Questions about the continued popularity of a play

Example: What is it about *Richard III* that has made it popular on the stage?

In most cases you will only have your imagination to rely on, but if you have seen a production, it is a good idea to refer to how a particular scene was done. You should, however, remember that all productions are interpretations and therefore don't have a final authority.

Preparing for questions on effectiveness can best be done by thinking through the kind of resources available in the theatre. You may, for instance, like to consider the following points.

- The number of characters on the stage will have an impact on the audience; consider the difference between the lonely Hamlet of the soliloquies and Claudius enjoying the power of a crowded court.
- The opening and closing scenes of a play will have a greater impact than many of the intervening ones.
- Contrasts will have a big impact, whether they be of mood, action or speech.
- Dramatic language will be embodied in the actions and gestures of the players.
- The relationship of the audience to the action will be a major factor in determining the mood of the play.

It's a good idea to keep a separate set of notes on how the plays you are studying make use of the opportunities of the theatre.

(4)   Questions about genre

Closely related to questions about dramatic effectiveness are questions about how a play stands in relation to the traditional theatrical genres. A *genre* is a type of literature: for instance, both comedy and tragedy are genres. Questions about genre are very unlikely to use the word, but they will invite you to write about the common expectations of audiences when faced with a play in a specific genre. Three sorts of question are often set.

- A definition of the genre is provided, and the candidate asked to discuss whether it applies to the play under discussion

Example: 'In comedy there is always confusion, but we never doubt that the outcome will be happy.' To what extent is this true of *Much Ado about Nothing*?

- The question that invites discussion about the extent to which a play can be regarded as belonging to a particular genre.

Example: Can Willy Loman be said to be a tragic figure?

- Students are invited to discuss whether there is a suitable way of describing a play. (This is very popular when the subject is Shakespeare's problem plays.)

Example: '*Troilus and Cressida* is too cynical for tragedy and too painful
for comedy.' Discuss.

What is at stake in these questions is just how useful critical categories are.
Many students are encouraged to write essays as if there were set, unchangeable
definitions of what tragedy and comedy are, and that all authors slavishly treat
these as rules to follow. Many essays start with a dictionary definition of, say,
tragedy and proceed to tick off the features in the play against it. There's one
thing that needs to be said about that: Don't do it!

We can't do without definitions, but we mustn't be misled into thinking that
they can perfectly and neatly apply to a whole multitude of plays. Nor should we
assume that because plays are called comedies or tragedies they have specific
qualities in common – a set of core features which will be found in every work
in the genre. There is, moreover, a cultural factor here: the English (unlike, for
instance, the French) have never tried to write according to rules. (French
writers have often experienced problems with Shakespeare, because he doesn't
fit into the rigid categories of their critical formulae.)

It's wise therefore not to regard definitions as scientific formulae. Nor should
we look for a 'lowest common denominator' in plays that are described as being in
the same genre. There is no 'essence' of comedy or tragedy that must be found in
any play that bears those names. What we find instead are links between individual plays that justify us in regarding them as being in the same family. Consider,
for instance, three Shakespeare plays: *The Comedy of Errors* has links with *A
Midsummer Night's Dream*, and *A Midsummer Night's Dream* has links with *The
Taming of the Shrew*, yet these plays don't share a common essence or core. One
play shares characteristics with another, though no single play has all of them.

The best thing you can do is recognise that genres are baggy and that within
each there is the possibility of a good deal of variation. That way you will be
able to recognise how a play extends the 'boundaries' of a genre.

- A Note needs to be added about Aristotle

His *Poetics* has often been regarded as a set of rules about what constitutes
tragedy. Generations of students have been encouraged to write essays in which
they discuss what he said about tragedy and then compare the play they are
studying to the Aristotelian formula. This is better than going to the dictionary,
but it's still mistaken. One reason has already been given: definitions of genre
are not precise and hard-edged. The second reason is that it's a misunderstanding of Aristotle. He was not trying to give hard and fast definitions but to
describe the kind of plays that he knew. It was only later generations that
thought of him as writing a rule book.

19.6 Coursework

Most examinations now have an element of coursework. This is both sensible
and just; sensible because students spend a lot of time working on essays, so it's

silly not to include them in the assessment process; and just because it's unfair to judge two or three years' work on a few hours of writing in an examination. This is not to say that everyone will do better at coursework than exams (though most do), but that any examination system must be trustworthy, and one that's neither sensible nor just is not worthy of trust.

Coursework puts the responsibility on you; here is a chunk of the exam that you have some control over. It pays you therefore to take it seriously. What advice then can be given about coursework? Here are some points that it might be helpful to bear in mind.

- In coursework you often have the opportunity of writing about a topic that particularly interests you, so, as you study, think about the enticing and intriguing aspects of a book that call for further thinking.
- Essays in coursework can in their topics and range be more adventurous than in an examination, so try to be ambitious.
- It's worthwhile working on several drafts of an essay; some Examination Boards do not allow you to re-write essays once they've been marked, so your improvements and refinements must be done beforehand.
- Don't neglect coursework by leaving it to the last minute.
- Because some examiners are obsessed with word limits it's not worth writing essays that exceed the word limit.
- In the light of the above point, remember that what matters is intelligent response and a clear argument; coursework essays should not try to impress merely because of their length.
- Remember that although the written work must be yours and yours alone, course work allows you to talk to teachers and friends about your ideas.

What those points are trying to stress is that coursework is an opportunity for you to do some hard thinking. Quite often those who have thought hard about their coursework essays will say it was the most rewarding part of their study. Even if the proportion of marks given for coursework is as low as 20 per cent (too low in my view), it's still worth putting in a great deal of effort.

19.7   Argument and evidence

There's one piece of advice that needs to be underlined. It's this:

- When answering a question, you should maintain a balance between argument and evidence.

The most important thing to show is that you have seen the issue or problem in the question. Too many essays (both for coursework and in examinations) are unfocused. What teachers and examiners welcome are essays that identify the main issue, develop and assess arguments about them and come to a conclusion.

To do this satisfactorily, you need evidence. It's wise to refer to specific passages, so that you can show how what you say is borne out by the text.

Many students are anxious (particularly in exams) about quotations. If you are worried, remember the following points.

- Long quotations are not required; a line or even a phrase will usually serve the purpose.
- A lot of students 'learn' quotations without trying; if you read a passage several times, something usually sticks.
- Most students know more than they think they do; what is usually lacking is confidence to use what they do know.
- Most quotations are insufficient on their own, so you need to discuss what has been quoted; this can be done by commenting on phrases or even single words.
- You can refer closely to a scene in a novel or play without quoting a single word.
- Quotations are usually less important than the argument.

In other words, quotations are not as important as many people think, so it's pointless getting worked up about them. My usual advice is that if a student has worked well throughout the year and concentrates on arguments, the quotations will look after themselves. This is not to say it's bad to learn things by heart, but that such learning often happens as a matter of course.

___ **Exercises** ___

19.1 Look through the questions you've been asked to do and see if you can understand what exactly is required of you.

19.2 Prepare revision notes for all your set books in the light of the kind of questions that you may be asked.

19.3 Try to work out what would be good questions on the books you are studying. (This is harder than you think!)

19.4 Make a list of the passages that are likely to be used in extract questions, and practise answering questions on them.

19.5 Make detailed essay plans in answer to the kind of questions you are likely to encounter in the exams.

⬡20 Examinations

20.1 Revision

It is foolish to leave revision to the few weeks before an examination.

- **Throughout your course of study you should find time to look through your work.**

The best thing to do is to look through what you have done every week. You should read through the material, do any writing that you think is necessary, and try to relate the new material to what you already know of the book.

- **Re-reading**

Once you have finished your first study of a book you should re-read it. (More advice on this is given in Chapter 16). You can do this in one of two ways:

- read the book through without taking notes
- make further notes as you read

It is wise not to exclude the possibility of making more notes, as new ideas may occur to you as you read. You can also turn to criticism to give you more ideas.

- **Making notes**

Throughout your course you will be making notes. As the examination approaches, you should make some that are specifically concerned with it. The best thing to do is to make separate notes on the important aspects of the book:

- its themes
- its style
- its characters
- its plot
- its effectiveness

It is also wise to look through the kinds of question that are usually asked and prepare notes on these. A convenient way of compiling revision notes is to buy a cheap exercise book and devote two or three pages to each of the topics. But you should not forget that it is the book upon which you are going to be examined and not your notes! Therefore, make sure that in your revision notes you keep a record of the page numbers of important passages.

- **There are a number of ways in which you can revise.**

- You can read through the books. This is particularly helpful in the case of poetry; because many poems are short, you can read several each day.
- You can look at your books in the light of your notes. If you have both open on the table, the one can illuminate the other.
- You can also look through your notes with possible exam questions in mind.

- **When you are revising, you should remember two things.**

 (i) Even if you are doing an open book exam, you still need to know your books very well.
(ii) You must never become so dependent on your notes that you can't respond to questions in the exam that have a different focus from the thinking with which you are familiar.

- **It's important to do some writing as part of your revision.**

You can plan answers, write about extracts and practise writing timed essays (if you're not asked to do this in class, do it in your own time). When doing timed essays, it's a good idea to find ones that have been set in an examination. You don't have much time (usually between half an hour and an hour), so you will need to practise getting down all you need to say.

- **Learning quotations**

The point was made in Chapter 19 that learning quotations can be a problem. In fact, it's not as much of a problem as most students think, but if you do an exam that requires it, here is some advice.

- Try recalling what you know (or nearly know) just from your reading. If you half know a quotation, it's not difficult to learn it properly.
- When you deliberately set out to learn passages, make sure they are ones you can use in a number of ways.
- When memorising a passage, try as soon as possible to do without the book. Read the passage three or four times, and then close the book and try to recall the words. Actively trying to remember fixes things much more firmly in the memory than passively reading the text.
- To keep quotations in the memory, repeat them regularly. You may like to pin them up on your bedrooms walls or put them on tape.
- Remember that even phrases can be very useful; for instance, someone studying *Macbeth* can do a lot with 'fair is foul' and 'light thickens'.

20.2 Examination technique

Examination technique helps you to make the best of what you know in an examination. Although the subject here is English Literature, the following advice is applicable to nearly all examinations.

- **Make sure you are not tired when you take the examination.**

If you have revised thoroughly, there is no need to stay up late the night before an examination. Even if the examination is in the afternoon, late night revision is both unnecessary and undesirable. The plain fact is that you should be fresh and alert before the examination.

- **Answer *all* the questions**

Teachers are never tired of telling their students this! The advice is so obvious as to seem almost unnecessary, but every year hundreds of candidates ruin their chances either by failing to answer all the questions or by only answering some of them in part.

This is where the value of doing timed essays as part of your revision comes in. If you are used to writing essays of the required length, you are much less likely to mis-time your efforts. If you do find you are spending too much time on an essay (this can easily happen with the first one you do), you must stop and start another.

- **Above all, you must decide at the very beginning of the examination which questions you are going to answer.**

When you are allowed to look at the paper, read through *all* the questions and decide there and then which ones you are going to do. This method has two advantages.

(i) It quickly gets rid of all your anxiety about the paper. Naturally, you will be worried about what is in the paper and you will probably be troubled about which ones you should do. If you can get over all that anxiety by deciding which questions you are going to answer, you can then use all your mental energy on the questions themselves.

(ii) You will find that your unconscious mind is already thinking about the questions you are to do. You may find an important idea about a question you are yet to do pops into your mind as you are answering another. You should briefly jot the idea down in case you forget it, and immediately return to the essay you are doing.

20.3 In the examination room

Some of the aspects of writing in the examination room have already been covered in Chapter 19, but some advice still remains to be given.

● **Make sure you are answering the question.**

To do this, you should read it through three or four times to determine what it is asking. It will be helpful in answering that question to look out for two things.

(i) You can look at what *kind of a question* it is. Study of the previous chapter will prepare you for that.

(ii) You can also look for the *key words* – the words that tell you exactly what the examiner requires of you. Popular key words are:

● effective
● successful
● aims
● purpose
● dramatic
● contrast

If a question asks you to write about the effectiveness of a character, you will have to make sure you don't give a character sketch. Unless you take note of the presence of the word 'effective', you may just write about what a character is like and so fail.

● **Sometimes a question can easily be broken down into parts.**

If you decide to do such a question, you usually have the shape of the essay sorted out for you.

─ **Example** ──────────────────────────

Look at this question on *Macbeth*.

Consider the role of the witches, and comment on their contribution to the play and the appeal they have for audiences.

Any answer to this question should be in three parts. There should be a lengthy part on the role of the witches, for which you will have to think about their place in the plot and the problem of what effect they have on Macbeth. There should then be a section on their contribution. You could write about how they create atmosphere and how they are similar to, or different from, other characters who appear to influence Macbeth. Finally, there should be a section on why they appeal. You could write about the opportunities they offer to a producer, and the effect that is created by the fact that they open the play.

When you are writing quickly, it is not always easy to be clear.

- **Remember that you are communicating with the examiner, and that you should produce what he or she wants.**
  Examiners look for four things in an essay:

- *an understanding of the issues of the question*
The best way of showing this is by writing a brief opening paragraph in which you explain the problems behind the essay and say what you are going to argue about them.
- *coherent argument*
You should make sure that you move from point to point in a logical way.
- *evidence that is discussed in detail*
You must show that you know which parts of the book are necessary for answering the question and you must be able to show how and why they are necessary.
- *a conclusion*
You must draw together all that you have said and show what it adds up to.
Practice at writing essays like this is, of course, necessary.

You must remember to write in a way which is appropriate to the wording of the question. If you are asked to discuss critical terms, you must show that you can handle them. An essay on imagery, for instance, requires you to use terms such as figurative, simile and metaphor.

- **Make sure you are answering in the right person.**

If you are asked about Shakespeare's treatment of a character, you should write in the third person. If, however, you are asked what *you* think about a book, you must answer in the first person. Examiners often complain that students don't write in a personal way. To say 'I felt this' or 'I think that' certainly helps.

20.4   Some warnings

- **You should never reproduce in an examination an essay you have written during the course of study.** Unless, that is, the wording of both questions is exactly the same.

You will, of course, use material from essays you have done, but whatever you use, be it argument or evidence, you must frame it according to the demands of the question. For instance, both the following questions are about Jocelin, the central character in Golding's *The Spire*:

Do you find Jocelin a likeable character?

Do you think that Golding is inviting the reader to approve of Jocelin?

Answers to both questions would include common material, but if you had done the first during a course of study and reproduced it in answer to the second in an examination, you would fail. The first asks you for your response to the character of Jocelin; the second asks you to think about whether the author invites the reader to judge Jocelin favourably or unfavourably.

- **In poetry answers you are expected to show that you can talk about a number of poems in the light of the question.**

Some students find answering questions on poetry difficult. Because of this they often get stuck with just one or two poems. That is not good enough.

When you are answering a poetry question, you should ensure that you can mention six or seven poems in some detail and refer more generally to others. It is also desirable to refer to two or three poems *together* when you are dealing with an aspect of the poet's work rather than looking in detail at one poem and then leaving it to look in equal detail at another. Examiners are rightly impressed by students who can move with ease from one poem to another when they are making a point about the poet's style or interests.

- **Answers should frequently mention the name of the author, particularly with novels and drama.**

Weak students often ignore the author altogether. You should mention the author because, as was stressed in Chapter 6, works of art are not just 'ordinary life' but objects specially made by authors. To use the name of the author indicates to the examiner that you understand that point. You can prepare for this by practising writing about how, for instance, Orwell presents, develops, or views what happens in his books.

- **You should avoid speaking of the characters as if they were real people.**

Again, this point has been made before. Characters in novels or plays only exist in the words on the page and should, therefore, only be spoken about in terms of them. A way of avoiding treating a character as if he or she were real is to speak of him or her in relation to the author or the reader.

- **When you are thinking through an examination question, you should not be afraid to disagree with it.**

Students are often worried about taking their own line because they wonder whether the examiner will like what they have written. The point to remember is that you must answer the question. If you are asked to say why you think a play has proved popular on the stage, you can't deny that it has been popular. If, however, you are asked whether you think a play is dramatically effective, you must tell the examiner what you think.

There is an alternative to either agreeing or disagreeing. In quotation questions you are given a view of the work. Quite often the view is true in parts but not wholly true, in which case you can say that you agree to a certain extent. Even if you take an unusual line of argument, you will be rewarded as long as you can produce a good case, backed up by evidence. Examiners are concerned that you should argue clearly, not that you should agree with them.

- **Leave yourself time to look through your answers.**

This applies in most examinations. When you are writing quickly, you tend to miss out words, mis-spell common words and make simple grammatical errors. If you leave yourself sufficient time to read through your paper, you can correct these. Because you think you know what you have written, you may not see the mistakes you have made, so you must read with great care, looking at every word.

Part IV
Glossary

⬡ Glossary

Abstract and Concrete   A word is abstract when it refers to a quality such as goodness or evil, and concrete when it refers to something that can be detected by the five senses. Literature needs both kinds of words. Ideas are abstract but they are made real by concrete examples. The opening of R. S. Thomas's 'Poetry for Supper' has an abstract word followed by concrete ones :

> Listen, now, verse should be as natural
> As the small tuber that feeds on muck...

The concrete words, 'tuber', and 'muck', give body to the abstract, 'natural', thus making it more effective. (See also **Image and imagery**.)

Act and Scene   The major structural divisions of a play are called acts, and their sub-divisions scenes. An act or scene changes to indicate either the passage of time, a new action or a change of place. Shakespeare's plays have five acts, whereas most modern plays have two or three.

Allegory   A story which seeks to demonstrate philosophical or religious beliefs. Each element in the story stands for an aspect of the belief that the story is seeking to explain. There could, for instance, be allegorical figures representing Truth, Goodness or Virtue. In Bunyan's *Pilgrim's Progress*, the central figure, Christian, is the Christian soul who sets out from the City of Destruction (man's fallen state) as a pilgrim travelling towards the Heavenly City (the eternal home of the redeemed).

Some works are very near to being allegory. The novels of William Golding have many allegorical elements. In the *Lord of the Flies* Simon is a Christ-like figure who is killed because the boys do not want to listen to the good news that he brings.

Alliteration   The repetition of the same consonant sound. Alliteration is usually both pleasing and memorable; pleasing because readers enjoy the pattern of sounds, and memorable because repeated sounds impress themselves upon the mind. There is no point in just mentioning that alliteration occurs, unless you can go on to discuss its effect. To help you describe the effect of alliteration you can ask whether or not it produces a distinctive tone, and whether or not it is regularly spaced. The former effect is the more important, because alliteration, whether or not it is regularly spaced, is always capable of contributing to the tone of a poem. For instance, the alliteration of the 'f' sound is regular in one line from Owen's 'Exposure', – 'With sidelong flowing flakes that flock, pause, and renew' – and irregular in another – 'Pale flakes with fingering stealth come feeling for our faces' – yet both create a furtive tone. The flakes may seem delicate but they are sinister in the way they bring a deathly cold to the exposed soldiers. (See also **Assonance** and **Consonance**.)

Allusion   A reference to another book, event, person or place. The allusion is usually implied or hinted, so the reader is given the pleasure of seeing it and understanding the effect it creates. Sometimes the effect is to make what is being said more significant, more ambiguous or more amusing. In Pope's *The Rape of the Lock*, Belinda is shown to have bright and sparkling eyes:

> Bright as the sun, her eyes the gazer strike,
> And, like the sun, they shine on all alike.

It is a radiant picture but one qualified by the allusion to St Matthew's Gospel, where Jesus says that God sends the sun to shine on everybody. The presence of that allusion suggests that those fascinated by Belinda, and maybe Belinda herself, have a distorted sense of values in that they confuse the human with the divine.

Ambiguity   The capacity of a word or words to mean two or more different things. In poetry this capacity is valued, because the meanings of poems are thereby enriched. When discussing ambiguity, you should show that the same words could have different meanings. For instance, in Blake's 'London' there are the lines:

> How the Chimney-sweeper's cry
> Every blackening Church appalls...

'Blackening' is ambiguous. Does it meant the soot from chimneys has blackened the Church, or is the Church actively blackening society? You will also probably need to discuss the tone of the poem, because a poet often makes it clear that a poem is deliberately ambiguous.

Assonance   The repetition of vowel sounds in adjoining words. The effect of assonance is similar to that of alliteration; that is to say, it helps to create tone. It is also worthwhile noting whether or not it is regularly spaced. Assonance is rarer than alliteration yet it can be very effective. In these four lines from Donne's 'Song', the repetition of the 'i' vowel creates a tone of lamentation and regret:

> When thou sigh'st, thou sigh'st not wind,
>   But sigh'st my soul away,
> When thou weep'st, unkindly kind,
>   My life's blood doth decay.

(See also **Alliteration** and **Consonance**.)

Audience   Those who view a play, and, by extension, those for whom any work is written. When you are reading a play, you will have to put yourself in the position of being the audience. The best way to do this is to be aware of all the resources of the theatre – actors, staging, scenery, costume, lighting and music – and imagine how these could be used in the production of a play. Then you will be imaginatively close to the experiences of the audience.

Ballad   A poem, usually of simple construction, that tells a story. Many English and Scottish ballads are quatrains, in which the first and third lines are longer than the second and fourth. Many of them are traditional and deal with love, war, travel and adventure. They are enjoyable because they are direct, fast moving and contain brief but telling details. For instance, the repeated line 'And no birds sing' from Keat's 'La Belle Dame sans Merci' is sufficient to convey the poem's terrible bleakness.

Black Comedy   Comedy that invites laughter at serious or painful aspects of life such as disease, pain, failure and death. Joe Orton's comedies can be described as black, and some moments in Shakespeare's problem plays – *Measure for Measure, All's Well that Ends Well* and *Troilus and Cressida* – come near to it.

Blank Verse   Poetry that is written in lines of unrhymed iambic pentameters. It is very common in English and can be used for telling a story or thinking about ideas and feelings. It is worthwhile noticing how regular and insistent its rhythms are.

Shakespeare uses blank verse in his plays. There is usually no point in drawing attention to this, unless there are very interesting variations in the rhythm of a line. Such variations are usually the expression of deep emotion. For instance, Hamlet's order to his mother, 'Look here upon this picture, and on this', could be scanned in the usual way, but that would not reflect its emotional quality. To do that justice, the line should be scanned:

> Loók heŕe uṕoń thiś pićtuře, and ŏn thîs ...

It is also important to notice when Shakespeare uses verse which is *not* blank verse. For instance, the witches in *Macbeth* and the fairies in *A Midsummer Night's Dream* speak in trochees rather than iambs. Trochees sound different, thus making the witches and fairies seem strange, non-human creatures. (See also **Metre**.)

Bravado   The outlandish and extravert way in which a tragic hero or heroine acts out his or her role. There is relish and even enjoyment in the whole-hearted embracing of the danger, bravery and immorality of the tragic path he or she has freely undertaken. In Shakespeare the bravado is seen in terms of a self-conscious adoption of theatricality. Hamlet, for instance, zestfully plays a number of teasing roles (including the staging of a play) in order to distract those who are trying to investigate his strange behaviour. The bravado of a tragic figure is what makes him or her both attractive and reprehensible.

Cadence   The rise and fall in pitch the voice makes when at the end of a line, a sentence or caesura. The emotional impact of poetry is often created by cadences. There is no technical language to describe their effect, though they are often said to be 'rising', 'falling' or 'steady'. When you write about cadences, you should try to characterise the emotional effect they create. For instance, the close of the passage about skating from Book I of Wordsworth's *The Prelude* is effective because the steady cadence enacts the peace of untroubled sleep:

> and I stood and watched
> Till all was tranquil as a dreamless sleep.

Caesura   The break in a line of poetry. The convention for marking a caesura is ‖. Caesuras are important because they mark changes in tone, in argument and emotion. They can also produce comic effects, particularly when what follows the caesura is very different from what preceded it. When writing about a caesura, you should never just point to its existence but try to describe the impact that it has. For instance, the caesura in the last line of Yeats's 'An Irish Airman Foresees His Death' is effective because there is no break in the previous line (there are very few in the poem) and because it enacts the clear-sighted thoughtfulness of one who has come to a momentous decision:

> A waste of breath the years behind
> In balance with this life, ‖ this death.

Caricature   The deliberate distortion or exaggeration of a character's features or manners in order to ridicule or amuse. The reaction of reader or audience is often affectionate amusement. Sometimes the term is used against an author when it is suggested that his or her characters are near to caricature. But this criticism can only be used if the author aimed at creating a fuller character and failed.

Character and Characterisation   Character is the name we give to the figures we encounter in narratives; characterisation is the way in which the character has been created.

Code   A fashionable term that has at least two distinct meanings. (i) It can refer to the set of beliefs by which a character in a book tries to live his or her life. For instance,

Great Expectations is about Pip's attempts to live by what he regards as the code of a gentleman. (ii) Its second meaning is the set of conventions of meaning authors employ and readers recognise. Allegory is a code because the author directs the reader, usually through names and representative actions, to read the book in a particular way.

The term can be used in a wider sense to refer to any means by which an author creates his or her meaning. Understanding a work therefore can be said to be a matter of recognising the code of meaning the author is employing. **A word of warning is however necessary:** many books are subtle in the way in which meaning is made, so any simple idea that once a reader has got hold of the 'code' the meaning can be 'cracked' is a grossly misleading one.

Comedy and Tragedy   A comedy is a play in which the confusions of characters, often prompted by love and furthered by deception or misunderstanding, eventually work out so that the play closes happily. The action of comedy is usually amusing, and the plot intricate.

Tragedy is a play in which a character (often called the hero) falls from power, influence or happiness towards disaster and death. Often a hero is wilful and seems to bring destruction upon himself. This wilfulness is called *hubris*. The action arouses feelings of awe in the audience, who often leave the theatre with a renewed sense of the seriousness and significance of human life. The word *catharsis* is often used to describe the audience's feelings. It means the purging from the mind of the feelings of pity and fear the play has aroused.

You should be careful not to impose these, or any other definitions of comedy and tragedy, upon Shakespeare's plays. All definitions should be used as general guides and not as rules. Though comedy and tragedy usually apply to plays, the terms can be used of both poems and novels.

Complex   A line, sentence, image, scene or whole work which consists of several closely connected ideas or feelings. You can use the term when you are trying to stress that the meaning, emotion or construction of a work is rich and varied. It is important to understand that the term implies that though a work has many elements, it is still unified. Therefore, it is often used as a term of praise. You should not, however, assume that only complex literature is good. There is also a pleasure and a value in simplicity.

Compression   A term used when talking about poetry to indicate the way in which writers concentrate meaning by cutting down the number of words. The experience therefore is of meaning concentrated in a few words. In many metaphors the whole figurative force is compressed into one word. Sometimes, as in these lines from Browning's '"Childe Roland to the Dark Tower Came"', compressed writing is direct, concentrated and close to notes or shorthand.

> grey plain all round:
> Nothing but plain to the horizon's bound.
> I might go on; nought else remained to do.

Conceit   A highly elaborate image that seems on first acquaintance far-fetched but yet which, with thought, is seen to be appropriate. It is strange but true. You should try to convey the sense of shock, the challenge to thought, and the pleasure of discovering that the image is apt. The most famous example is from Donne's 'Valediction: forbidding mourning', where he speaks of a husband and wife's souls as being a pair of compasses:

> If they be two, they are two so
> As stiff twin compasses are two,
> Thy soul the fixed foot, makes no show
> To move, but doth, if the other do.

The shock is that the insubstantial soul should be compared to 'stiff twin compasses'; the challenge to thought comes when the third and fourth lines are read, and the pleasure is of seeing that the image is delightfully logical – she is stable but will move as he moves, because they are really one.

Consonance The repetition of the same consonant sounds in two or more words in which the vowel sounds are different. The effect is of interest when the words are related in meaning as well as in sound. In W. H. Auden's '"O where are you going?" said reader to rider' there is a line: 'Behind you swiftly the figure comes softly.' The consonance of 'swiftly' and 'softly' is interesting because both words are concerned with the stealthy and slightly sinister approach of the strange 'figure'. (See also **Alliteration, Assonance** and **Half-rhyme**.)

Consonants and Vowels A consonant is a sound produced by stopping the breath, and a vowel by allowing the air to pass through the mouth without stoppage. Vowels are a, e, i, o, u and, in some cases, y; all other letters are consonants. The terms are useful when writing about the effects of sound in poetry.

It is often important to note whether a vowel is long or short. For instance, the long vowels of Herbert's 'Sweet day, so cool, so calm, so bright' create a meditative and tranquil effect, whereas the short 'i's in the following lines from T. S. Eliot's 'The Love-Song of J. Alfred Prufrock' are nervous and slightly irritable.

> Oh, do not ask, 'What is it?'
> Let us go and make our visit.

Convention An agreement between author and reader or audience that a device, form or procedure stands for the reality of what is being conveyed. A convention is never 'true to life', but reader and audience accept that it represents that feature or aspect of life. For instance, a stage is accepted by the audience as being a battlefield, a palace or a drawing room. Conventions are present in all types of literature, and as long as the reader understands that that is what they are, no difficulty is caused.

Sometimes the word 'conventional' is used to indicate disapproval. This is a different use. It means that an author is in no way original but simply uses other people's ideas. You must be careful not to confuse the two uses of the word.

Counterpoint A word borrowed from music to indicate how some syllables in an otherwise regular line produce variations on the set rhythm. You should only use the term if you want to discuss the emotional or intellectual effect of the variation. The opening of Larkin's 'Church Going' is basically iambic until the last three emphatic words of the second line, which have the effect of enclosing the poet in the church, the poet's thoughts in his head, and the reader in the poem:

> Once I am sure there's nothing going on
> I step inside, letting the door thud shut.

The counterpointing of the rhythm fixes poet and reader in one place and prepares them both for the serious and sensitive meditations that are to come. (See also **Metre** and **Scansion**.)

Denotations and Connotations The denotations of a word are its standard range of meanings, the connotations its additional meanings that emerge through association, suggestion, and emotional undertones. Writers, particularly poets, often exploit a word's connotations, so you should look to see if their words work in this way. For instance, the denotations of the word 'flat' are a smooth, unbroken surface; its connotations are lifeless, dull and uninteresting.

Denouement   A term that may be used of both novels and plays when talking about the way the tangled elements of a plot are untied. Denouements are often linked to discoveries, because it's often in the light of a discovery that a plot can be wound up. Because plots are more important in comic rather than tragic works, their denouements are more complex and, often, more intriguing. The unveiling of Hero in *Much Ado About Nothing* (a discovery) leads to the hoped for denouement – the publicly declared love of Beatrice and Benedick. (See also **Discovery**, **Resolution** and **Reversal**.)

Diction   The selection of words used in a work. The term is only useful if you can characterise the diction. For instance, an author may use words drawn from everyday life (John Betjeman often does this in his poetry), from religion, from politics or from another academic subject, such as a science. When you write about diction you should try to show the effect of selecting a particular range of words.

Discovery   The moment, usually towards the close of a plot, when something is disclosed which alters the situation and allows the plot to be resolved. In *Jane Eyre*, for instance, her discovery that Rochester's wife is dead enables the plot to end with the marriage that both Jane and the reader desire. In *Twelfth Night* the discovery that makes possible the winding up of the plot is the public realisation that Sebastian and Viola are twins. (See also **Resolution** and **Reversal**.)

Disjunction   The event which by disturbing or rupturing the customary pattern of life initiates the main elements of a plot. The arrival, for instance, of Mr Bingley in the opening chapter of *Pride and Prejudice* is the disjunction that makes possible the subsequent events of the plot.

Empathy/Sympathy   Empathy is the imaginative act in which we put ourselves in somebody else's place; sympathy is the feelings we have (usually of understanding pity) for someone's plight. Literature need not demand either of these responses from a reader; quite often it's differences and distance rather than similarity and closeness that characterises our reactions to the characters in literary works. (It's hard trying to imagine what it must feel like being Cleopatra or Macbeth.)

When we are asked to respond, the feeling that is demanded is usually sympathy (we might pity the terrible misunderstanding of Othello) but sometimes characters invite us to see their plight as ours. There are elements of this in Hamlet when he speaks in plurals rather than in singulars: 'Thus conscience does make cowards of us all'. By speaking of 'us' rather than 'me', Hamlet invites us to see his state as ours and so empathise.

Enactment   This word stands for the way in which all aspects of words – their sounds, rhythms, and the shapes they make in lines and stanzas – contribute to the meaning of what is being said. You should use the word to avoid the idea that poetry is just made up of form and content. Enactment insists that words are not divisible into what they say and *how* they say it, and that how something is said shapes *what* is said, and vice versa. In Byron's 'So, we'll go no more a-roving', the repetition of the 'o' sound, the heavy stresses on 'go' and 'roving', the casual 'so' at the beginning of the line, and its repetition at the start of the second line enact the langour of one who is wearied by much experience:

> So, we'll go no more a-roving
> So late into the night,
> Though the heart be still as loving,
> And the moon be still as bright.

End-stopped and Run-on Lines.   An end-stopped line is one in which the grammatical unit, be it clause or sentence, is coterminous with the line. Thus, there is the satisfaction of finding the line and the sense ending together. A run-on line (sometimes called an *enjambed* line) is where the grammar, and thus the sense, is left unfinished at the end of the line. Run-on lines create pleasurable feelings of expectation, as the reader has to look further for the full sense of what is being said.

Epic Simile   The comparison of one thing in terms of another in which the idea introduced to make the comparison (the vehicle) is developed in a lengthy passage to form a vivid picture. Epic similes are effective when there is an appropriateness in the comparison. For instance, in Book I of Milton's *Paradise Lost* the fallen angels rising from the burning lake of Hell are compared to the plague of locusts brought down upon Egypt by Amram's son – Moses:

>   As when the potent rod
> Of Amram's son in Egypt's evil day
> Waved round the coast, up called a pitchy cloud
> Of locusts, warping on the eastern wind,
> That o'er the realm of impious Pharaoh hung
> Like night, and darkened all the land of Nile:
> So numberless were those bad angels seen
> Hovering on wing under the cope of hell...

The appropriateness is not just a visual one; Milton shows that both the locusts and fallen angels were a plague – the former upon Egypt, the latter upon the whole of mankind.

Epigram   Either a brief, usually witty, statement or a short poem which makes a simple but often dramatic or humorous point. You will probably use the first meaning more than the second. Often it is useful to call a deft line or remark epigrammatic. By that you are saying it is punchy and memorable. T. S. Eliot's 'Whispers of Immortality' has a grimly epigrammatic thrust:

> Webster was much possessed by death
> And saw the skull beneath the skin;
> And breastless creatures underground
> Leaned backward with a lipless grin.

Epiphany   James Joyce used this word to indicate those moments of illumination that often come to characters, particularly those in short stories, at the climax of the plot. An epiphany can be something seen or understand or something familiar which, for the first time, is seen for what it is. It's useful when writing about those moments of insight that come to Katherine Mansfield's characters, often at the very end of the story. (See also **Discovery**).

Expectation   The effect of being led to think that something is going to happen. Short stories, novels and plays all build up expectations in readers and audiences. Expectations are built upon what is known about events and characters, and also on what the characters themselves expect to happen. Whenever you write about expectation, you should stress that it is the author, or playwright, who is responsible for creating it. (See also **Surprise** and **Relief**.)

Farce   A branch of comedy in which the characters are reduced to stock figures, and the action is often frantic and even violent. Thus, in farce characters can be beaten or humiliated and the audience reacts with laughter, because it has not been invited to see the characters as having any sort of distinctive personality. Elements of farce creep into some plays.

For instance, the middle scenes of *Dr Faustus* can be said to be farce, and the innumerable beatings of servants in Shakespeare's *The Comedy of Errors* introduce farce into a carefully constructed comic plot. (See also **Tragedy and Comedy**.)

Fictionality   Although the idea that literary works draw attention to their own fictional status is currently popular, the idea of fictionality – that literature is art and therefore specially made – is a traditional one. When Victorian novelists addressed their readers directly they were drawing attention to the fact that literature is not the same as everyday life. Nowadays this term is used of those works which deliberately play upon their own conventions. In *The French Lieutenant's Women*, John Fowles talks about himself as the novelist and discusses other, usually nineteenth-century, writers. (See also **Reflexivity**.)

Flat and Round Characters.   Terms introduced by E. M. Forster to indicate characters in novels who have little personal identity (flat), and those who are given much more individuality (round). You should use the terms with care, because characters in novels are rarely simply flat or round. (See also **Stock character**.)

Focus   A useful term to deploy when talking about how an author is presenting something. For instance, one of the ways in which *Wuthering Heights* works is though the difference in focus between the steady Nelly who narrates events with a broad, though not necessarily deep, understanding and Cathy and Heathcliff who are almost obsessive in their preoccupations with their own feelings.

Foregrounding   A term that may be used when discussing the interest an author takes in a character or issue. To foreground is to single out for special interest or treatment. For instance, Lawrence usually foregrounds the intense and fluctuating inner lives of his characters. Sometimes it's useful when you are trying to bring out what does or does not interest an author: for instance, Wilkie Collins pays very little attention to his characters' states of minds but foregrounds their strenuous attempts to understand and outwit each other.

Frame   You have to be careful when using this term because in Theatre Studies it has a quite specific meaning, which is concerned with the perspectives an audience is given when viewing a set of events. In English the term is broader and simpler. It is used of any action that provides a context for a subsequent action. Its most popular use is in drama when there is a play within a play, as in the Induction of *The Taming of the Shrew*; or in novels where one narrative leads to another, as in the incidents at the start of *Heart of Darkness* which provide the frame for Marlowe's narrative.

Genre   A word taken from the French which means a literary type or kind. Comedy, tragedy and satire are genres, but nowadays it is also common to speak of poetry and the novel as genres, too.

Half-rhyme   The effect that is created when the consonants of two words in a rhyming position have the same sounds but the vowels do not. In effect, it is consonance functioning in the place of rhyme. The effect of half-rhyme (or *para-rhyme*, as it is sometimes called) is to make the ear expect a rhyme which is denied. The result is that the words often sound strangely out of tune with each other. In Owen's 'Futility' the feeling that death has distorted the natural progress of life is enacted in the half-rhymes. He is speaking of the sun:

> Think how it wakes the seeds,
> Woke, once, the clays of a cold star.
> Are limbs, so dear-achieved, are sides,
> Full-nerved – still warm – too hard to stir?

Whenever you write about half-rhyme, you should try to bring out how it leads you to expect a rhyme which you do not get. (See also **Consonance** and **Rhyme**.)

Heroic Couplets   These are lines of iambic pentameters that rhyme in pairs. They are assertive and self-affirming and are consequently appropriate for argument. For instance, Pope in *An Essay on Criticism* neatly conveys the ideal of economy in verse in a heroic couplet which is itself economical:

> Words are like leaves; and where they most abound,
> Much fruit of sense beneath is rarely found.

They are, however, also used in narrative poems. Many people do not find them easy to read, because they seem repetitious. They should be read slowly, and it is often interesting to note whether the sentences of the poem are coterminous with the couplets. When they are not, and run-on lines occur, readers usually enjoy the variation. (See also **Metre**.)

Image and Imagery   Any figurative or descriptive language that appeals to one of the five senses is called an image. Images could also be metaphors, similes, symbols and personification, as well as examples of non-figurative description. Images are impressive because they make ideas concrete. They also create atmosphere and can be used to establish a pattern within a poem. It is sometimes helpful to show how an image works in some detail. For instance, in *Macbeth* Macduff tries to put into words the horror of finding that Duncan, King of Scotland, has been murdered. He uses a very complex imagery to do this:

> Confusion now hath made his masterpiece!
> Most sacrilegious Murther hath broke ope
> The Lord's anointed Temple, and stole thence
> The life o' th' building!

The death of Duncan is first seen in the image of 'Confusion' as an artist or craftsman, making his 'masterpiece'. Then 'Murther' (murder) is seen as a thief breaking into a religious building. (See also **Abstract and concrete**, **Metaphor and simile**, **Personification** and **Symbol**.)

Intrusion   A term usually used when discussing the way in which a narrator enters his or her own narration, usually for the purpose of commenting upon the events. George Eliot frequently does this in her novels. The effect is sometimes called *narratorial intrusion*.

Inversion   Inversion occurs when an author, usually a poet, changes the 'natural' or 'standard' word order. For instance, Milton's line from *Paradise Lost* – 'Now came still evening on, and twilight grey' – inverts the normal order of words, so that the verb 'came' comes before the noun 'evening'. Inversion draws attention to the crafted nature of literature and also foregrounds certain words and ideas. For instance, in the line from Milton the inversion allows the interesting (and even paradoxical?) idea of a still evening moving by juxtaposing the words '...came still...'

Irony   The effect produced when a reader sees that there is a gap between the words that are being said and the real significance of those words. There are different kinds of gaps. The gap between words and truth occurs when something the reader knows to be mistaken is said. A second type of gap, or discrepancy, is between the words and meaning. This occurs when the reader sees that the real significance of what is being said is very different from what the speaker supposes. The gap can lie between intention and result. A speaker can intend something but the reader will see that the result will not be what is expected. This is also called dramatic irony. There is also the irony of one character interpreting the world one way, whilst the reader is led to see that this is false. In all cases of irony, someone is put at a disadvantage because others, usually the author and reader, can see more clearly than he or she can.

When you write about irony, you should make clear who is placed in a position of advantage and who is at a disadvantage. You should also remember that irony can produce different emotional effects. It can be bitter, comic, serious, tragic, sad, and so on. In your writing you should try to bring over how irony can make the reader or audience change attitudes to a character. For instance, you may be horrified by the callous inhumanity of Lady Macbeth, who believes that, after the murder of Duncan, 'A little water clears us of this deed'. When, however, she walks in her sleep and is seen to be perpetually washing her hands, you may see the terrible irony that 'a little water' can't clear her of guilt. When you see the irony, your horror may turn to pity.

Knowledge   Knowledge in literature means what it means in any context – that which you have good reason to think is true. In literature it's sometimes important to keep in mind what characters know and what they think they know. Such knowledge is often to be seen in relation to what other characters know and what the reader knows. Usually knowledge gives a character advantage and power. There is a chilling moment in *The Woman in White* when it's disclosed that one of the villains has dishonestly come by all the knowledge that the heroine has painstakingly gathered. From that moment the reader knows that she is at his mercy.

Lyric   A poem, usually of no more than forty or fifty lines, and often much shorter, which expresses the thoughts and feelings of the poet or of an imagined speaker. The tones of such poems are varied, but they are often personal, reflective, and frequently deal with love or other powerful emotions. Sometimes writing that is smooth, fluent and intimate is described as lyrical. Most people's idea of poetry is lyrical. It is useful to remind yourself that poetry can be narrative, didactic and satiric as well. (See also **Song**.)

Masque   A highly elaborate entertainment in verse and song with lavish costumes and sets that was popular in the sixteenth and seventeenth centuries. The characters are often gods or allegorical figures. Shakespeare's *The Tempest* contains a masque to celebrate the betrothal of Ferdinand and Miranda. Milton's *Comus* is also a masque. If you have to write about masques, you will have to imagine the visual impact that they make on stage. (See also **Allegory**.)

Mental Landscap   The effect created when a landscape is portrayed in terms of the feelings of the author or character, who views it. The outer world thus reflects the inner world of thoughts and feelings. The effect is particularly prominent in late eighteenth-century and much of nineteenth-century literature. Mental landscapes are often strangely impressive. In Wordsworth's *The Prelude* there is a passage in which the poet descends from the Alps through a deep ravine; the vast and sublime landscape echoes the workings of his own imagination. Sometimes a mental landscape works by using words appropriate to both the external scene and the state of mind. In Tennyson's 'Locksley Hall' the protagonist speaks of the 'dreary, dreary moorland'; the word 'dreary' applies to what he can see and how he feels.

Metaphor and Simile   The comparison of one thing in terms of another; in metaphor there is an implicit identity, whereas in simile the comparison is introduced by the words 'like' or 'as'. Metaphors are thus more compressed and economical than similes, though similes are closer to ordinary speech, and there is a distinct pleasure in following through the comparison from the object being presented to that in terms of which it is presented. If you wish to distinguish one from the other, the terms 'tenor' (the object presented) and 'vehicle' (that in terms of which it is presented) can be useful. Thus, in the metaphor for a church from Larkin's 'Church Going' – 'this special shell' – church is the tenor and shell the vehicle, or in Larkin's simile from 'Ambulances' – 'Closed like confessionals' – the tenor is ambulances and the vehicle confessionals.

Metre The regular rhythms of poetic lines, created by a sequence of stressed or unstressed syllables. A recurring unit of stressed and unstressed syllables is called a *foot*. Special names are given to these recurring feet, and also to the number of feet in a line. Common English metres are the following:

> *iambic:* an unstressed syllable followed by a stressed syllable
> *anapaestic:* two unstressed syllables followed by a stressed syllable
> *trochaic:* a stressed syllable followed by an unstressed syllable
> *dactylic:* a stressed syllable followed by two unstressed syllables.

The names for the number of feet in a line are as follows:

monometer	one foot
dimeter	two feet
trimeter	three feet
tetrameter	four feet
pentameter	five feet
hexameter	six feet
heptameter	seven feet
octameter	eight feet

There is usually little point in merely labelling a metre. If you wish to discuss metre, you should try to characterise the effect it has by showing how it helps to enact the meaning of the poem. (See also **Blank verse**, **counterpoint**, **Heroic couplets**, **Scansion** and **Stanza**.)

Monosyllabic and Polysyllabic   Words of one syllable such as 'did', 'good', 'said' and 'would' are monosyllabic. In poetry and verse drama they are effective in making the lines feel emphatic, forceful and strong. Consider the force of the opening of Donne's 'Hymn to God the Father':

> Wilt thou forgive my sin where I began
> Which was my sin though it were done before.

The monosyllables enact the dark, serious strength of the poet's plea.

Words of more than one syllable are polysyllabic. When a number of polysyllabic words are used in a line the effect is likely to be flowing, lyrical and sometimes even majestic. Notice how the polysyllabic words in Hopkins's 'The Windhover' help to enact the flowing and majestic movements of the falcon in flight:

> I caught this morning morning's minion, king-
> dom of daylight's dauphin, dapple-dawn-drawn Falcon...

Multiple Narration   A story that is told by more than one narrator. Sometimes, as in *Wuthering Heights*, interesting problems of reliability and perspective are raised when the events are seen from several viewpoints. The reader must be alert to what each narrator knows and aware of the different ways in which they present, interpret and judge what is going on. (See also **Narrator**, **Primary narrator** and **Reliability**.)

Narrative   A set of events that are related by an author to a reader or listener. Sometimes the term is used to cover the nature of fiction itself – what it is for a story to be told – and, by extension, it's also used of the kind of problems readers encounter in narratives. In these latter senses the emphasis is always on how the narrative is made.

Narrator   The narrator is one who tells a story. The narrator can, but need not, be the novelist. Narrators can tell their stories, or narratives, in the first or the third person. If the story is told in the first person, there is only access to the mind of the narrator. If, however, the story is narrated in the third person, it is possible to see into the minds of all the characters. When an author knows everything that goes on in characters' minds, he or she is called an *omniscient* (all-knowing) narrator. (See also **Primary narrator** and **Retrospective narrator**.)

Naturalism –   See **Realism and Naturalism**, below.

Onomatopoeia   The effect that is created when the sounds of words mime or resemble the sounds of the object being described. Individual words such as 'crash' or 'buzz' are onomatopoeic, but the term is more generally used of an effect created by a number of words. Onomatopoeia is usually worth discussing when it creates atmosphere. In Keats's 'Ode to a Nightingale' one stanza closes with this line: 'The murmurous haunt of flies on summer eves.' The onomatopoeic 'murmurous' combines with the long vowels and the alliteration on 'm' and 's' to produce an atmosphere of languid ease.

Overtones and Undertones   The associations of a word or words. Overtones are the clear and obvious associations, while undertones are those meanings which are hinted and implied. However, the two words are often used interchangeably to refer to words' wider meanings and emotional colouring. It is often very useful to point out the overtones and undertones of a word. You can do this by pointing to the number of ways in which a word is used in ordinary speech.

Pathetic Fallacy   The way in which a writer gives human feelings to an object that could not possibly have them. The effect it creates is very close to personification. Its origin is probably in the very common practice people have of transferring their own feelings about something to the thing itself. Therefore, pathetic fallacy is often an indication of what the writer or character is feeling. In Tennyson's 'Ulysses' the sea 'Moans round with many voices'. The word 'moans' indicates the state of mind of the protagonist. (See also **Mental landscape** and **Personification**.)

Pathos   The arousing of tenderness, pity or sorrow in a reader or an audience by the presentation of a sad or moving scene. The pity of reader or audience is often due to the helplessness of the characters. Thus, the distraught Ophelia's speech about the sad decline of Hamlet at the end of Act III, Scene 1 is full of pathos. When writing about pathos, you should strike a balance between showing how the emotions are aroused and recording what you feel about the scene.

Persona   A specially created voice or self in a poem, novel or short story. In most cases a persona speaks in the first person singular, though in some cases, particularly poems, this need not be so. Personas give works unity by showing the reader that everything in the work is the expression of a particular viewpoint. Because of this, it is wise to discuss personas in terms of tone and attitude. You should remember that a persona is not to be identified with the writer, and that a writer can adopt as many personas as he or she chooses.

Personification   The effect created when a non-human object or quality is written about as if it were a human being. Keats personifies the Grecian urn when he calls it a 'still unravished bride of quietness', and Gray personifies wealth and beauty when he writes of 'all that beauty, all that wealth e'er gave'. You should always try to characterise the effect of personification. Often, it makes the object seem close to both author and reader, and, in some cases, it can make the object or quality personified seem more lively and engaging. (See also **mental landscape** and **Pathetic fallacy**.)

Plot The pattern of events that constitutes the main business of a narrative. Because plot is a literary idea, it's best to define it as the order of events as they are known to the reader. It's often helpful to look at the problem or situation out of which the plot grows and think about the various ways in which plots can be constructed.

Primary Narrator In multiple narrations the primary narrator is the first that the reader meets. Subsequent narrators may be called *secondary, tertiary* and so on, though usually there's no need. The point about the primary narrator is that even if the role is a minor one, as in Lockwood in *Wuthering Heights*, the term is still the one to use. (See also **Multiple narration**).

Problem Plays A group of plays written by Shakespeare which, though they have a comic form, deal with dark and serious aspects of life. They are sometimes called the 'dark comedies'. *Measure for Measure*, for instance, has the comic form of confusion working towards a happy ending, and many comic conventions such as disguise and deception. Yet it deals with a man sentenced to death, and the attempts of a corrupt official to seduce a nun. Other problem plays are *All's Well that Ends Well* and *Troilus and Cressida*. Sometimes *Hamlet* is said to be closer to a problem play than a tragedy.

Prolepsis/Proleptic An event the full significance of which is only realised in the future. The term can be used of those events that are only seen in their true light later on in the book. There is, for instance, a proleptic element in the way in which Dickens presents Orlick in *Great Expectations*. After she's been attacked, Pip's sister wants to see Orlick. This is puzzling, but when we discover towards the end that Orlick was her assailant we can appreciate why she wants to see him.

Protagonist Originally the hero in a Greek play, but now it is also used to mean the speaker in a narrative poem or dramatic monologue. The protagonist is usually a specially created voice. The poet can thus explore a realm of experience different from his or her own. When writing about the protagonist of a poem, you should make sure that you don't confuse him or her with the author of the poem.

Realism and Naturalism Sometimes these terms are used interchangeably to refer to narratives that try to evoke the sense that what is being conveyed is a direct transcription of actual events. Historically, the terms have different origins; realism is any fiction that presents everyday characters in their usual settings, whereas naturalism was a more philosophical kind of fiction that presented characters as solely the products of their biological inheritance and social circumstances. Since there aren't in English many novels that follow naturalistic presuppositions, realism is the more useful term.

Whenever you use the words 'realism' or 'realistic' you should remember three things : (i) most literature isn't realistic (Shakespeare, for instance) – in fact, it's a difficult term to use of literature written before the nineteenth century; (ii) realistic literature isn't, by virtue of being realistic, better than literature that isn't; (iii) although the aim is to reproduce the surface appearance of everyday life, realistic literature is itself a specially made form of art that depends upon a careful selection and arrangement of details.

Reflexivity the manner in which a book draws attention to its own status as a created work. Sometimes, reflexivity can suddenly distance a reader from the events, because he or she is reminded that the characters only exist in a book. On other occasions, reflexivity can awaken the reader to the fascinating topic of what an author does in creating a work of art. In this sense many works are implicitly reflexive; for instance, Keats in 'Ode on a Grecian Urn' is writing about the poem he is writing about the Grecian urn.

Reliability   The extent to which what a narrator says can be trusted. In much fiction the issue doesn't arise but when it does, as in for instance Lockwood's and Nelly's narratives in *Wuthering Heights*, it raises interesting questions of perspective, contrary judgements and the extent to which the reader endorses what the narrator is saying. (See also **Multiple narration**, **View** and **viewpoint**.)

Relief   The effect experienced by readers and audiences when the tension created by expectation is released. Sometimes a reader or audience responds to relief by laughter, but on other occasions, as in tragedy, a feeling of seriousness is left when the anticipated event has occurred. (See also **Expectation** and **Surprise**.)

Resolution   A term for the ways in which a plot is sorted out, usually at the close of a book. Resolution usually has two aspects – a human one and a formal one. Audiences and readers want to know how the lives of characters work out, so they take an interest in whether or not the plans and hopes of the characters are fulfilled. The formal aspect is not detached from this interest. Characters form groups and are often very similar or interestingly different from each other. Such grouping prompts a desire in the reader for a balance, or at least a discernible pattern, in the working out of their respective lives. A simple case of this is the desire to see the good rewarded and the bad punished.

The close of Shakespeare's plays are an interesting balance of the human and formal interests; audiences want to see the lovers married off and they enjoy the way in which the pairings are carefully contrasted with each other. The marriages at the close of *As You Like It* form a set of interesting contrasts as well as engaging our sympathies to varying degrees. The term can also be used of poetry, to describe the way in which the passage of feelings in a poem or an argument are brought to a satisfying close.

Retrospective Narration   A form of narrative (usually in the first person) that makes use of the past, often to allow the narrator to reflect on what has happened and to discern the differences between past and present. In *Great Expectations* Pip the narrator often allows himself to think about the mistakes of his youth and, without giving away what has happened to him, indicate how different he is from the former self about which he writes. What is interesting about *Great Expectations* and several other retrospective narrations is their inconsistency. For much of *Jane Eyre* there is no retrospective distance between narrator and the young Jane, only occasionally does she slip in a remark about how difficult she must have been as a child. Some retrospective narrations deliberately avoid exploiting the distance between the older narrator and the younger narrated self. In *Huckleberry Finn* the narrating Huck is as naïve and prejudiced as the self whom he presents. (See the entries on **Narration**.)

Reversal   A term originally introduced by Aristotle to discuss drama but which can be used when talking about other sorts of narrative. It refers to the event, usually towards the end of a work, when the fortunes of the central figures are changed. In tragedy the change is for the worse, whilst in comedy reversal paves the way for the happy ending. Because Shakespeare works through expectation rather than surprise, his reversals don't function as dramatic turnabouts. In many nineteenth-century novels, however, secrets are important, so their disclosures work more like those in the plays that Aristotle used for his examples. Reversal is often indistinguishable from discovery. In *Great Expectations* the return of Magwitch functions as a discovery which brings about a reversal in Pip's fortunes. (See also **Discovery**.)

Rhyme   The identity in two or more words of the final vowel and any consonants that follow it. When the rhyming words are monosyllabic, the rhyme is said to be masculine, as in 'bold' and 'old', and when they are polysyllabic, they are said to be feminine, as in 'ending' and 'bending'. (You will also note that in the feminine rhymes the last syllable is unstressed.)

Whenever you write about rhyme, you should bring out the effect it creates. Rhyme creates harmony and also the pleasing effect of completing or resolving an idea. When words rhyme, they tend to be more noticeable and hence more important in the poem. When the words rhymed are important, the whole meaning of the poem can be focused. Rhymes, particularly feminine ones, can also be funny. (See also **Half-rhyme**.)

Satire   The art of exposing folly or wickedness by mocking it. Sometimes a whole work is called a satire, but more often it is thought of as a quality or function of an author's writing. For instance, Dickens satirises the civil service in *Little Dorrit* by creating the Circumlocution Office – a massive department whose aim is to prevent anybody from doing anything. You should remember that satire is a moral art. That is to say, it does not merely poke fun at something but ridicules it in the name of important values.

Scansion   The examination of metrical patterns in verse by noting the sequences of accented and unaccented syllables. If you wish to draw attention to a pattern, you should mark accented syllables with a ´ and unaccented ones with a ˘. There is usually no point simply in labelling a line (see **Metre**) unless you can discuss any variations, or show that it effectively enacts the meaning of the line. (See also **Blank verse**, **Counterpoint**, **Heroic couplets** and **Stanza**.)

Setting   The context in which the events in a literary work take place. Settings are often significant because they reflect in a number of ways the characters and events. The nature of characters, the moods of characters, the plight of characters and the significance of what is going on are often evident in the locations and surroundings. The abrasively new buildings of Alec D'Urberville's home indicate his *nouveau riche* status; the wild and threatening marshes of *Great Expectations* echo the guilt of young Pip; the lonely moors of *Jane Eyre* reflect her abandonment, and the hollow in which Sergeant Troy demonstrates his sword play to Bathsheba evokes the sexual potential of their relationship.

Soliloquy   A speech delivered when a character is either alone or isolated on the stage. A soliloquy can be *public*, in which case the character directly addresses the audience, or *private*, in which case the audience overhears the character talking to himself or herself. In Shakespeare, soliloquies are usually only given to important characters. For instance, Hamlet has a number of private soliloquies, and Iago a number of public ones. Characters very rarely tell lies in soliloquies, so you should pay particular attention to them.

Song   Either a lyrical poem which might be set to music or verses intended to be sung in a play. In the first case, you could ask yourself whether the rhythm and sounds of the poem are appropriately light or flowing. In the second, you should ask how it contributes to the mood or meaning of the play. When you are imagining what a play would be like on stage, you can ask yourself what kind of tune would be suitable. (See also **Lyric**.)

Sonnet.   A poem of fourteen lines. A number of forms have been created, but the two most popular are the one constructed in an octave (eight lines) and a sestet (six lines), and the one in three quatrains (four lines each) and a couplet (two lines). When you write about a sonnet, you should look for the tightness of the argument and the depth of the emotional range. It is worth noticing how they end: is the end artificial, or does it naturally arise out of the rest of the poem and satisfactorily conclude it?

Stanza   A group of lines in a poem that form its basic, structural unit. The shape of a stanza is formed by the number of lines and often by the rhyme scheme. If you choose to write about the stanza form of a poem, you should seek to show how it moulds the meaning of the poem. You can also ask whether the stanza is appropriate to the mood and meaning of the poem.

Famous stanza forms are *terza rima* (three lines, usually rhyming ABA,BCD); *quatrain* (four lines); *rime royal* (seven lines, rhyming ABABBCC); *ottava rima* (eight lines, rhyming ABABABCC); and the *Spenserian stanza* (nine lines, rhyming ABAB-BCBCC). The last line of the Spenserian stanza is an *alexandrine* – a line of six (a hexameter) rather than five stresses; this line closes the stanza in a leisurely, even languid manner. (See also **Rhyme**).

Stock Character   A character in a play or novel who is no more than a representative type. Such characters have no individuality and usually possess only one or two characteristics. They are often comic. (See also **Flat and round characters.**)

Subjective and Objective   A thought is subjective when it is concerned with the personal reaction of somebody, and objective when it ignores what the individual feels about something but concentrates on the object itself. Writing about literature should always be a blend of both. You should write about the words of a poem, novel or play, and about your subjective reactions to these.

Sub-plot   A minor plot which often echoes the concerns of the major plot. You can use the term of both novels and plays. The relation between major and minor plots deserves attention.

Subversion   A popular word for any way in which the language of a book allows the reader to see the events critically and thereby make judgements about the characters. One of the teasing aspects of *The Great Gatsby* is the way in which Nick's enthusiasm for some aspects of Gatsby's life subverts him in the eye of the reader and makes him a narrator whom we think carefully about when it comes to the issue of trust.

Surprise   The effect created when expectation is not fulfilled. It can, therefore, only be discussed in relation to expectation. Novelists often spring surprises upon readers by unusual coincidences or the reappearance of a character. Shakespeare rarely works by surprise. The rejection of Falstaff and the last scene of *The Winter's Tale* are rare exceptions. (See also **Expectation** and **Relief.**)

Suspension of Belief   A term introduced by Coleridge in relation to the conventions of the theatre. When a member of an audience accepts stage conventions, including things like ghosts or witches, he or she willingly suspends belief or disbelief. That is to say, conventions are accepted as real in the theatre, and the issue of whether or not they can be believed in outside the theatre is not raised.

Symbol   An object that stands for, points to and shares in a significant reality over and beyond it. Blake's 'The Tyger' stands for and points to creative energy but it is also an instance of that creative energy. Some symbols are traditional, while other symbols are specially created by authors.

You can learn about traditional symbols, but need to be alert to the resonances of words and their context to recognise ones that are newly made by a poet or novelist. For instance, when you read Shelley's 'Ode to the West Wind', it is important to know that the wind is a symbol for inspiration. When, however, you read Ted Hughes's 'Hawk Roosting' you should try to see that the way the hawk is presented makes it a symbol of the terrible destructiveness that Hughes believes is at the heart of nature.

Syntax   The construction of sentences; that is, the order of words and their relation with each other. As the construction of a sentence controls the meaning and emotional impact of what is being said, it is always wise, particularly when thinking about poetry or verse drama, to study syntax. It is important to see whether the sentences are long or short, whether they have many or few clauses, and whether, as is usual in English, the subject comes before the object, or the other way round.

Theme   The subject, concerns, issues and preoccupations of a poem, novel or play. The word is usually spoken of as meaning the significance of events rather than the events themselves.

Tone   The emotional and intellectual attitude, manner, or poise of a piece of writing. A useful way of assessing the tone of a work is by asking how the author is speaking to you – the reader. In ordinary conversation you would pick up the tone from the way the words were delivered; when you are dealing with words on the page, you should allow their diction, rhythm and sounds to do this for you. Because tone is emotional, you must always try to characterise it. Thus, you may say the tone of a work is intimate, sly, innocent, hectoring, aggressive or fierce. You should remember that all literary works have a tone, and though it is sometimes difficult to detect, you can always try to discuss it.

Trajectory   The direction of a plot. The term is useful when discussing how the initial conditions of a plot can be expected to develop. Quite often the delight we have in literature lies in the way in which the trajectory of the plot is other than what we were led to expect. In *The Winter's Tale*, for instance, there is an interesting change from a plot preoccupied with the difficult relationship between the two Kings to one which centres on the loves of their two children.

Unities   At one time it was believed that a good play should comprise one action, should take place in a day, and should happen in one place. These three requirements were called the unities. Most English drama ignores them, although Shakespeare's last play, *The Tempest*, comes quite close to observing them.

View, Viewpoint   How an author regards and thereby invites the reader to regard the events of a narrative. The interesting questions to ask are the closeness of the author to the characters and events, the moral light in which they are regarded and any changes that occur in the author's perspective. Charlotte Brontë is very close to *Jane Eyre* but distant from most of the other characters; George Eliot views everything as a matter of moral concern but is always deeply understanding of human failure, and Dickens shifts the perspective in *Great Expectations* so that we are sometimes invited to look at things morally and at other times only as the material for comedy.

Villanelle   A verse form (originally from France) of five three-line stanzas and a final quatrain, in which the first and third line of the first stanza appear alternately in the following stanzas and form a couplet in the final one. A popular modern example is Dylan Thomas's 'Do not go gentle into that good night'.

  When writing about villanelles, you should bring out the pleasure of finding that the recurring line has an appropriate place in the succeeding stanzas. Sometimes its new place brings out fresh meanings in the line. For instance, the line from Dylan Thomas is an order in the first stanza and a statement of fact in the second. In grammatical terms it changes from the imperative to the indicative mood.

Part VI
Suggestions for Further Reading

Suggestions for further reading

GENERAL BOOKS

The following books deal with a number of literary topics; some are in the form of glossaries, some general introductions, and others show how literary thinking can illuminate non-literary matters.

M. H. Abrams, *A Glossary of Literary Terms* (New York: Holt, Rinehart & Winston)
John Peck and Martin Coyle, *Literary Terms and Criticism: A Student's Guide* (Macmillan)
Ian Robinson, *The Survival of English* (Brynmill)
W. W. Robson: *A Prologue to English Literature* (Batsford)

POETRY

Most of the following books are introductions to practical criticism; that is, to the reading of individual poems. Suggestions about editions of individual poets can be found in the section headed LITERARY WORKS below. A number of the books listed above also deal with the reading, appreciation and interpretation of poetry.

Charles Barber, *Poetry in English: An Introduction* (Macmillan)
Paul Fussell, *Poetic Metre and Poetic Form* (Random House)
D. W. Harding, *Experience into Words* (Chatto & Windus; Penguin)
Philip Davies Roberts, *How Poetry Works* (Penguin)
Allen Rodway, *The Craft of Criticism* (Cambridge University Press)

NOVELS

Of the following books, some are general introductions and others, in addition to general material, discuss individual novels.

Walter Allen, *The English Novel* (Phoenix; Penguin)
Wayne C. Booth, *The Rhetoric of Fiction* (University of Chicago Press)
Ian Milligan, *The Novel in English: An Introduction* (Macmillan)
John Peck, *How to Study a Novel* (Macmillan)

DRAMA

The following list includes general books on drama and some works on Shakespeare and his theatre.

John Russell Brown, *Shakespeare's Dramatic Style* (Heinemann)
S. W. Dawson, *Drama and the Dramatic* (Methuen)
J. L. Styan, *Shakespeare's Stagecraft* (Cambridge University Press)
G. J. Watson, *Drama: An Introduction* (Macmillan)

LITERARY WORKS

Works set in public examinations are usually available in a number of editions; the ones listed below all have notes and critical comments.

Macmillan Shakespeare
Macmillan Students' Hardy
Macmillan Students' Novels
The Penguin English Library
Penguin English Poets
The New Penguin Shakespeare
The Signet Classic Shakespeare
World Classics (Oxford)

CRITICISM

The following series are either short books dealing with literary works or concepts, or collections of essays by a number of writers.

Casebooks (Macmillan)
The Critical Idiom Series (Methuen)
Macmillan History of Literature
Macmillan Master Guides
Macmillan Modern Dramatists
Penguin Critical Anthologies
Studies in English Literature (Arnold)
Text and Context (Sussex University Press)
Text and Performance (Macmillan)
Twentieth-Century Interpretations (Prentice–Hall)

General index

Index of authors and works